Nations

What are the origins of nationalism and why is it capable of arousing such intense emotions? In this major study Azar Gat counters the prevailing fashionable theories according to which nations and nationalism are modern and contrived or "invented." He sweeps across history and around the globe to reveal that ethnicity has always been highly political and that nations and national states have existed since the beginning of statehood millennia ago. He traces the deep roots of ethnicity and nationalism in human nature, showing how culture fits into human evolution from as early as our aboriginal condition and, in conjunction with kinship, defines ethnicity and ethnic allegiances. From the rise of states and empires to the present day, this book sheds new light on the explosive nature of ethnicity and nationalism, as well as on their more liberating and altruistic roles in forging identity and solidarity.

Azar Gat is Ezer Weitzman Professor and Chair of the Political Science Department at Tel Aviv University. His more recent publications include *A History of Military Thought: From the Enlightenment to the Cold War* (2001); *War in Human Civilization* (2006), named one of the best books of the year by the *Times Literary Supplement*; and *Victorious and Vulnerable: Why Democracy Won in the 20th Century and How it is Still Imperilled* (2010).

Nations

The Long History and Deep Roots of Political Ethnicity and Nationalism

Azar Gat
With Alexander Yakobson

CAMBRIDGE
UNIVERSITY PRESS

CAMBRIDGE UNIVERSITY PRESS
Cambridge, New York, Melbourne, Madrid, Cape Town,
Singapore, São Paulo, Delhi, Mexico City

Cambridge University Press
The Edinburgh Building, Cambridge CB2 8RU, UK

Published in the United States of America by
Cambridge University Press, New York

www.cambridge.org
Information on this title: www.cambridge.org/9781107400023

© Azar Gat 2013

First published 2013

Printed and bound in the United Kingdom by the MPG Books Group

A catalogue record for this publication is available from the British Library

Library of Congress Cataloging in Publication data

Gat, Azar.
    Nations : the long history and deep roots of political ethnicity and nationalism /
Azar Gat ; with contributions by Alexander Yakobson.
        pages   cm
    Includes bibliographical references.
    ISBN 978-1-107-00785-7 (Hardback) – ISBN 978-1-107-40002-3 (Paperback)
    1. Nationalism. 2. Ethnicity–Political aspects. I. Yakobson, Alexander. II. Title.
    JC311.G44 2013
    320.54–dc23
                                                                            2012025021

ISBN 978-1-107-00785-7 Hardback
ISBN 978-1-107-40002-3 Paperback

CONTENTS

ACKNOWLEDGMENTS

While writing this book I constantly exchanged views with Alex Yakobson. The fruits of this exchange are scattered throughout the book and go much beyond the specific references mentioned in the text. In addition, Alex read each chapter after it was finished and made helpful comments. He also wrote Chapter 7. His wisdom and brilliance are unmatched.

My friends and colleagues at Tel Aviv, Yossi Shain and Uriel Abulof, read some of the chapters and made useful suggestions. So did also Aviel Roshwald and Steven Grosby in their capacity as (initially anonymous) readers for Cambridge University Press. The Ezer Weitzman Chair at Tel Aviv University, of which I am the incumbent, helped to sponsor this project. The Israel Science Foundation supported it with a grant. The Alexander von Humboldt Foundation made possible my research stay at Konstanz. I am deeply grateful to them all.

1 INTRODUCTION: IS NATIONALISM RECENT AND SUPERFICIAL?

This book is the result of my deep dissatisfaction with the study of nations and nationalism as it is currently framed. Undergoing a spirited revival since the 1980s, the literature on the subject is marked by a great fault line which runs through the field. On one side of that line stand those who regard the nation as a creation of modernity. In their view, the nation emerged in Europe during the nineteenth century with the French and Industrial revolutions, or possibly sometime before, during the early modern period. For modernists, nations are a product of processes of social integration and political mobilization, which have welded together large populations hitherto scattered among parochial and loosely connected small rural communities spanning extensive territories. According to this perspective, it was only in the modern period, with the advent of print technology, wide-scale capitalist economies and, later, industrialization, urbanization, mass education, and mass political participation that such social integration and mobilization became possible, with active solicitation by the state. On the other side of the fault line stand those who defend, adapt, and develop the more traditionalist view of the nation (labeled "primordial" or "perennial"). They believe that nationhood, as a reality and a sentiment, is older, existed before modernity (even if not universally), perhaps as far back as antiquity, and not only in Europe but throughout the world.

This debate is further accentuated as it reverberates across the wider circles which have been drawn to the subject as it gained popularity. In the social sciences, history, philosophy, literature, and cultural studies, scholars working on related subject matters cite fashionable theories of nationalism, all too often radicalizing them even beyond their original form. Furthermore, cohorts of undergraduate and graduate students of an impressionable age, who are particularly receptive to sweeping pronouncements and criticism of accepted assumptions, are regularly exposed to exciting theories of nationalism as part of their disciplinary socialization and professional initiation. In this process the rift between the modernist and traditionalist schools is constantly reproduced. False dichotomies and captivating hyperboles have become the norm in the study of nationalism, to the degree that they are barely recognized as such.

While fully acknowledging the tremendous growth of modern nationalism in response to the massive forces of transformation generated by modernity, I am closer to the view of those who criticize and reject the exclusive identification of the nation with modernity. Certainly, nations emerged at a certain (early) point in history, they form and disappear, and are therefore not "primordial" in this sense. Furthermore, the national phenomenon has evolved in history, so even the term "perennial" is insufficiently reflective of historical change. And yet, if one accepts modernist theorist Ernest Gellner's definition of the nation as a rough congruence between culture or ethnicity and state, then nations are not confined to modern times. Nor are they as sharply distinct from other highly potent forms of political ethnicity, as modernists would have it. Indeed, as this book suggests, the traditionalist position, although generally correct, is not sufficiently comprehensive. The existing debate needs to be transcended by a substantial broadening of perspective. The crucial question of what makes ethnicity and nationalism – be they old or new – such potent, indeed, explosive forces has scarcely been asked, let alone answered.

Nationalism is the elephant in the room whose huge presence has been consistently overlooked, unaccounted for, and downplayed by the major social theories of the modern period, such as liberalism and Marxism. As a result, scholars, media commentators, and the public in general are repeatedly surprised when its movements shake and often shatter the room. The cause of this recurring, systematic blindness recalls the ancient Indian tale of wisdom where blind men gather to examine an elephant. Each of them feels a different part of the animal and thus arrives at a different conclusion as to its nature and form, depending on whether it is the trunk, tusk, ear, leg, belly, or tail that he examines. The phenomenon of nationhood must be perceived in its entirety. Otherwise, theory becomes an elephant in a china shop.

Ethnicity has always been political

Our point of departure is the following propositions: nationalism and ethnicity are closely associated; by and large, nationalism is one particular form of a broader phenomenon, that of political ethnicity; and ethnicity has always been highly political, ever since the emergence of the state and even before. *By ethnicity I mean a population of shared kinship (real or perceived) and culture* (for a more detailed discussion see "Concepts and definitions," below). Historical states are commonly classified into the following categories: petty-states, states, and empires. And in *all* of them ethnicity was a major factor.

As a rule, the people of petty-states, of either the rural or urban type (city-states), were ethnically related. They tended to belong to the same ethnic space, although encompassing only part of that wider ethnic space, which was usually divided among a multiplicity of petty-states. Conflict was commonplace among petty-states that shared ethnic traits. Yet, when threatened by a foreign enemy, more often than not they tended to cooperate against the outsider. When aliens lived in the petty-state and in those rare cases wherein the petty-state was home to more than one major ethnic group, this too tended to have political consequences, as we shall see.

A space inhabited by an ethnically related population was also conducive to the growth and expansion of larger states, facilitating a process of unification. Of course, the state, in turn, greatly reinforced the ethnic unity of its realm: by the reality of unification itself and through deliberate leveling and fusion efforts. Ethnicity made the state and the state made ethnicity, in a reciprocal and dialectical process. Indeed, *both* these threads of causation reveal how highly political ethnicity has always been. Why would the state strive to homogenize its realm where possible, were it not for the fact that a sense of common identity immeasurably fostered the people's loyalty? In those historical circumstances where the state roughly encompassed and remained largely confined to an entire generally distinct ethnic space, was identified with a particular *Staatsvolk*, the result is known as a national state or nation-state.* For geopolitical and historical reasons explored later in the book, this particular template of political ethnicity was more prevalent and survived better in Europe. Furthermore, it has become a more typical (but far from the exclusive) form of modern political organization because of greater social integration and the empowerment of the masses. Still, the national state was also quite prevalent during premodern times and outside Europe. Nations and national states can be found wherever states emerged since the beginning of history. What sociologists have labeled territorial states (a rather meaningless concept, as all states have territory) or dynastic monarchies in fact tended to be *national* monarchies. This term has long been used by historians, and for good reasons given the close, non-accidental link between ethnos and state in most of these states and the significance of this link in shaping state boundaries and cohesion.

In yet other cases, different ethnic and national communities were forced into a larger state structure, either because they were coerced by a dominant ethnopolitical group, or because they were too weak to fend for themselves in a violent world and were therefore sheltered, or allied with other groups, within a larger multiethnic union (various combinations of the above processes were at work). Still, within such larger multiethnic unions – called empires when they were large enough – ethnic existence was also widely political, formally or informally, usually both. Informally, the more the state was dominated

---

* The difference between these two concepts in most usages is slight to non-existent. Charles Tilly has suggested that national states are "states governing multiple contiguous regions and their cities by means of centralized, differentiated, and autonomous structures," whereas a nation-state is "a state whose people share a strong linguistic, religious, and symbolic identity": Tilly, *Coercion, Capital, and European States,* AD 990–1992, Cambridge, MA: Blackwell, 1992, 2–3. However, the first category is not at all national but simply a state, which can be national or not. Furthermore, *contra* Tilly, I hold that his first category was not historically new, nor was the second category historically rare. S. E. Finer, *The History of Government from the Earliest Times,* vol. 1, Oxford University Press, 1997, 4, makes more sense in calling fourteenth-century England and fifteenth-century France national states, while reserving the term nation-states to the modern breed, where "sovereignty is democratically exercised by the nation." The drawback in the latter part of this definition is that it seems to be restricted to democracies. To avoid this untenable restriction, many scholars regard popular sovereignty as the legitimizing principle and distinctive mark of the nation-state. Still, whether national state or nation-state, Finer clearly identifies the nation as the cornerstone of many premodern European states.

by a paramount ethnic community, the more power relations and benefit allocation were skewed in its favor, and the state's symbols of identity reflected its particular ethnicity. It was mainly this ethnic core upon which the state relied to establish its rule, because it was this ethnic core's loyalty that could be counted in a way that could scarcely be said for other ethnicities or peoples within the realm. Other ethnic communities within the state were well aware of, and more or less acquiesced to, their secondary or subordinate status, for the reasons mentioned above. It often helped that their status could incorporate some positive elements. Above all, their separate identity could be respected and protected to some degree. Their particular institutions and system of law were often recognized and retained within the larger state structure, and considerable cultural tolerance tended to prevail.

Historical sociologists of the modernist persuasion hold that premodern empires were elite power structures, wherein the ruling elite were indifferent to the ethnic composition of its subjects. Yet this widely held view is highly simplistic, for very few historical empires, if any, were so construed or were ethnically blind. This is one of many false dichotomies – misplaced either/or distinctions – that we encounter in the scholarly literature. In reality, empires were indeed elite power structures, yet, at the same time, nearly all of them were grounded in and relied upon a dominant ethnic nucleus. Thus, ethnicity has always been highly significant in determining identity, solidarity, and political organization within and between states. It is only that most ethnic communities were too small and weak to achieve and retain statehood, that is, national independence, whereas more powerful ethnic communities went on to conquer others, assuming a dominant position within a multiethnic state or empire. National states appeared only in those cases in which a rough congruence between an ethnos and a state occurred.

This must not be interpreted to mean that ethnicities were homogeneous or clear-cut, coming neatly sealed in distinct and fixed packages; far from it. We are dealing with populations that share a significant, albeit variable, number of kin–culture traits, giving rise to variably heterogeneous, "punctuated" continuums. Subpopulations within an ethnic space are variably distant from one another in terms of such traits. And these distances can produce intermediate, graduated, and compound ethnic affinities within a larger ethnos, as well as developing into more significant cleavages and even splits.

New similarities and differences continuously emerge, and processes of ethnic fusion and fission occur, shaping and reshaping group boundaries and identities.[1] However, greater internal similarities generally separate one ethnic population from its neighbor, as with the sometimes substantially different dialects of one lingual space, which are nonetheless much closer to one another than to a distinctly separate lingual space, again with considerable variation. The fact that there are no neatly fixed ethnic packages, where culture, kinship, and identity are wholly homogeneous and fully overlapping, does not mean that there are no such significant and quite enduring packages at all. The charge of "essentialism" has become the ultimate detraction in the humanities and social sciences, and for good reason, given the dangers of crude conceptualization. However, "family resemblance," relative distances within and between groups, and continuities versus change in temporal transformation are a perfectly valid, indeed indispensable, way of thinking about very genuine realities.

And yet notions such as ethnicity having been central in historical states and nationhood generally meaning statehood for a people predominantly defined in terms of a shared kin–culture identity have become largely out of step with the recent discourse on nationalism. Because of deep concern over the horrendously violent expressions of ethnicity and nationalism, there is a strong aversion toward the idea that ethnicity and the nation are intimately related. Nationalism and ethnicity are often studied as separate subjects, and from different books. Some scholars, such as Walker Connor, have protested that "a nation is a nation, is a state, is an ethnic group."[2] I diverge from Connor in some significant respects, as discussed in the section "Concepts and definitions," below. All the same, other leading modernist authors have also recognized the intimate connection between nationalism and ethnicity, a point lost on many of their followers. Karl Deutsch defined the nation as "the coming together of a state and a people," regarded in ethnic terms.[3] Ernest Gellner similarly and more famously referred to it as a congruence of culture or ethnicity (he used the terms intermittently) and state, a definition I generally share.[4] Of course, both men believed such a congruence to have emerged only with the advent of industrial society.

Gellner regarded ethnicity as synonymous with culture, although on occasions he also mentioned conspicuous genetic-biological traits that may create ethnonational distinctions.[5] But even cultural attributes are widely rejected nowadays as inadmissible to the concept of the nation. "Civic nationalism," supposedly based solely on common citizenship and shared political institutions, is habitually contrasted to "ethnic nationalism," both historically and normatively. However, as quite a few scholars have noted, this distinction is greatly overdrawn.[6] Civic institutions have been variably central to the make up of nations. But there have been very few nations, if any, whose existence was divorced from ethnicity, that is, which did not share cultural and at least some kin affinities. In reality, civic nationalism too – indeed, civil nationalism *in particular* – generates assimilation into the ethnonational community, either as an explicit ("republican") requirement or as a tacit assumption. This applies not only to old ethnicities and nations, but also to new ones. These are born and formed all the time, most strikingly in immigrant state societies, through processes of integration, hybridization, and amalgamation. A more helpful distinction between "ethnic" and "civic" nationalism is that the former emphasizes descent and shared culture, while the latter emphasizes state territory and culture. It should be noted, however, that in many so-called civic nations a feeling of kinship is created with cultural integration and intergroup marriages even in the absence of a sense of common descent. Thus, both ethnic and civic nationalism incorporate elements of ethnicity, albeit with some significantly different emphases, *inter alia* between the twin elements of kinship and culture. In the absence of a shared cultural matrix and sense of kinship, there can be common citizenship in a multiethnic and multinational state; but there is very rarely a notion of common national identity, especially in free societies where people are given a choice in the matter. Ultimately, nationalism is a state of mind, a sense of shared communal-political identity, affinity, and destiny, a "daily plebiscite," as Ernest Renan called it.[7] Yet in reality, this state of mind is strongly associated with other shared contents of the minds involved, most notably a common culture and sense of kinship.

A most sensible pioneer of the modernist view, Carlton Hayes, very early rejected the conceptual confusion he saw developing between national affiliation and citizenship.[8] Similarly, Connor deplored the misconception which had gained currency in the 1950s and 1960s, under Deutsch's influence, that "state building" and "nation building"

were practically synonyms. This misconception gave rise to expectations that nations could easily be welded together in new states
in Africa and Asia, irrespective of their ethnic heterogeneity. Indeed,
Deutsch himself found it necessary to caution in the 1960s that such
processes were inherently slow.[9] This crucial misconception, and its
policy implications, are as much with us today as they were then.

All modernist writings can be regarded as footnotes to Hans
Kohn's seminal work.[†] In his view, nationalism is an artificial historical
construct, built in the nineteenth century on older and more natural
feelings of love for one's place, language, and customs (remarkably
Kohn does not mention one's people, though he later adds commᴗn
descent).[10] Eric Hobsbawm holds a similar view. To the question of
how such a powerful emotion like nationalism, which profoundly stirs
people's souls, causes them to kill and be killed, could have suddenly
emerged in the nineteenth century out of thin air, Hobsbawm replies
that nationalism mobilized earlier, "protonational" sentiments, such as
those of shared religion, language, and ethnicity.[11] If so, however, were
ethnicity and nationalism two distinct and separate phenomena, one
old and possibly more "natural" and the other new and artificial, as
Kohn and Hobsbawm have it, or is this yet another false dichotomy,
where in reality a deeper connection existed? Indeed, Kohn concedes
in a brief remark in his introduction that a weaker national sentiment
existed here and there before modernity.[12] Gellner mentions the same
point in his conclusion.[13] And Hobsbawm, despite a great deal of forced
argumentation, concludes that "a proto-national base may be desirable,
perhaps even essential, for the formation of serious state-aspiring
national movements."[14] After all, if nationalism was not grounded
in ethnicity, why did it involve the disintegration of multiethnic empires
as one of its most distinctive manifestations, rather than the creation of
new "all-imperial" national states?

Thus, contrary to rhetoric and image, a narrower gulf than the
one generally perceived separates modernists and more traditionalist
critics with respect to the relationship between ethnicity and nationhood, and even regarding the existence of premodern (albeit weaker)

[†] The pioneering modernist theorists of nationalism from the 1930s on, Hans Kohn,
Carlton Hayes, and Karl Deutsch, are currently overshadowed by the later exponents
of modernism of the 1980s. But except for the fanfare, the latter added little that was
new to their predecessors' work.

forms of the nation and nationalism. There is in effect only a short distance between the ideas cited above from Kohn, Deutsch, Gellner, and Hobsbawm (let alone Hayes, and, as we shall see, Tom Nairn) and those of one of the major exponents of the more traditionalist view, Anthony Smith, who has stressed the ethnic roots of nations. Modern nations, he maintains, usually did not crystallize *ex nihilo*. In most cases they emerged from earlier ethnic communities which shared traits such as language, traditions, memories, a belief in common descent, and a sense of collective identity which often reached far into the past.[15] In the absence of an accepted noun in English, Smith has suggested the adoption of the French term *ethnie*, derived from the Greek *ethnos*, to denote those ethnic entities from which nations emerge. All the same, while stressing the premodern ethnic roots of nations and the role of "ethno-symbolism" in national identity formation, Smith too was generally inclined to view the nation itself as a modern phenomenon. He has become more open to the possibility of premodern nations only in recent years.[16]

Smith was circumspect on this point because of his acceptance of the generally correct and significant modernist precept that it was only with the technological, economic, social, political, and legal developments of modernity that mass popular participation in the state increased momentously. The masses were integrated into and mobilized by the state. Popular sovereignty and equal citizenship, inaugurated by the French Revolution, were the hallmarks of this process, and they are regarded by many as necessary conditions for the formation of a true national community. According to the standard sociological depiction of premodern societies, most of their populations consisted of peasants. In large states these populations were scattered across the countryside in small rural communities, isolated from the outside world and from the politics of the state, except as subjects to its dictates. Kin, tribal, and local affiliations dominated their lives. They were mostly illiterate. They possessed inherently parochial cultures which formed a mosaic of local and regional "low cultures." These differed markedly from place to place and often had little in common with the "high culture" of the elite, especially that which dominated the capital and ran the state. A major element of this cultural heterogeneity was the diversity of mutually barely intelligible dialects that separated communities from one another and from the standard "high language" of the state. Class differences were rigid and deeply entrenched, with the overwhelming majority of the population completely excluded from political participation. Given these pervasive divisions, argue the modernists, if there was any sense of shared identity, affinity and solidarity in premodern states, it was mainly confined to the elite (which according to Gellner, however, was cosmopolitan in outlook, closely tied by culture and interest with its peers across political boundaries). The common identity did not spread to encompass the masses. In this view, the elite hardly regarded the masses as part of a shared collective entity, nor did the masses feel part of, or affinity toward, such an entity. In fact, although never made explicit, what many modernists call into question is not merely premodern nation-hood, but the existence of premodern *peoples*.

While there is a large grain of truth in the standard picture of premodern societies, it simplifies, omits, and distorts much of the historical reality. The fundamental question is two-pronged: to what degree there existed a broader array of common ethnic, kin–culture traits within many large states, which went far and deep enough to encompass the wider strata of the people, made them *a* people; and, in turn, to what degree the people felt affinity, identification, and solidarity with such states, in the ethnic attributes that they shared. Answering this question is particularly tricky, however, as a seemingly insurmountable empirical obstacle stands in the way, long recognized by students of nationalism.[17] As the masses were mostly illiterate, there exists almost no direct record of their thoughts and feelings, and precious little indirect evidence. The masses are barely represented in the premodern record. They have no voice. To make progress in our investigation, it is therefore necessary to find ways around this obstacle, to penetrate, if only a little, the veil of silence.

How deep did premodern ethnonational identity reach?

The question of how widespread was the diffusion of culture to the lowest levels of state-societies can be tested, for example, by examining the most significant of cultural attributes, language. Did states' official language in premodern societies invariably remain confined to the center and the elite, making little headway in displacing local dialects and indigenous languages? This is what sociological theorists posit, based on select European historical cases which have gained paradigmatic status.

However, as we shall see, in some other, no less prominent yet largely overlooked premodern cases, the state's language expanded throughout the realm, driving out, and at times entirely eradicating, its competitors all the way down to the grassroots level. Similarly, dialect differences were strong in some countries but much slighter in others, where they constituted no obstacle to mutual understanding across the realm.

Religious ideas and cults were another central cultural form. Indisputably, local cults, myths, and deities flourished in premodern societies, most notably in rural environments. Still, higher religions, pantheons, and mythologies were shared across ethne, penetrating the most remote of rural communities, even where no unifying state existed, let alone where it did. Indeed, the network of cultic and congregational sites with their clergy extended to every town and village and was a major vehicle of cross-country socialization. It was customarily used to inculcate loyalty to the state and rulers; yet it was equally capable of serving as a bastion of opposition and agitation against them, *inter alia* if they were perceived as foreigners or subservient to foreign domination that threatened the national culture and identity. Where an ethnic or national religion was involved, as was almost invariably the case, it typically preached common identity and solidarity. When universal religions emerged and spread, cutting across state and ethnonational boundaries, they sometimes became a separate focus of identity and allegiance, competing with ethnonational loyalties. More typically, however, official or unofficial national churches of the universal faith were very much the norm wherever a multiplicity of national states existed. Overwhelmingly, such churches tended to champion the patriotic cause in case of a threat or conflict. As Michael Petrovich, Connor Cruise O'Brien, Adrian Hastings, Steven Grosby, Anthony Smith, Philip Gorski, and Anthony Marx have shown, perceptions of one's people and country as holy and chosen were prevalent throughout history.[18] Rather than conflicting with the national idea, as it is conventionally and erroneously assumed to have been, religion was one of its strongest pillars. It was, in fact, the most powerful and all-pervasive mass medium of the *premodern* "imagined community," which Benedict Anderson has failed to recognize.

Anderson has coined the enormously successful phrase "imagined community" to describe the impact since the late fifteenth century of print technology. Allegedly, print created large-scale networks of shared culture based on the printed vernacular beyond the "real," face-to-face communities of the local village and town.[19] However, although the advent of print technology undoubtedly represented a quantum leap in communication, large-scale "imagined communities" of shared culture had existed before, infused with a sense of common identity and solidarity. Major cultural features, such as language and religion, demonstrate that ideas and other cultural forms could diffuse widely and deeply in premodern societies. Indeed, language and religion were in themselves major *vehicles* of common national identity and solidarity. Anderson shares the common view that universal religious identity (Christian, Muslim) preceded national identity. Powerfully connecting the believers across countries and continents, these were premodern "imagined communities" in Anderson's sense of this concept. However, he argues that they were united by a literary language not understood by the masses.[20] This ignores the national religions of most peoples *before* the rise of universal religions, as well as the strong national character and usual ethno-national bias of the local churches of universal faiths, which found expression in their preaching to the faithful in the vernacular. In reality, religious identity dovetailed with, rather than preceded, ethnonational identity, powerfully contributing to the cohesion of the national *cum* religious "imagined community."

Thus, the emphasis on literacy has been largely misleading, because illiterate societies had their own potent means of wide-scale cultural transmission. We have already mentioned the dense network of cultic-clerical centers planted everywhere across a country. Oral epics recited by wandering bards celebrating gods, kings, heroes, and the people – always *ours* – served as another major vehicle of cultural dissemination. Their effect on the consolidation of large-scale "imagined communities" cannot be overstated. Dances, plays, games, and festivals, often infused with ritualistic significance, were equally influential. Moreover, it is all too often forgotten that although the masses in historical state societies were illiterate, they were commonly read to by the literati, and for very distinctive purposes. Such public readers included the state's agents in public summons, priests in rituals and festivals, and artistic performers of various sorts.[21] In addition, peasants carrying produce for sale in markets and towns, or frequented by traveling traders, were exposed to, and eagerly absorbed, echoes from the outside world. That meant their region and province, and also their people, country, and state writ large. Finally, institutions such as military service and even the school, the great agents of the modern nation, were variably present in some premodern states societies as well, to much effect.

This was not an all or nothing proposition. No one is arguing that premodern peoples and nations were as closely integrated as those of modernity. Yet it is erroneous to assume that they were not bound together at all by a sense of common culture and kinship, with considerable variation, of course, depending on the case. There was far greater variation among premodern societies in terms of their cultural unity than that portrayed in the reductionist standard sociological picture. These societies were not all *equally* fragmented by class, locality, and dialect. Neither were the rural communities of the countryside entirely isolated and disconnected, again with considerable variations.

The most tangible test for the existence of premodern national affinities is the following: did premodern peoples view foreign intrusion and rule with total indifference and apathy, as modernists claim, because their horizons were wholly parochial and they regarded the elite that exploited them as alien and foreign as the foreigners? Or did they very well feel that the foreigners were foreigners, resented them for this reason, and were prone to express that resentment in action, even if they often had to submit to superior brute force? Indeed, although common identity and solidarity in premodern societies are seemingly difficult to record because of the elusiveness of the evidence concerning the masses, they are nevertheless clearly exposed by political realities. Deeds are indicative of, more indicative than, thoughts. This brings us back to the elephant in the room that somehow remains invisible. The submission or acquiescence to foreign conquest by peoples and other ethnopolitical entities was often achieved only after desperate popular resistance. Stubborn struggles for independence habitually evoked acts of mass patriotic devotion and heroic sacrifice of life, property, and so much else that was dear. Furthermore, renewed mass uprisings were ever to be expected even after independent statehood was lost. All these were very far from being purely elite matters. For this very reason, foreign rulers often made supreme efforts to cultivate a native image, conspicuously adopting local customs and appearance. It is hard to ignore such major features of political history, or fail to see how they impinge upon our enquiry regarding the existence and manifestations of premodern ethnic and national identity, solidarity, and political mobilization. Irrespective of whether they were ruled by their own elite or by foreign conquerors, people in many premodern state societies lacked individual freedom. Thus, the purpose of their struggle and sacrifices against foreign rule could only be *collective* freedom, that is, national independence.

True, the more despotically ruled and rigidly stratified a state was, the more reluctant its rulers and aristocracy were to call upon the masses for fear that they would become dangerously empowered domestically. Correspondingly, the more oppressed and disenfranchised the masses, the more alienated and accustomed to passivity they tended to be. Here, too, historical states varied in the degree of their political and social exclusion and, hence, in their ability to tap and mobilize popular energies. Nonetheless, in serious emergencies the tendency to appeal to the masses by invoking ethnic and national sentiments of solidarity regularly manifested itself. It pointedly indicates that the state authorities believed such sentiments actually existed and were potentially powerful. More significantly, it is often reported that support for an uprising against foreign rule came *mainly* from the popular strata of society, with the wealthy and privileged, who were more inclined to cooperate and acquiesce, brushed aside by popular enthusiasm. Notably, too, it was the lower clergy, closer to the masses in background and outlook, that tended to figure prominently in such popular ethnic and national uprisings. They often went against the higher clergy, which could be more closely tied to a foreign rule by interest and sociopolitical cooptation.

This brings us to another pertinent point with respect to the national phenomenon. So-called "instrumentalists" emphasize manipulation by state authorities and social elites as the cause of nationalism. They cast the masses in a wholly passive role, an object to be carried in any direction desirable to those at the top. Most instrumentalists are also modernists, and the two positions are commonly conflated because they both convey a picture of nationalism as contrived. And yet leading modernist theorists have well recognized that the emergence of nations and nationalism was a deeper and more comprehensive sociopolitical process. As Hobsbawm has found it necessary to caution:

> *While governments were plainly engaged in conscious and*
> *deliberate ideological engineering, it would be a mistake*
> *to see these exercises as pure manipulation from above. They*

were, indeed, most successful when they could build on already present unofficial nationalist sentiments, whether of demotic xenophobia or chauvinism ... or, more likely, in nationalism among the middle and lower middle classes.[22]

Indeed, a one-sided, top-down model of national incitement is as fatuous as single-blade scissors or one-handed clapping. For how could such manipulation succeed in evoking the most powerful, stormy emotions in populations that had always been and remained suspicious of, or apathetic toward, the state authorities and often hostile toward the social elites? How could manipulation be effective unless it appealed to a genuine and deep popular sentiment?[23] Moreover, national eruptions were often directed *against* state authority which was deemed alien. As already mentioned, nationalism regularly involved the breaking up of multiethnic states and empires, thereby triumphing against state power and all its instruments of control and manipulation. This glaring fact is strangely overlooked in the "instrumentalist" discourse. In fact, nothing except the most deeply-rooted and potent popular emotions could be incited from the top, cynically or not, in either modern or pre-modern societies. For uncovering the roots of national sentiment and allegiance one has to look at the broader community of culture and kinship – population, elites, and leaders alike.

Modern national identity was famously forged in, and propagated from, the cities – the hubs of power, education, and communication – by intellectuals and the middle classes. But as some leading modernists have noted in a sort of afterthought, it was the countryside that was perceived as the true repository of national identity, and it was mainly from rural materials of language and custom that it was forged. Whereas the elite and urban middle class often assimilated into a hegemonic foreign culture, the countryside retained the traditional culture and identity. As Tom Nairn wrote in criticism of Gellner:

Czech nationalism was "made in Prague", undoubtedly; but its ethnic characteristics came out of Bohemia, Moravia and the Sudetenland, and were not themselves "made" in the familiar sense of invented ... "traditions" are also a real matrix borne forward from past times by individuals and families ... not creation ex nihilo *... And the past which has mainly counted here ... is that of peasant existence.*[24]

Indeed, one little noted reason why nationalism became so potent in modernity is that the masses – more mobile and largely concentrated in the cities, near the centers of power – were now far more able to voice and enforce their preferences, which were almost invariably nationalistic. Rulers had to be much more responsive to these wishes than they had been obligated to when the masses were impotently scattered in the countryside. They were now riding a tiger. Thus, at the risk of some oversimplification at this stage, one may suggest that more than being elite manipulation of a new sentiment, the surge of modern nationalism was a function of old popular sentiments empowered by democratization. Indeed, rather than nations and nationalism being a modern invention, the superficial product of political manipulation, this idea itself is a modernist (or sometimes postmodernist) invention, spurred by and riding high on the ideological-political agenda of our times.

The underlying dispute

What are the origins of, and explanation for, such a powerful, often explosive sentiment, capable of stirring people so deeply, of generating tremendous willingness to sacrifice, moving people to kill and be killed? As a number of critics have noted, this is perhaps the most glaring lacuna in modernist theorizing. Ultimately, this book's dispute with modernists and instrumentalists is broader than the question of how old the nation is or of nations' ethnic underpinning. Central to the modernist message, either implicitly or explicitly, is the proposition that due to their novelty nations and nationalism are pure historical constructs, more or less arbitrary and thus bear little more significance than a fashion or a craze.

There are various reasons for this predilection to downplay the ethnic and national phenomenon. Both liberalism and Marxism, the dominant social theories and ideologies of our times, lack the conceptual frameworks within which the deeper roots of ethnicity and nationalism can be comprehended. Famously, what one cannot conceptualize one does not see, even if it is an elephant in the room. Furthermore, it is probably not a coincidence that the pioneering modernist theorists – Kohn, Deutsch, Gellner, Hobsbawm – were all Jewish immigrant refugees from central Europe (and Elie Kedourie from the Middle East) during the first half of the twentieth century. All of them experienced changing identities and excruciating questions of self-identity at the time of the most extreme, violent and unsettling nationalistic eruptions. It was only natural that they reacted against all this.

Thus, although many modernists have been well aware of the difference between nations as "imagined" (in Anderson's sense of collective consciousness) and "invented," quite a few could not resist the temptation to play on the semantic ambiguity in their rhetoric. It has been all too easy to mix metaphors with nationalism's "invention of tradition," the catchy title of Hobsbawm's book. Here, too, however, as Nairn, for one, has reminded fellow modernists, the inherently fanciful processing and reprocessing of tradition did not mean fabrication *ex nihilo*. Rather, it primarily involved selective reworking of existing historical materials and folk memories which often had at least some basis in reality.

Gellner, the proponent of the starkest form of functionalism in his conception of modern nationalism as a necessary tool of industrial society, has been typical in contending that "nationalism does not have any very deep roots in the human psyche."[25] Tellingly, however, in response to criticism, he later admitted to be deeply moved by his native Bohemian folk nationalism.[26] Indeed, could such a profound emotion as nationalism suddenly spring up in nineteenth-century Europe from no apparent source in the human psyche? And even if we accept that the national sentiment was based on earlier ethnic allegiances, where did *they* come from? What is the source of Hobsbawm's "demotic xenophobia and chauvinism"?

One cannot begin to comprehend the enormous appeal of nationalism, its "spell" and combustive nature (which shook the above modernists' lives), unless it is understood as the tip of an iceberg. Ethnopolitical formations, including premodern and modern nationalism, permeate political history and history in general; and while diverse and subject to sweeping historical transformations, they spring from deep within the human psyche. At the heart of the debate is not merely the semantics of what constitutes nations and distinguishes them from other forms of communal political identity. The underlying dispute is where do *all* these forms of identity, affinity, and solidarity come from, how deeply and closely they interrelate, and how genuine and significant they have been, past and present. At the beginning of this chapter I suggested that in the main nationalism is one particular form of political ethnicity. Our next step is to inquire what ethnicity itself is, why it has always been political, and what explains its strong hold on human emotion and behavior. In the following chapter we turn to the notion of human nature, long regarded as taboo in the humanities and social sciences, and explore its intricate interrelationships with culture from the early beginning of our species. But first, some discussion of key concepts and definitions is in order.

Concepts and definitions

Believing in diversity, punctuated continuums, and the flow of phenomena into one another, I am not a great advocate of formal definitions. Still, some principal concepts used in this book may be in need of more systematic elaboration. While attempting this I strive to avoid pedantry, because concepts and definitions are merely intellectual frameworks superimposed on reality and cannot substitute for it, are construed by agreement, and regularly change semantics.

Ethnos and ethnicity

The concept of the ethnic group, ethnos, or *ethnie* has been advanced by Anthony Smith as the substratum of nations (opting for the Greek etymology, I use ethnos in the singular form and ethne in the plural). As pointed out by Gellner, only a minority of ethnic groups achieved their own state and, therefore, nationhood, mostly because the majority of them were too small and weak. Presently, there are about 7,000 languages in the world, the large majority of them spoken by miniscule ethnic communities, but less than 200 states.[27] Although highly affected by ethnicity, most historical states did not exhibit a rough congruence between state and ethnos, that is, most of them were not national states. Some were large multiethnic states or empires, whereas other, petty-states, shared and divided among them a larger ethnic space. However, the great majority of national states are so categorized because they roughly exhibit such congruence.

Modernists claim, with some justification, that the state created the nation more than the other way around. But this was far less the case with respect to the state–ethnos relationship. To be sure, once states existed, they regularly and profoundly affected ethnicity, with the two shaping each other in a close and reciprocal interrelationship. Furthermore, new ethne have emerged throughout history, often heavily mediated by the state. Individual ethne are no more "primordial" than the nation, though ethnicity as a general category has a better claim for being primordial. In most cases, however, ethne tended to predate the state (and quite often proved highly resistant to its intrusion), with their original formation sometimes stretching far back into prehistory. Ranging from tens of thousands to hundreds of thousands and even millions of people, an ethnos should not be confused with a tribe, as it often is (e.g., not the Latin, Celt, Zulu, Kikuyu, or Pashtun tribe, but, rather, tribes, tribal ethnos, or ethnos). Prestate ethne were invariably comprised of a multiplicity of separate tribes and tribal confederations – smaller, close-knit kin units, which nonetheless were frequently in conflict with one another. This tribal composition of the ethnos was eroded and often eradicated with the emergence of the state.

At the same time, ethne also differed from nations, more substantially, indeed, than Smith allows for. He lists the following as characteristic of the *ethnie*: a collective name; common myth of descent; shared history; distinctive shared culture; an association with a specific territory; and a sense of solidarity.[28] My own concept of the ethnos as a population of shared kinship (real or perceived) and culture is broader in some respects and narrower in others. It diverges in various ways not only from Smith's, but also from a few other accepted definitions of ethnicity in the scholarly literature. An explanation is necessary for why I believe it is more in accordance with both reality and common parlance.

Although a perception of common descent is often defined as a constitutive element of ethnicity, for example, by Max Weber and Walker Connor,[29] the concept advanced here specifies kinship rather than descent. Common descent is only one, albeit prevalent, subcategory within the broader category of shared kinship or "blood relation." This is a subtle but important and generally overlooked distinction. It is the notion of extended family which is typical of an ethnos and ethnicity, and this notion often, but not always, includes common descent. In many cases there is a strong sense based on tradition that the ethnos was originally made up of separate groups that came together and amalgamated into one. The Romans, for example, had strong traditions that they originated from Latin and Sabine groups which joined together at the founding of Rome. Initially speaking different Italic languages, they fused almost without a trace, including the adoption of the Latin language by the Sabines. This tradition of mixed origin helped to legitimize Rome's policy of incorporating many of the conquered into its citizen body, which went hand in hand with cultural Latinization and common identity formation. Similarly, the English have a strong perception of descending from both the Anglo-Saxons and Normans. Except in some nineteenth-century class prejudices and a few characteristic family names, these distinct ancestors are generally regarded as having been completely fused together in terms of language, other cultural traits, identity, and, indeed, "blood." The French also have a tradition of their mixed origins from Gauls, Romans, and Germans. This has nothing to do, in either reality or perception, with the heterogeneous composition of the French nation in later medieval and modern times, because the above original ethnic groups of descent blended without a trace. Much the same applies to Castile in Spain. Moreover, similar processes continue to occur all the time, as in the common ethnic and national identity variably forged from diverse ethnic roots in individual Latin American countries.

Indeed, going farther than Smith, I argue that shared ethnicity is the substratum of nations not only in historical, but even in new immigrant states. Ethnic formation is an ongoing process. Immigrant states habitually integrate newcomers into a broad cultural and kin community as a prerequisite for the creation of a common national identity. The key to the fusion of a shared ethnic identity, even in the absence of a belief in common descent, is extensive intermarriage among the founding groups and the adoption of a common culture. Over time these processes both turn the populations in question into self-perceived kin or a "community of blood" and make them scarcely distinguishable from one another. Note that the very notion of the ethnos as a family implies individuals and groups joining together in "blood" and loyalty through marriage ties (and even adoption). Generations of anthropologists, from Claude Lévi-Strauss on, have stressed that in-laws are everywhere considered as kin.[30] We shall see more about the rationale behind this in Chapter 2. Connor, who insists that a national state is the political expression of an ethnos defined in terms of common descent alone, does not only err with respect to a sense of common descent among the English or Castilians, both of which he rightly regards as real nations; his concept also goes against the genuine self-identity and self-definition of Americans, Mexicans, or Argentineans, each of whom have no sense of common descent yet feel themselves to be new and very real nations.

The concept of ethnicity employed here might also be disputed from another direction. Some regard the sense of kinship (or descent) alone, and not common culture, as the defining element of ethnicity. The term ethnocultural is often used to emphasize the cultural element as distinct from, and additional to, the ethnic aspect. For those espousing this concept of ethnicity the inclusion of culture in ethnicity may appear as an unwarranted stretching of the concept beyond recognizable meaning. In reality, however, ethnicity overwhelmingly tends to combine *both* kinship and a common culture. I suggest that this is what people usually have in mind when thinking about ethnicity. The two elements combined were also central to the historical concept of race, which the new term, ethnicity, replaced from the 1950s onward precisely because race had assumed a strictly biological meaning since the late nineteenth century. Indeed ethnography is the field that studies the culture of kin–culture communities. Furthermore, ethnic and linguistic communities are terms used almost interchangeably. To be sure, distinct ethne sometimes have a similar culture, most notably language. However, this relationship scarcely works in the opposite direction: despite sometimes considerable internal diversity of culture and language, an ethnos very rarely includes populations from different linguistic spaces. Furthermore, fusion of a shared culture, most notably among populations living in the same territory, is often a prerequisite for, and an intermediate step in, processes of intermarriage and formation of a sense of kinship.

If the concept of ethnicity suggested here is broader than some other definitions with respect to the twin elements of kinship and culture, it is narrower in other respects. Most notably, I do not regard features such as a collective name or even a *sense* of kinship or commonality as constitutive elements of all ethne. Many ethne lacked such features until late in their history. Although clearly sharing distinctive ethnic traits, such as kin relatedness and similar language, customs, and a pantheon, they did not possess a conscious common identity. They typically developed such identity only with increased contact with outsiders, who often were also those who gave the ethnos its common ethnic eponym. Famously, it is contact with an alien "Other" that impresses upon a fragmented ethnic population its common traits and forges its separate identity. The prehistoric Celts, Germans, and Slavs are cases in point, as were many ethnic populations in nineteenth-century Africa, which only became defined as such by contact with the European colonial powers. Contrary to a widespread misconception, by categorizing a population living in a territory in terms of its common language and culture, the colonial authorities did not "invent" these ethnicities, but rather made them conscious. Referring to the ancient Greeks, who shared ethnic attributes and increasingly developed a conscious sense of common identity during the archaic and classical periods, Friedrich Meinecke called such self-aware ethne "cultural nations" (*Kulturnationen*).[31] In this book, ethne covers both weak and strong consciousness of common identity, and even a total lack thereof. For a conscious sense of identity and common fate, as well as other traits, as *constitutive* elements, one needs to proceed one step further, to peoples.

Peoples

Peoples are strangely rare in the literature on the nation and nationalism, despite common usage of the term in ordinary parlance. There have been peoples everywhere (Hebrew *am*, *goi*, Greek *laos*, Latin *gens*, German *Volk*, Slavic *narod* are a few, randomly chosen, ancient synonyms), but scarcely in the scholarly discourse. The concept was employed as a matter of course by Deutsch and is sensibly used by Hobsbawm. Yet, as the debate has gathered momentum, modernists have tended to avoid anything that suggests something other and earlier than modern nations. Furthermore, the concept of a people has been increasingly regarded as if it were devoid of ethnic content and indistinguishable from population or populace.[32] From the other side, a traditionalist author like Anthony Smith has concentrated on ethnicity. More recently, Rogers Smith has pointed out this lacuna.[33] Like him, I propose reinstating peoples as a common and distinctive historical entity between ethnos and nation. In order to be categorized as a people, an ethnos should have a sense of common identity, history, and fate. Furthermore, such a sense should exist even if the people does not achieve independence or other forms of political self-determination, and, hence, nationhood. Moreover, that sense should compete successfully with other allegiances, bridging tribal cleavages, political disunity among multiple states, or cohabitation with others (either coerced or voluntary) within larger states. Thus, there is a people in every national state, but there can also be a people without one.

By the same token, the various people in a country do not necessarily constitute *a* people, as English speakers often and all too cavalierly assume.

Nation and national state

A people becomes a nation when it is politically sovereign, either as a dominant majority, *Staatsvolk*, within a national state, or as the politically central element within a multiethnic state or empire. Short of independent statehood, a people can be regarded as a nation if it possesses elements of political self-determination and self-government, or actively strives to achieve them. By and large, national states are a particular form or template of political ethnicity, in which a rough congruence exists between a single, dominant people and a state. In this I share Gellner's formula, with a few reservations. Principally, I take issue with Gellner regarding the historical time depth of ethne, peoples, and nations. As this book aims to show, all of them long predate modernity, are as old as the state itself, and stretch back to the dawn of history. In this I am closer to Anthony Smith, especially in his later works, which increasingly allow for the existence of pre-modern nations and national states.[‡] Second, while I maintain that the link between ethnicity and nationhood is a very close one, there are a few exceptions, most famously the Swiss, where a distinct sense of common national identity unites very different ethnic communities.[§]

To clarify this point, let us go back to Renan and see what was right and what was wrong about his voluntary and subjective concept of the nation, developed in reaction to the stripping of Lorraine and (German-speaking) Alsace from France and their annexation, against their people's will, by Germany in 1871. Indisputably, there is an

---

[‡] Surprisingly though, Smith's updated definition of the nation ("The Genealogy of Nations," in Ichijo and Uzelac (eds.), *When is the Nation?*, 119, also 97–98) omits the political element, most commonly statehood, probably because he regards this element as inherently modern. In my view, such an omission collapses the distinction between a people and a nation, much the same as Smith partly conflates the characteristics of the ethnos and the nation.

[§] However, note that the joint ethnic composition of Switzerland does not at all mean that Swiss nationhood is purely civic or lacks very distinctive ethnic elements. The country's constitutive cantons are strongly ethnic in their public character, and the Swiss have always been very unfavorably disposed toward the naturalization of foreigners and ethnic aliens.

intrinsically voluntary element in national self-identification and affinity. People may choose to belong to this or that nation on the basis of whatever criterion, including Renan's shared memories and vision of the future. However, as Marx put it with respect to action in history in general, people's choices are not *purely* voluntary, but are made within the conditions and circumstances they find before them. Renan's claim that people are not "slaves" of their race (ethnicity), language, religion, or territory has become commonplace in the study of nationalism, as national identity cannot be *reduced* to any of the above. Nonetheless, there is a very strong correlation – and causal connection – between these features and national identity, with ethnicity being by far the most significant factor. In his zeal Renan fell victim to that most common intellectual trap, the false dichotomy. While nations are indeed politically sovereign/state communities of common affinity, self-identity, and solidarity, these bonds overwhelmingly correlate with and relate to shared kin–culture traits.

Thus, language, the most distinctive marker of ethnicity's cultural element, correlates very closely with national identity. In Europe, the densest concentration of national states for geopolitical and historical reasons examined in Chapter 5, all states except for a very few have a dominant shared language at either the vernacular or literary level.[34] True, there are many small ethnic/linguistic minorities and a few larger ones in practically all these countries. Yet it is precisely their difference that marks distinct identities and fuel demands for national self-determination among quite a few of these groups, most notably the larger ones and those that have territorial contiguity. In other parts of the world, where states have no clear *Staatsvolk* and are truly multi-ethnic/multilingual, common national identity is an ongoing and uncertain project which largely depends on the adoption of a common language and other forms of shared culture (as well as elements of kinship) for its success. As we shall see in Chapter 6, this is the process that has more or less materialized in both the English-speaking immigrant countries and Latin America, is much in evidence in South Asia and the Southeast Asian archipelago, and less so in sub-Saharan Africa.

Territorial contiguity is another major determinant of an ethnonational community.[35] The same territory can be home to separate ethnonational populations, but, as with language, the inverse relationship is rarer, and ethnonational communities tend to be territorially contiguous. Not only is contiguity necessary for political sovereignty;

the close interaction that comes with a shared territory also constantly sustains and reinforces the commonality of culture and kinship. Conversely, great territorial non-contiguity is likely to result in a separation of ethnonational identities, as occurred, for example, with the English-speaking countries in relation to their former mother country.

The role of a common religion in the formation of national identity has been significant, albeit considerably less than that of language and territorial contiguity.[36] The significance of religion stems from its historical role as a major element of culture, and hence of ethnicity. The greater the salience of religion in the culture of a people, the more a defining element of the nation it has been. *Inter alia*, a distinct national religion has been the most salient influence. On the other hand, shared religion in and of itself rarely trumps linguistic differences to create a common ethnic or national identity. Thus, historically, more than creating ethnic and national communities, religion's greater effect has been in either reinforcing them, if it was shared, or sometimes undermining them, if it was not.[37]

Shared historical memories and a sense of common fate for the future were rightly regarded by Renan, and have been accepted ever since, as central to national identity. Notably, however, a shared history is conducive to the creation of a common identity precisely to the extent that it generates a common culture and sense of kinship. This was true of Renan's France with its uniquely successful, centuries-long process of French acculturation and common identity formation. And as we shall see throughout this book, the same causal relationship existed, with remarkably few exceptions, in most other places. Common acculturation has not always been a sufficient condition for overcoming earlier distinct ethnic and national identities and for forging a joint identity; yet almost invariably it has been a *necessary* condition. In the absence of common acculturation and a creation of a sense of kinship, peoples that were held together for many centuries often split apart at the first possible opportunity. A sense of common fate for the future rests on the same preconditions.

Finally, many modernists regard equal citizenship and popular sovereignty as inseparable from the concept of the nation. As both these principles are a modern creation which emerged on a country-size scale with the American and French revolutions, modernists thereby define the nation as modern, rather than regard both principles as elements of *modern* nationalism. Definitions are an intellectual grid laid over reality, and they can thus be sliced in any number of ways.** Being largely subjective, semantics is ultimately beyond dispute as long as the conceptual grid maintains internal coherence and consistency. There is, however, one more relevant criterion for judging concepts: the degree to which they correspond to common-sense usage and understanding of the reality they describe. I suggest that in ordinary parlance a nation means *a political/state community of common affinity, identity, and solidarity, the association of a people, usually defined by a certain culture and kin sentiments, with a particular state.* The question is whether or not such affinity and solidarity existed in premodern times, even in the absence of equal citizenship and popular sovereignty. Precisely because equal citizenship, popular sovereignty and nationalism have tended to go together during the modern period, they should not be confused but carefully distinguished from one another.

Nationalism and patriotism

Nationalism conventionally denotes the doctrine and ideology that a people is bound together in solidarity, fate, and common political aspirations, a doctrine and an ideology which became the paramount principle of political legitimacy in the nineteenth century. This doctrine or ideology is often confused with the *existence* of nations and national sentiment, affinity, and solidarity, which is also widely attributed to the nineteenth century. In reality, premodern people also felt and exhibited love and devotion for their ethnopolitical community, which again, when an ethnos and state converged, can be referred to as national. In the same way that the national phenomenon was merely one template of political ethnicity, such national devotion was merely one particular form of the well-recognized phenomenon of patriotism, one's attachment and devotion to one's state and people. In pettystates this implied an affinity and devotion to a kin–culture ethnopolitical community that was usually smaller than the entire ethnos. In multiethnic states and empires, it meant affinity and devotion to the state, predominantly exhibited by its dominant people or ethnos, although possibly also by others, depending on their communal or individual status within the state.[38]

** For "national state" as distinguished from "nation-state" see note 4.

2 THE EVOLUTION OF KIN-CULTURE COMMUNITIES

The concepts of ethnic group and ethnicity were coined in English in the wake of the Second World War to replace the concept of race that had lost its legitimacy with Nazi racial doctrines and their horrendous application. Although race assumed a predominantly biological meaning from the late nineteenth century onward, it had traditionally denoted large communities of both cultural and "blood"-kin relatedness. Hence, the English race, French race, Japanese race, and so forth. Vaguely, the concept of ethnicity incorporates both the above meanings of a shared culture and kin relatedness. But it has retained semantic ambiguity because of lingering uneasiness regarding either of these elements, with the result that one or the other is often disregarded. As suggested here, both elements are integral to ethnicity, with their relative weight differing in each individual case, and they have been largely interconnected. I begin with kinship.

The application of evolutionary theory to explain basic human emotions, desires, and behavior – popularly known as "sociobiology" – has gained ground rapidly since the late 1970s, profoundly revolutionizing the study of man. Its relevance to our subject can be summarized as follows: people tend to prefer closer kin, who share more genes with them, to more remote kin or "strangers." As a propensity this is not necessarily conscious. Like any natural predisposition, it evolved because those who acted upon it increased their genes' representation in the human population and, consequently, also that predisposition itself. Obviously, kinship is not the only medium of human affinity and loyalty, but it is a major one and closely tied to the others. The argument that here lay the root cause of tribalism, ethnocentrism, and, at least partly, nationalism has been advanced by several scholars, of whom at least one, Pierre van den Berghe, is regularly cited in the scholarly literature on nationalism.[1] And yet even when cited, the evolutionary message has had little impact on that literature.

There are various reasons for this neglect, rejection, and even down-right hostility. Early, crude attempts to extend the Darwinian revolution to the understanding of human behavior and society, carried out in the late nineteenth and early twentieth centuries and known as social Darwinism, leaned toward racism and class bias. In reaction, the social sciences and humanities completely moved away from anything that suggested a biological basis for human behavior. Massively reinforced after the horrors of Nazism and with the dismantling of public racism in the West, this tendency reached its apogee in the 1960s and 1970s. Thus, scholars from the above fields have found themselves totally unprepared as revolutionary breakthroughs in the decipherment of the genome coupled with a great revival of evolutionary theory generated one of the most significant scientific developments of the era. Nothing in their professional training enabled them to relate to the new perspective and insights. Indeed, everything they had learned served to predispose them against it. For in their reaction against social Darwinism, the social sciences and humanities veered too sharply in the opposite direction. With a few exceptions, they rejected the idea that anything like human nature existed or was meaningful to the understanding of society. Instead, they adopted the view that people and human societies were wholly determined by culture and history. This, however, was just another false either/or dichotomy. It meant turning a blind eye to a whole side of reality, for it is *both* nature and nurture, indeed, precisely the *interaction* between them that has always shaped people and human societies. Genes are not everything, of course, but they are hardly irrelevant, or disconnected from culture.

Kinship, or a strong sense of it, has been recognized by not a few authors as a major constitutive element of most nations. Yet whether or not this sense was warranted and where it came from remains mostly undetermined. Family ties are an obvious social reality, though the source of this most powerful bonding has never been clarified in the social sciences either. Without an evolutionary rationale, the question of what explains this basic human bond could not be answered, if it has been asked at all. It has been regarded as a "just-so" fact, the way the world is.

Kin ties extended in prestate societies and on the peripheries of some
state societies from nuclear and extended families to tribes. Still, there
is mainly confusion as to whether or not nationalism related to tribalism is a further extension of the same affinity through widening
circles and in the domain of political communities. Tribalism is regularly invoked in the media and public discourse when ever-surprised
and shocked western societies are confronted with the eruption of
ferocious ethnic and national conflicts somewhere in the world. Yet
there are always those who rush to dismiss that concept as irrelevant.

 The leap from family to tribe to people and nation strikes
scholars as much too big, as problematic and questionable in many
ways. Thus, it is necessary to clarify what in kinship remains relevant to
such a complex phenomenon as the nation up the long march of history
and the growth of political organization. Our starting point predates
the state and even agriculture, which are very recent events in human
history. The first states appeared only 5,000 years ago, and in most
parts of the world much later. Agriculture, too, first appeared only
about 10,000 years ago and took thousands more to spread. By comparison, the genus *Homo* goes back some 2 million years, and our own
species *Homo sapiens*, people who practically are biologically us, about
150,000–200,000 years. Thus, 99.5 or 95 percent, respectively, at the
very least, of humans' time on earth was spent before agriculture and
the state. During that time, people lived in small kin groups as hunter-
gatherers (also called foragers). And it is to this mode of life over vast
time spans that evolutionary theory looks for the roots of human
natural predispositions. What proved adaptive then constitutes our
biological inheritance, around which our spectacular and multifarious
cultural development over the past few millennia has been built and
with which it constantly interacts.

Kinship and culture in the past 150,000 years

Evidence about the aboriginal human way of life comes from archaeology and even more from the variety of forager societies that survived
into or close to our times and have been studied by anthropologists.
I have devoted hundreds of pages to them elsewhere,[2] and the following
is a simplified but fairly adequate abstract of their social structure. As
the evolutionary literature has swelled momentously, I cite it only

sparingly, limiting myself to what is strictly necessary for the subject and relevant for most readers. I develop the still underdeveloped theme of how culture fits into human evolution from as early as our aboriginal condition and how in conjunction with kinship it defines ethnicity and ethnic allegiances.

Foragers lived in extended family groups or clans, also known as bands or local groups in the anthropological literature. These consisted of a few dozen people of several generations, including elders, male siblings with their wives, and children. Dispersed over large territories to subsist, clan groups were part of a larger association: the regional group, or tribe, which on average consisted of about 500 people. They assembled seasonally in festivals, where rituals were performed and marriages were agreed upon and celebrated. Thus, the tribal group was both an endogenic marriage pool, wherein the vast majority of marriages took place, and a culture unit. The regional group, or a number of related regional groups, were often a "dialect tribe," if they did not speak an altogether separate language. They also had their own name and a distinct sense of self-identity as a "people."

It is easy to understand in evolutionary terms why members of family groups show solidarity among themselves: one's genes are passed on to succeeding generations not only through one's own offspring, but also through other close kin who share the same genes.[3] Siblings share, on average, 50 percent of their genes, the same percentage as parents and offspring. Half-siblings share, on average, 25 percent of their genes, as do uncles/aunts with nephews/nieces. Cousins share, on average, 12.5 percent of their genes.* Thus, those who possessed a trait to care for their close kin increased their genes' representation over time, and with them that trait itself. This is the

---

* There should be no confusion here. More than 99 percent of the genes are identical in all people. All the variations among individuals are due to the remaining less than 1 percent, and it is to this variation in the genome that the shared genes above refer. It should not be thought that this less than 1 percent difference in genes is so small as to be insignificant. Humans share more than 98 percent of their genes with chimpanzees, yet crucial changes in a small number of genes trigger very substantial differences. See, e.g., W. Enard et al., "Intra- and Interspecific Variation in Primate Gene Expression Patterns," Science, 296 (2002), 340–343; Galina Glazko et al., "Eighty Percent of Proteins are Different between Humans and Chimpanzees," Gene, 346 (2005), 215–219.

basis of the long-held notion that "blood is thicker than water." It is mostly with these primary groups that people's allegiance rests.

Members of the regional group or tribe were not as closely related as primary family members (or as a colony of social insects, which are clones or near clones which descend from one mother and often father). Still, the rationale of kinship does not end with close kin, although it declines along a steep curve as it expands. Since the large majority of marriages took place within the regional group, there was a wide gap between the "us" of the tribe and outsiders.[4] The evolutionary logic suggests abstractly that an individual would be willing to risk his or her life for two siblings or eight cousins, who together have the same number of genes in common with one's self. This, of course, is only the mathematical logic to which reality more or less approximates. And in principle, the same logic holds true for 32 second cousins, 128 third cousins, or 512 fourth cousins – which is, in fact, roughly what a regional group was. This is a major reason why members of the group tended to prefer other members of the group to outsiders.

Moreover, although not every member of the regional group was a close kin of all the others, the regional group was a dense network of close kinship through marriages. When a daughter of one family was given in marriage to another family, the couple and their offspring became a "shared investment" and "joint venture" that allied the two "in-law" families (as it does today). If you are unaccustomed to this language and find it alien, recall that this evolutionary rationale accounts for the well-recognized fact that kin relations and marriage links constitute the primary social bonds in "primitive" and not so primitive societies. Political treaties and alliances throughout the ages were cemented by marriage.

Notably though, kin ties in humans do not end at the gene level. There is a crucial cultural twist here, which is not separate from our biology but partly built into it. How do we know who our kin are? In nature, from microorganisms to humans, there are biological and social cues for recognizing close kin.[5] Humans grow up together with their close kin, remember marriages and births, and are told about kin relations. For more distant kin, however, people have rougher indications. Similar physical features (phenotype) are one such indication of genetic relatedness. Thus, different and unfamiliar racial groups are likely to appear more alien. Moreover, apart from biology, humans have culture, and are differentiated by their cultures. Since culture,

particularly among hunter-gatherers, was local and thus strongly correlated with kinship, cultural identity became a strong predictor of
kinship. Those around me in the tribal group who dressed, behaved,
and looked like me were also most likely to be more related to me than
aliens. Therefore, humans are distinctively inclined to side with people
who share the same culture with them against foreigners.[6] The more
different another culture is, the "stranger" and less part of "us" it
would be regarded. Even between relatively close ethnic groups people
are acutely attuned to the subtlest of differences in dialect, accent,
dressing style, and behavior, and tend to give preference to what is
most akin to them. This is the key to what a perplexed Freud
confusedly described as the "narcissism of minor differences" between
close ethnicities.[†]

The Yanomamo hunters and horticulturalists from the Orinoco
basin between Brazil and Venezuela demonstrate this universal trend.
They believe "all other people are inferior ... explaining their strange
customs and peculiar languages." Even within the Yanomamo themselves, "any difference between adjacent groups is exaggerated and
ridiculed. Language differences in particular are promptly noted and
criticized by the Yanomamo ... The characteristic reaction of any
group to a tape recording made in another area was this: 'They speak
crooked; we speak straight, the right way!'"[7]

Culture sharing is crucial in another way too. Not only was it
in itself a strong predictor of kin relatedness in aboriginal communities;
it is also a highly significant tool of human social cooperation.
Cooperation is dramatically more effective when cultural codes – above
all language, but also customs, values and other patterns of thought
and behavior – are shared. Culture, cultural diversity, and, hence, the
facility of shared culture cooperation are unique to humans and differentiate them from other social animals. Cultural–linguistic diversity

[†] Sigmund Freud, "Group Psychology and the Analysis of the Ego" (1921) and
"Civilization and Its Discontents" (1930), in *The Complete Psychological Works of
Sigmund Freud*, London: Hogarth, 1953–1974, vol. 18, 101–104, and vol. 21,
108–116, respectively. Freud confessed his puzzlement over the reasons for group ties
in general. He tried to explain the "narcissism" as a bottled-up expression of an
elementary aggressive drive, thus turning the matter on its head and denying it any
logic, evolutionary or otherwise. Why aggression should express itself in this
particular domain remained wholly obscure. In actuality, it is ethnic differences, even
minor, that may trigger aggression, rather than the other way around.

among forager groups varied markedly, depending on their history and geography. For example, among both the Eskimo-Inuit of the Arctic and the Bushmen of southern Africa more or less similar languages are shared across thousands of kilometers. But in Australia, whose human habitation is very old, going back some 50,000 years, linguistic diversity among the hundreds of regional/tribal groups was much greater. There were more than 200 different languages and far more dialects.[8] Similarly, scores of linguistically different foraging "peoples" and hundreds of tribes lived in the lush coastal strip of the American northwest. Finally, the natives of Highland New Guinea were not hunter-gatherers, but the world's largest and most isolated surviving concentration of primitive horticulturalists (together with Amazonia). Inhabiting valleys separated by rugged and forested mountains, they speak about 850 different languages (out of the world's roughly 7,000 extant languages).

Thus, the regional group, or "dialect tribe," differing from its neighbors in language and customs, was by far the most effective framework of social cooperation for its members. Outside it, people would have found themselves at a tremendous disadvantage, as any immigrant knows (even in today's far gentler conditions). Once acquired in youth by a long process of socialization, cultural forms become extremely difficult to replace. Brain structure consolidates in adults, losing most of its earlier elastic ability to rearrange itself through learning. Therefore, a shared culture in a human reality characterized by cultural divisions further increased the social stake of a tribal group's members in their group's survival. A threat to the existence of the group and its particular culture was a genuine threat to one's own existence. For this reason, people tend to cherish the closely knit web of symbols, codes, and practices that mark them as a community of kinship, culture, and mutual cooperation. Hence, also the predominance of language, the chief culture form and medium of communication, as by far the most prevalent cultural marker of ethnicity and nationhood.

Note that this major cultural factor is not confined to a "purely cultural" sphere. As a strong selection force in the life of aboriginal people over thousands of generations, throughout the history of *Homo sapiens*, a non-specific preference for whatever culture group within which one happens to grows up and be socialized became encoded in our genes in the same way as the preference for kin was. The point here needs to be clearly understood. While culture forms, including complex languages, are highly diverse and are transformed largely randomly, the *potential* to create them is universal and inborn in our species. Similarly, by all evidence, the *capacity* for regional/tribal group relations (with which advanced symbolic capability is intimately linked) is a trait that evolved biologically with our species. Symbolic culture, complex language, and regional grouping, as a minimum, have existed over eons wherever *Homo sapiens* lived. Experts have become increasingly aware that culture and nature in humans coevolved in a reciprocal, mutually affecting symbiosis.[9] Still, the special role that culture played in the evolution of kin–culture communities has not been sufficiently recognized in evolutionary accounts of group relations, ethnicity, and nationalism. Culture, cultural diversity, and the vital role of shared culture in facilitating social cooperation – all uniquely human – increased people's attachment to their extended kin group.

Preference for one's kin–culture group was a very strong selection force over geological times in the aboriginal human way of life because competition and conflict between individuals and groups were very intense. Recent studies have conclusively shown that the Rousseauite image of prestate abundance and peacefulness, which dominated anthropology during much of the twentieth century, was embarrassingly wrong.[10] Hunter-gatherers experienced critical scarcities, which fuelled competition and conflict among them. The violent mortality rate among their adult males ranged at around 25 percent, far higher than in the overwhelming majority of historical state wars. Whole groups were occasionally wiped out in natural catastrophes or in conflict with one another.

To be sure, competition and even conflict among close kin were also ubiquitous. Evolutionary logic explains why this is so: the closer the kin, the greater the reward for caring for them, but only as long as they do not threaten the prospects of even closer kin. For example, one is genetically doubly closer to one's self than to a sibling. Therefore, in case of severe competition between them, sibling rivalry can become intense and even deadly. The story of Cain and Abel demonstrates both the intense competition and strong inhibitions against the killing of kin involved in such occurrences. Similarly, while uncles/aunts are evolutionarily inclined to favor their nephews/nieces, they doubly favor their own offspring. Hence, the all too familiar jealousy, tensions, and antagonism between relatives.[11] In extreme cases this may even result in cooperation with outsiders against kin, which sometimes happens but which has always carried the moral stigma of betrayal. By and large, however, family members tend to support one another, *inter alia* in disputes and clashes with members of other families. In interclan rivalry, clans which were intermarried were likely to support one another against other clans. Finally, the clans of one regional group normally supported one another against other regional groups. A traditional Arab proverb expresses this evolutionary rationale: "I against my brother; I and my brother against my cousin; I and my brother and my cousin against the world." This is somewhat more complex, and realistic, than the simple ingroup-cooperation/outgroup-rivalry suggested by Herbert Spencer and William Graham Sumner. Cooperation and even alliance with non-kin and strangers takes place all the time, for the attainment of common objectives and on the principle of reciprocity.[12] Yet they come more easily where cultural codes are shared and kin trust is stronger.

The interrelationship between kinship, culture, and social cooperation in the aboriginal hunter-gatherer regional group sheds light on the roots of group solidarity and ethnocentrism. As scholars are becoming increasingly aware after protracted controversies, selection took place not only at the gene and individual level, but, to some extent, also among groups. It is agreed that genes for self-sacrifice on behalf of the group could not have been selected if they had the effect of annihilating those who possessed them faster than aiding them through improved group survival. There is a fine balancing act here. Still, as Darwin himself suggested, under conditions of intense competition, a group which was biologically endowed with greater solidarity and with individual willingness to sacrifice for the group would defeat less cohesive groups.[13]

The adaptive functions of some non-utilitarian forms of cultural life, such as communal rituals and ceremonies, and even the communal aspects of art, which are otherwise quite mysterious, might at least partly be explained by the evolutionary advantages of large group cooperation. All these cultural forms first appeared with *Homo sapiens*, have been universally present in every society of our species throughout its long existence, and seem to be mutually connected. Rituals, cults, and religion are a mystery to those in the Enlightenment's tradition who regard them as hugely wasteful superstitions. Some scholars, invoking an analogy from artificial intelligence, have suggested that religion is a "bug," a "parasite," or "virus" on *Homo sapiens*' advanced intellectual software. This proposition expands on an older view according to which religion is a by-product of the much wider scope of our species' powers of imagination and comprehension, which make people ponder, fear, and attempt to come to terms with death and the cosmic forces of nature and the universe.[14]

Conversely, religion may have constituted, evolutionarily speaking, more than worthless expenditure of resources and time. From Émile Durkheim's *The Elementary Forms of the Religious Life* (1915), which concentrated on the Australian Aboriginal hunter-gatherers, functionalist theorists have argued that religion's main role was fostering social cohesion. Machiavelli, Rousseau, and the nineteenth-century French positivists held more or less the same view. As Richard Dawkins observes, discussing the same idea in evolutionary terms: "What a weapon! Religious faith deserves a chapter to itself in the annals of war technology."[15] We know this from history only too well. Obviously, religion is a complex phenomenon, and many threads of causation probably combined to generate it. The factor pointed out here means that in those tribal groups in which common ritual and cult ceremonies were more intense, social cooperation became more habitual and spiritually legitimized. This was probably translated into an advantage in intergroup competition and conflict. The ancient Greeks' amphictyonic, religious–military alliance has become a generic term denoting a very common historic, and prehistoric, phenomenon.[16]

It should be realized that the aboriginal human condition is not an exotic piquantry, tucked in the remote beginnings of time. Quite the opposite. History's short span is illuminated by the bright light of written records. But beyond that very limited area under the lamppost, shrouded in the thick darkness of prehistory, real people of our species – for whom we have no known names or a concrete record of events – lived over thousands of generations. We know from archaeology and anthropology that they were anatomically like us, created exquisite art, possessed a symbolic and linguistic capacity as advanced as ours, and belonged to regional groups divided by kinship and culture. Ethnicity – kin–culture reality and a sense of identity – is a human-specific and universal extending far back to the beginning of our species.

Surviving foraging societies illustrate the familiar characteristics of ethnocentrism. The "Eskimo" (a name the American Indians gave to their Arctic zone neighbors) called themselves by a variety of words which usually meant "real people." They regarded themselves literally as the real people, as a class apart from all other human beings.[17] The Yanomamo also

> *believe that they were the first, finest, and most refined form of man to inhabit the earth ... Yanomamo in fact means "humanity," or at least the most important segment of humanity. All other peoples are known by the term* naba, *a concept that implies an invidious distinction between "true" man and "subhuman" man ... A foreigner is usually tolerated if he is able to provide the Yanomamo with useful items ... but apart from that he is usually held with some contempt.*[18]

Evolutionary inheritance and historical transformation

Assuming all the above to be true, what are the residues of our evolutionary inheritance in historical ethnicities and nations, whose conditions are so radically changed from those of aboriginal hunter-gatherer family groups and tribes? After all, although aboriginal groups also underwent constant transformation and were subject to processes of fission and fusion, ethne and nations appear to be even more subjective, elusive, and in a state of flux. Among the most enduring human cultural forms, they nevertheless appear and disappear, with people and groups mixing with others, shaking off one identity and adopting another, changing their allegiance and often sharing in a multiplicity of identities. To be sure, ethnicities and nations are complex, composite, multilayered and multifaceted historically developed phenomena.

Are ethne and nations kin groups? Given the complex historical processes of group amalgamation, identity formation, and transformation, scholars usually refer to a "myth" of common descent or kinship shared by ethnic groups and nations. But what does "myth" stand for? In both scholarly and colloquial discourse it often implies falsehood, but more discriminately it means a legendary communal story or tradition about great past events, which may have a greater or lesser base in reality. In fact, exponentially growing in number and sophistication in recent years, scientific studies reveal that most ethnic communities tend to be genetically related.[19] This is not that surprising because massive population movements were rare before the advent of modern means of transportation. As we shall see in Chapter 3, the roots of most populations go back to the original settlement of their territories during the Neolithic agricultural expansions and even before. Present-day populations tend to be descendants of these founder groups, and have mostly intermarried locally, within themselves, over millennia. Foreign migrations and conquests usually took the form of elite takeovers, with the majority of the population remaining unchanged.

Just as clearly, however, genetic studies show that genetic continuums regularly flow into or are split between different – occasionally hostile – cultures, ethnicities, and nations. People are sometimes genetically more related to their neighbors across the border than to other people of the nation to which they belong and express allegiance. Contrary to superficial either/or reasoning, this does not mean that kinship is irrelevant. Rather, the picture is more subtle and other factors are involved. In the first place, what matters, of course, is the *perception* of kinship (which, again, more often than not has a genuine basis in reality). The significance of the "myth" of common descent is precisely that peoples throughout history have been so prone to generate it as a supreme bond. When different communities fused together, they tended to create an often fictitious genealogy of common ancestry and descent. People everywhere have been strongly inclined to extend the images and idioms of kinship over those with whom they shared cultural identity, territory, and political community, and not only metaphorically.

As noted in the Introduction, in some cases the people of an ethnos are quite aware that they originated from diverse groups and did not all share a common descent. Still, common descent is not the only source of kinship. The more ethnic and national collectives integrate through marriages over generations and centuries the more they feel themselves to be a kin community in which the various founder groups have been immersed. Furthermore, as we have seen, a common culture binds people together, functioning not only as a cue for kinship but also as a shared system of codes and symbols. People acquire that system in a protracted process of social learning in youth, function best within it, and find it exceedingly difficult to replace. For this reason, they are heavily invested in, and are strongly attached to, that culture and the collective that embodies it. Sticking to the things that one knows best and is unlikely to replace successfully – language, social values, patterns of behavior, and belief – is largely imposed on people as their superior option. Similarly, the intimately familiar landscapes of one's native land, engraved in one's consciousness for the very same reasons, evoke great attachment and devotion.

Needless to say, rather than "blind instincts," these are all deep-seated but highly modulated predispositions, whose particular expressions are largely circumstantial. Moreover, there are other, sometimes conflicting, considerations that feed into people's calculations. Thus, people regularly adopt foreign cultural forms, sometimes eagerly, and they might also migrate from their native land (where conditions might be harsh) provided they consider these acts to be beneficial to them and believe that they can carry them out successfully. Notably though, similar processes of identity formation tend to occur in their new and adopted homeland. Processes of cultural amalgamation, to the extent that they take place over time, have bound together not only historical peoples and nations, but also modern immigrant ones. People relate to the ethnos and nation in familial terms as a reality and metaphor. But, significantly, it has been through *any* of the following means for joining the "family" – birth, marriage, or "adoption" – that admission to these kin–culture collectives has always taken place. Joining ethnic and national collectives has never been as easy as some liberals imply, but neither has it been as insurmountably difficult as some conservatives make it out to be, with great variation, of course.

This is the deep root of tribalism, ethnocentrism, xenophobia, patriotism, and nationalism. With the coming of agriculture, state societies, and modernity, and as ethnic communities expanded from hundreds and thousands to millions, often many millions, the sentiment of kin–culture solidarity expanded far beyond its original setting and scope. One's people or nation can evoke the greatest devotion, indeed, *fraternity* within a *motherland* or *fatherland* (the words are revealing), no matter how genetically related its members actually are (and they often are). Individuals have been genuinely prepared to risk and sacrifice themselves for these large shared-culture, semi-, and sometimes pseudo- or "imagined" kin groups. This is the "atavistic" element which has baffled modern observers and is often evoked vaguely in order to explain people's willingness to kill and die for seemingly remote causes. Liberals and Marxists, tied to an economic concept of rationality as a quest for material reward, have lacked the analytical tools for comprehending these seemingly "irrational" preferences: in the liberal case, that of the collective over the individual (or humanity); and in the Marxist, that of the nation over class (or humanity). In reality, however, the "false consciousness" that theorists often ascribe to people may apply more to themselves, because people's notions of their interests and prosperity are simply different than the theorists' concepts. People care about their individual interests, to be sure, but, as we saw, these extend into, and are intertwined with, their broader kin–culture communities.

Thus, to the bewilderment of the ideologues of the Second International, when the First World War broke out the workers in each of the belligerent countries enthusiastically threw their lot in with their conational middle- and upper-class "exploiters" and against foreign "fellow workers." A Frenchman or a German was prepared to kill or be killed for Alsace-Lorraine, whose possession appeared to have no practical bearing on his daily life. In the great extension of culture groups and consciousness boundaries, these provinces were perceived by him as something like the neighboring home territory of his immediate close-kin group.

Certainly, what was adaptive in small aboriginal kin–culture groups has not necessarily remained so as human conditions changed radically through history. And yet in this, as in so much else, our natural predispositions, shaped during our species' long aboriginal existence by tremendous forces of selection, remain extremely potent. Cultural takeoff since the advent of agriculture and the state has been much too recent to significantly affect human biology. Biologically we are virtually the same people as our Stone Age forefathers. Thus, where radically new conditions sever the original link between a human behavior pattern and the original evolutionary end it evolved to achieve, it is this pattern rather than the evolutionary end that people are tied to by powerful emotional stimuli. People's desire for sweetness serves to illustrate originally adaptive propensities that have gone astray in altered cultural conditions. Indicative of ripeness and high nutritious value in fruits, it is now artificially produced and harmful. Obesity, when appetite that was adaptive in an environment of food scarcity is indulged in a society of plenty, is another illustration. On a happier note, people continue to intensely pursue sexual gratification, even though effective contraception has made most of this obsessive activity irrelevant in terms of the reproductive success it originally evolved to achieve. Indeed, this does not make sexual gratification any less enjoyable, valued, or, for that matter, rational.

One final example, often quoted in the sociological literature, brings us closer back to our subject. It demonstrates how our mechanism for identifying kin can misfire under altered cultural conditions. In Israeli village communes, *kibbutzim*, children used to be raised together from birth in communal nurseries rather than in their own families' homes. It has been found that when these children grew up, they treated each other as siblings, at least in the sense that they rarely got involved romantically among themselves and even more seldom intermarried. Unexpectedly, they instinctively applied to their pseudo-kin the universal, biologically rooted, taboo against incest which runs through nature.[20] (This taboo, too, is not merely a human "social construct," for in other social mammals as well, the males or females leave the group at puberty to avoid inbreeding with its genetic risks to the offspring.)

All this does not mean that we are the slaves of our genes and unaffected by culture. But nor should our biological inheritance be impatiently dismissed as irrelevant to social realities, as generations of scholars from the social sciences and humanities have been schooled to believe. Undoubtedly, accelerated cultural development has dramatically changed and diversified human behavior throughout history and around the globe. And yet historical cultural development did not operate on a "clean slate," nor is it capable of producing simply "anything." Although highly diverse and multifarious, human cultural forms have been built as a range of variations around a clearly recognizable deep core of innate, evolution-shaped human propensities. In the process, while never disappearing, these propensities have been greatly modified, assuming novel and widely varied manifestations. Such gene–culture interactions are the stuff from which human history is made, including kin-preference, ethnicity, and their many derivatives. With historical transformation all genetic bets are not off; they are hedged.

This point also needs emphasizing in order to allay other often-voiced concerns regarding the application of evolutionary theory to human affairs. The evolutionary logic in itself has no normative implications. It can inform us about natural human predispositions, whose often ignored effects we would be wise to take into account but which are frequently variable and even contradictory. (Both late nineteenth- and early twentieth-century social Darwinists and *tabula rasa* liberals erred here in two opposite directions.) We may choose to follow natural predispositions or work to adjust them so that they better suit our changed circumstances. There is nothing sacred or morally compelling about maximizing gene propagation. This is merely the blind, algorithmic mechanism of natural evolution. The human brain – itself a product of evolution and a powerful instrument of conscious, purposeful, and future-oriented, rather than blind, design – may come up with more satisfactory arrangements. Apprehensive of the often explosive and horrendous manifestations of ethnicity and nationalism, scholars in these fields have been prone to confuse the descriptive and the normative. But while the normative perspective is not only legitimate but also vital, it must not distort our vision of reality.

"Primordialism" is a label that has all too often substituted for a deeper scholarly understanding. Ethnicity in general, as opposed to any specific ethnos, is primordial in the sense that it has always been a defining feature of our species. Nationalism is not primordial in that sense, if only because that particular form of political ethnicity is historically intertwined with the rise of state societies, premodern or modern. Indeed, both ethnicity and nationalism in all their wealth of forms have been bound up with cultural–historical developments. And yet they are not reduced or *reducible* to these developments without roots in an innate human preference for one's kin–culture group. The modernists' fallacy here amounts to breathtaking naiveté. Traditionalists, too, emphasizing the longer historical roots of the nation, have not gone further, because to suggest anything about human nature meant venturing into forbidden land and violating disciplinary orthodoxies. On the other hand, evolutionary studies of ethnicity and nationalism, though very cognizant of the role of culture, have not realized how uniquely ingrained in our species it is and how it reinforces kin relatedness in creating large group identity and solidarity. Nor have they traced the transformations of such inborn propensities through the ages. An ever sensible theorist such as Anthony Smith has withheld judgment on van den Berghe's evolutionary account of the basis of the national phenomenon. He has suggested that in order for the abstract evolutionary logic to have conviction, one would have to demonstrate how it operated in the actual historical reality of changing cultural boundaries and identities, and how it extended from small kin communities to nations.[21] It is the interconnections between kinship, culture, and identity formation, and the interface between human propensities and historical development that this book sets out to explore. So far our discussion has unfolded in the abstract. Henceforth, we delve into the world of actual tribes, ethne, peoples, states, and nations.

3 FROM TRIBES TO STATEHOOD

Between 10,000 and 5,000 years ago, agriculture and animal husbandry were independently pioneered in west and east Asia, Central America, the Andes, and a few other minor centers. From there farming spread out to cover most of the world's surface that was suitable for it. Its impact was profound. Both tribe and ethnos were deeply affected. Furthermore, within a few millennia, states emerged where agricultural society had taken root, building on, and then transforming, existing kin–culture populations. States eroded and supplanted tribal structures. At the same time, ethnic bonds of affinity, identity, and solidarity remained central to state existence and politics throughout history. In what follows we shall trace the increase in the size of tribes and the formation of large-scale ethne due to the spread of agriculture and animal husbandry. We shall then trace the transformation of kin–culture bonds as they lost their tribal form and became intertwined with the politics of evolving states.

Tribal growth and ethnic expansion

Agriculture's far greater productivity in comparison with foraging meant that human population, and hence demographic density, increased by leaps and bounds. World population, estimated at somewhere between 5 and 15 million before the advent of agriculture, grew by a factor of 100 by the eve of industrialization.[1] This was a gradual process, of course, but from the start it meant that agricultural tribes were larger than the hunter-gatherer regional/tribal group. Wider kin circles now lived closer together. Still, agricultural tribes remained relatively small-scale societies, normally consisting of anywhere between two thousand to a few tens of thousands of people.

Tribal societies were mostly pre- or protohistoric, that is, they lacked writing systems. Good evidence about them comes only from historic state societies, premodern or modern, that left records of their tribal neighbors. The following is a brief survey of evidence, intended to demonstrate the form and size of tribal societies. The classical Greek and Roman sources are an invaluable source of information. In the middle of the first century BC, during his conquest of Gaul, Julius Caesar mentions about a hundred Celtic tribal communities (*civitas* or *populus*), already undergoing the beginning of urbanization and in the process of transition away from tribalism.[2] Over thirty main tribal groupings are identified in Britain during the Roman conquest of the first century AD.[3] Some fifty tribal entities are mentioned in Tacitus' *Germania*, whereas sixty-nine are recorded by the geographer Ptolemy in the second century AD.[4] Classical sources mention between fifty and a hundred Thracian tribes (roughly in today's Bulgaria).[5] Much the same picture emerges for the Greeks and Romans themselves in their pre- and early state times: Athens originated from a confederation of elements from the four Ionian tribes; Sparta from elements of the three Dorian tribes; Rome from three Latin tribal entities with an admixture of Sabines and others.

European contact with a large variety of tribal societies world-wide during the modern period offers another invaluable source. In North America, the Iroquois League of five tribes in upstate New York is estimated to have numbered 20,000–30,000. Only a little smaller were the Huron tribal confederacy, their neighbors; the Powhatan confederacy in Virginia; and the Cherokee of the southeast.[6] There were twenty-seven tribes and tribal confederacies on the Great Plains. The four tribal confederacies that dominated the northern Plains (Dakota, Blackfoot, Cree, Mandan-Hidatsa) similarly consisted each of an estimated 15,000–25,000 people.[7] In Central America, the Aztecs were one among seven Nahuatl speaking tribes that immigrated into the Valley of Mexico from the north. Their original tribal composition was still evident in the internal borough division of Tenochtitlan, the city they built in the fourteenth and fifteenth centuries, as they grew into statehood and later into an imperial power.

In Polynesia, a few thousand people to a tribe was the standard, though in Hawaii, Tonga, and Samoa, tribes were tens of thousands strong.[8] In New Zealand, a total native population of a few hundred thousand was divided among some forty, often warring, tribes.[9]

In Africa, studies of prestate ethne in the first half of the twentieth century registered the following results. The Dinka of southern Sudan numbered some 900,000, divided into twenty-five main tribal groups. Their neighbors, the Nuer, totaled 300,000, with tribal size varying considerably. The Logoli and Vugusu Bantu of western Kenya comprised about 300,000, divided into some twenty tribes. The Konkomba in northern Togo comprised 45,000 people, divided into several tribes. The Lugbara of Uganda and Congo numbered 250,000, divided into some sixty tribes. The Tallensi of the Gold Coast totaled about 35,000, out of a larger lingual and ethnic stock of about 170,000. The Zulu "nation" of a few hundred thousand people was united in the early nineteenth century from many previously independent tribes, each totaling a few thousand.[10]

In Eurasia and Africa the domestication of large animals gave rise to a semi-pastoralist and pastoralist way of life (which because of the scarcity of suitable breeds did not exist in the Americas and Oceania).[11] Occupying the arid and semi-arid land on the peripheries of the agricultural communities, pastoralists were also bound together by tribal, kin-based ties. Again the ethnographic record is extensive. In mid-twentieth-century east Africa, for example, the pastoral Datoga numbered 30,000, divided between several tribes or subtribes. The Maasai totaled close to 250,000, divided between seventeen tribes.[12] The Dodoth numbered 20,000,[13] as did the Karimojong.[14] The Basseri tribe of southern Iran comprised an estimated 16,000 people, divided into twelve kin groups, which were further divided into large extended families.[15] The pastoral Bedouin tribes who inhabited the area around the middle Euphrates in northern Syria in the early twentieth century numbered a few thousand "tents" each, and up to 10,000 for tribal confederations.[16]

The excavated archives of the ancient kingdom of Mari in the same region, relating to the nineteenth and eighteenth centuries BC, offer the most extensive picture we possess of the pastoralist population in the ancient Fertile Crescent. Of the three major Amorite pastoral tribal confederations in the Mari domain, ten Hanean, five Benjaminite, and three Sutean tribes are mentioned by name, and they were further divided along kin lines.[17] The ancient Israelites' presence in (pre- or proto)history starts as they appear coalesced, in a process whose origins remain mostly obscure, into twelve tribes. These had various sizes, internal clan divisions and closeness to one another, and they were coming together in a loose military–amphictyonic alliance. In the light of archaeological surveys, estimates of the early Israelite population have now been sharply revised downward to considerably less than 100,000 people.[18]

This ethnographic survey can teach us a great deal about both tribe and ethnos, because cross-cultural similarities are striking. Europeans found to their surprise that there was a close resemblance between the tribal societies they encountered during their Age of Discovery and those with which they were familiar from their classical education.[19] First, tribal structure was remarkably similar. Nuclear and extended families were linked with related families in clans (Greek *genos*; Roman *gens*). The principal body of social interaction in tribal societies, the clan, was actually or supposedly descended from a common founding father, who was generally believed to have had a supernatural and heroic origin. Related clans within the tribe often came together in higher associations or fraternities (Greek *phratria*; Roman *curia*). These successive subdivisions have different names in different anthropological studies as well as in different societies, but the general structure was fairly similar. Surviving in name and some residual functions in the Greek and Roman poleis, these kin tribal subdivisions were identified by Lewis Morgan in the Iroquois, as well as in Aztec Tenochtitlan. More recently, they have been described by anthropologists in the small-scale horticultural societies of Highland New Guinea.[20]

The term "segmentary society" is often used to describe this social structure. Loyalty was extended above all to family and clan, but clans, fraternities of clans, and whole tribes habitually came together in alliances to counter external threats. The same applies to tribes cooperating in tribal confederacies. On all these levels, the language of kinship and ancestry was regularly invoked to enlist support. Ancestry and genealogy were orally recorded many generations back. When new links and alliances were forged through processes of tribal fusion, common ancestry was often "faked" or "invented." This, however, should not obscure a deeper reality: even when an element of fabrication, sometimes perhaps conscious, was involved in such acts, tribal people grew to believe in these imagined projections, often deeply so. Indeed, their strong propensity to generate and uphold them is unmistakable. Cultural fusion completed the process as expanding and interlocking kin circles correlated with locality and a common culture. Ancestral, matrimonial, local, and linguistic ties were reinforced by other common cultural traits, most importantly those of ritual networks and amphictyonic alliances.

There should be no misunderstanding: although exhibiting considerable endurance over time, tribes and ethne were far from being "primordial" or static. New tribes and ethne branched out and evolved into separate existence as they grew over a certain size and part of them moved into new localities. They also split because of internal strife, and were sometimes dispersed, eliminated, or absorbed by others. Because of the segmentary nature and fluidity of the tribal groupings, anthropologists have become less confident than they used to be in the concept of the tribe. Skeptic influential anthropologist Morton Fried has gone as far as suggesting that the tribe is a "secondary phenomenon," only created under pressure from more complex social entities (states).[21] In the same vein, it has been argued that modern Western imperial powers actually created in their colonies tribal organization that had not existed before. This was allegedly done because colonial authorities imagined indigenous societies to be so composed; because they needed more clearly defined local entities to work with; and/or in pursuit of divide-and-rule tactics.

Such views vastly exaggerate genuine realities. True, clans were more loosely connected and experienced greater friction among themselves when facing little outside pressure. Common bonds and a sense of shared identity and solidarity among them tightened when such pressure increased. Yet such pressure often came from other *tribal* groups, long before state encroachments began. For example, the Iroquois League of five tribes became famous for its fierceness and military prowess in the seventeenth-century colonial and native wars. But the evidence from archaeology and native traditions shows that the League predated the arrival of the Europeans in North America. Its member tribes, which had earlier existed separately and in a state of endemic conflict, joined together in alliance against other emerging tribal conglomerations, such as the Huron Confederacy.[22] The processes of tribal conglomeration continued under increasing contact with states. For example, two of the major latter-day Germanic tribal entities, the Franks and the Alamanni, appeared as such only in the third century AD, presumably from processes of confederation involving earlier known tribes on the Roman frontier. The Franks apparently crystallized from some eight loosely connected Lower Rhine tribal groups.[23] The name Alamanni (= all men) hints at similar processes among tribal groupings of the Upper Rhine. This was the same well-known formula that would later apply to nations: outside pressure brought together and galvanized disparate and often conflicting communities that became conscious of greater kin–culture similarities only in the presence of an alien "other."

The above ethnographic survey illustrates the fact that tribal communities existed within a wider ethnic space. Such ethne shared kin–cultural attributes, but, unlike tribal groupings, had little or no ties that would make them a *social* entity.[24] These ethnic spaces also tended to grow in size after the transition to agriculture. Historically, there have been three major mechanisms of ethne expansion. States would be a major vehicle of ethnic leveling and assimilation. But they would themselves rely on preexisting ethnic realities, as both agricultural and pastoral expansions tended to generate large-scale ethne expansions well before states arose. The reason for this ethnic expansion is that those who adopted agriculture early on often experienced massive population and territorial proliferation. As agriculture translated into great demographic growth, the pioneering agricultural groups tended to spread out into uncultivated lands, in most cases pushing out, or absorbing, the much thinner local populations of hunter-gatherers.

A striking instance of this pattern, which took place relatively late in time so leaving particularly clear marks, is the expansion of the Bantu-speaking farmers. Spreading from west Africa from the first millennium BC on, they gradually colonized central and southeast Africa. In the process, they pushed out into arid lands the Khoisanid populations of hunter-gatherers (today's Bushmen and Khoikhoi/Hottentots), who earlier appear to have inhabited the whole of east Africa. This expansion, long attested to by the existence of the Bantu family of languages, has been documented by archaeology and more recently by the new methods of population genetics.[25]

Although the evidence is buried much deeper in the past and is far more complex and open to different interpretations, a similar process seems to have taken place in the oldest center of agriculture, southwest Asia. Europe was one direction into which Near Eastern farming spread. Most archaeologists agree that migrating colonists from Anatolia and the Middle East spread into the Balkans and central Europe at a mean rate of one kilometer per year. The beginning of agriculture in central Europe is associated with a uniform archaeological culture (LSB), which emerged fully out of no visible indigenous origins. Furthermore, it turns out that the most significant genetic gradient on the population map of modern Europe goes from southeast to northwest, apparently recording the wave-like shape of the Neolithic farmers' colonizing advance.[26]

To be sure, Bantu is not an ethnos but a large family of over 500 languages. As for the original Neolithic expansions, their great time depth, going back 10,000–5,000 years into the past, ensures that the populations involved diversified even more. Our knowledge about these developments, shrouded as it is in the mists of prehistory, is scant and conjectural. Both cases are cited here only to illustrate the process of agricultural ethnic expansions. The following two examples of this process are more directly associated with the formation of particular prestate ethne.

As in other early centers of farming, original rice cultivators spread widely in east and southeast Asia.[27] One instance of this spread was the population now known as Japanese, which apparently arrived from Korea around 400 BC, bringing wet rice agriculture with them. They gradually pushed the earlier, foraging inhabitants (Jamon) up the archipelago due to their greater numbers, a function of dense agricultural settlement. A moving frontier separated the two ethnic populations for thousands of years, and is almost as distinctive today. Inhabiting Japan for many millennia and citizens of the Japanese state, the around 150,000 Ainu – the remnants of the Jamon, who live in Hokkaido and other northern islands – are hardly considered Japanese by either Japanese or themselves. A Japanese ethnos, although obviously diverse locally in dialect and custom, predated, and underlay, the Japanese unified state that began to emerge after AD 500.[28]

Russia is another telling example. The vast expansion and diversification of the Slavs is historically and archaeologically documented from around AD 500. Scholars still debate where their original homeland was, but it is generally agreed to have been somewhere between the upper Vistula and upper-middle Dnieper rivers, with recent evidence increasingly pointing toward the latter location. Partly an agricultural expansion, the Slavs' remarkable spread was largely due to the great migrations associated with the fall of the Roman Empire. There were Slav migrations westward into the lands of east-central Europe vacated by Germanic tribal formations which had moved into the collapsing empire. Other Slavs migrated southwestward, harassing and settling among the Balkan populations of the Eastern Roman Empire. Yet other Slavs expanded eastward: in the Ukraine, Slav agricultural settlement seems to have taken over from the pastoralist Germanic Goths and Iranian-speaking Sarmatians which had moved into the empire; in today's Belarus and Russia, Slav settlers apparently displaced and/or absorbed the thin foraging Finno-Ugric-speaking populations, as well as Baltic-speaking agriculturalists, both of which are believed to have lived there earlier.[29]

The northern boundaries of the Russian people and nation are revealing in this respect. Along the Baltic coast, where natural resources were more plentiful and settlement denser, the Baltic and Finno-Ugric populations held their own and survived in today's Lithuania and Latvia (Baltic-speaking), Estonia and Finland (Finno-Ugric speakers). The survival of these peoples is evident linguistically and, indeed, also genetically,[30] despite the presence of mighty neighbors and centuries of foreign rule and assimilation pressures. To prevent any misunderstanding, the genetic differences between the Baltic and Finno-Ugric populations and their Slavic neighbors are wholly insignificant in terms of their humanity and culture. If people are carried from one culture to another in infancy they grow up adopting the culture of their new environment and are indistinguishable from it culturally. Such extensive population mix has in fact taken place throughout history on both sides of the above (and any other) boundaries. The differences in gene frequency simply indicate that neighboring populations today lived separately from one another as far back as the Bronze and even the Stone Age. Because of this, they developed different linguistic–cultural complexes, which have kept them pretty much distinct from one another for millennia during historical times. Their different languages and separate sense of identity at present do not arise from differences in gene frequencies *per se*, but from these parallel historical routes. Along these routes the populations concerned remained distinct from one another even as their respective languages have been greatly transformed and their cultures completely changed.

Again, as with Japan, the emergence of Russian states later in the first millennium (under Nordic leadership) and their eventual political coalescence were crucial for consolidating various tribal groups of

East Slavic speakers into a Russian people and a nation. Needless to say, all the above processes were anything but preordained, and ethnic divisions different to those that actually emerged could have developed under different circumstances and given other historical contingencies. Indeed, due to various developments that we shall discuss later, Russian, Byelorussian, and Ukrainian national states, speaking related East Slavic languages, exist as this book is written. Still, the developments that actually occurred and those that could have occurred were all constrained to a large degree by the ethnic realities formed on the ground by the Slavic agricultural expansion in the east. The formation of an ethnic space of related kin–culture traits was the substratum upon which the huge Russian national state could be forged. The effect of such expansion and ethnic formation should not be regarded as an all or nothing proposition. A factor can have decisive effects without being wholly deterministic.

Pastoralism was a second vehicle of massive ethne expansions. Scholars have emphasized the symbiosis that existed between neighboring farmers and herders, who traded with and were dependent on each other to complement their diets and obtain utility goods. Still, the pastoralists' mobility and the farmers' vulnerability tended to give the former a military advantage that they often used to exploit and dominate their sedentary neighbors.[31] This was true even before the domestication of the horse on the Eurasian steppe, which made the pastoralists the terror of civilizations across the landmass. For example, even though the horse was absent in east Africa, arriving Europeans widely noted that the pastoralists of the region tended to prey on their agricultural neighbors. During the second millennium, pastoralist speakers of Nilotic languages continuously expanded from southern Sudan into southwest Ethiopia, Kenya, Tanzania, Uganda, and Rwanda-Burundi, harassing, sometimes displacing, and sometimes dominating the local Bantu-speaking farmers. This pattern often became out-and-out political domination. The best known case is Tutsi rule over the Hutu in Rwanda and Burundi.*[32] The dominant

---

* In the spirit of the skeptic 1960s, it has been alleged that these ethnic distinctions in Rwanda and Burundi were actually created by the Belgian and German colonial powers and reflected their prejudices and administrative needs. But the precolonial history of the region reveals that at most the colonial authorities built on, formalized, and sometimes accentuated long existing ethnosocial divisions and hierarchies.

pastoral ethnos in these dual societies consisted of only about 10–15 percent of the population. To be sure, in the same way that in Norman England the local Germanic language was eventually adopted, somewhat changed, by the conquerors, the pastoral elite sometimes adopted the language of the local and much larger farming population. In Uganda and Rwanda, for example, Bantu languages are spoken. However, in many other cases the pastoralists' languages took over.

Pastoralist takeover may also have occurred in the original source of pastoralism, the pre- and protohistoric Near East, long before the introduction of the horse and camel. From the mid third millennium BC, the city-states of Sumer, whose inhabitants spoke a language with no known relatives, began to face pressure from Semitic-speaking pastoralists from the east. In the twenty-fourth century BC, the Semitic Sargon of Akkad, "whose fathers had lived in tents," rose to rule the old Sumerian domains. Later, at the turn of the millennium, came wide-scale infiltration and harassment by western Semitic tribal pastoralists from northern Syria, whom the locals called Amurru, that is, "Westerners," the Amorites of the Hebrew Bible. By the beginning of the second millennium, Amorite ruling dynasties and ruling elites had taken over throughout the region: in Larsa, Babylon (the famous Hammurabi), Marad, Sippar, Kish, Mari, and Assyria.[33] A similar process of pastoralist takeover of the urban centers may have taken place further west, in the Levant, where the absence of written records leaves the archaeological finds mute.[34]

As with the great expansion of the Nilotic languages in east Africa, it has been suggested that the spread of the Semitic languages in the ancient Near East was connected to these pastoralist expansion and takeovers. As written records increasingly appear throughout the region, Semitic languages are documented to have been widely diffused. The similarity between the earliest known Semitic languages suggests that their spread and diversification could not have begun much earlier.[35] Obviously, such a large family of languages could not have come into being just by accident, without some spreading mechanism. Traversing much greater distances than the land-bound farmers, opportunistically aggressive pastoral societies were ideal vehicles for linguistic spread by means of "elite dominance." Indeed, the spread of Semitic languages supposedly resulted in the displacement of the original languages of the farming communities. Sumerian was displaced by Akkadian and survived only in liturgy. In the ancient Levant, most place names were of non-Semitic etymology, a sure sign of an earlier linguistic presence in the region. Language replacement of this sort did not mean population replacement. The language change would have been mostly affected by the dominant social position achieved by the pastoralists and reflected the transformation of culture and identities.

The spread of the Indo-European family of languages is veiled by even thicker prehistoric darkness. However, it presumably took place around the same time as the expansion of the Semitic languages and may have been carried out by a somewhat similar agent. As the British in late eighteenth-century India noticed with amazement, the ancient language of India, Sanskrit, from which nearly all the languages of the subcontinent (except for the Dravidian south) had branched out, revealed many similarities to Latin and to European languages in general. It was soon detected that the same family of languages extended from Europe through Iran to India. And again, this similarity could not have been accidental. People must have carried the languages with them. Linguists tracing the similarities between and branching out of all historically known Indo-European languages, and archaeologists tracking the material and historical evidence, generally agree: the source of the spread appears to have been pastoralists from the Ukrainian steppe. Domesticating the horse and inventing the ox-drawn wheeled wagon toward 3000 BC and the horse-drawn chariot around 2000 BC, they set in motion long, gradual, and highly complex processes of expansion and diffusion.[36]

This is not the place to go into a highly conjectural reconstruction of these processes, whose details are largely lost in prehistory. It should be reemphasized, however, that the spread of Indo-European languages did not mean the displacement of all others by a particular population or race, as nineteenth- and early twentieth-century (often racist) theorists held. Although the original speakers of Proto-Indo-European (PIE) were probably an ethnos of sorts, the subsequent, protracted, and multilayered spread of the Indo-European languages mostly occurred through elite dominance over indigenous populations. The historically known speakers of the Indo-European languages do not constitute a genetic community, as nineteenth-century theorists were disappointed to discover in India, where they went in search of blond Aryans. Nor did Indo-European speakers enjoy any particular "genius" that would account for their spread apart from a contingent military superiority derived from pastoralism, the horse, and the chariot.

Moreover, the speakers of Semitic and Indo-European languages, respectively, do not constitute an ethnos any more than the speakers of Bantu languages. Again, the purpose of looking at these early expansions is to shed light on some major processes that created larger ethnic spaces before the state, and often facilitated its formation. Some later instances of pastoralist expansion are not only far better documented historically, but are also more directly relevant to our subject. Such, for example, were the vast expansion of Turkic from its origin in the Altai throughout central and western Asia, and that of Arabic from Arabia throughout the Middle East and North Africa. In both these cases, unfolding from the second half of the first millennium AD on, the conquering elite was very small in number. The vast majority of the inhabitants of Anatolia (or even central Asia) are not Turkish by descent. Nor did the vast majority of the population in the Middle East descend from Arabia. In both cases, large indigenous populations, which in the main go as far back as the Neolithic agricultural expansions, have changed language, culture, and identity through processes of elite dominance.* Geographic–cultural diversity among speakers of Turkic languages is very considerable. This, together with the particular historical trajectories of the societies in question, contributed to the fact that visions of pan-Turkic nationalism have not been successful. Still, such visions were based on genuine affinities and sentiments that are central to the identity of Turkic-speaking countries, individually if not collectively. Despite much local diversity, Arab kin–culture identity is stronger, so that it is more meaningful to speak about an Arab ethnic space or even "nation" (*ummah*). This has been the cornerstone of both pan-Arab and individual Arab states' nationalism. Both compete with other, confessional, local, and tribal sources of identity, as we shall see.

To further illustrate the significance of all the above processes for large-scale ethne formation: pre-Columbian America, where no herding societies existed and where the two other vehicles of ethnic expansion – agriculture and states – were slower to develop, was extremely fragmented linguistically. With 23 language families and

---

* Again, the opposite also occurred, as with the Altaic Bulgarian horse pastoralists, who adopted the language of the Slavic farming communities they had conquered in the eighth century.

375 different languages in North America alone (some 2,000 languages in all of the Americas), it was linguistically four times more diverse than Eurasia.[37]

From tribes to states

With property accumulation and growing social status differences, tribal society increasingly experienced a concentration of political power, which eventually led to the emergence of state authority. Livestock, land, servile labor, metals, and other utility and prestigious goods could be accumulated with the transition to agriculture. Skill- and kin-based differences in status which had prevailed in relatively "egalitarian" foraging societies were thereby magnified.[38] Jean-Jacques Rousseau, who was the first to bring this process into focus, was on far firmer ground here than in his portrayal of aboriginal innocence. The more affluent a society was, the more power relations within it became skewed in favor of the rich and mighty.

Originally, the clans' elders carried particular weight, and collective decisions were reached by tribal assemblies of all free men. The clans were sometimes ranked genealogically, according to real or fictitious seniority in the main male line. As economic and social differentiation began to open up, two types of distinctive status emerged in many tribal societies. They have been labeled "chief" and "big man" in a paradigmatic study of Polynesia.[39] The "office" of chief possessed very limited authority. The chief was either openly elected or, more commonly, the office was inherited within the senior clan, though not necessarily from father to son and often through elections. The chief served as a social arbiter, fulfilled ritualistic functions, and was sometimes the leader in war. In all these activities he wielded little coercive power. In contrast to the chief, the "big man" held no office. His status derived from his social astuteness and entrepreneurial spirit, charisma, prowess, and skillful use of his property. He stood in intricate social relations with a group of followers from his own clan and often from others, to which he offered patronage, protection, economic assistance in times of stress, and other benefits. In return, he received their allegiance and support.

As the process ran its course, property accumulation increasingly "objectified" status differences, turning "ranked" societies into "stratified" ones and chiefs and "big men" into nascent aristocracy. Communal tribal possession of the land, periodically rotated between the clans – Marx's "archaic communism" – gave way to forms of private property. Tribal society was transformed. Power and power relations were no longer grounded solely in kinship. A new element was introduced. Chiefs and "big men" now made use of their retinues, dependants and clients to throw their weight around in social dealings. These hosts largely came from their own and related clans, but also from other clans and even from outside the tribe altogether. They were bound to their patron by the supra-kin ties of economic and social benefits and obligations. Young warriors in search of fortune joined the retinues of famous war leaders. In some cases, the followers of particularly successful war leaders crystallized and settled down as new tribes. Elite ties, too, cut across tribe and kin relations. Chiefs and "big men" from different tribal communities cemented alliances between them, sometimes against "tribal interests."[40] The Classical authors' depictions of their tribal neighbors were remarkably paralleled throughout the tribal lands encountered by modern Europeans in America, the Pacific, and Africa.

Julius Caesar's observations of the Celtic and Germanic societies in the mid first century BC and those of Tacitus of *Germania* more than a century later provide some of the earliest and clearest anthropological accounts of the transformation of tribal society. By the first century BC, urban centers or towns (*oppida*) had emerged in Gaul for the first time. Society had become highly stratified, with chiefs and "big men" transformed into a powerful aristocracy. The old tribal assemblies had been reduced in significance. Many of the poor became clients of the aristocratic families, while young warriors joined their retinues. This state of affairs was characteristic of a society already on the road away from its older tribal form, something of which Caesar (*The Gallic War*, esp. 6.11–15) was well aware. He contrasted Gaul with the Germans of his time, among whom ancient, more primitive, and more egalitarian tribal society was still the norm (6.21–26). However, by Tacitus' times, Germanic society had also changed considerably. There was still no urban settlement of any sort in *Germania*, nor would there be until late in the first millennium AD. However, Germanic chiefs and "big men" now attracted retinues of young warriors, creating supra-tribal foci of power around them.[41]

The classical authors were regularly confounded as to how exactly to render tribal institutions and offices in terms that would correspond to those of their own civilizations. Tacitus called the Germanic powerful in possession of retinue *principes*, which was a reasonably good rendering (akin to the English adjective/noun principal = chief, rather than "prince," both deriving from the Latin). However, elsewhere (*Germania*, 7), when describing the traditional tribal offices, he used the Latin designations kings (*rex*; *reges*) and war leaders (*dux*; *duces*): the former appointed on account of high birth, the latter for valor. While *dux* was a neutral rendering for a war leader (unlike the later European duke, it was not an official title in Tacitus' Rome), *rex* was a more problematic term. Tacitus made it very clear that both offices had very limited authority and even less disciplinary powers, and that they mainly led by reputation and example. Still, the confusion of tribal chiefs with state kings has been commonplace among people from state societies coming into contact with tribal ones. Indeed, in many colonial situations, from Roman to modern times, the colonial power, preferring to work with a centralized client authority, actually turned chiefs into kings, investing in them power and authority that they had previously lacked.[42]

Interestingly, the difficulties of comprehension and terminology also extend to the Greeks' and Romans' past in their own prestate period, whose memory only dimly survived in myth, epic, and tradition. The main literary source for this past, for the ancient Greeks as well as for us, is the Homeric epics. While the *Iliad* preserved a faint memory of the glory of the then collapsed Mycenaean world, the *Odyssey* was more reflective of social conditions during the late Dark Age (eighth century BC), before the reemergence of Greek civilization and the rise of city-states.[43] We are conscious of the existence of the Dark Age Greek tribes, albeit vaguely, because they left traces in historical times and in the polis. In the world of Odysseus, tribal society was highly stratified and dominated by the households of rich local chiefs and "big men" with their retainers and clients. The kin network was transformed to the extent that the powerful heads of the household estates (*oikos*) extended their clan (*genos*) names to encompass and subsume their clients and dependants. It was now only *their* clan names and *their* genealogy that counted, and only they claimed ancestry from gods and semi-legendary heroes. The title of these chiefly heads during the Dark Age, *basileus*, is better understood in terms of its meaning in the earlier, stately, Mycenaean written records. It then denoted the relatively lowly office of a village head, rather than the meaning it was to assume during the rise of the polis, that of a king. The *basileis* were powerful tribal and local chiefs and "big men." They held military leadership as well as communal ritualistic and judicial functions in a segmented tribal society.[44] While popular tribal assemblies declined in importance, the counsel and support of the elders of the main clans was necessary for any general action. Only during the emergence of the polis did some *basileis* work to transform their limited chiefly status into more centralized authority ("chiefdom") and into true kingship.

Morgan was the first to outline this process in his pioneering study of tribal society, both with respect to the Greek *basileus* and to the early Roman *rex*. The office of the first semi-legendary Roman *reges*, traditionally dating from the eighth century BC, essentially meant confederate chiefs who acted as war leaders and high priests. It was the same chiefly title preserved in the prestate stratum of other Indo-European languages: Sanskrit, *raj*; Gaulis, *rix*; Old Irish, *ri*; Tracian, *rhesos*; Greek, *aregon/archon*; Gothic, *reiks*.[45] Only with emerging statehood and the beginning of urbanization in the sixth century BC did the later Roman *reges* attempt to achieve what we now understand as true kingship. Consequently, the last, "proud" *rex* was deported from Rome in 510–509 BC by the former tribal powerful already turned into a nascent aristocracy.

The later Romans' knowledge of these early times was very dim and shrouded in myths. Not even an early Roman epic source like the *Iliad* and *Odyssey* exists. Still, here too, down into historical times, these aristocratic families dominated society through their hosts of retainers, clients, and dependants, over whom their clan (*gens*) name was called. They claimed divine and heroic descent and vigorously vied with one another for dominance. The republic they established after the abolition of kingship was a means through which they successfully strove to institutionalize their domination over society while regulating the internal competition between them. Some early Roman traditions kept the memory of how the rudimentary state period had actually been. For example, in 479 BC, one of the most powerful of the Roman clans, the Fabii, took it upon itself to carry out the war against the Etruscan city of Veii, "as if it were our own family feud." According to Livy (2.48–9), 306 clan members, accompanied by a large host of kinsmen (*cognati*) and friends (*sodales*), participated in the affair.

Such power in the hands of a major clan leader could become overwhelming. Caesar (*The Gallic War*, 1.4) writes about one of the most powerful among the Helvetii who was called to trial on a charge of conspiring to achieve absolute rule. He came with "all his retainers, to the number of some ten thousand men, and also assembled there all his clients and debtors, of whom he had a great number, and through their means escaped from taking his trial." Caesar (2.1) commented that "The more powerful chiefs, and such as had the means to hire men, commonly endeavored to make themselves kings."

Indeed, there often arrived a point when chiefly power was no longer merely dominant within society, but grew to control it. On the strength of their retinues, chiefs, "big men," and war leaders were able to secure a type of authority that they had not possessed in simpler tribal societies. Overpowering and rising above their peers, they established what anthropologists call chiefdoms. In a process whose first steps are described by Tacitus in *Germania* (15) and by Hesiod (*Works and Days*, 37–39) with respect to the "gift-eating *basilees*" of about 700 BC Greece, such chiefs established a rudimentary resource extraction system. Like Mafia dons, they demanded "gifts" and contributions from their subordinates. Henchmen were employed to supervise the countryside, and authority was exercised through minor, subordinate chiefs, and family and village heads. Although the semblance of kin and tribal fraternity was preserved, these centralized, multilayered, "complex" chiefdoms were far more hierarchic and authoritative than ordinary tribal or chiefly societies.[46] Chiefdoms survived into modern times in the Scottish Highlands and Islands, associated with clan names such as Macleod, Macdonald, Clanranald, Campbell, and MacGregor. The same applied to some of the largest islands of Polynesia, including Tonga, Society Islands, Tahiti, and, most notably, Hawaii, as well as to much of pre-Columbian America and Africa.[47]

The most centralized and complex of these chiefdoms were only a short step from states, with the main difference being their tribal form and scale. Several interrelated processes were responsible for the erosion of the tribe and the growth of state authority. As we have seen, socioeconomic relations increasingly cut across tribal networks in propertied societies. Although class and status hierarchies did not supersede kin affinities, they became increasingly dominant. Related to the above was greater territorial mobility, as people moved from their native places in search of opportunity: young warriors joined the retinues of great leaders; poor and rich came to seek employment and fortune where prosperity prevailed; and people emigrated from the countryside to emergent towns and cities. As they moved to denser nucleated settlements, they continued to stick together in extended families and maintain tribal affiliations. However, the dynamism and constraints of urban housing, property possession, and professional occupation necessarily resulted in a great erosion of older tribal boundaries and identity.

The rise of the state fed on and further reinforced these trends. The state's leaders interchangeably suppressed and coopted the tribal elite. The state's apparatus was a hierarchy based on the remuneration of office, and the old tribal elite was absorbed into it and/or eliminated. Moreover, state law, sanction, and administration took over functions earlier fulfilled by kin–tribal collectives. To give the most elementary example: there was no personal security in tribal society except for that offered by the threat of blood-revenge by one's kin. Much the same applied to larger warlike activity and to all sorts of collective projects. The more the state took over such functions, the less people relied on tribal institutions and affiliations, and the more the latter declined and faded away. Finally, reflecting the socioeconomic and political processes outlined above, tribal domains were replaced by state territorial–administrative units and often survived in name only.

Such shifts are attested to in the formative period of the most famous city-states of antiquity: Athens and Rome. Athens of the sixth century BC experienced widening socioeconomic gaps as it transformed from tribal society to commercialism, urbanism, and statehood. Riding on popular unrest against the dominance of the great aristocratic clans, one aristocrat, Peisistratus, made himself tyrant or autocratic leader. During his long reign he greatly diminished the power of the old tribal elite, and many of them were forced to leave. After the fall of tyranny, Peisistratus' work was followed by a democratic reformer, Cleisthenes. His reforms (508–507 BC) were intended to break the hold of the tribal elites over society and state; incorporate immigrants from outside Attica, who had moved to prospering Athens but had remained outside its tribal institutions; and accommodate the shift of a previously rural population to urban living. Although Cleisthenes did not abolish the old four Athenian tribes with their kin-based *phratriai* and *gene*, he left them with only ceremonial functions. Side by side with them he established ten new territorial units, also called tribes but so designated in name only. Each of the new tribes was composed of villages and urban borrows (*demoi*) from the three geographic zones of Attica. Correspondingly, Cleisthenes reshaped the citizen council, so that membership in it now came from the new territorial tribes instead of the old kin ones.*[48]

A similar process took place in sixth-century BC Rome, as it became increasingly urban and socially stratified, and as state authority increased. Protohistoric King Servius Tullius seems to have represented an increase in the status and power of the old chiefly *reges*. Roman traditions attribute him with a series of interrelated reforms. Unlike Cleisthenes, he did not superimpose new tribes on the old, but transformed the original tribes themselves. To undermine the political kin basis of the powerful aristocratic clans and integrate newcomers into the Roman polity, he reconstituted the Roman tribes as territorial units. He also established the assembly of the citizens in arms, the *comitia centuriata*, as the principal institution of the Roman state in place of the kin-based *comitia curiata*.[49] When kingship was abolished in 510 BC and a mixed aristocratic–popular republic evolved, the Roman tribes remained territorial–political units. Their number increased over the centuries from the original three to thirty-five as a pure state administrative expediency, as Rome expanded in and colonized Italy and absorbed and assimilated local populations.

Finally, not only city-states but also evolving large states underwent similar processes. Taking place sufficiently late in time to be well recorded by arriving Europeans, the formation of the Zulu kingdom under Shaka in early nineteenth-century South Africa is a popular case study of state emergence,[50] as well as being a model of nation formation. The Zulu state emerged within the realm of a single ethnic stock, or ethnos, the Nguni-speaking Bantu. As mentioned previously, an ethnos is not a political entity. Until the late eighteenth century, the Nguni were divided among many different chiefdoms which incorporated separate tribes and sub-tribes. The chiefdoms' small kinship-based structure precluded wars of subjugation. However, at the beginning of the nineteenth century, one chieftain, Dingiswayo, succeeded in breaking away from the power constraints of kinship, to create a formative kingship. By force of arms coupled

---

* D. Roussel, *Tribu et cité*, Paris: Belles Lettres, 1976, has stressed the invented nature of many tribal institutions during the early polis. But this hardly means that tribal reality itself was invented rather than transformed by nascent states, as the ancient sources clearly testify. Otherwise, it is impossible to explain where the tribal concept came from. For an overview of the debated kin–tribe evidence see John Fine, *The Ancient Greeks*, Cambridge, MA: Harvard University Press, 1983, 34–36, 56, 59, 183–188; Anthony Snodgrass, *Archaic Greece*, Berkeley, CA: University of California Press, 1980, 25–26.

with moderation, he gradually extended his control over other chiefdoms, retaining their ruling clans but often substituting the former chief with a junior member of the same clan, who thus owed him his position. He also dismantled the old clan-based militia, establishing in its place permanent units from mixed localities with appointed officers at their heads. Eventually, some thirty tribes came under Dingiswayo's overlordship.

After Dingiswayo was killed in 1817, his nascent kingdom was taken over by one of his best military commanders, Shaka of the Zulu clan, which gave the new realm its name. Shaka continued with Dingiswayo's methods, only supplementing them with proverbial cruelty and massive conquests. Shaka's troops were posted around the realm, away from their original tribes, so that they could not serve local tribal resistance. His kingdom expanded to perhaps as much as 80,000 square miles – roughly the size of England – and its population numbered in the low hundred thousands. Among the means Shaka used to consolidate his realm was the institution of communal rituals. Associated with and presided over by himself, they supplemented the traditional family ancestral worship and village cults. A more moderate successor, Mpande, continued to pursue the consolidation of the kingdom. He transformed tribal domains into state territorial administrative districts and placed his many sons from polygamous marriages in important administrative positions. At the same time, he married off his daughters to local chiefs while marrying their daughters, thus further tightening the ruling kin network around the crown. An increasingly stronger sense of Zulu identity and unity was thus being forged and gradually coming into being. However, not long after Mpande's death in 1872, the Zulu state came to the end of its independence as the British Empire established control over it.

As we shall see, the Zulu case is typical of state and nation formation throughout history. But before we go further, we need to summarize more clearly the interrelationship in this process between state, tribe, and kin–culture identity.

State formation, tribal erosion, and ethnicity

There was a strong tension between emerging states and existing tribal organization. Clan elders and tribal heads were forced to forfeit power. A previously segmented society became subjected to the dictates of a state bureaucracy, which imposed taxes, corvée work, and military service. People who had cared only about their own were now obligated to shoulder all this burden for the benefit of self-serving and far-away authorities, or, at best, in the service of remote collective ends, with most cases falling somewhere in between. For these reasons, the emergence of the state was a coercive and violent process, spurred by the dictates of power. Domestically, the state's larger and more concentrated instruments of power generally proved superior and capable of subduing or crushing resistance. Outwardly, they were essential for coping with the greater power of other states that were putting pressure on segmented tribal society.

Propelled forward by these twin pressures, states proliferated. But the process was far from being straightforward. In the first place, a state's emergence could easily reverse, and early states were prone to disintegrate. For example, the biblical tradition in the books of Samuel and Kings depicts typical tensions between tribe and state in the formative Israelite kingdoms of Saul, David, and Solomon. Ultimately, the kingdom is alleged to have split because of the new heavy burden imposed by the state and because the northern tribes found it difficult to accept a ruler from the southern tribe of Judah. Second, the state's victory was often incomplete and tribal entities survived and maintained an autonomy of sorts under or on the peripheries of the state, as they still do in some less developed areas of the world. Mobile pastoralist tribes were particularly resilient, because they experienced the social processes described above far less and because the state found it difficult to pin down and subdue them. The already cited records of the city-state of Mari in northern Mesopotamia in the early second millennium BC reveal that the state authorities successfully controlled the peasant and urban communities, while maintaining uneasy relations with the pastoralist tribes within their realm. The latter enjoyed great autonomy and only vaguely recognized the state's suzerainty.[51] Thousands of years later, the same duality between state and nomadic tribe was highlighted by political theorist Ibn Khaldun, who composed his *Prolegomena to History* (1377) in Muslim North Africa. Indeed, a similar balance prevailed wherever pastoralist populations lived within the state's realm, from North Africa and the Middle East through the Russian steppe and central Asia to China.[52] In some of these areas it still does. Poorly developed agricultural tribal communities also survived on the peripheries of states, and a tribal zone extended outside many of them through much of history.

Over all, however, the kin-based tribe declined and disappeared with the rise of the state. Yet it would be wrong to think that ethnicity in general was not a constitutive element of premodern states. The above-cited examples are telling. Although the Athenian polis eroded the old tribes to insignificance, it remained based on the ethnically related population of Attica, which shared kin–culture attributes. True, Athens attracted many immigrants. Yet notably, although at the height of the commercial empire immigrants included non-Greeks, most of the immigrants were ethnically Greek. Furthermore, as a rule, the immigrants adopted the Attic dialect and assimilated into the local culture in a few generations. Further still, the large numbers of them who arrived during the fifth century BC were denied political rights and remained in a status of non-citizen residents (*metics*). Only "autochthonous" Athenians, descended from two Athenian parents, qualified for citizenship.[53] In Rome, too, one of the most open polities ever in terms of the expansion of citizenship, ethnicity mattered a great deal. Rome first spread through Latium, an area inhabited by people of the same ethnic stock as Rome itself, the Latins, many of them absorbed into the Roman state. Further expansion in central Italy involved a thorough Romanization of native communities. Ultimately, Rome expanded into an Italian and, later, Mediterranean empire. And as we shall see, in every step in this centuries-long expansion the diffusion of a common culture was a major political factor which went hand in hand with the spread of Roman citizenship.

The Zulu case demonstrates the major effect of ethnicity in pristine large states. As mentioned above, the Zulu state emerged and rapidly expanded within the realm of a single, Nguni-speaking ethnic stock. Precisely for this reason the Zulu realm was not merely a political domain, but proved so malleable to processes of nation-building. Although there was obviously considerable diversity within this ethnic space, strong shared ethnic features made the state's work incomparably easier. It was on a common ethnic substratum that the standard state-building techniques could become effective: the expansion of nucleus state power by the combined coercion and cooptation of formerly independent chiefs; the assumption of supreme military, judicial, and religious authority by the overlord; and, over time, the welding of the realm into an increasingly unified state through increasing bureaucratization and processes of cultural fusion involving religious syncretism, joint military service, and common identity formation.

Certainly, not all states remained confined within a common ethnic space. Many of them, called empires if they were big enough, ruled over other ethnic populations. We now proceed to examine the interrelationship between ethnicity and statehood in premodern polities: city-states, states, and empires.

4 PREMODERN ETHNE, PEOPLES, STATES, AND NATIONS AROUND THE WORLD

With the rise of the state we are entering a more familiar territory, at least for one side of the debate on the nation. Modernists have scarcely dealt with premodern states, except for pronouncing that such states did not rest on national or ethnic foundations, sentiments, and identity. According to this view, ethnicity, while existing, was largely devoid of political significance. States were allegedly based on other principles and were supra-ethnic. In reaction, traditionalists have sought to show that nations and national sentiments existed before modernity. Scholars mostly concentrated on early modern and late medieval Europe. But some of them, such as Anthony Smith, Steven Grosby, and Aviel Roshwald, went further, to the ancient Near East and classical Greece. I share many of their views, and wish to broaden the perspective as much as possible, to other continents, civilizations, and historical periods. Although the heavy European bias in the study of nationalism is well recognized, too little has been done to correct it. What follows is an examination of premodern polity types: petty-states, states, and empires. It intends to establish how central ethnicity and political ethnicity – including its national form – were to states' existence and conduct from the very beginning of statehood. To add to the confusion, there are modernists also with respect to the state who claim that the state is a modern creation. But in my vocabulary states are old and the modern state is merely a new stage in their development.[1]

A   ETHNOS AND CITY-STATE

The city-state was the most glorious type of petty-state.[2] Its urbanism
was sometimes associated with commercialism, far-flung interests, and
a measure of cosmopolitanism, which makes it particularly interesting
for our subject. The city-state's small size meant that it encompassed
only part of a common ethnic space, divided among a multiplicity of
city-states. Therefore, in Gellner's definition, and in mine, the city-state
was not a nation, in the sense that it did not proximate a congruence
between a state and an *entire* culture/ethnos (a congruence which is
never perfect, of course). And yet, as some scholars have pointed out
with respect to ancient Athens, the city-state did exhibit a congruence
between state and culture/ethnos in the sense that its people tended to
belong to the same ethnos (which also encompassed a large number of
other polities). Indeed, they have stressed that Athens constituted a
kin–culture political community of great solidarity. These scholars have
reasonably argued that this should be regarded as nationhood.[3] Different definitions are a matter of semantics and, therefore, largely a matter
of choice. However, although I adopt a different conceptual grid,
I agree with these scholars on the realities behind the concepts: the
patriotism associated with the city-state derived directly from its
people's sense of common kin–culture identity and solidarity. Certainly,
participatory political institutions, where they existed, contributed a
great deal to the strength of patriotism. But contrary to some views,
civic institutions and a creed of freedom were not the root of patriotism. Throughout history patriotism has also revealed itself in the most
brutal of tyrannies.[4] The little noticed fact is that city-states, while, of
course, not wholly homogeneous, were ethnically constituted. As in all
other polity types, ethnicity was thoroughly political and highly
significant.

It should come as no surprise that as a rule city-states were
composed of an ethnically related population. After all, city-states
crystallized from the people of a particular area who coalesced from
the surrounding countryside into an urban center.[5] Furthermore, as
city-states tended to crystallize against one another, each with a small

territory, they together formed a kin–culture cluster, dividing among them a shared ethnic space.[6] Thus, not only the individual city-state but also the multiplicity of city-states in a particular area typically consisted of an ethnically related population, a reality which did not prevent frequent antagonism among them. This follows a familiar pattern, captured by the already cited Arab proverb: "I against my brother; I and my brother against my cousin; I and my brother and my cousin against the world." As in tribal systems, conflicts and belligerency among city-states of the same ethnos were the most common. The simple explanation for this is that the majority of conflicts and wars take place among neighbors, who live in close proximity to one another and have a lot to fight over in terms of adjacent territory, resources, and other interests.[7] Thus, the city-state's people, while themselves being deeply divided domestically, viewed their ethnically related neighbors as their most threatening "other." However, when a more starkly foreign threat loomed, city-states which shared ethnic attributes more often than not tended to cooperate against that threat, typically coalescing into formal alliances and confederacies.

To be sure, this pattern was far from being unequivocal and tidy, and many other factors were involved. And yet a broad survey of historical city-state systems demonstrates that it was real enough. It also reveals that although immigrants and foreigners were sometimes present within city-states, especially in the largest and most prosperous among them, the ethnic identity of such immigrants and foreigners overwhelmingly affected their social, civic, and political status. Some excellent comparative studies of city-state systems, most notably those edited by Mogens Hansen under the auspices of the Copenhagen Polis Centre, make our job easier.

The cradle of civilization

Sumer, the earliest city-state system and earliest literary civilization together with Egypt, exhibited many of the above features. From the late fourth millennium BC, a few dozen Sumerian city-states emerged in lower Mesopotamia (today's southern Iraq). They shared a language, Sumerian, which has no known relatives. Although each city-state had its own patron god, they also shared a pantheon, ritual texts, a script, and culture in general. In short, the Sumerians were an ethnos politically divided into separate and often antagonistic units. Occasionally, some city-states rose to dominate others.

Sumer was a prosperous and magnificent urban culture, with trade contacts reaching far away into foreign lands. But as one scholar put it: "resident aliens ... were apparently very few in number."[8] In the twenty-fourth century BC, the Land, as it was called, was transformed. As mentioned in Chapter 3, Semitic-speaking pastoralist populations began infiltrating Sumer from upper Mesopotamia and the west. One entrepreneurial leader from among them, Sargon of Akkad, rose to dominance in the land neighboring Sumer. He defeated a coalition which united against him encompassing practically all the Sumerian city-states (fifty-one in number) and conquered the cities one after the other. The above-cited scholar explains their reasons for collaborative resistance to Sargon: "One is that the Sumerians considered Sargon and his 'sons of Akkade' to be foreigners; another, that the cities had lost their relative autonomy."[9] Obviously, *both* ethnic identity and balance of power considerations mattered. After Sargon's death, the Sumerian city-states "revolted in a victory-or-death rebellion" against his successor, Rimush. In the crushing suppression of the revolt, the cities apparently lost between a quarter and a third of their men.[10] Rather than being confined to the cities' rulers and elite, the revolt seems to have been a mass popular affair.

Sargon's empire succumbed to outside invaders some fifty years later. All the same, continued settlement and dominance by Semitic-speaking pastoralists over the following centuries changed the linguistic character of the Land. Notably, its dual ethnic character did not survive for long, as Sumerian was displaced as a living spoken language by Akkadian (Eastern Semitic). Mesopotamia, or Babylonia, as it is known after its greatest city-state at that time, again became a common sphere of language, ritual, literacy, and culture in general. For some periods the city-states were able to retain their independence, but eventually they were absorbed by the successive imperial powers that took over the ancient Near East.[11]

City-state clusters existed further west in Syria and the Levant almost as early as in Mesopotamia. But because literacy developed there later and was occasionally lost as the city-states collapsed and the region plunged into dark ages, the evidence about them is elusive. Only during the second and first millennia BC do Egyptian, Hittite, and Assyrian, as well as some local, sources offer clearer snapshots. Some of the city-state cultures known from these sources have had their celebrity enhanced by their appearance in the Hebrew Bible. Such were the Canaanite city-states, which shared a language, pantheon, and material culture.[12] They incessantly fought among themselves, with some of them occasionally gaining ascendancy over their neighbors. However, as Egypt revived and reasserted its power after a period of decline, a grand coalition of Canaanite city-states assembled to repel the foreign invader. Again, this act of "balancing" against a powerful threat also had a clear ethnic dimension. The Canaanites were defeated in the battle of Megiddo (1479/1457 BC) by the great warrior Pharaoh Tuthmosis III and fell under Egyptian rule which exploited the divisions among them. As Egypt's power again waned, they found themselves squeezed between the rising power of the Sea Peoples/Philistines and the Israelites, respectively.

The Sea Peoples came from the Aegean cultural sphere: the islands, the Anatolian seashore, and possibly also the Greek mainland. They apparently consisted of tribal groups, war bands, and fugitives from invasions and rising state power. Around 1200 BC they devastated the Levant coast, but their invasion of Egypt was defeated. Some of them, including the Biblical Philistines, were settled down by the Egyptians as mercenary garrisons on the coastal plain of Canaan. When Egypt's central government declined, they took over as lords where they had been stationed. The Philistines established five city-state polities on the southern plain. Although independent, these city-states cooperated in order to dominate their neighbors. In turn, the hill tribes to their east reportedly crystallized under their pressure into an Israelite religious–military alliance, and later kingdom. Thus, ethnic divisions had a clear political significance. Indeed, revealing processes took place within the Philistine polities themselves. They began in the form of elite rule by foreign warrior bands over the local populations, and their Aegean origins are well documented in the archaeology of their sites. However, as in Norman England, ethnic differences between rulers and ruled gradually eroded, and within a couple of centuries the Philistines had largely assimilated into the local Canaanite language and culture.[13]

Phoenicians, Greeks, and Rome

The Phoenicians were another Canaanite city-state culture, located further north on the Levant coast. Specializing in long-range maritime commerce, they established trading posts and colonies across the

Mediterranean from 1200 BC onward. This expansion brought the Phoenicians in touch first with the Greek city-states and later with the city-state of Rome. Each of these major historical players will now be examined separately, as well as in their mutual interactions.

The Phoenician city-states were often in conflict with one another. But with the rise of the great empires that successively took over the ancient Near East, they came under their suzerainty and lost their independence. They provided these empires with naval contingents, most famously for the failed Persian invasion of Greece. They continued to carry the burden of the naval warfare against the Greeks down to Alexander of Macedonia's conquest of the Persian Empire, when he stormed the city of Tyre (332 BC) and conquered all the other Phoenician cities. Notably though, the rivalry between the Phoenicians and the Greeks did not arise solely from the services demanded by an imperial master. Antagonism grew as the Greeks themselves began establishing colonies across the Mediterranean from the eighth century BC onward and expanding their trade. The western Mediterranean was one area where these spheres of colonization and trade collided. The Phoenicians established dozens of colonies along the coasts of North Africa, Spain, western Sicily, and Sardinia. The Greeks founded an even larger number of colonies in "Magna Graecia": Sicily, southern Italy, Sardinia, and Corsica, as well as on the coasts of southern France and northeast Spain. There were rivalries among the Phoenician colonies-turned-city-states, and one of them, Carthage, in today's Tunisia, succeeded in securing control over them. Similarly, there were endemic conflicts and vicious wars among the city-states of Magna Graecia, and some of them grew to dominate others. In Sicily it was Syracuse that tended to dominate the other Greek city-states by force. Still, in the intermittent conflict that developed over centuries between Carthage and the Greek city-states of Sicily (and also in Sardinia and Corsica), only in a very few cases did Greek city-states ally with the Phoenicians.

The logic that we have seen in previous cases, whereby a system's coalescence against a large foreign invader can be attributed to pure balance of power considerations, barely holds here. Obviously, the Phoenician city-states were not always happy with Carthaginian hegemony, whereas the Greek city-states in Sicily resisted domination by Syracuse. And yet in the face of an alien threat, the battle lines were strikingly drawn along ethnic divisions (with the native Sikeloi as a third category squeezed in between). Indeed, successive tyrants of

Syracuse effectively beat the pan-Hellenic drum to stir Greek public opinion in Sicily their way. Major coalitions between Carthage and Greeks would occur only when their own rivalry was eclipsed by the threat of a third power, Rome.[14]

The ancient Greeks are a quintessential case study for the political role of ethnicity.[15] In historical times they had a strong sense of being a single ethnos, which shared blood ties, language, a pantheon, mythology, traditional texts (Homer and Hesiod), cultic centers (Delphi) and, not least, the Olympic Games. All the others, non-Greeks, were barbarians. At the same time, Greek was divided into four major dialects (each with its own subdivisions): Ionic, Doric, Aeolic, and Arcadian. There is no precise evidence as to how these somewhat different but mutually intelligible dialects developed before literacy and the rise of the polis.[16] But each dialect group also tended to possess a distinct sense of kinship, and each still carried a legacy of similar tribal names shared by various city-states in the group.[17] This brings us to a third level of the Greek composite ethnic identity: the division into separate city-states. These kin–culture–civic communities were unquestionably by far the most significant politically. Still, the other levels of Greek ethnic identity also mattered a great deal politically.

We begin with the Greek subgroup identities, and with the Dorians. In Sparta, ethnic identity underpinned the polis in a way that was unparalleled anywhere else. Domestically, Sparta was uniquely built as an oppressive military regime by a Spartans minority over an enslaved helot majority. The roots of this structure are protohistoric and shrouded in myth. But it is widely believed to have resulted from the subjugation of a native Achaean population by invading Dorians. Non-Spartan Dorian elements in Sparta's territory, the *perioeci*, were not enslaved and enjoyed economic and other freedoms, as well as a measure of communal autonomy. Thus, while economic exploitation was at the root of Sparta's unique character, it was starkly construed along ethnic lines.

Much the same applied to outside relations. The Dorian city-states in the Peloponnese were often at war with one another. The rivalry between Sparta and Argos, for example, was one of the most bitter and enduring in Greek history. And yet a sense of common Dorian identity was strong and politically potent. In the sixth century BC, Sparta succeeded in consolidating most of the Peloponnese into a political–military league under its hegemony. Sparta's military supremacy and coercion were central to the formation of the league, but Dorian kin sentiments were also significant. The league cultivated the cult of the Dorian hero Heracles, and held religious festivals like the Olympic Games in Dorian Elis, which, although open to all Greeks (and only Greeks), were celebrations of the Dorian sentiment. As always, these realities revealed themselves most strikingly when outside "others" were involved.

Athens was one beneficiary of Spartan military intervention, which expelled the tyrant Hippias. Yet, although not far away, it was neither in the Peloponnese nor Dorian. When the Ionian Greeks of Asia, on the Anatolian coast and islands, revolted against their Persian imperial master, it was Athens, not Sparta, which came to their aid. Kin sentiments of common descent were uppermost in Athens' response to the Ionian plea for help, as the Ionians had emigrated to establish their colonies across the Aegean from the southeastern seaboard of Greece, including Attica, a memory shared by both sides. The failed Athenian intervention triggered Persian military incursions into Greece itself, including a full-scale invasion (480–479 BC).

For the first time in their history the Greeks faced the threat of subjugation to a foreign imperial power, and they haphazardly allied to ward off the invasion. Admittedly, those in northern Greece most exposed to the massive Persian invasion chose to submit to and collaborate with the invaders rather than risk annihilation. Inter-Greek rivalries, the interests of individual tyrants, and connections with the East were other causes of collaboration. Notably though, the collaborators were stigmatized by the charge of Medism (an eponym of Persia), or betrayal of the Hellenic cause, by those who chose to resist, which included Sparta and its allies and Athens.[18] Assuring Sparta of its unwavering loyalty to the common cause, Athens attributed it, according to Herodotus, to "the kinship of all Greeks in blood and speech, and the shrines of gods and the sacrifices that we have in common, and the likeness of our way of life, to all which it would ill beseem Athenians to be false."[19] Again, balance of power considerations were never isolated from ethnic identity, affinities, and solidarity.

In the century that followed the Persian defeat, Greece experienced successive attempts by three leading city-states to convert their hegemony of a regional alliance into a vehicle for establishing a coercive and exploitative empire. These were Athens and the Attic–Delian League, formed to liberate the Ionians from Persia and spanning the

Aegean; Sparta and the Peloponnesian League; and Thebes and the Boeotian League in central Greece.[20] The Greeks exhausted themselves in these struggles, allowing the Persian Empire to reassert itself. The king of Persia became the arbiter of Greek politics, negotiating peace between the antagonists and bringing the Greek cities of Ionia back under his rule (387 BC). It was in these circumstances that pan-Hellenism, a call for Greek unity against Persia, gained currency, articulated by the publicist Isocrates. Such sentiments were taken up by King Philip II of Macedonia, followed by his son Alexander. Macedonia itself was an ambivalent case. Bordering on Greece, with a Hellenized royal house and elite, it was barely considered genuinely Greek by the Greeks. Opposition to imperial subjugation and foreign rule thus combined in the formation of a Greek coalition against Macedonia. Greek resistance was crushed by Philip and Alexander. At the same time, it was the rhetoric of pan-Hellenism and the actual mobilization of a Macedonian–Greek army for a great invasion of the Persian Empire that constituted the legitimizing basis for Macedonian hegemony.

With Alexander's conquest of the East, the Greek world was no longer dominated by the independent city-state. Yet Greek identity remained the defining feature of that world and its politics. We shall return to this in our discussion of empires. Eventually, both the remaining Greek city-states leagues and Hellenistic empires would succumb to Rome.

Rome was the most successful city-state ever, owing primarily to its ability to transcend the inherent size limitations of the city-state and dramatically expand its citizen body.[21] Still, as mentioned in Chapter 3, although Rome exhibited an unusual openness to the incorporation of others, this massive process of expansion was not divorced from ethnic realities but was closely interwoven with them. Unlike Greece, Italy did not consist of a single ethnos, or even a preponderant one. As the darkness of prehistory lifts, the peninsula was home to some thirty different Italic languages/ethne, plus Etruscans, Greeks, and Celts. Conflict and war were rife among tribes and among city-states both within and between ethne. However, many of these ethne formed an alliance or a league of their ethnos to cooperate against foreign challenges, again demonstrating how pivotal ethnic identity was to politics. Rome started out as the leader of one of these alliances, that of the Latins in west-central Italy. The Latin city-states belonged to the same ethnic stock as Rome, speaking the same language, Latin, and sharing a culture. The alliance was forged in the protracted struggles between the sixth and fourth centuries BC against incursions by the Etruscans to the north, the Sabellic hill peoples to the east, and invading Celts.

As Roman military ascendancy grew, central Italy was progressively Romanized. In the first place, defeated communities were forced to cede part of their lands to Rome and its Latin allies. Rome's settlement of these lands made possible a steady internal demographic increase of its citizen body. Second, as with so many other hegemons of city-state leagues, only more successfully, Rome eventually transformed its hegemonic alliance with the Latins, directly annexing many of them and establishing stricter hegemony over the rest (338 BC). Third, the same process was progressively extended beyond Latium, initially in central Italy and later further afield in the peninsula. Rome had no pronounced policy of cultural assimilation, but its presence, prestige, and centuries-long hegemony facilitated such processes, first among the Italian elites and then among the people. The gradual extension of citizenship to selected communities (though, indeed, initially often without political rights) and Roman acculturation went symbiotically hand in hand. In this way, the territory of the Roman state itself (not including its satellite "allies") and its citizen population grew steadily. It is estimated at 26,000 square kilometers and some 900,000 people in 264, at the outbreak of the First Punic War.[22] Roman citizen population was about four to five times larger than that of the largest Greek polis, Athens.

The Roman alliance defeated the strong league of Samnite tribes and city-states in southern Italy. It also brought the many Greek city-states of that region under its hegemony. To free themselves, the latter, normally disunited, enthusiastically allied with the Hellenistic king-general-adventurer Pyrrhus of Epirus, who landed in Italy in a quest for empire but was finally driven out by Rome (280–275 BC). Clearly, ethnic identities played a significant role in all these alliances. This is most strikingly revealed in Rome's gravest trial: the Second Punic War with Carthage, when the Carthaginian general Hannibal invaded Italy, annihilated one Roman army after another and shook the foundations of Roman hegemony.

Empires are often more vulnerable on their own territory, where an invader might spur a rebellion among their subject peoples. Indeed, after his crushing victory at Cannae (216 BC), Hannibal succeeded in breaking up the Roman hegemonic alliance. The Samnites, many Greeks, and other peoples of southern Italy (as well as Greek Syracuse in Sicily) deserted Rome and joined Hannibal in the hope of regaining their liberty. The Celts and Etruscans in northern Italy were in either open or subdued rebellion. Only the Latins and other thoroughly Romanized communities of central Italy remained loyal to Rome (though, exhausted by the war, some of them eventually refused to contribute more troops to the war effort). Indisputably, Rome's presence and deterrence by terror were strongest in its immediate vicinity; but the threat of Hannibal's armies was no less potent. *Two competing hegemons were involved, which helps to neutralize, or "control for," the effect of power balancing.* Ultimately, the communities of central Italy preferred a hegemon from their own ethnic stock to a foreign one. More or less the same applied to Carthage's own empire. After a long grinding struggle, Rome turned the tables by invading Carthage's home territory in North Africa (205–202 BC). Here too, Carthage's subjects, most notably the Numidians, took the opportunity and defected, joining forces with the invader. Only the other Phoenician city-states remained loyal to Carthage, until its armies were crushed and the war was lost. We shall discuss the later stages of Rome's imperial expansion later on.

Premodern America, Africa, Asia, and Europe

There is an unavoidable risk of tedious repetition as we proceed to examine other city-state systems throughout history and around the globe. Thus, I shall try to keep this survey concise, highlighting both the systems' internal affinities and divisions. While coming in kin–culture clusters, they were politically fragmented among often antagonistic units. The presence of a foreign challenge was the most significant motivation for cooperation among them, whereas excessive conduct by a hegemon tended to have the opposite effect.

There were many city-state cultures in pre-Columbian America. One of the most glorious, which possessed a script and therefore written narratives, was the Maya of the Yucatan in Central America. The Maya were divided among some sixty city-states during the height of their civilization between the third and ninth centuries AD. Still, despite considerable regional diversity, they shared a great deal in terms of culture, religion, and script. As in other city-state cultures, vicious warfare took place among the Mayan polities. Their mysterious collapse, probably due to ecologic overstretch, leaves us with little evidence as to what they might have done in the face of a major foreign threat. When the Spanish arrived, desperate but uncoordinated resistance by Mayan communities, spreading over vast territories, lasted for centuries.

Further northwest, the Aztecs, or Mexica, were one among several Nahuatl-speaking tribes that took over in most of the city-states of the Valley of Mexico before Spanish arrival. Tenochtitlan, the Aztec city-state, founded in the early fourteenth century, allied with neighboring Nahuatl-speaking Texcoco and Tlacopan in a Triple Alliance which the Aztecs increasingly dominated. The Alliance established its rule over the fifty-odd city-states of the valley, and further expanded throughout central Mexico to create one of the largest multiethnic empires of pre-Columbian America.[23] The Aztecs' conduct toward their subjects and enemies became proverbial for its harshness and cruelty. Indeed, one of the main reasons for their empire's collapse before a few hundred Spanish *conquistadors* was that its enemies (chiefly Tlaxcalla) and some of its subjects along the Spaniards' route joined the invaders in order to liberate themselves. There were some defections in the Valley of Mexico itself, including one member of the Triple Alliance, Texcoco. The Spaniards exploited a rivalry over the throne between two brothers from the royal house to install one of them as a Spanish protégée. Nonetheless, part of the city's people remained loyal to the Aztecs.[24]

The most urbanized city-state system in sub-Saharan Africa was that of the Yoruba in today's western Nigeria, which lasted for hundreds of years until the nineteenth century.[25] The Yoruba were (and are) an ethnos that shared a language and culture, but were divided among independent and antagonistic city-states. One of them, Old Oyo, achieved imperial hegemony over the others during the seventeenth and eighteenth centuries. But as its power waned, the city-states resumed independence and regularly fought among themselves, revealing a measure of cooperation only in warding off heavy raiding by the mounted Fulani herdsmen from the north. Other major city-state systems emerged in west Africa around the same time. The Hausa are an ethnos of similar language and culture, whose city-states flourished in northern Nigeria and Niger from the fifteenth to the early nineteenth centuries.[26] The Fante, on the Gold Coast (southern Ghana) – another ethnos, culture, and language – were often in conflict with one another. However, in the eighteenth century they formed a federation to defend against and conquer their neighbors, actively participating in the Atlantic slave trade.[27] Similarly prospering on the slave trade were the city-states of the Ijo ethnos of the eastern Niger Delta.[28] The city-state polities of the Kotoko ethnos, southeast of the Lake of Chad, coalesced in the nineteenth century into two separate federations – north and south – each with a distinctive dialect.[29]

The often rival caravan city-states of Arabia experienced a remarkable development in the seventh century AD. They were united by Muhammad, the armed prophet of the new religion of Islam, who then brought the pastoralist Arab tribes under his mantle. Unity was cemented not only through a powerful creed and a shared ethnicity, but also by a foreign challenge. Rather than a defensive response to a threat, in this case the challenge presented itself in the form of an offensive opportunity offered by the rich civilization to the north. In the wake of their great conquests, Arabs became the ruling elite throughout the Middle East. Formally, Islamic doctrine recognizes no ethnic distinctions. However, the Arab people and language, gradually assimilating most of the population of the Middle East, hold a special place in Islam.

The southeast Asian archipelago that encompasses today's Malaysia and Indonesia is as large as western Europe. During the fifteenth and sixteenth centuries it was the sphere of a flourishing trade network and numerous prosperous city-state polities. Across the area's great expanse there were various neighboring ethnicities, most notably Malay, Thai, Javanese, and Makassarese. How significant these ethnic distinctions were in the politics of the city-states is an interesting question. Whatever the predominant language and culture in each of them, the mercantile cities contained substantial foreign elements, including Chinese and Japanese traders. The ruling elites in particular are claimed to have been cosmopolitan in outlook. Obviously, I am not arguing that in *all* city-state systems without exception ethnicity was equally potent and politically significant. Still, as one sensible and nuanced study of the Malay put it: "the Malays seem to be associated with most of the early states of the western archipelago of the Malay Peninsula and Sumatra … While politically fragmented … the populations of these polities were broadly identified as 'Malays.'" All these Malays shared a language, an Indic culture, and the Hindu religion, replaced in the fifteenth and sixteenth centuries by Islam. "When it was necessary for a Malay to differentiate himself from a Muslim Javanese or Acehnese, the usual resort would be to that of a separate *bangsa*, that is, all those descended from a different (putative) social line." While the concept "also has overtones of shared culture, this is secondary in the emic view to the solidarity acquired through common descent or origin."[30]

That this feeling of kinship, common identity, and solidarity was politically significant is suggested by strong negative evidence. As another highly circumspect scholar writes about the most prosperous and cosmopolitan Malay city-states, such as Melaka, citing sixteenth- and seventeenth-century Portuguese observers, they: "suffered militarily from their pluralism, since loyalties were fragmented and only the minority *malayos* (Malays) could be counted on to fight with the king."[31] Indeed, the king himself was invariably Malay, surely not an accidental political fact.

Finally, we turn to medieval and early modern Europe. Hundreds of city-states emerged in northern Italy from the eleventh century on, fiercely competing with one another. However, as their budding independence was threatened by the German emperor Frederick Barbarossa, they formed an alliance, the Lombard League, which defeated him at Legnano (1176). Unquestionably, local civic identities counted far more than Italian or even Lombard identity, and a balancing act against an overpowering imperial threat was the most important factor determining the city-states' behavior. Still, the threat was also foreign and the emperor's "oppression of Italy" was one element mentioned by the civic orators.[32] In an era when imperial dynastic legitimacy was a sacred principle, the claim that the sovereign violated local customs, freedoms, and privileges was the only normative way to formulate calls for rebellion against foreign rule.

Later, and as the threat of Imperial rule subsided, intracity factions and intercity rivalries split the Italian city-states between the opposite camps of Imperial and Papal supporters (Ghibellines and Guelphs). Furthermore, having each established its rule over the other city-states in its area and pursuing its own policy, Florence, Milan, Venice, and Genoa fell divided rather than standing united against the new French and Spanish national states around 1500. As in fourth-century BC Greece, humiliation and occupation by foreign powers spurred calls for national unification and liberation. The most famous was Machiavelli's plea, in the conclusion of *The Prince*, to liberate Italy from the barbarians, even if this was to be carried out by a native autocratic ruler. Machiavelli's appeal was clearly meant to arouse and vastly underestimated the countervailing forces. Nonetheless, it leaves little doubt that, despite Italy's great regional diversity and deep divisions, foreign powers were viewed as alien and that this view had widespread emotional appeal:

> *The opportunity to provide Italy with a liberator ... must not be missed. I have no doubt at all that he would be received with great affection in all those regions that have been inundated by the foreign invasions, as well as with a great thirst for revenge, with absolute fidelity, with devotion and with tears of gratitude. What gate would be closed to him? What people would fail to obey him? What envious hostility would work against him? What Italian would deny him homage? This foreign domination stinks in the nostrils of everyone.*[33]

The Hanseatic League in north Germany and the Baltic (thirteenth to seventeenth centuries) incorporated scores of merchant city-states which allied to advance their commercial interests and establish an effective trade monopoly in northern Europe. Conspicuously though, this quintessentially commercial league admitted German city-states only. Even their commercial outposts in foreign cities and countries were run as closed ethnic enclaves. In the end, even this powerful city-state alliance was incapable of standing up to the new European national states, Sweden, Denmark, Poland, England, and the Netherlands, whose rise heralded the Hanse's demise.

The Swiss Confederation is another interesting case. It was founded in the fourteenth and fifteenth centuries, when Alpine German peasant communities allied with neighboring German city-states to defeat the German nobility's attempt to subjugate them. A socioeconomic struggle thus gave rise to a separate German-speaking political entity that would eventually evolve into a separate nation. Although expanding to include both French- and Italian-speaking cantons, the German-speaking element dominated the Confederacy, and practically ruled over the Italian parts. Only in the nineteenth century did Switzerland develop into a truly multiethnic nation, one of the world's very few, as we shall see.

In summary, city-states were kin–culture communities which invariably belonged to a city-state cluster sharing an ethnic space; and both these features had profound political implications. Domestically, the city-state's population overwhelmingly belonged to the same ethnos. Where foreigners were present, their identity regularly affected their civic and legal status, with processes of acculturation and assimilation facilitating political integration. Outwardly, too, although often highly antagonistic toward one another, the city-states of a similar ethnos tended to cooperate against outsiders, typically forming a common alliance or league for that purpose. There were many other significant factors at work, but ethnic identity and solidarity were anything but insignificant.

Indisputably, from among the various graduated levels of identity and solidarity in a common ethnic space that of the city-state community itself was by far the strongest. As the city-state was the effective political unit, intercity-state cooperation was inherently tenuous and fragile. This, together with the city-state's small size, meant that even confederated city-states were ultimately unable to hold out against large states and empires. For this reason, the city-state was a particularly transient phenomenon in polities' evolution. Its glory in its prime tends to obscure the fact that nowhere did it survive for more than a few centuries.[34] The United Dutch Provinces, confederating the Netherlands' mercantile cities, were the exception, largely due to their ability to shelter behind water barriers. The Swiss Confederation, shielded by its mountain fortress, was another successful survivor. In the process, however, both confederations increasingly assumed the form of a national state themselves.

B   THE PREMODERN NATIONAL STATE

The city-state was one course of polity formation, which was ultimately absorbed into states and empires. But large states emerged as early
as city-states, constituting a parallel avenue of state formation which
issued directly from an environment populated by tribes, chiefdoms,
and rural petty-polities.[35] As mentioned previously, states tended to
emerge within an ethnic space which shared kin–culture attributes. The
existence of such a space greatly facilitated the unification of the realm,
and had a deep and enduring influence on the state's survival and
politics.

   We have seen that prestate ethnic spaces, created most notably
by pristine agricultural and pastoralist expansions, were common.
Certainly, once existing, state sovereignty greatly reinforced the ethnic
leveling of its realm and often generated ethnic fusion and assimilation
of diverse ethnic groupings. States shaped ethnicity almost as much as
ethnicity shaped the state. Indeed, this also testifies to the crucial
political significance of ethnicity. Still, contrary to an all too common
view, state-building in a preexisting ethnic space was very much easier
than ethnos-building. Most states were built upon a population of
common ethnicity and depended on its sense of shared identity, affinity,
and solidarity. They centered on a particular majoritarian *Staatsvolk*.
Such states differed from empires on precisely this point: whereas the
former generally remained confined to a specific people (in the main
and never purely, of course), the latter expanded beyond their more
dependable ethnic core to rule over a larger multiethnic realm.

   Historical sociologists refer to premodern states as "territorial
states." As all states have a territory, this is an awkward label. It is
obviously intended to denote a scale larger than that of city- and other
petty-states. Sociologists also commonly use the designation "dynastic
kingdoms" in reference to premodern states. This designation implies
that such states were held together by state power and monarchic
legitimacy alone. However, as argued here, premodern and not only
modern states tended to be national states. In the great majority of
cases, the "territorial state" or "dynastic kingdom" was in effect a

national monarchy, wherein ethnos/people and state converged. Obviously, I am not claiming that the people of premodern national states were as closely integrated and highly mobilized as the people of modern national states are. Modernity made a difference, indeed, a huge difference. And yet to the extent that premodern states exhibited a rough congruence between ethnicity and statehood – which, far from being accidental, resulted from ethnic bonds of affinity, solidarity and mutual cooperation – they were by that very definition national.[36] Similarly, the intentional and unintentional processes of ethnic leveling and common identity formation generated by these states can only be described as nation-building.

The Zulu state- and nation-building described in Chapter 3 is both remarkable and typical at the same time. I will not repeat its details except to reiterate that the Zulu state and nation were forged from the ethnically related Nguni-speaking Bantu. These were subjected to the rule of a unified state apparatus and then to processes of cultural fusion, involving religious syncretism, joint military service, and common identity formation. All this took place in the first three-quarters of the nineteenth century, and yet there was nothing modern about it. Indeed, the great significance of the Zulu case, which has earned it a paradigmatic status in the anthropological literature on state- and nation-building, is that the whole process unfolded in an illiterate, preurban, Iron Age society. It was virtually untouched by Europeans, except for the occasional visitors who were able to observe and record it. As state formation in protohistory is inherently shadowy, typically taking place before literacy (itself a product of the state), the Zulu case is particularly illuminating. Among other things, it belies the view, shared even by traditionalists, that literacy, at least among the elite, was a necessary prerequisite for the formation of a sense of national identity. Finally, from the theoretical point of view, the Zulu society which underwent the processes of state- and nation-building also has the advantage of having been as far removed from European conditions as can be imazined.

Indeed, as the scholarly debate concerning the existence of premodern national states has centered almost exclusively on late medieval and early modern Europe, we will avoid Europe altogether in this section and turn our attention to other regions and periods. These have been strangely neglected in the study of nations, except by the few scholars cited at the beginning of this chapter. Europe's premodern national states will be examined separately in the following chapter.

Ancient Egypt: the first state – and first national state

There can hardly be a more appropriate case to begin our survey of premodern national states than the first large state, ancient Egypt. It has already been highlighted in this connection by Anthony Smith. From around 3000 BC, ancient Egypt was the world's first literate civilization, together with Sumer. However, unlike Sumer it was not divided politically into many city-states, but emerged quite early as a unified state, congruent with a distinct people of shared ethnicity. Both the state and the people, and the congruence between them, lasted for nearly three millennia. A very large state and people by the standards of the ancient Near East, Egypt would exercise imperial overlordship over some of its neighbors, mainly in the Levant. But there was never any doubt that the empire was merely the periphery of the state and people of Egypt, with their distinctive culture or civilization. Nor was there any doubt about Egypt's identity when the country was periodically taken over by foreign invaders from the Levant, Libya, or Nubia (Sudan). Furthermore, when central rule disintegrated into so-called "intermediate periods" between the Old, Middle, and New kingdoms, the ethnic unity of the country, and the prevailing sense of that unity, facilitated reunification.

The united kingdom of Egypt did not emerge full-blown. It had to be created, unified from a multiplicity of petty-polities in a proto-historic, preliterate process that is only vaguely recorded in tradition and by archaeology.[37] The archaeological record suggests that during the fourth millennium BC agricultural tribal/chiefly society along the Nile Valley coalesced into small regional polities. Egyptologists tend to believe that the later Egyptian administrative districts, or *nomes*, preserved the original layout of these petty-polities, in the same way that county and province names in England and much of continental Europe do. Subsequently, archaeology reveals the formation of two cultural spheres, one in the south and the other in the north, in Upper Egypt and the Delta. Of the two, the former appears to have been the more centralized and hierarchical state, with its urban walled center at Hierakonpolis. Although everything about protohistory – Egyptian included – is partly conjectured, the archaeological finds increasingly tend to confirm the general outline of later Egyptian traditions, according to which the Nile Valley was unified by the kings of Upper Egypt who had conquered Lower Egypt.

The Nile highway and the all-round protection offered by desert and sea facilitated and secured the new union. State- and nation-building could be successfully pursued by the country's mighty autocratic rulers, aided by a powerful bureaucracy and clergy. Smith has excellently described the main contours of this process.[38] But although the ethnic origins of nations is his general theme, he has left out that aspect: how much of an ethnos the inhabitants of the Nile Valley had been before the unification. Smith had very good reason for doing so, for the short answer is that we do not know. It stands to reason, however, that they were. The population of the Nile Valley seems to have emerged from a Neolithic agricultural expansion, growing the same kinds of domesticated plants and animals. Although there were surely different dialects, especially between Upper and Lower Egypt, there is no evidence from the Egyptian records of any significant linguistic or ethnic differences within the realm. It is unlikely that such differences, had they existed before unification, would have been totally eradicated without a trace so fast. It can be argued with some justification that the state's authorities were interested in suppressing evidence of such differences. Still, from what we know about other literate civilizations, linguistic and ethnic differences, where they exist, come up in the records because of their saliency. Indeed, the Egyptian texts and visual representations keenly highlight any difference between Egyptians and foreigners – each depicted in their typical look and dress.[39] Finally, large ethnic spaces regularly existed even in the absence of unified states, as we have seen with respect to city-state cultures. They are also widely recorded by literate civilizations among their prestate tribal neighbors, as, for example, along the Greek–Roman northern frontier in Europe: Thracians, Illyrians, Celts, and Germans, among others. Thus, there is no compelling reason to think that the preunification population of the Nile Valley could not or did not constitute an ethnos.

This is not to underestimate the ethnic leveling and nation-building accomplished by the early Pharaohs, but only to put them in the right context. Ethnicity and state action were mutually affecting. Upon unification a new capital was established at Memphis, on the former border between Upper and Lower Egypt. The symbols of power – the titles, crowns, and royal icons of the former kingdoms – were combined. Religious syncretism of the earlier local deities was initiated from above, creating a state religion with a divine king at its center. Local dialects were subsumed under an official (Upper Egypt) state language. Internal peace was enforced. Royal administration, taxation, economy, justice, and military systems were imposed. Monumental state construction, state art, and state literacy evolved rapidly to record and run the extensive state affairs.

Skeptics may raise all the customary objections to the common-sense proposition that Egypt was a national state. For example, did the peasants who constituted the vast majority of the population really share in the elite culture propagated by the state and religious authorities? Did they actually feel a sense of identification with a despotic and exploitative state? We again run into that almost intractable problem: the sources on the illiterate masses are close to non-existent. And yet, although answers to the above questions must always be qualified and seen as a matter of degree, they generally appear to be affirmative. It is widely accepted that state, religion, and civilization in Egypt were inextricably related, indeed, that they were remarkably congruent. All the evidence shows that the Egyptian masses were no less absorbed in cult and ritual than, and cherished their traditions as much as, any other premodern people. Nor were even the most remote rural communities unexposed to the thick religious, cultural, and political messages that came from the temples and their clergy in the perpetual cycles of cult and ritual that formed people's spiritual world. These were the makings of the premodern "imagined community" which Benedict Anderson has failed to consider. The Egyptian state, religion, and civilization were all national. As always, a foreign threat made this clearer.

True, in despotic Egypt the people were not involved in the public domain except as subjects to the state's demands and were habituated to passivity. The peasants were immersed in their daily toil, preoccupied with the struggle for survival, experienced mainly their village community, and were powerless to influence remote political events even if they wanted to. Still, national identity was not an all or nothing proposition. A looser sense of it and weaker popular mobilization than during modernity were precisely these: less potent forms of similar attachments. People knew very well that foreigners were foreigners and they resented them as such, especially if Egyptian identity was under threat. In desperate circumstances, Egyptian rulers did not shrink from appealing to these popular sentiments with a nationalist message. Clearly, they would not have done so had they not believed that such an appeal was potentially effective. Such circumstances occurred, for example, when the Asiatic-Semitic Hyksos, or "chiefs of foreign countries" in Egyptian, took advantage of the weakening of central power to establish their rule over the Nile Delta and much of the rest of Egypt during the mid seventeenth to mid sixteenth centuries BC. When the prince of Thebes raised the banner of revolt against them, as well as against invaders from the south, his rhetoric was unmistakable:

> One prince rules in Avaris, another in Ethiopia, and here
> I am, associated with an Asiatic and a Negro. Each has his
> slice of Egypt ... None can rest in peace, despoiled as all are
> by the imposts of the Asiatics. I will grapple with them ...
> I will save Egypt and overthrow the Asiatics.[40]

The prince succeeded in driving out the foreigners and reestablishing Egypt's unity, independence, and territorial integrity in the New Kingdom. We know very little about the course of the war, but his victory was surely not unconnected to his ability to appeal to and mobilize popular and – there is no other word – national support and legitimacy. It apparently did matter to people whether the despotic ruler to which they were subjected was foreign or native.

After two millennia of almost uninterrupted indigenous rule, Egypt was successively taken over during the early first millennium BC by Libyan and Nubian invaders, whose leaders made themselves pharaohs. Later, the country lost its independence altogether, as it was conquered by and incorporated into the Assyrian and Persian empires. Following Alexander's conquest of the East, Egypt became the center of the Ptolemaic Hellenistic kingdom. Notably, foreign rulers were careful to adorn themselves in the guise of the pharaohs and assume the role of defenders of Egyptian traditions, religion, and civilization. Much of this was directed at appeasing and coopting the Egyptian elite, especially the powerful religious establishment. But the fear of a popular revolt was equally potent, as we shall see. A sense of distinctive Egyptian national identity – a congruence of a people and culture, and its political implications – survived indigenous Egyptian state rule. Altered by Christianity, it would eventually be radically transformed by Islam and the adoption of the Arabic language.

Nascent national states in the ancient Near East

Bordering on Egypt, the Levant is the next part of the ancient Near East that draws our attention. As we have seen, it was dominated during the third and second millennia BC by city-state systems. However, in the first half of the first millennium BC the region experienced processes whose significance has been well exposed by Grosby.[41] The northern part of the Levant, today's Syria, was home to Aramaic regional polities. Like the Greeks, the Aramaeans were an ethnos that shared a language, pantheon, script, and culture in general, as well as a sense of kinship and shared identity, yet remained divided politically. The Aramaean states cooperated against the rising threat of Assyria, but ultimately succumbed to it. Developments were not very different in the southern part of the Levant, except for one crucial element: the peoples of the states that emerged there – those of the Israelites, Ammon, Moab, and Edom – spoke closely related and mutually intelligible dialects (which as a modern Hebrew speaker I am still able to understand without any special study); and yet they developed into separate peoples, each with its own culture, sense of identity, and state. Although the Hebrew Bible presents a fictitious genealogy of kinship among them (as part of its genealogy of all of humanity), it shares the perception that these were separate peoples.

The early evolution of these peoples is shrouded in the mists of protohistory, so it is difficult to tell what realities preceded the emergence of the various states, what set them on their separate courses, and what was generated by the activities of the respective states once they arose.[42] The differences in culture and sense of identity among the peoples concerned were largely grounded in religion, and some of them may have developed before the states' period. The Israelite tribes seem to have variably participated in an amphictyonic–military alliance centering on the cult of Jehovah and his shrine at Shiloh prior to the state period. There is little evidence on whether the same was true of the cult of Chemosh in Moab, Kos in Edom and Milcom (Molech of the Canaanite pantheon) in Ammon. Obviously, there was a variety of worship of largely overlapping deities among these peoples. Equally clearly, each of the rising states made a conscious effort to institutionalize a state religion around a central national deity. Again, preexisting ethnic differences apparently contributed to, and were then massively reinforced by, the growth of these small national states.

The idea that ancient Israel was an example of a premodern nation has gained currency even among those who believe it to be a rare if not an isolated case, including the father of modernism Hans Kohn.[43] The claim has even been made that its model, as projected through the Bible, played a decisive role in sparking early modern European national consciousness (a claim I believe to be overdrawn, although the people and nation of Israel were undoubtedly a very strong idiom).[44] Scholars of ancient Israel fiercely debate the questions of when Israelite state formation occurred, what form it took, when the notion of an Israelite people became rooted, and how deep and widespread it was. There is also controversy over the existence of a united kingdom under David and Solomon in the tenth century BC. There were two separate kingdoms, Israel and Judah, from the ninth to late eight centuries BC, when the northern and stronger kingdom of Israel was destroyed by Assyria. The writing of the most important of the historical books which would be incorporated into the Hebrew Bible is traced to the seventh century BC. They were inspired by the vision of a united people of Israel with its unified national history and special relationship with God. That went hand in hand with the Judean kings' efforts to fuse the refugees from Israel and their own people into one and prepare them for a struggle to break the Assyrian yoke. In this context, royal propaganda, ancient myth, oral traditions, and history are difficult to separate from one another.[45]

Still, whether one dates the process before or after the exile and return from Babylon, it is hardly denied or deniable that a strong sense of Judaic self-identity as a nation became pervasive and very potent. The ancient Judaic case has a rare element which supposedly gives it a modern quality: the national–historical epos, the *Torah*, was also the canonic religious text, popularly internalized by recitation in congregation by the masses throughout the year as routine worship. In order to be able to learn the *Torah*, Jews acquired literacy at a much higher rate than was usual among premodern societies. And the illiterate were also thoroughly exposed to the oral recitation. The Hebrew

Bible divides humanity into peoples (*am*; *goi*) as a matter of course and views them in kin terms as "families of the earth." Some scholars believe that this is a special derivation from, and projection of, the Bible's concept of the people and nation of Israel. But there is no reason to think that this view was special to the Bible. In Israel's vicinity, Ammon, Moab, and Edom were examples of the crystallization of small national states that exhibited a congruence of state and ethnicity or peoplehood. All these small national states would be conquered by and absorbed into the Assyrian Empire and its successors. The particularly strong features of Judaic identity as a people and a nation, rooted in a monotheistic national religion and literate culture, only explain how this identity uniquely survived the loss of political self-rule and diasporic existence over millennia.

To crush forever indigenous revolts, Assyria, followed by Babylon, carried out a policy of massive deportations throughout their realm.[46] They gave special attention to the elite and population of the fortified cities and towns, the centers of resistance, whose people were also easier to round up after resistance had been broken. But they also uprooted whole populations from their homeland and settled them elsewhere in their empire. Clearly, they would not have gone to all this trouble were it not for the fact that indigenous resistance by ethnopolitical communities living in their native country was endemic, persistent and, indeed, encompassed the population at large.

The emergence of national states also took place further east and north in the ancient Near East, in Babylonia and Assyria themselves, as well as in Elam, Media-Persia, possibly Urartu (Ararat), and Lydia, to name only some major cases. For example, although almost as old as Sumerian civilization, Elam, located in what is today's southwest Iran, is less well known because of the paucity of the sources. Still, it emerges from prehistory in the third millennium BC as a distinct culture with its own language, unrelated to any other, and script (later replaced by Akkadian). Dynasties rose and fell in Elam, and we have little precise information about the country's internal make up and changes of boundaries. Nonetheless, it seems pretty clear that during most of the period from sometime in the third millennium to the seventh century BC – nearly two millennia – Elam was a unified realm where state and culture converged.[47] This time span is not much shorter than that of the Egyptian state, and that without Egypt's geographical isolation and in a most exposed and volatile area. Evidently, some very potent and resilient bonding element held Elam together for so long and through relentless historical upheavals.

Mesopotamia was even more exposed, and its incipient national state formations more vulnerable and more tentative. After the fall of Akkad, Ur of the Third Dynasty affected a revival of Sumerian culture and a unification of the Land (twenty-first to twentieth centuries BC). The city-state system of southern Mesopotamia gave way to central state power, which created a realm wherein state and culture converged. As a leading historian of that period, obviously unaffected by modernist theorizing, has written: "The Third Dynasty of Ur ... must be given credit for having established a new concept of rule – the first bureaucratic national state."[48] This process of state- and nation-building was cut short by defeat at the hands of Elam. However, in the seventeenth century BC Mesopotamia was again unified by Hammurabi of Babylon. The kingdom was destroyed by a Hittite invasion in the following century. Nonetheless, the realm henceforth known as Babylonia, remained a single linguistic and cultural sphere, which facilitated repeated unifications. Babylonia was unified by the foreign tribal Kassites from the Zagros Mountains and turned into a single country-state, where city-state autonomy was lost for good (sixteenth to twelfth centuries BC).[49] The state was destroyed, again by Elam, but Babylonia was reunified by native kings shortly thereafter. The ebbs and flows of their power came to an end with the rise of the Assyrian Empire.

Developing from the city-state of Assur to a nascent national state in northern Mesopotamia during the second millennium BC, Assyria further expanded in the eighth and seventh centuries BC into an imperial juggernaut that swallowed all the other polities throughout the ancient Near East, including national states. Ushering in a new era, Assyria became the first in a series of empires that henceforth would constitute the standard in southeast Asia, replacing one another over millennia down to the twentieth century. Assyria was replaced by Babylonia and then by Persia, both incipient national states themselves which grew into empires. Thus, the existence and proliferation of national states in southwest Asia was interrupted by imperial expansion, either by a foreign power that eliminated local independence or by the national state itself that expanded to rule over others. For this reason, empires have become identified with this region in the literature on state and nation. I postpone further discussion of this process until my treatment of empires later in this chapter. We now switch across the continent to another pristine cradle of civilization, east Asia.

China: the largest and most enduring ancient people and state

China is one of the world's oldest civilizations and states, singular in having survived and exhibited a virtually unbroken cultural and political continuum since its inception. It has also been the world's most populous civilization and state, again continuously, over millennia. Furthermore, it has profoundly affected the development of its neighbors throughout east Asia. Thus, the question of whether or not premodern China ought to be regarded as a national state should have been central to the controversy concerning the nation. And yet this question has been given only minimal attention on the very margins of a European-centric debate. Modernist precepts are not alone in their responsibility for this marginalization. The Chinese have also contributed to it. In the late nineteenth and early twentieth centuries, China was dominated and thoroughly humiliated by the Western powers and Japan. Chinese intellectuals, patriots, and political leaders acutely felt that together with their industrial–technological superiority these powers manifested national cohesiveness and zeal unknown in China. They regarded the creation of modern-style nationalism a top priority if China was to survive. A dichotomous view of nationhood, as either modern or none at all, took root in the discourse about China. Unquestionably, as already emphasized, modern nationhood was greatly changed and far enhanced in comparison with premodern forms of the nation. Still, was the congruence between state and culture in China – alias nationhood – irrelevant in terms of identity, affinity, and solidarity? Did it have nothing to do with the country's unique continuous cultural and political existence over millennia? This notion surely sounds absurd, and yet it has been very pervasive. Fortunately, a reaction against the solely modern concept of Chinese nationhood has been gathering momentum among scholars.[50]

It is widely argued that premodern China was a "civilization" rather than a nation. But as with ancient Egypt, this only dodges the question. Civilization means a wider cultural framework that may encompass various national cultures, separate peoples, and separate states. Western, Muslim, and Hindu civilizations are some examples of such diverse cultural units. However, unlike the above, Chinese civilization was fundamentally congruent with a unified Chinese state and a Chinese people. Surely, as with almost any national state, there were minorities within the state; China experienced periods of political disunity; and Chinese civilization enjoyed enormous prestige and influence throughout east Asia, among non-Chinese people. Yet none of these points alter the fact of China's remarkable millennia-long cultural–political coherence.

True, there has been considerable linguistic diversity among the Chinese. Chinese civilization emerged in the north, along the Yellow River, a sphere of Neolithic agricultural expansion unified politically by China's first dynasties during the second millennium BC. They introduced the Chinese script, and their language, historical Mandarin, encompassed the entire north and extended southward. During the first millennium BC, the Yangtze River basin in the south was culturally and politically absorbed by the north. Chinese political domination was accompanied by massive colonization from the north (mainly male settlers who married local women), as well as by thorough Sinification of the indigenous populations. Both historical and genetic evidence attest to this.[51] In the process, Mandarin diversified in the south into several sister languages. The significance of this diversity should not be exaggerated, however. Dialects of Mandarin are the native tongue of more than 70 percent of the population in today's China, with the other six Chinese languages comprising about 20 percent. Despite the leveling efforts of modern state education, these proportions are probably not very different from historical realities. All the above, the ethnic Chinese, are often referred to as Han Chinese, after the name of the first dynasty that exercised prolonged rule over unified China. Indeed, non-adoption of a Chinese language as a native tongue is one of the hallmarks of the fifty-five non-Han ethnic and national minorities (together comprising 7 percent of the population) which survived in the remote corners of the south, in the northeast, and elsewhere. Last, but not least, the Chinese pictographic and ideographic script transcends dialect and language differences.

Literary culture, mass education, and universal military service are famously regarded as the tools that forged modern national identity. Yet all of them were largely present before modernity in that fifth of humanity that China has always comprised. Since the time of the Tang Dynasty (618–907), China was uniquely ruled by a body of literate Confucian bureaucrats, the mandarins, a meritocracy selected through highly competitive examinations held in all the provinces and open to candidates of every class. To prepare people for the examinations, the imperial authorities established schools in the towns and villages. Although only a minority attended these schools, the significance of their deep penetration into the farthest reaches of the country and of their uniform cultural and political message is not difficult to understand. Moreover, the imperial authorities stipulated that decrees of national significance would be read aloud in mandatory public gatherings regularly held in every village. Thus, although the peasant population of the provinces was habituated to passive obedience to the imperial rulers, they were neither entirely ignorant about far-away events nor wholly disconnected from a national culture beyond that of their own locality. "High" and "low" cultures certainly existed, but their interface was much greater than Gellner would have it. As a leading historian of Chinese nationhood put it:

> *In privileging modern society as the only social form capable of generating political self-awareness, Gellner and Anderson regard national identity as a distinctively modern mode of consciousness ... The empirical record does not furnish the basis for such a strong statement about the polarity between the modern and the premodern.*[52]

> *The long history of complex civilizations, such as that of China, does not fit the picture of isolated communities and a vertically separated but unified clerisy. Considerable research about complex networks of trade, pilgrimage, migration, and sojourning shows that villages were linked to wider communities and political structures ... The exclusive emphasis on print capitalism as enabling the imagining of a common destiny and the concept of simultaneity ignores the complex relationship between the written and spoken word. In agrarian civilizations, this interrelationship furnishes an extremely rich and subtle context for communication across the culture.*[53]

Another leading scholar on China has expressed a similar view:

> *Earlier attempts to explain China's remarkable record of*
> *unity focused, inevitably perhaps, on the super elite of*
> *scholar-bureaucrats ... One must consider the role of*
> *ordinary people: farmers, artisans, shopkeepers, midwives,*
> *silk reelers, and laborers ... who were engaged in the*
> *construction of a unified culture ... In this view, peasants are*
> *not, as some have claimed, "easy material for ideological*
> *molding"; they are leading actors in the performance that we*
> *have come to call Chinese culture.*[54]

Both scholars have highlighted the role of mass pan-Chinese myths and rituals, tightly regulated by the state, as a strong constitutive element of premodern Chinese national identity.

One example of the interface between "high" and "low" culture is the image of the emperor. The Confucianism that became China's state ideology posited the emperor as the supreme – strict but benevolent – head of the family, to whom the people owed not only obedience but also devotion and love. However, this image was not invoked unnaturally or without striking a real chord among the emperor's subjects. Such an image was common in other large and despotic national states (such as Czarist Russia), but scarcely in multiethnic empires.

Unified China under the Han introduced universal military conscription for all men at the age of twenty-three. After one year of training in their native provinces, the conscripts moved to spend another year in garrison duty, frontier armies, or naval service. They were then discharged and called up for training every eighth month until the age of sixty-five (later lowered to fifty-six).[55] China was the only notable power before the nineteenth century to adopt such a comprehensive system of conscription and reserve duty. And at least some of the effects attributed to modern armies of universal conscription as the "school of the nation" surely applied in this case too. These included: a wider national perspective gained by travel and service far away from one's locality; contact and fraternization with comrades from other provinces; and indoctrination to serve the emperor and country. Both the ruthless and despotic Ch'in Dynasty which unified China in 221 BC after a long period of fragmentation, and the more moderate and enlightened Han Dynasty which succeeded the Ch'in, safeguarded the class of small freeholder peasants, which they regarded as the economic and military backbone of the state. Only during the later Han did land accumulation in large estates bring about a decline of the small peasantry, which in turn contributed to the decline of the conscript-militia armies. Such armies were revived during China's second golden age under the Sui and Tang Dynasties (AD 581–907).[56]

The dichotomous view of China as a civilization rather than a nation confuses the picture in another way too. It is a widely accepted truism that a sense of shared ethnic and national belonging crystallizes and manifests itself only in the presence of a foreign "other" that highlights the similarities rather than differences within a closely related ethnic population. Thus, confident hegemonic peoples whose identity is not threatened often seem to exhibit little national self-awareness. Their identity and pride as a collective tend to be transparent to them and taken as a matter of course. Hence, for example, the supposed absence of nationalism attributed to the English, mainly by English writers, in much of the nineteenth and early twentieth centuries, during Britain's zenith. In this respect, nothing came close to China's unique position. Unlike in other state systems, the Chinese state nearly monopolized the east Asian agricultural space. So universal was it that, famously, both the people and state almost lacked distinctive eponyms. The Han or any other general designation were rarely used. What we call China was known to its people as the "Middle Kingdom" at the center of the acumen, which had no equal and whose emperor ostensibly ruled "everything under the sun." Its small neighbors often were, and in any case were regarded as, lowly dependants and satellites. China denoted universal civilization, and Chinese identity – confident and unchallenged – essentially meant humanity writ large.

Yet not entirely. Even before imperial unification barbarian tribesmen harassed and threatened China from several directions. As early as the first millennium BC, Chinese writers regularly contrasted superior Chineseness with foreign barbarism. Scholars have pointed out that some of these writers treated the foreigners as a "biological," barely human, race apart. Others regarded the differences as fundamentally cultural, which the barbarians could overcome if they assimilated into Chinese civilization.[57] Either way, both views fall within our concept of ethnicity, in which culture and a sense of kinship interact in various measures. As we have seen, much of China itself was created in a process of cultural assimilation in which non-Chinese populations were Sinified.

One dedicated study, based on a rich variety of source material, has demonstrated that even when China was at the height of self-confidence and hegemony under the Tang Dynasty, the Chinese people felt a strong sense of ethnic difference – both racial and cultural – between themselves and non-Chinese. The author of the study expresses his dismay at "an extremely narrow base of politicized or outmoded theories, unspoken or unproven assumptions, and a penchant for compartmentalizing or simplifying the role of ethnicity in Chinese history."[58] And what was true of Chinese identity during the zenith of Chinese power became all the more true when this power declined, as the foreign challenge to China intensified over time. The mounted archer peoples of the steppes to the north proved to be a menace against which China had little effective remedy. Like later-day Egypt, China was ruled by foreigners during most of its history after the fall of the Tang in AD 906.

The Manchurians in particular repeatedly seized control over China, or its northern part, establishing rule, successively, by the T'o-pa Wei (AD 386–556), Khitan-Liao and Jurchen-Chin (AD 907–1234), and Manchu-Qing (AD 1616–1912). The second name in each of the above represented the Chinese dynastic title adopted by the foreign conquerors, respectively. The Mongol conquest, which began in 1211 under Chinggis Khan and was completed under the leadership of his grandson Kublai, lasted until 1368, taking the Chinese dynastic name of Yüan. Each of China's Manchurian and Mongol conquerors exhibited similar ambivalence about their difference from the conquered. On the one hand, they sought to preserve their distinct identity and culture, both because it was theirs and because their military superiority and rule over China depended on their unique culture as mounted pastoralists and their status as a warrior caste. On the other hand, the conquerors' assumption of Chinese dynastic names was only one aspect of their efforts to appear fully Chinese culturally in order to gain public legitimacy.[59] As in Egypt, their efforts indicate that this factor mattered a great deal. Furthermore, over time, the conquerors were irresistibly allured by and assimilated into Chinese culture. Nonetheless, to many Chinese they remained foreign conquerors, and as such objectionable. There were quite a few popular political expressions demonstrating this.

For example, scholars have noted the rise of Chinese patriotic nationalism in Sung China (969–1279), the dynasty that had lost the north to the invading Manchurian Jurchen but was able to hold on in the south.[60] Most notably, despite mistrust by the imperial authorities which feared disobedience, popular militias, known in Chinese as "loyal and righteous-minded troops" and "people army," sprang up spontaneously in the provinces to resist the Jurchen. Thus, for example, "Chang Jung, a fisherman from the Liang-shan moor in Shantung province, assembled between 200 and 300 men equipped with boats, and 'attacked the Chin constantly.'" As an official imperial commander reported: "The societies for loyalty and righteousness have existed for many years in all districts of this prefecture."[61] According to a modern study, the sources "contain numerous accounts of bravery in the min-ping, and numerous statements by officials confirming the superiority of these forces over the regular troops ... it is probably fair to say that among the majority of the Sung Chinese hatred for the Chin overshadowed all internal social tensions ... Ethnic contradictions outweighed class contradictions."[62] Indeed, "The documentation on the Fang La rebellion suggests that the 'loyalty' of the rebels, so mistrusted by the court, was no longer interpreted primarily as loyalty to the ruler or to the dynasty, but as loyalty directly to the state." "One of Fang La's purported speeches to his associates during the uprising of 1120–1122 complains bitterly about Sung tribute to the barbarian states."[63] These realities of political action, as well as rare occasions such as this when the voice of the masses is heard in the documentation, confirm unsurprisingly that popular devotion to the patriotic–national cause was often stronger and more authentic than the more calculating attitudes of rulers and elites. Furthermore, while peasant uprisings were common in premodern history, so were also popular and popularly supported rebellions against a foreign rule. Although the two motives – the socioeconomic and ethnonational – often reinforced each other, there is no reason to conflate them, as the rebels' rhetoric amply demonstrates.

Both the Jurchen and Sung were subsequently destroyed by the Mongol conquest. However, the Mongols themselves were eventually driven out, and by Chinese. While repeated famines were the trigger for popular unrest and anarchy during the Yüan decline, these were fully exploited by the rebel Zhu Yuanzhang, who beat the nationalist drum. Coming from a poor peasant family, he became leader of one of the armed gangs that rose up against the Yüan. Assuming the mantle of defender of Confucianism, he achieved national ascendancy. Again, in a country and era in which dynastic legitimacy, even foreign, was a sacred principle, the claim that the rulers lost their mandate by violating local culture and customs was the normative way to formulate nationalist calls for rebellion. Defeating other rebel armies and the Yüan, Zhu Yuanzhang made himself emperor in 1368. He took special care to eradicate everything Mongol and foreign, nominating only Han Chinese officials and restoring Chinese customs and practices. The new dynasty which he established, the Ming, ushered a new golden age for China, expressed among other things in an expansive and nationalistic foreign policy.

The Ming were the last native dynasty to rule China. Their reign ended in 1644 with another Manchurian takeover. The invading Manchu, who became the Qing Dynasty, ruled with an iron hand through the traditional Chinese bureaucracy. But the story of an otherwise insignificant attempt at a nationalist rebellion during the 1720s and 1730s is illuminating in many respects. In the manifesto of the planned rebellion, the conspirator Zeng Jing drew on the ideas of earlier Chinese authors, especially Wang Fuzhi (1619–1692) who during the Manchu takeover had revived the view of the foreigners as beasts: "The barbarians are a different species from us, like animals; it is the Chinese who should stay in this land, and the barbarians who should be driven out."[64] The plot was discovered, and Zeng Jing was arrested. However, the Manchu Emperor Yongzheng decided not to execute him, but in a rather bizarre and fully documented episode drafted a response to the rebel's allegations and later engaged in correspondence with him. The former rebel was made to see his error and admit the Manchu were not beasts, ruled China according to Chinese ways, and were its only hope. Furthermore, the emperor ordered that a book incorporating his correspondence with the rebel should reach everyone in the country. He explained that if he did not: "how would I be able to face my officials at court and in the provinces, and those who live across the country?"[65] Having been read before large gatherings of mandarin bureaucrats in Beijing, the book was mass copied and made mandatory in all the schools and examinations for office throughout China. Clearly, opinion and legitimacy among the literati-bureaucrats who ran China mattered a lot. Yet the emperor did not stop there, but ordered the book to be read in public gatherings in every village in China.

Given that popular echoes from premodern societies are so scarce, this episode strikingly demonstrates both the great sensitivity surrounding foreign rule (about which the Qing rulers were constantly nervous) and the remarkable channels of cross-country communication that existed in China. Furthermore, while the whole affair was certainly unusual, the practice was not. For example, in 1724, Emperor Yongzheng issued a Confucian tract of maxims of good conduct for his subjects. A version in colloquial style "was read aloud at yamen [official's office] throughout China on the first and fifteenth of each moon."[66] True, wood-block and stone-block printing (less developed than European movable metal type) had been invented in China and used for distributing the imperial books and decrees. But indeed, already appearing during the Han period around the beginning of the Common Era and widely in use during the Tang period later in the first millennium, these means of communication practically spanned the entire history of the premodern Chinese empire-state. For example, the founder of the Ming Dynasty in the fourteenth century, Yuanzhang, sought to protect the commoners from being abused by officials:

> *His discourse on sound government and the justification of severe penalties for wrong-doing was published in a pamphlet called* Grand Monitions, *of which each household must retain a copy . . . In every community two pavilions were constructed . . . The good and bad deeds of the villagers were . . . posted at these pavilions. Twice a year, in the first and tenth lunar months, every community held its local banquet. Attendance by all households was compulsory. Before food and drink were served there were chants, lectures, the reading of imperial laws, and the reprimanding of individuals who had committed misdeeds in the village.*[67]

Confucian tenets of good conduct were "repeatedly cited in every school in every village and even passed on to the illiterate."[68]

China's masses were undoubtedly immersed in their daily toil and disenfranchised politically. Scattered as they were in the countryside, most of the time they were impotent to resist the dictates of the imperial authorities, including ruthless foreign rulers at the head of superior foreign armies. Local and provincial identities were strong and diverse. National bonds of identity, affinity, and solidarity were much weaker than they would become during modernity. And yet to argue that they did not exist or were politically insignificant before modernity, *inter alia* with respect to the question of foreign rule, is simply untrue. One scholar, reacting against the idea that premodern China was a culture but not a nation, has arrived at this common sense conclusion:

> For the majority [of the population, culturalism] ... would have been less important than their primary ethnic identification. It seems likely that most Chinese thought of their cultural and political community – their nation – as a Chinese one, and that culturalism, to the extent that they understood it, reinforced their sense that the empire was properly Chinese.[69]

The author of another major study, *The Rise of the Chinese Empire*, has unabashedly titled his first volume: *Nation, State and Imperialism in Early China, c. 1600 BC–AD 8*. He also regards the Chinese state, nation, and civilization as having been inseparable, welded together by imperial rule and expansion. As early as the time of the Han, China's first enduring imperial dynasty, a popular song proclaimed:

> Within the Four Seas,
> We all are brothers,
> And none be taken as strangers![70]

The author of yet another exhaustive scholarly study, of Manchu China, has stated as its purpose "to demonstrate that ethnicity has an important role to play in historical analysis; that it is neither an exclusively modern concern nor a peripheral one."[71] The Taiping Rebellion (1850–1864) was the greatest popular revolt against the Manchu and the most lethal and destructive conflict of the nineteenth century, in which an estimated 25 million people were killed. The China of the time was still entirely premodern and its people were scarcely affected by the increasing encroachments of the European powers. And yet the spirit of the rebels' proclamation was unmistakable, restating the same themes we have encountered throughout Chinese history:

*O you masses, listen to our words. It is our belief that the
empire is China's empire, not the Manchu barbarian
empire ... Alas! Since the Ming's misrule, the Manchu
availed themselves to the opportunity to throw China into
confusion; they stole China's empire, appropriated
China's food and clothing, and ravished China's sons
and daughters ...*

*The Chinese have Chinese characteristics; but now the
Manchus have ordered us to shave our hair around the head,
leaving a long tail behind, thus making the Chinese appear
like brute animals. The Chinese have Chinese dress; but now
the Manchus have ... discarded the robes ... of former
dynasties, in order to make the Chinese forget their
origins ... The Chinese have the Chinese language; but now
the Manchus have introduced slang of the capital and
changed the Chinese tones, desiring to deluge China with
barbarian speech and barbarian expressions ...*

*We have carefully investigated the Manchus' Tartar
origins and have found that their first ancestor was a
crossbreed of a white fox and a red dog, from whom sprang
this race of demons.*[72]

Thus, centuries of Manchu imperial propaganda proved to be incapable of preventing the resurfacing of powerful popular sentiments
against foreign rule in a mass popular rebellion.

In the giant's shadow: national states around China

If Chinese nationhood, one of the world's most ancient and the most
enduring, can be dismissed with the claim that for the Chinese
their civilization was so universal as to denote humanity writ large,
the same can certainly not be said about China's neighbors. Existence in
the shadow of the giant was a major catalyst for efforts by neighboring
ethnic communities to establish themselves politically in order to withstand China's military pressure and overwhelming cultural hegemony.
And it did not matter, or rather it mattered dialectically, how much of
Chinese culture they were eager to adopt. Of course, as noted before,
many ethnic communities were absorbed by and assimilated into early

"China" as it expanded. Yet all around the periphery of what became historical China, better protected by distance and geography, national states – comprising their own people and culture – emerged, largely in reaction to China.

In Mongolia and somewhat less so in Manchuria, populations were nomadic and societies tribal. But even if larger political conglomerations there were also shifting to count as national, the admittedly patchy evidence nevertheless suggests that they exhibited an unsurprising link between ethnicity and statehood. In Mongolia two different languages of the Altaic language family were spoken, Mongolian and Turkic, both probably arising from pristine pastoralist expansions, including the adoption of the riding horse. As China became a united imperial power in 221 BC, a huge tribal confederation, known as Hsiung-nu in the Chinese sources, formed on its northern frontier. Whether it was (proto-)Turkic- or (proto-)Mongolic-speaking, or both, remains unknown. Later on, the Sui and Tang dynasties in China (AD 581–907) faced the emergence of vast Turkic confederations on the steppe. In contrast to many other ethnonational consolidations, the stimulus for these great unions of the steppe was offensive rather than defensive. They conglomerated in order to take on China and plunder its wealth.[73] Chinggis Khan's Mongol Empire, exceptional in both its ability to unite all the peoples of the steppe and its massive conquests, falls under our discussion of empires later on.

The exact ethnic and linguistic composition of pre- and proto-historic Manchuria is unknown. But as most of the country was unified by the Jurchen people, their language, a member of the Tungustic family of eastern Siberia, became standard. First occupying China, later falling under Mongolian suzerainty, then defending their independence against the Ming, the Jurchen, known as Manchu, again took over China in the seventeenth century. Assimilation, both voluntary and involuntary, into Chinese culture has since largely eradicated a distinct Manchurian identity.

Bordering on Manchuria, but more sheltered from China by the Yellow Sea, Korea is a classic case for our subject. In protohistoric Korea three separate kingdoms emerged during the first millennium AD. Withstanding Chinese invasions in the north, they absorbed many features of Chinese culture, including script (changed into an indigenous one in the fifteenth century), Buddhism, and state Confucianism. The kingdom of Silla unified the country in the seventh century, and it was apparently its language that became standard. The Goryeo Dynasty replaced Silla in 936, and thereafter until modernity Korea retained a more or less uninterrupted unity and independence despite Chinese, Mongolian, and Japanese incursions and periods of domination. Korean culture, identity, and statehood have overlapped more than a thousand years. Again, why should this remarkable congruence have endured for so long and so persistently, withstanding mighty neighbors, if collective identity did not matter politically in premodern state societies ostensibly defined by elite rule and class divisions? This is a mystery that modernist theorists of Korean nationhood do not seem to recognize. However, as traditionalists have cautiously suggested: "the organizational activities of the state may have created a homogeneous collectivity with a sense of shared identity much earlier than happened in the countries of Western Europe that provide the model for 'modernist' scholarship."[74] And to this one should add the admittedly little known early common ethnic underpinning of the Korean state, which would in turn be reinforced by the state's activities. In any case, Koreans have long been imbued with a sense of being a separate and distinct ethnos or "race," people, and culture.[75] As modernist theorist-historian Hobsbawm has admitted: China, Korea, and Japan are "among the extremely rare examples of historic states composed of a population that is ethnically almost or entirely homogeneous."[76] We shall see about the claim of rarity later on, but first we turn to Hobsbawm's third cited case, Japan.

No less influenced by Chinese civilization than Korea, but even more protected by sea from China and the continent, and filled with a sense of its separateness and uniqueness, Japan should have been paradigmatic in the study of premodern nationalism. And yet it barely figures in it. It is on par with China in both its significance and neglect. As with China, Western modernist notions have been adopted by some Japanese scholars, for in Japan the change from the premodern to the modern era was even starker than in China.[77] Faced with pressure from the Western powers, Japan revolutionized itself in the Meiji Restoration (1868). The Meiji reformers institutionalized a strong central state, pushed for rapid industrialization, and cultivated an intense nationalist ethos, propagated through universal education and every other means. Again, no one is denying the huge impact of modernization in Japan, as elsewhere. Still, this hardly means that a strong sense of nationhood had not existed in premodern Japan and had not been pivotal to Japanese politics. Did the Meiji "manipulators" invent, rather than adapt from the central tenets of Japan's traditions, the nationalist ethos which they themselves so passionately espoused? Did this ethos, centering on Japanese kin–cultural uniqueness and the divinity of the emperor, have any chance of being embraced by the people as intensely as it was if it had not corresponded very deeply to their own sense of their culture, people, and country? And were these three not congruent as far as mythological and historical memory could reach?

Far more than China, the population of Japan has been ethnically homogeneous ever since the emergence of a unified Japanese state around the middle of the first millennium AD.[78] As we have seen in Chapter 3, a Japanese ethnos, apparently originating from rice-cultivating colonists from Korea, expanded up the archipelago of Japan, predating and constituting the substratum of a unified Japanese state. In turn, the growth of the state helped to further homogenize the realm. From the third century AD, from its center on the Nara-Osaka plain, the Yamato state progressively expanded and consolidated that realm. And from the late sixth century, with increasing agricultural intensification and growing Chinese influence and threat, Chinese-modeled religions, literacy, architecture, urbanism, and a centralized bureaucratic state inaugurated Japan's historical era. With them came also state armies of national conscription, in which the peasant population was trained and served away from home.[79]

True, by the twelfth century Japan had undergone feudal fragmentation, which would occasionally deteriorate into anarchy and protracted civil wars. And yet central government was repeatedly reinstituted by military rulers (shoguns): the Kamakura shogunate (1185–1333); more weakly and at the end only nominally, the Muromachi shogunate (1336–1573); and finally, the most powerful and centralized state rule of the Tokugawa shogunate (1603–1868). While resting on military force, the shogunate (*bakufu*) relied as heavily on the country's deeply-entrenched sense of ethnic oneness, which, significantly, no autonomous or even rebellious feudal lord ever challenged. Furthermore, although depriving the emperor of any real authority, the shoguns derived their legitimacy from an imperial mandate, supposedly given voluntary. Indeed, holding the reins of power, the shoguns never dared to usurp the imperial title itself. The Japanese royal house is the oldest in the world, going back one and a half millennia.

The sacred horror surrounding the emperor as a deity and the symbol of the nation did not start with modernity, but was by its very nature profoundly premodern.

Like China, Japan is claimed to have lacked a sense of the "other" and hence national self-awareness. This was supposedly due to insular isolation rather than exclusiveness. However, extensive cultural imports as well as threats of invasion from Tang China made the Japanese very much aware of their otherness. And the Mongol invasions launched by Kublai Khan's China in 1274 and 1281 were repulsed by mobilization on a national scale. True, mobilization involved mainly the samurai warrior class. The political exclusion of the masses in feudal Japan grew steadily, and was fully institutionalized under the Tokugawa. Then, too, however, the deeply felt Western presence in Japan after 1540, including significant conversion to Christianity of both nobles and commoners, led to the Tokugawa rulers' decision to banish all foreigners and close the country completely to outsiders. They feared their subversive effect on local customs and loyalty. Thus, it was the foreign impact on Japan, rather than a lack thereof, that fed Japanese isolation.[80] Japan's strong sense of cultural separateness, which today expresses itself in, among other things, the most restrictive immigration policy and lowest rates of foreign immigrants of all the developed countries, did not begin with modernity.

On the other side of China, Vietnam offers another typical example of national state formation. China's early expansion absorbed and assimilated most of the populations in what became south China. So the question of where China ends in the south was basically determined by a balancing act involving distance, mountainous terrain, limits of political and military power projection, and ethnicity. The early Vietnamese speakers populated the Red River basin in today's north Vietnam as part of the Neolithic spread throughout southeast Asia of wet-rice cultivators speaking so-called Austro-Asiatic languages. Later, the powerful Han and Tang dynasties invaded the region, subjecting it to a 1,000-year rule (111 BC–AD 938). Nonetheless, the survival of the indigenous language and identity despite sweeping cultural borrowing from China made it possible for local leaders to unify the realm and consolidate it into a national state, independent and distinct from China. This was not just another splinter province of China, drifting apart during times of anarchy and reunited at times of Chinese dynastic revival. The distinct Viet ethnicity sustained and, in turn, was protected by its enduring political separateness, despite repeated Chinese invasions and periods of domination.[81] As in Japan (and Tibet), the Viet rulers assumed the title of emperors to emphasize that they were equal rather than subservient to the sovereign of China. From the eleventh to the eighteenth centuries, the Viet state, language, and people expanded through conquest and peasant colonization into the central and southern parts of the coastal plain down to the Mekong Delta, assimilating the local populations except for a few in remote mountain enclaves. The existence and congruence of the Viet state, people, and culture long predated the French colonial occupation in the nineteenth century.

Here lies the answer to the question raised by Benedict Anderson: why did French Indochina disintegrate into separate national states with decolonization, rather than become a single realm as in Dutch Indonesia. This was so because the various new states in Indochina rested not merely on precolonial states or ethne, but on premodern national states that combined both.[82] Each of these premodern national states had a long history and an ethnic core, or *Staatsvolk*, identified with it for many centuries. Each survived dynastic changes, border expansion and contraction, and periodical political disintegrations while institutionalizing and spreading its culture.[83] These national states included: a Cambodian–Khmer state since the sixth century AD (with the Khmer constituting 90 percent of the population today); a more or less unified Siamese–Thai state since the fourteenth century (with the Thai constituting 85 percent of the population today); and a Myanmar–Burman state since the tenth century (with Burman comprising 68 percent of the population today). The postcolonial Vietnamese, the strongest of the region's peoples, opted for independence over an Indochina union precisely in order to preserve their distinctive identity. And the others certainly did not wish to be subsumed in a Vietnamese-dominated state.[84] Ethnic Vietnamese make up 86 percent of Vietnam's population. Hobsbawm has evidently exaggerated the extreme rarity that he attributed to China, Korea, and Japan as historic states whose population was ethnically almost or entirely homogeneous.[85]

Needless to say, in each of the above cases there have been serious minority problems. Furthermore, in each of them there has been extensive "creative" reworking of existing traditions, memories, and myths by modern nationalists and state authorities, the so-called "invention of tradition." Yet scholars have been overly impressed by this common process. They have sweepingly assumed that the constant adaptation of materials that is intrinsic to the flow of tradition, including fabrication and manipulation, wholly invalidates the nationalist claim, whereas it often merely tints genuine realities. The following quote from Anderson is typical of this seemingly sophisticated deconstruction of national traditions: "That today's Vietnamese defend a Viet Nam [name] scornfully invented by a nineteenth century Manchu dynasty reminds us ... of the imaginative power of nationalism."[86] The uninformed reader is left with no inkling that, rather than being invented in 1802, the Viet name and distinct identity go back between 1,000 and 2,000 years.* Indeed, in all the above-described cases, congruence between state, people, and culture prevailed from the early history of state existence, and was anything but a coincidence. It was precisely because of their bonds of affinity, identity, and solidarity that these premodern national states were that much easier to unify, to keep united, and defend their independence, while at the same time reinforcing that common identity and homogenizing their realm.

Geography emerges as a major factor here. Although ethnicity is far older and more deeply rooted than is commonly recognized, it is also malleable and subject to processes of assimilation and conversion. Geographical barriers have played a major role in determining the limits of power projection, communication, and hence the survival and boundaries of ethnic and political communities. Premodern political boundaries have been the subject of considerable misunderstanding, already criticized by Grosby. A recurring assumption in the literature on nationalism is that boundaries among premodern states were not clearly defined. The source of this assumption is probably the fragmented nature of, and overlapping authorities in, the European feudal system, another example of the European bias in this field. However, the record from around the world is more diverse: boundaries in many state systems, and often among prestate societies, were clearly marked, strictly kept, and mutually exclusive. As the anthropologist who studied the Mae Enga horticulturalists of New Guinea has reported: clan territories were "defended, literally, to the last yard."[87] A study of African tribal societies similarly stresses that in many cases territorial

---

* As Anderson himself writes, the argument with the Chinese was actually over whether the kingdom should be called Nam Viet, meaning Southern Viet, which implied a potential claim on the part of the Vietnamese to southern Chinese provinces, or Viet Nam, south of Viet, meant to deflect such claims.

boundaries were clearly defined, recognized, and exclusive.[88] Another recent study of tribal boundaries has found them to be remarkably "robust."[89] And the same has been found to be the pattern of state boundaries in the first state system, the ancient Near East.[90]

To avoid tedious repetitions, I will not present further cases of premodern national states outside Europe. The above should be sufficient to refute the widely accepted claim, originally made by Elie Kedourie, that nationalism and the national state were alien to Asia.[91] This claim was based on a one-sided selection of periods and regions. Anderson also generalized from his area of specialty, the southeast Asian archipelago (today's Indonesia and Malaysia), where premodern national states had failed to take root, and downplayed the obvious significance of such states in shaping modern national identity in other parts of east and southeast Asia.[92] Certainly, an opposite bias must equally be avoided. Some, but hardly all, or even the majority of, premodern states – in Asia or elsewhere – were national states. Others were petty-states, dividing among them a wider ethnic space. And yet others were empires, wherein most typically one people or ethnos expanded to rule over foreign peoples and ethne.

C WERE EMPIRES ETHNICALLY BLIND?

There is no single widely accepted definition of what constitutes an empire. But it generally denotes a very large state that dominates subject peoples (and its neighbors). China is an example of an empire that succeeded in assimilating most of its realm in terms of culture and identity. It thereby doubled as a gigantic national state, wherein state, people, and culture converged. With ancient Egypt, too, the Egyptian national state dwarfed its non-Egyptian imperial periphery. However, the majority of empires were not like these two. In this book on nationhood as a particular form of political ethnicity, empires interest us for two reasons. First, they were the powerful engines which through superior force destroyed national states that had been budding everywhere from early on in the process of state formation. Empires were the "black holes" into which many national states were swept and in which they disappeared. This is a major source of the prevalent optical illusion regarding the absence of such states in premodern times. Conversely, empires' pressure sometimes served as a catalyst for the crystallization of national states around them.

The second reason why empires interest us here is that although they have been described by many historical sociologists as pure elite and class power structures, ethnicity was at least as significant in their make up. Almost universally they were either overtly or tacitly the empires *of* a particular people or ethnos. The military might and political dominance of that people/ethnos was the cornerstone of the empire. The empire's rulers and most of the elite came from it. For its survival the empire relied on the loyalty and devotion of that core. And the state symbols and official culture tended to reflect those of the imperial people/ethnos even when cultural tolerance and pluralism prevailed. Of course, when the imperial people/ethnos came from the undeveloped periphery and took over rich and refined civilizations, some processes of cultural assimilation of the conqueror into the conquered culture also tended to occur. Empires sometimes downplayed their core ethnic character, consciously projected an inclusive, all-encompassing image and ideology, and coopted parts of the elite from other peoples and ethnicities within the realm as their loyal servants. To do otherwise was often counterproductive, if not suicidal, for them. All the same, the realities of power and benefit allocation were only thinly masked.

From Assyria to Persia

As we have seen earlier, southwest Asia, the cradle of civilization, is most typical of the process whereby empires swallowed burgeoning national states. We interrupted our discussion of that region with the rise of Assyria, the first in the long succession of empires that conquered and ruled the Near East. Starting from the city-state of Assur, Assyria developed into an incipient national state in the second millennium BC, stamping the eastern Semitic population of the north Mesopotamian ethnic space with the marks of its state culture and patron deities. Outside pressure contributed to this process of territorial expansion and state- and nation-formation. In the middle of the second millennium BC, Assyria intermittently fell under the suzerainty of two powerful empires, those of Mitanni and the Hittite. Despite the paucity of the evidence, these two are themselves of paradigmatic value: they may have been early examples of empires wherein a ruling ethnic elite doubles as a sociopolitical class.

Information about Mitanni (sixteenth to fourteenth centuries BC) is very scarce. Located in eastern Anatolia to the north of Assyria, its people were Hurrian, a distinct ethnos and language, neither Semitic nor Indo-European. However, Mitanni was evidently ruled by an Indo-European kingship and feudal-military equestrian aristocracy (*mariyannu*). These apparently arrived from the north, via Iran, as part of the movement of tribal war bands that introduced the war chariot, a great novelty at that time, into Iran, India, and the ancient Near East. This process of elite conquest is believed to have been the engine that propelled the southeasterly spread of the Indo-European languages. How the conquering Arian elite stood in relation to the local Hurrian population in Mitanni remains obscure.[93] However, while Mitanni was obviously not a national state, ethnicity seems to have been far from irrelevant to its social and political structure.

Although the evidence on the Hittite Empire is more plentiful, the role of ethnicity in it remains largely unknown. As in Mitanni, the original non-Indo-European population of the land of Hatti in central Anatolia was ruled by a royal house and elite who spoke an Indo-European language called Nesili. As it expanded in Anatolia, the empire encompassed the speakers of related Indo-European languages, Palaic and Luwian. At its height during the fifteenth to twelfth centuries BC, the empire was semi-feudal and the elite rode war chariots.[94] But to what extent social and political status in the empire mirrored ethnicity is unknown. According to one theory, both empires of Mitanni and Hatti collapsed suddenly and completely in the upheavals of the twelfth century BC because of their narrow sociomilitary (possibly ethnic) elite base. By contrast, Assyria survived because it was a national state which raised mass peasant infantry armies.[95]

This was the tool which enabled Assyria to subjugate the entire ancient Near East for the first time. The Assyrian monarchy succeeded in mobilizing its free peasant population into military service, thereby adding first-class infantry to the equestrian arm and creating an unbeatable military machine. This meant that the Assyrian freeholder, although living in a highly stratified society and subject to the state's dictates, retained a higher social status than was common in other polities of the region. The army fought for the spoils of war, to be sure, but it was also a national army bounded together by the culture, deities, and patriotic sentiment of the land.

As the empire expanded over the entire Near East, its national Assyrian core inevitably changed. Initially, the empire was hegemonic, that is, it more or less left in place the existing states and rulers, only forcing them to pay heavy tribute to Assyria. However, from the time of King Tiglath-pileser III (744–727 BC), the system switched from hegemony to direct imperial rule. Former subject states lost their semi-independence and self-rule, and their territory was transformed into administrative provinces directly administered by Assyrian governors and the imperial bureaucracy. The same king also initiated the massive deportations of rebelling peoples, which greatly mixed ethnicities across the entire region.[96] In these proverbially cruel processes, existing ethnopolitical entities were mercilessly crushed. Yet Assyria, too, was deeply affected. Exiles from the empire, mostly Aramaeans, filled its major cities. The army, turning increasingly professional, incorporated various auxiliary contingents, again mostly Aramaeans. The masses of Assyrian freeholders that formed its backbone were progressively eroded by war and the enormous inflow of wealth which accentuated social polarization in Assyria.[97]

In some senses, then, the Assyrian Empire became more cosmo-politan, if this term is appropriate at all in view of its horrendous ruthlessness. The Aramaean element in particular was incorporated as a junior partner in the empire. The Aramaic language, with its far easier to learn alphabet script, would become the lingua franca in the Near East for more than a millennium, until the rise of Islam and adoption of Arabic. Still, nobody ever doubted that the empire was Assyrian, as were its royalty, aristocracy, and the people that remained its mainstay. It was the total destruction of this core, the land, and cities of Assyria in the late seventh century BC by a coalition of Babylon and Media that brought an end to the Assyrian Empire.

Babylon, ruled by Chaldaean dynasties and tribesmen from the south of Babylonia, replaced Assyria as the imperial master throughout the Near East. But it was itself soon defeated and replaced by Persia (539 BC), an even larger and more enduring empire, and of particular interest to our subject. The process of state-building on the Iranian plateau, northeast of the ancient kingdom of Elam, gathered momen-tum only during the reign of Assyria. Iran was home to various tribal formations and petty-polities, whose people spoke related languages and dialects of the Indo-Iranian branch of Indo-European. As already mentioned, the formation of this ethnic space is attributed to the sweep of such speakers in the second millennium BC from the Eurasian steppe across Iran to India. Media was the first large-scale state to emerge on the Iranian plateau. It was created from six tribes and dozens of petty-states unified under dynastic rule in the seventh century BC in response to Assyrian pressure. According to Herodotus: "Deioces collected the Medes into a nation [*ethnos*], and ruled over them alone. Now these are the tribes of which they consist: the Busae, the Pareta-ceni, the Struchates, the Arizanti, the Budii, and the Magi."[98] The authoritative standard scholarly translation quoted here (Loeb), from 1946, was evidently uninhibited from using the term nation in this context. Moreover, historians on both sides of the debate over the authenticity of Herodotus' early history of Media, adopt the term national as applied to it.[99] After allying with Babylon for the destruction of Assyria, Media further expanded its suzerainty over the various peoples of Iran and eastern Anatolia. However, as the Median aristo-cracy grew dissatisfied with the monarch Astyages, who had attempted to curb its power, it switched its allegiance to his grandson (550 BC). This was the Achaemenid Cyrus of Persia, a country neighboring and hitherto dependent on Media and of a close Indo-Iranian ethnicity, who became the ruler of a combined Persian–Median Empire.[100]

Cyrus defeated and conquered Lydia in western Anatolia, another empire dominated by a particular people (Herodotus, 1.28). He then defeated Babylon and took over its Near Eastern empire. His successors further expanded the Achaemenid Empire, which extended from the gates of India to Egypt and the Aegean. The empire was famously tolerant toward local ethnicities, customs, and cultures. And yet it was anything but ethnically blind. The formation of a Persian–Iranian national state, with its incipient cultural and linguistic core and national religion (Zoroastrianism), was superseded by imperial expansion. But it was hardly in question whose empire it was. There was a clear hierarchy here: the Medes came very close to the Persians as co-partners in the empire, and other Iranian peoples constituted the next circle, quite distinct from the rest. This was not an abstract matter. Not only the royal house, but also the top provincial governors (*satraps*), generals, and other high-ranking officials were Persian–Mede and, second, Iranian. Locals were mostly coopted into lower levels of the administration.[101] Furthermore, as Darius I turned the empire more bureaucratic, he also reinforced the centrality of Persian identity as its official culture.[102] All this meant that the Persians, Medes, and other Iranians were both the main beneficiaries of the empire and by far its most trusted element (although, of course, hardly free from personal ambitions among the elite, which could turn treacherous).

The same logic applied to the army, the instrument that made and sustained the empire. Levied contingents from the various peoples of the empire were called up for large-scale campaigns. These massive imperial armies were engraved in historical memory by the Greek historians (who also wildly exaggerated their numbers).[103] "Driven into battle with lashes," they could not be relied upon to do any serious fighting, nor were they expected to. Rather, they served as auxiliaries and cannon fodder for the core of the army. This core consisted, first, of the central standing army and imperial guard (mistranslated "the Immortals" by Herodotus) of 20,000 troops, half of them horse and half foot, derived solely from Persians and Medes. Second, there was the Persian–Mede and Iranian cavalry called up for campaigns. They clearly figure as the empire's main fighting force in the great battles of both Xerxes' invasion of Greece and Alexander's invasion of the Persian Empire. Third, since the Persian infantry was found to be no match for the Greek hoplites, the Empire increasingly relied on mercenary Greek infantry, even as it fought Greeks. Indeed, whereas the first two elements of the Persian army demonstrate the significance of the Empire's core ethnicity, the Greek element is a reminder that material profit and not only ethnic allegiance motivate people for action.

Alexander the Great conquered the Achaemenid Empire and occupied Persia and Iran. These were ruled by his Seleucid successors for another century. Still, the collapse of the vast Achaemenid Empire left the Persian–Iranian ethnic core very much in place. Indeed, Iranian political independence and unity were soon revived, with statehood and the Persian cultural sphere closely overlapping. Both the Parthian and Sassanid states that successively encompassed the whole of Iran (247 BC–AD 224 and AD 224–651, respectively) are widely referred to as empires and variably expanded beyond the Iranian plateau. However, their territory and population always remained overwhelmingly Iranian, as were their language, culture, and state-cultivated Zoroastrian religion.[104] Their realm was perhaps just a little too heterogeneous to fully merit the designation national state, but it was not very far from it. It retained a two-tier structure, which is still characteristic of modern Iran: Persian speakers constituted the majority; and the Persian culture was hegemonic, in which other Iranian ethnicities largely participated and were partly absorbed.[105]

The Arab-Islamic conquest of the seventh century was a turning point in Iranian history, and led to the country's conversion to Islam in the following centuries. However, unlike elsewhere in the Middle East and North Africa, the Arab language and identity did not take over, and the Iranian cultural sphere remained very distinct under Islam. Revising his early great book *The Arabs in History* (1950), the doyen of Middle Eastern studies, Bernard Lewis, has written revealingly:

> *In the 19th century, that age of liberalism and nationalism, it was assumed generally by scholars that the great struggles of the early caliphate were basically national: especially Persian nationalism in revolt against Arab domination. By the time I was writing this book, these ideas have been generally abandoned and we were all quite sure that nationality did*

not matter very much, that ethnicity was of secondary
importance, that what really mattered were the economic
and social factors ... Looking at the world in 1992, who
would have said that ethnicity didn't matter?[106]

Rather than a relativist postmodernist lesson, the obvious, common-sense conclusion to be drawn from the above is the following: *both* ethnonational and socioeconomic factors mattered a great deal, and were often overlapping, depending on the case, but they were hardly reduced or reducible to one another.

As elsewhere in the Middle East and Asia, Turkic and Mongol hordes and dynasties established their rule over Iran from the late first millennium by virtue of their military superiority. One such dynasty, the Safavid, again unified the country (1501–1736), and was followed by another, the Qajar Dynasty (1794–1925). However, almost as in China, these Turkic dynasties ruled over a distinct Persian–Iranian cultural sphere and were largely assimilated into it. Clearly, there have always been large minorities in Iran, constituting close to half of the population today. Furthermore, what Iran meant territorially expanded and contracted throughout history. As with other countries, Iran was largely defined by state power. Still, Iranian statehood itself was very much defined by ethnic realities. Precisely because of this reciprocal relationship, a Persian–Iranian ethnic sphere and statehood have existed despite interruptions for more than two and a half millennia.

With its semi-arid, sparsely populated landscape and largely pastoralist economy, Iran was dominated by the horseman throughout its history. This increased the power of the semi-feudal aristocracy that dominated all the Iranian states successively from Median and Achaemenid times up until the twentieth century.[107] Many scholars regard elite rule as antithetical to nationhood. They believe that only the elite who participated in the body politic shared in a wider notion of the state (if they were not actually cosmopolitan in outlook, according to Gellner). However, although popular participation vastly increased both identification with the nation and national energies, the above distinction is too simplistic historically. Premodern Czarist Russia, discussed in Chapter 5, is a major example of a despotic country where national sentiments were strong. Tribal identities, where they existed, as in Iran, were a far greater obstacle than despotism and elite rule to the formation of a national identity.

As it happens, much greater equality and sense of political participation existed in the Hellenic world that defeated the Achaemenid Empire. This was true not only of the classical Greek polis but also of Europe's first national state, ancient Macedonia, also discussed in Chapter 5. But what about the Hellenistic empires that replaced Persia in ruling the East after Alexander's conquests?

The Hellenistic and Roman empires

Hellenic civilization has a reputation for being rational, enlightened, and highly attractive to those who came within its sphere of influence. Still, the Hellenistic empires – the Seleucid in southwest Asia and the Ptolemaic in Egypt and its periphery – were empires of and by the Greek–Macedonian element. Alexander had reportedly wished to incorporate the Persian elite into the structure of his empire and encountered strong opposition from his people. Yet whatever the exact nature of his plans, little remained from them after his death. On the whole, both the Seleucid and Ptolemaic empires were despotic, ruling with few checks on the monarchs' actions. But the mainstay of both empires was the Greek–Macedonian population, which was settled in colonies throughout the realm and enjoyed both citizen rights and partial autonomy within their respective poleis. They lived by Greek laws, were tried in Greek courts, and were educated in Greek schools. "Ethnic segregation" is the expression used by one scholar to describe their position in these multiethnic empires.[108] Literacy was apparently widespread among the Greeks, a significant fact given the role attributed to literacy and schooling in advancing modern nationalism. The army is accredited with a similar role as the "school of the nation," and the Greek–Macedonian population was the loyal element from which the army was raised. There were also Greek mercenaries and some auxiliaries from non-Greek warlike ethne. But as a rule the native population of the Hellenistic empires was kept out of the army, and for a very good reason.

This was particularly true of Ptolemaic Egypt, ever concerned about a native Egyptian uprising. After all, the kingdom centered on one of the world's oldest nations. As we have seen, the Ptolemaic rulers took special care to present themselves in the image of the Pharaohs, and as the protectors and benefactors of traditional Egyptian religion and culture. Yet the Egyptian people were the most underprivileged element in their country, where even other non-Greek ethnic groups were favored as being more trustworthy. The Egyptians' legal status was inferior, *inter alia* in taxation.[109] Obviously, economic exploitation was the basis of the system, but it was notably structured along ethnic lines. The Ptolemaic kingdom's problem is strikingly exposed by a major historical episode. Heavily pressured by the Seleucids who invaded their territory in coastal Syria and Palestine, the Ptolemaic rulers resorted to desperate measures. They raised troops from the native Egyptian population to bolster their army, a step they had never taken before. The invading Seleucids were defeated (217 BC). But in the wake of that victory, the Ptolemaic kingdom experienced a widespread revolt of its native Egyptian people, now trained for war. The south seceded under a native dynasty with the support of the clergy. The rebellion lasted a generation before being suppressed. Native Egyptian troops were never conscripted again.

The Hellenistic kingdom's officials and higher administration also came from the Greek–Macedonian element. Historians rightly point out that the boundaries between the categories of Greeks and non-Greeks were not watertight and inflexible. Non-Greeks could achieve a preferential Greek status if the state wished to favor them. More importantly, people could change identities by a process of acculturation, fostered by intermarriage.[110] Hellenization, the adoption of the Greek language, culture, and identity, went on throughout the Hellenistic East, particularly in the major cities, but far less in the countryside. Descent was an important element of Greekness, but not the exclusive one. All this granted, the Hellenistic empires were Greek in a deep political sense. And politicized native Egyptian identity and sentiment were hardly non-existent either.

One of Rome's major advantages, which contributed to its victory over both the Greek poleis and the Hellenistic empires, was its ever-growing body of citizens. We interrupted our discussion of Rome when it had completed its domination of Italy and was about to expand into an empire that encompassed the entire Mediterranean basin. As already pointed out, Rome was one of the most open polities ever in granting citizenship. And yet this was a very protracted process that unfolded over centuries and was closely intertwined with Roman acculturation.[111] It was the cultural component of ethnic identity that triumphed in Rome's expansion.

Italy was the first step in this process. When brought under Roman hegemony as "allies" during the fifth to third centuries BC, the ethnically diverse communities of the peninsula wanted to retain their semi-independent status and internal autonomy. However, by the first century BC things had changed. As mentioned before, Rome had no policy of acculturation. Still, Roman acculturation throughout Italy had been steadily advancing, through Roman and Latin settlement, elite connections, military service, and the increasing attraction of belonging to the Roman state. Indeed, as the empire grew, there were great benefits to being a Roman citizen. When their demands were turned down, the allies rose in arms in the so-called Social War (91–88 BC) and gained inclusion in the Roman state. And if ethnic differences in Italy were still noticeable at the beginning of the first century BC, they had practically disappeared by the end of that century. By the time of Augustus, the concepts of Roman and Italian had become virtually identical. Roman acculturation and political integration reinforced each other in creating what had become in effect a Latin-speaking Italian people. As Edward Gibbon put it, as early as 1776, in his classical *The Decline and Fall of the Roman Empire* (1.ii.2):

> *From the foot of the Alps to the extremity of Calabria, all the natives of Italy were born citizens of Rome. Their partial distinctions were obliterated, and they insensibly coalesced into one great nation, united by language, manners, and civil institutions [emphasis added] ... Virgil was a native of Mantua; Horace was inclined to doubt whether he should call himself an Apulian or a Lucanian: it was in Padua that an historian [Livy] was found worthy to record the majestic series of Roman victories. The patriot family of the Catos emerged from Tusculum; and the little town of Arpinum claimed the double honour of producing Marius and Cicero.*

Writing before the French and Industrial revolutions, Gibbon was evidently unaware that the nation, "united by language, manners, and civil institutions," would supposedly be born only with those revolutions. A modern historian of Roman citizenship has independently expressed himself in the same terms as Gibbon: "Italy was now identical with the Roman State, which after a period of cultural and social fusion provided the closest parallel found in antiquity to a large national state in the modern sense, with a universal language and a single system of local government and civil law."[112] Another distinguished historian, surely familiar with the controversies surrounding the antiquity of the nation, did not shy away from titling his book: *Culture and National Identity in Republican Rome.*[113] The concept of the *populus Romanus*, the Roman people, as the sovereign, politically active agent during the republic reinforces the modern parallel. This aspect of Roman citizenship was largely lost during the reign of the emperors.

Still, more or less the same dual process of Roman acculturation and expansion of citizenship took place throughout the Empire, most notably in its western parts, again taking several centuries to unfold. The Romanization of these parts was so thorough that Latin completely replaced the local languages in both Gaul and Iberia, and not only in the cities and towns but also throughout the countryside. Barely any Celtic residues remained in French, Provençal, or the Iberian tongues, the daughter languages of Latin which developed after the fall of the Empire. Even in Dacia (today's Romania), where Roman rule lasted only about 150 years, Latin took over (and would evolve into Romanian). As the leading expert on the subject put it: "In the western Empire Latin came into conflict with a number of vernacular languages and eventually affected their death."[114] Such cases of complete language replacement throughout western Europe strikingly negate the picture of rural isolation posited by the modernist literature on nationalism. In this picture, the state's language was supposedly confined to the centers of power and did not penetrate the countryside. As we shall see with other examples as well, this model is based on a lopsided selection of cases that have been accorded paradigmatic status, and was far from applying universally in the premodern world. Certainly, as in any language, differences of accent and expression in spoken Latin, according to social status and locality, were evident both inside and outside Italy.[115] And yet there is no evidence in the classical sources that one Latin speaker had any difficulty in understanding another. In this respect, the variation of Latin in the Empire was much closer to that of modern English or Spanish than to the often mutually unintelligible dialects of modern German or Italian.

Hand in hand with Roman acculturation, citizenship was gradually extended to the provincial elite, to whole civic communities, and to discharged soldiers of the auxiliary forces after many years of service beside the Roman legions. Finally, in 212, the entire free population of the Empire was given citizenship. The Christianization of the Empire, as well as outside pressures, contributed to the crystallization of a wider Roman identity. During the third to fifth centuries the barbarian threat to the Empire increased so much that the fearful provincials clung to their Roman identity with greater fervor. After the barbarians took over Gaul, the dominant distinction in the country was between the invading Germans and "Romans," as the population of Gaul was now called. The making of a Roman people inhabiting the entire Western Empire had been well advanced and would have become a fully-fledged reality had Rome survived like China. As Gibbon (1.ii.2) summed it up: "A nation of Romans was gradually formed in the provinces ... The grandsons of the Gauls, who had besieged Julius Caesar in Alesia, commanded legions, governed provinces, and were admitted into the senate of Rome."

Reality was somewhat different in the eastern part of the Roman Empire. The cultural weight and prestige of Greek resulted in its survival as the elite language of learning and government in the East alongside Latin. Indeed, linguistic and ethnic diversity and mixed identity were far greater in the Roman East, where substrata of ancient civilizations remained and split identities had been the norm throughout the Hellenistic period. Below Greek and Latin, there was also Aramaic as the lingua franca of the Levant and Mesopotamia since Assyrian, Babylonian, and Persian times. And in addition, there was a variety of local languages, many of them literary as well as spoken, including Egyptian (Demotic, later developed into Coptic), Hebrew, and many others. Thus, the East was Greek more than it was Roman, but people variably shared in several linguistic mediums and a diversity of local identities.[116] These realities contributed to the partition of the later Roman Empire into the Latin-speaking West and the Greek East. They also meant that despite the spread of Christianity, shared identity was weaker in the East when the Arab-Muslim conquerors took over in the seventh century.

The Arab, Ottoman, and Mughal empires

We have already noted that Islam is a pronouncedly universalistic religion which recognizes no ethnic distinctions among the faithful. Indeed, the powerful ideal of the Islamic *ummah* (Arabic for nation) embraces all the believers and is presented by Islamic devotees as antithetical to national and ethnic divisions. Reality, however, has been far more complex. From the start, the Islamic faith has been closely intertwined with Arab identity, the people of the prophet among whom the new religion was founded and in whose language the Koran and later Islamic religious texts were written. As they conquered the Middle East and North Africa in the seventh century, Arabs established themselves as a ruling elite throughout the region. True, anyone who converted to Islam gained a privileged status (including tax exemptions). But, indeed, such conversion practically meant the adoption of the Arabic language, the language of religion and government. In a process that took centuries to unfold, Arabic supplanted existing languages in the cradle of civilization, pushing those that survived into a minority status on the margins of an Arabic-speaking society.[†] With this transformation, not achieved in the East by either the Greek or Roman civilizations, came a profound change of identity. Although the Arab conquerors of the Middle East amounted to no more than a small percentage of the population of the societies they ruled, their identity took over. Both the Arabic language and the founding story of Islam nestled in Arabia, and the Arab people played a role in this development. The local populations of the Middle East, which on the whole had existed in their places since Neolithic times, adopted not only religion and language but partly also the belief in their Arabian descent.

To be sure, this picture is far from being complete. Minority religious and ethnic communities survived throughout the Arab Middle East, as did distinct memories of autochthonic roots and separate identities competing with the Arab identity. The diversity and significance of local identities among Arabs is also very considerable. Moreover, Islam spread far beyond the Middle East, to Iran, central, south and southeast Asia, the Balkans and sub-Saharan Africa. And in all these places the local populations did not adopt the Arab language and identity, and, indeed, retained separate ethnopolitical identities. Finally, like all the great civilizations of Asia, the Arab Middle East itself experienced

---

[†] Although traditional literary Arabic is considerably different from the modern vernacular variants, these variants are very close to one another and present no obstacle to mutual comprehension among modern Arabic speakers, except for those of the Maghreb, particularly Moroccan.

takeovers by militarily superior nomadic horse peoples from the central Asian steppe. From the eighth century on, Turkish tribesmen and war bands constituted the armies of the Arab caliphate. Soon after, they took over as rulers. Their position, however, was much more deeply entrenched than that of the Manchu in China. Like the Manchu, the Turks retained their language and identity while embracing much of the local culture. At the same time, Islam as a comprehensive popular faith to which the Turks converted provided a far more potent legitimization and a shared identity than the Confucianism upheld by the Manchu ever could. Furthermore, Turkish settlement and dominance in Anatolia resulted in a gradual adoption of the Turkish language and identity by the far more numerous local population of that land. These processes culminated in the Ottoman Empire, which dominated the Middle East from the fifteenth to the early twentieth centuries.

The Ottoman Empire was explicitly Islamic-universalist, with its sultan doubling as the caliph of all the believers. Muslim elites throughout the realm, in Anatolia, the Balkans, Mesopotamia, and Syria were coopted into the higher administration of the empire and incorporated into its armed forces. The empire also exhibited a high degree of toleration toward non-Muslims. Thus, the Ottoman Empire was at the same time multiethnic, tolerant, and outstanding in the degree to which it made religious identity its underlying principle. However, the limits of Ottoman multiethnicity should also be remembered. Like all empires, the Ottomans rested on forceful coercion, which ultimately relied on the military superiority of its Turkish element. This was by far the strongest – and most loyal – element in the Empire, to which all the others joined in recognition of this fact. Turks comprised both the standing household cavalry and the majority of the empire's semi-feudal cavalry (*sipahis*). The standing elite infantry force, the janissaries, was famously raised from abducted Christian children trained as Islamic warriors. But it was in Turkish and into Turkish identity that they were raised. Most of the non-Turkish troops were frontier irregulars.[117]

Ethnonational identity was manifested in other ways too. The Ottomans granted extensive legal and administrative autonomy to each confessional community (*millet*) in the realm to run its affairs according to its own laws and customs. Yet these confessional communities – Greek Orthodox, Syrian Orthodox, Armenian, and Jewish – were in reality ethnic as much as religious communities.[118] Finally, given that old national identities had been eradicated by the successive empires that had ruled the Near East since Assyrian times, infra-state tribal and local identities constituted the main focus of people's allegiance.[119] All together, it was the dominance of a despotic empire, supra-ethnic religious identity, confessional-ethnic communities, and local kin ties that informed Kedourie's claim that nationhood was alien to the Middle East and his complaint that it was artificially imported into it by the West. However, whether or not a non-national Middle East could survive without highly coercive regimes and with the erosion of tribalism and other features of traditional society is quite another question, which is likely to remain extremely relevant for the foreseeable future.

India is our last and most intriguing case. Like Europe, the people of the subcontinent constituted a multiethnic and multistate civilization, and these two features were interconnected. Unlike China, imperial unifications in India, most notably by the Maurya (322–185 BC) and the Gupta (c. AD 320–550), did not endure. As a result, to a greater degree than Mandarin Chinese, Sanskrit, the language of the Aryan invaders who took over most of the subcontinent in the second millennium BC, diversified into a family of separate Indic languages. Rather than state-generated ethnic leveling on a grand scale, there was ethnic diversification at the local state level. The great variety of Hindu cults was highly polytheistic and therefore even less unifying than Christianity was in Europe. Obviously, there were many common elements in Indic culture, but a sense of common identity was weaker in India than it was in Christendom. Still, as is often the case, threat perception caused by foreign invaders created a sense of distinction between "them" and "us."

The foreign invaders, beginning from the eighth century, were Muslim, so both ethnic and religious differences fueled the clash of identities. Both differences had independent existence, and the two should not be conflated, but nor were they entirely separate: the Muslim invaders and rulers were variably Arab, Persian, Afghan, and Mongol-Turkic. By contrast, although substantial conversion to Islam took place in India, the great majority of the people remained Hindu (with significant Sikh and Buddhist communities). Again, the military superiority of tribal horsemen from the lands northeast of India was the foundation of their elite rule. Thus, in addition to religious and ethnic identities, military cultures and elite politics each played a role, with all these elements being mutually intersecting. The Delhi Sultanate, established by tribal war bands from Afghanistan, dominated northern India from the thirteenth to the early sixteenth century. The Delhi rulers, intermittently Afghan and Turkic, carried out a policy of Islamicization and strongly discriminated against their Hindu subjects. Their Islamic and ethnic identity combined with their position as ruling military elite in a foreign country amid a foreign culture. The Delhi Sultanate was defeated and replaced by other invaders from the northeast, who created the glorious Mughal Empire that unified most of the subcontinent.

The Mughal Empire was at once more multiethnic and more tolerant than the Delhi Sultanate, which was one of the secrets of its success. It is often presented as a model of true multiethnicity, and, indeed, in the annals of empires the Mughal case is even more outstanding than that of their Ottoman contemporaries. The Emperor Akbar (1542–1605) steered the newly founded empire away from Islamic sectarianism and coopted the Hindu powerful. In a real sense, he had little choice. The power of his dynasty was based on a Turkic-Mongol war band from inner Asia, which first took over Kabul in Afghanistan and then invaded north India and defeated its former Afghan rulers. Following the defeat, Afghan chiefs joined the victor, but it was essential for him not to over-depend on them and broaden his support base as much as possible. With this in mind, Akbar incorporated the Hindu warrior chiefs of north India, the Rajputs, into the empire's ruling elite and army. The empire also relied on Indian infantry recruited in the countryside by local Hindu strongmen. Although power, status, and profit were the basis of the Mughal–Rajput connection, it was cemented by kin ties at the family level. As an explicit political act, the Rajput elite extensively intermarried with the Mughals, giving their daughters to the sultan and the Mughal grandees. Persians in the Mughal court, renowned for their literary, artistic, and administrative skills, completed the image of Mughal cosmopolitanism.

I am not disputing this image, nor claiming that ethnicity underlay all empires to the same degree. As already noted, the Mughal Empire stood at the far end of the spectrum in its multiethnic cooptation and was, indeed, rare in this respect. Still, it is important to realize that, like the Ottoman Empire, the Mughal Empire was not a partnership among ethnic equals. Mughal rule rested on an asymmetrical balance of power with a clear ethnic underpinning within a highly coercive military empire. Ultimately, the empire was based on the military superiority of its Turko-Mongol horsemen, to which Afghan tribal horsemen were coopted as their second best option in lieu of their own former empire. The Hindu Rajputs were essential but junior partners. Again, they shared in the rich benefits of the empire in lieu of their earlier status as independent rulers which they had been forced to forfeit.

This reality is strikingly revealed by the figures. Muslims, although only a small fraction of the empire's population, comprised some 80 percent of its aristocracy, while only 20 percent were Hindu. Non-Indians were a minuscule fraction of the population; and yet in the 80 percent Muslim aristocracy 23.3 percent were Turko-Mongols, 28.4 percent were Persians (the majority of them probably from Safavid Persia's ruling Turkic elite), 5.9 percent Afghans, and 14.7 percent Indian Muslims (with 6.6 percent other Muslims). The Hindu Rajputs comprised 16.5 percent. Furthermore, although many of them held very high offices in their domains, "the higher ranking Rajput held ranks ... in the third tier of great nobles ... Virtually no Rajputs served as provincial governors, for example."[120] Tolerant and inclusive as the Mughal Empire was, its ethnic realities cannot be more clearly revealed.

The Mughal Empire is arguably the hardest case for my claim that empires were anything but ethnically blind, and that as a rule they each had a dominant people or ethnos who held a "controlling stake" in it. This is therefore a good point to end our survey of extra-European empires before the reader is driven to exhaustion. We have concentrated on Asia, the oldest, largest, and most diverse arena of state existence. But the same is true of the Inca people in the Inca Empire, the largest and best documented "territorial" empire in pre-Columbian America. And much the same can be shown for sub-Saharan Africa. In the great empires of west Africa, the Soninke people, a subgroup of the Mandé ethnos, was the mainstay of the empire of Ghana (c. AD 750–1240). The Mandinka people, another branch of the Mandé, played a similar role in the empire of Mali (c. 1230–1600) that succeeded Ghana. The Songhai people to the east, speaking a Nilo-Saharan language, broke away from Mali and established their own Songhai-dominated empire (c. 1340–1591).

Conclusion

For those who regard equal citizenship, popular sovereignty and mass political participation as constitutive elements of the concept of the nation, this definition renders the present chapter practically irrelevant, except perhaps for Roman Italy during the late republic. They may choose a different designation for what I describe as premodern national states – ethnic states, for example. I have little argument with this position, because distinctions can be made and definitions sliced in any number of coherent ways. However, for many, possibly the major-ity, of the participants in the debate on the antiquity of nationhood, reality rather than semantics is at stake. What I take issue with is the view that premodern polities were fundamentally elite power structures in which popular sentiments of shared ethnic identity played no signifi-cant role. Furthermore, I dispute the claim that a rough congruence between ethnicity and state – Gellner's definition of the nation – hardly existed before the modern era.

As we have seen, individual city-states regularly comprised people of the same ethnos, and regarded foreigners, where they existed, as a distinct category. If at all, the latter were admitted into the citizen body usually in connection with social and cultural assimilation. In addition, although often highly antagonistic toward one another, city-states of the same ethnos revealed a marked tendency to coalesce into an alliance or a permanent league in the face of exterior rivals. More-over, city-states were not the only path of early state formation. Large, "territorial" states were just as ancient, and they tended to be national states, wherein state and ethnos overlapped. With major ethnos forma-tion going far back into the Neolithic agricultural and pastoralist expansions, it was immeasurably easier to create and sustain a large state within a common ethnic space which shared language, culture, and a sense of kinship. In turn, state formation itself greatly enhanced the ethnic leveling of the realm and often brought about the assimila-tion of foreign groups. Either way, the bottom line is that national states sprang up as early as, and hand in hand with, the process of state formation itself. They are as early as the state, and as a rule can be found wherever "territorial" states existed.

This strong tendency of the "territorial state" or "dynastic kingdom," in most cases a national monarchy, to center on a particular people or *Staatsvolk* – as extensively documented in this chapter – is a conspicuous political reality that is almost staring one in the face. It helps to overcome the problem of the muteness of the masses in the historical records. Indeed, if premodern states were pure elite power structures and did not derive legitimacy and solidarity from a pervasive sense of kin–culture community, why did their political and ethnic boundaries tend to converge so non-randomly? Recurring popular uprisings against foreign rule, with their wholesale sacrifice of life and property, strikingly point in the same direction. Reality speaks volumes, even though the illiterate masses rarely found somebody to record them. Such rare and illuminating written recording is provided, for example, by the Sung imperial officials with respect to the spontaneous popular-patriotic rebellions flaring up against the foreign Jurchen rule in China. Elite dominance and class oppression, although certainly affecting national cohesion and popular involvement adversely, hardly eradicated a deep-seated shared sentiment of kin–culture identity and solidarity. People could be, and were, economically, socially, and politically subservient yet could still identify with their ethnonational collective when faced by foreigners. This simple reality, which eluded the leaders of the socialist Second International on the eve of the First World War, had been true long before their day, even when the people were scattered in the countryside in supposedly isolated rural communities.

To be sure, tribal and local identities often threatened national states from below. Especially in the early stages of state formation these were frequently centrifugal forces, and political disintegration occasionally directed splinter parts into a separate ethnopolitical path. Kin–culture identities are often graduated, and they are susceptible to historical processes of fusion and fission. National states were also vulnerable to outside threats by way of conquest by powerful empires that deprived them of independence. Indeed, this process often led to desperate resistance and recurring uprisings, suppressed only through the bloody process euphemistically known as imperial "pacification." On the other hand, after long periods of imperial rule both elites and masses often lost much of their distinct identity, and sometimes underwent imperial acculturation and incorporation. The power and impact of empires have greatly contributed to the optical illusion that national states and ethnonational sentiments in general were not a prominent aspect of premodern history. In reality, however, such states and sentiments were very pervasive indeed, yet often succumbed to superior force.

King Agrippa II, ruler of a small principality in Galilee as a Roman protégé, addressed his agitated Jewish kinsmen in Roman-ruled Jerusalem and Judea in AD 66 to dissuade them from revolting against the empire. In his speech he pointed out what was obvious to everybody in the Roman Empire, yet is overlooked by modernists: peoples throughout the empire had desperately sought and fought to preserve their independence and liberty from Roman rule. Responding to the people's "passion for liberty" [*eleutheria*], Agrippa agreed that "servitude is a painful experience and the struggle to avoid it once for all is just." Patently, this notion was very much there in ancient antiquity. Furthermore, as the people Agrippa addressed were not slaves, he obviously meant *collective* as distinguished from personal freedom. However, Rome was simply much too powerful for the Jews to challenge: "Myriads of other nations [*ethne*], swelling with greater pride in the assertion of their liberty [*eleutheria*], have yielded ... are you wealthier than the Gauls, stronger than the Germans, more intelligent than the Greeks, more numerous than all the peoples of the world?" The Jews did not listen to Agrippa and were crushed after a desperate war, with Jerusalem and the temple destroyed. Indeed, it was quite often popular sentiments and passions, rather than the calculations of sometimes collaborative elites, that sparked massive popular rebellions against foreign imperial rule – in actuality, national wars of independence.[121] In the realm of political action one can hardly conceive of more concrete expressions of the "politicization of the masses" on a grand scale.

Certainly, ethnonational identities, although prominent, were far from being the sole or even the most prominent force in history. I am not arguing that they were omnipotent. Family and tribe as primary foci of kin solidarity, and religion as a powerful form of cultural identity, often reinforced but sometimes competed with ethnonational allegiances. Moreover, power, status, and material gain were the most powerful incentives that often trumped others. All the same, ethnonational identity and sentiments, more or less potent, were always present as a major factor of pivotal political significance. Political ethnicity – together with the politicization of the masses the hallmark of the national phenomenon – was far from being a modern invention.

Why was this so? As pointed out in the Introduction, this is another point on which I take issue with the widespread view exemplified by Gellner that, "nationalism does not have any very deep roots in the human psyche." Although highly diverse, nationhood and other forms of political ethnicity have been such common and powerful features of human reality from the very beginning of statehood because people had always been heavily biased toward those they identify as their kin–culture community. Innate evolution-shaped human propensities take a variety of forms in history and widely interact with other factors in a kaleidoscopic reality. But their presence and significance in historical reality are exceedingly hard to miss.

There are several reasons why this reality has in fact been missed by so many. And one of these reasons is Europe's unusual trajectory and thus the special role it has acquired in the history of the nation. Both Europe's extreme levels of feudal fragmentation during the Middle Ages and its pioneering breakthrough into modernity and highly advanced national states were unique.

5 PREMODERN EUROPE AND THE NATIONAL STATE

Europe dominates the study of nations and nationalism, being regarded as the exclusive hotbed of the national state. Modernists and the majority of traditionalists agree about this, even as they differ on when European national states emerged, whether it was only with the French and Industrial revolutions, or during early modern times, or the Middle Ages. As we have seen, this view of Europe's uniqueness is fundamentally untrue. National states have existed around the world for millennia, indeed, their emergence was everywhere closely intertwined with the emergence of the state itself as one of its forms. Thus, Asia (and adjacent Egypt), where states evolved the earliest, is also where some of the most ancient national states can be found. This reality is blurred by the fact that in southwest Asia in particular (but not in east Asia), the national state template of political organization was destroyed and supplanted by the imperial template from Assyrian times. Europe's uniqueness, while existing, was somewhat different than is usually construed. Failure to realize where the European experience was unique and where it was not has created misperceptions that have bent and distorted the scholarly discussion of the national phenomenon. The following are some major, both specific and non-specific, features of Europe's development with respect to our subject:

- As in other parts of the world, national states – wherein an ethnos or a people (*Staatsvolk*) and a state tended to converge – emerged in Europe north of the Mediterranean close on the heels of state formation itself. This dual process took place in the emergent European civilization from the second half of the first millennium AD. It was largely built on preexisting ethnic entities, and on the whole its effects have been remarkably enduring.

- Due to geopolitical reasons, which will be discussed below, the national state template was from the very beginning more typical of the emerging European civilization than it was in many other parts of the world, and it proved to be particularly resilient against imperial takeovers. Yet, because of their general backwardness in terms of socioeconomic development and administrative infrastructure, the emergent European national states went through feudal fragmentation which weakened the cohesion of both states and nations.[1]

- Shortly after European national states began to roll back feudalism and regain unity and central authority, Europe was the first among the world's civilizations to break into modernity. This rapid transition from feudal fragmentation to the far greater cohesion generated by the processes of modernization gave the growth of European nations and national states a particularly steep trajectory and the appearance of something completely new.* As Europe moved on toward industrialization and global mastery, its modern national states outshone everything else, overshadowing the prevalence and significance of the premodern national state both inside and outside Europe.

This European uniqueness, as well as Europe's special role in the scholarly literature on nations and nationalism, requires this specialized chapter entirely devoted to Europe's premodern national states, in addition to our global survey in Chapter 4. Although far from having been inaugurated in Europe, the national state did make a special career in it.

Geopolitics: statehood in the Classical Mediterranean and in emergent Europe

We begin with that most conspicuous fact about European history: the near absence on this continent of hegemonic empires that overwhelmed the state system. Alone of all the great civilizations of Eurasia, Europe

---

* For the very same reasons, not only the national state but also the state itself is often declared to be a wholly new, modern, and European phenomenon, disregarding its long history around the world since the dawn of history; cf. Chapter 4, n. 1, above.

was never united by force from within, nor was it conquered from outside. Rome, the only arguable exception, was fundamentally a Mediterranean rather than a European empire which mainly incorporated southern Europe. Moreover, while enduring for centuries and being highly influential, it lasted for only a fraction of European history. All other attempts at imperial unification – the Carolingian, Ottonian, Habsburgian, and Napoleonic – were geographically even more confined and short-lived. It has long been noted that the absence of imperial domination also meant a greater tradition of freedom in the West. This was so because a smaller political scale was generally less conducive to the concentration of autocratic power at the expense of both the aristocracy and the people, the so-called oriental despotism.[2] Montesquieu, who was the first to identify this European uniqueness, pointed out its political consequences and recognized that it owed a great deal to Europe's special geography and ecology:

> In Asia one has always seen great empires; in Europe they were never able to continue to exist. This is because the Asia we know has broader plains; it is cut into larger parts by seas; and, as it is more to the south, its streams dry up more easily, its mountains are less covered with snow, and its smaller rivers form slighter barriers. Therefore, power should always be despotic in Asia ... In Europe, the natural divisions form many medium-size states, in which the government of laws is not incompatible with the maintenance of the state ... This is what has formed a genius for liberty, which makes it very difficult to subjugate each part and to put it under a foreign force.[3]

Southwest and east Asia, and the north of the Indian subcontinent, incorporate large open plains, which facilitated rapid troop movement and imperial communications. By contrast, southern-western-central Europe is split throughout by mountain ranges and surrounded by seas that everywhere penetrated deep between its constitutive parts. Sheltered behind these obstacles and often benefiting from individual access to the sea, the many smaller political units that emerged in this fragmented landscape were able to defend their independence with much more success than those of Asia. Other geographical–ecological factors also contributed to Europe's distinct political development. Except for its eastern part, Europe was not exposed to a vast pastoralist steppe frontier, as were the civilizations of Asia. Nor, because of its temperate climate and even rainfall, was Europe internally divided into arable and more arid, pastoral strips and zones, as was the case in the Middle East and North Africa. Due to this circumstance, pastoralist tribal formations were a permanent feature in the lands of Islam and constituted separate foci of identity competing with both state and nation. By contrast, tribal entities in Europe did not survive the establishment of state authority, more developed agricultural settlement, and the growth of cities.

All this does not imply geographical and ecological "determinism." It simply means that, rather than being wholly accidental, salient features of European history were heavily affected by physical and ecological conditions that made the consolidation of large empires in Europe that much more difficult and the survival of tribal societies beyond a certain stage unlikely. Obviously, Europe was not a monolith, and there was a great diversity of geographical and ecological conditions within it. Thus, there were significant differences in geographical settings between the Classical civilization of the Mediterranean and the European civilization that emerged north of it after the fall of Rome. Indeed, these differences help to explain why of the three types of polities that sprang up everywhere around the world – petty-states, states, and empires – it was the middle-size state, rather than the smaller or larger templates, that from the very start figured as the most typical form of political organization in Europe north of the Mediterranean.[4]

Classical Greece, Europe's first civilization, is paradigmatic in many ways. Being Europe's most fragmented peninsula, criss-crossed by mountains and sea, Greece foreshadowed in miniature the political fragmentation of the peninsular and rugged continent as a whole. More than coincidence, memory, and cultural transmission connected the Greeks to later European history. Furthermore, the next geographic region into which civilization spread happened to be Europe's second most rugged peninsula *cum* archipelago, Italy.[†] Thus, in both Greece and Italy, a multiplicity of city-states dominated the fragmented landscape, even though at least Greece (but not Italy) was inhabited by

---

[†] I exclude Norway, for this was the part of Europe most distant from the cradle of civilization in the ancient Near East, which, as a result, civilization would reach last in its gradual northwestward advance.

people who regarded themselves as a single ethnos. It should be noted, however, that the same sea which sheltered and granted access to the open to the Greek and other Mediterranean polities could also serve as a communication highway (comparable to Asia's open plains) for prospective empires that succeeded in mastering it. Rome gained such mastery in the third century BC, and it is in this sense that we have described Rome as a Mediterranean empire. It was the communication and logistical highway of the Mediterranean *mare nostrum* that made possible the Roman Empire's large scale.

As polities established themselves farther north, away from the Mediterranean shores, the geographic settings changed markedly. More open plain lands lay in between and north of Europe's main Alpide mountain ridges. In addition, even where seas bordered on these lands, they constituted a much smaller part of their perimeter than was the case in Greece and Italy. It is not a coincidence, then, that political consolidations larger than the city-state emerged as the norm in these parts of Europe from the very beginning. Indeed, it has barely been recognized that Europe's earliest national state appeared in neither medieval nor early modern times, but was in fact ancient Macedon. As a historian of Macedon's emergence writes cautiously:

> I once wondered whether Macedon was Europe's earliest national state ... the Macedonians were an ethnic group derived from their predecessors, the Makedones, and defined in historical times by their service to their king ... In this sense they were a people, or ethnos, *with a common set of loyalties and a shared historical experience.*[5]

Scholars are not sure whether the language spoken by the Macedonian tribes on Greece's northern, semi-barbaric frontier was a dialect of Aeolic Greek or a separate language. Either way, economic contacts with and cultural imports from Greece greatly influenced the royal house and elite of the emergent Macedonian state. Established according to tradition in the seventh century BC in response to the pressure of endemic warfare with tribes of the neighboring Thracian and Illyrian ethne, the monarchy ruled tenuously over a thin, largely pastoralist Macedonian population. By the fourth century BC, however, more sedentary agriculture had taken root in the southern part of the country, and towns had grown and expanded with active monarchic support. Building on these developments, the monarchy was able to centralize power and intensify the processes of state- and nation-building in a way that brings to mind the European national monarchies of the late Middle Ages. Traditionally, the mounted aristocracy constituted the mainstay of the Macedonian army. King Philip II drew them closer to his court. Their children were educated there and formed the state's first-rate "companion" cavalry. More importantly, Philip II created an infantry phalanx army of peasants to complement the aristocratic cavalry. The freedom of the Macedonian peasant-soldiers was enhanced by, and became the cornerstone of, Macedonian power and monarchic authority. In turn, the king had to pay heed not only to the wishes of his aristocratic "companions," but also to the voice of the soldier assemblies.[6]

Herein were the makings of the Macedonian national state. Philip gradually expanded his realm, forcefully incorporating some Thracian and Illyrian tribes as well as Greek cities on Macedon's Mediterranean coast. He treated all these as part of Macedon proper, while, indeed, making a conscious effort to homogenize the realm, culturally as well as politically.[7] However, as he continued his string of military successes further afield, the "allies" coopted or coerced into his hegemonic empire in Thrace, Illyria, Epirus, Thessaly, and Greece itself retained formal independence and self-rule, and were not incorporated into the Macedonian state. Clearly, there was no question among either Macedonians or non-Macedonians that the state of Macedon rested on the Macedonian monarchy, aristocracy, and people. All others were clients or satellite allies, either willingly or not, as the non-Macedonian elements often revolted.

We have already mentioned the political realities that made Macedon not only Macedonian, but also a remarkably egalitarian, participatory, almost citizen state. The monarch was bound by tradition and power relations to listen to the advice of the Macedonian military aristocracy around him. Moreover, he was obliged to consult with and get the approval of the assembly of all Macedonians on all major decisions. There may also have been local assemblies in the various districts of the kingdom. But as practically all the Macedonian men during the reign of Philip and his son Alexander were engaged in almost continuous military service, the army doubled as a general assembly of the people in arms (similar to Rome's *comitia centuriata*). Popular direct participation, usually associated with the small scale of the city-state, could in such circumstances materialize on a country scale. Every Macedonian had the right to speak in the assembly, which regarded the king in a remarkably egalitarian manner as their appointed war leader. The issues discussed and approved by the assembly included the election of a new king from among the heirs to the throne and decisions about war and peace. The assembly also heard foreign delegations, ratified treaties, and had judicial rights, especially over capital offenses.[8] Although the king who chaired the assembly was usually able to steer things his way, this was far from a forgone conclusion. For example, we learn from the classical sources that Alexander faced open opposition in the army assembly to his wish to continue his campaigning deep into Asia. At the gates of India the assembly members decided they had had enough and turned the frustrated Alexander back. The Macedonians also openly expressed their resentment at Alexander's increasing reliance on non-Macedonians.[9] Thus, the modernist notion that the people of large-scale premodern societies lacked both a strong sense of corporate identity and political participation is not borne out in the case of Macedon.

Notably, the imperial power and fabulous resources gained by Alexander in the East enormously strengthened the hand of the conqueror and prompted him to transgress the traditional boundaries of his authority. He reacted with great displeasure and sometimes violently to dissent both among his aristocratic companions and in the army assembly, signaling that the old balance of power and old customs had changed with the changing circumstances.[10] The Hellenistic empires founded by his successors in the East assumed many features similar to earlier and later autocratic empires of that region. Macedon itself, reconstituted as a separate imperial national state under a new ruling house after the death of Alexander, preserved much of its old identity. However, never fully recovering from its population loss due to wars and the exodus east, Macedon was ultimately defeated by Rome and was absorbed into its empire, losing both its independence and identity.

And yet later developments would show that Macedon's course of evolution, whereby an ethnic-tribal space was consolidated into Europe's first national state rather than into a fragmented city-state system, did not represent an isolated case. More typically, it would constitute the *norm* north and west of the rugged Greek and Italian peninsulas, as this vast barbarian sphere was gradually drawn into contact with civilization. Thus, for example, the large national state of Dacia emerged in the lower Danube plain (the territory of today's Romania) during the first century BC to the first century AD. Its people, welded together by an increasingly powerful monarchy, consisted of the tribal Thracians who lived north of the Danube. They thereby avoided the early inclusion into and assimilation within the Hellenistic and Roman empires experienced by their southern kin. In the end, Dacian statehood and nationhood proved to be short-lived, as the Roman Emperor Trajan conquered the country in AD 106 and incorporated it into the empire, where it was thoroughly Latinized. However, as Rome preempted and disrupted other attempts at large state-building on her northern barbarian frontier, her downfall signaled the proliferation of national states throughout Europe.

A THE MUSHROOMING OF NATIONAL STATES
IN EMERGENT EUROPE

The barbarian invasions which put an end to the Western Roman Empire were the starting point of both a new, European civilization (which owed a great deal to the Classical–Christian heritage) and Europe's history of national states. There is nothing new in the idea that many peoples of Europe had their formative period in the so-called Middle Ages, and that the emergent European states both reflected and reinforced this reality. Modernists have been distinctively unsympathetic to this idea and have done their best to discredit it by exploding the myth-making that surrounded the processes of ethnogenesis and nation-building. This has been an all too easy exercise, because myth-making is indeed central to such processes for several interrelated reasons. First, ethnogenesis and incipient nation-building usually occur in protohistorical, preliterate societies, and are therefore mostly reflected in epic, legend, and other traditional forms of oral transmission. Second, national traditions are ever couched in the rhetoric of kinship, kin solidarity, and heroic sacrifice for the collective. Third, national traditions have been the object of propaganda, manipulation, and downright fabrications by mobilizing state and national agents from the very beginning, a process greatly intensified with modern nationalism. Fourth, lest it be thought that everything can be reduced to cynical manipulation by rulers and elite, national traditions have as strong an emotive power on leaders as they do on the people. As such, they are particularly prone to being conceived in quasi-sacred and biased terms by both.

Still, after acknowledging all the above, were ideas about European peoples' long history, and a close overlapping between states and peoples from the very beginning of state formation in Europe merely nineteenth-century nationalist myths and anachronisms? In contrast to the modernists, who scarcely studied premodern societies, traditionalists, such as Hugh Seton-Watson, John Armstrong, and Adrian Hastings, have sought to demonstrate that many European nations preceded modernity.[11] Moreover, some historians of medieval societies have responded to the debate, bringing to it their specialist expertise. As we shall see, the large majority of the historians who have addressed the subject tend to support the notion of medieval European nations. Skepticism is duly confined to the early medieval period of the barbarian invasions, settlement, and state formation.

Before delving into all this, the need to avoid both poles of common false dichotomies should be reiterated. No ethnic identity or people are primordial or come neatly packaged with an unchanging essence. Ethnogenesis, processes of ethnic and national fission and fusion, changes of identity, and cultural transformation take place all the time in response to many factors. In realizing all this we have progressed from the sometimes naive nationalist perceptions of earlier generations. On the other hand, it is equally important to bear in mind that ethnic and national identities are very strong human realities whose historical expressions are highly potent. Rather than being purely arbitrary, they are deeply rooted in human propensities and existing kin–culture formations, which while always in flux are still among the most durable of cultural forms. In this sense, traditional perceptions of ethnicity and nationhood were far from lacking validity.

The barbarian invasions by mostly Germanic and Slavic tribes and war bands into the Roman Empire were a salient development in the emergence of Europe, and had a seminal and lasting effect on its map of peoples and states. Before the invasions both the Germans and Slavs had been disparate tribal ethne, among whom state organization had not yet evolved or was only beginning to emerge. Both ethne underwent diversification into subgroups by geography, ecology, and history. During the centuries preceding the invasions the spread of the Germanic populations had already produced considerable differentiation in dialect: Old Norse in Scandinavia; West Germanic (already undergoing internal differentiation) along the North Sea coast and further inland; and East Germanic of the Goths (and others) who had migrated to the Ukrainian steppe and adopted its way of life. The Slavs would similarly diversify with their geographical spread after the invasions. Beyond their various tribal conglomerations German and Slav speakers possessed only a faint notion of a shared identity within their respective ethne. This was commonly impressed upon them only through contact with others, who often also gave them their common ethnic name. During the invasions both the Germanic and Slavic hosts experienced a great deal of fusion and fission, mixing older tribal entities and newly formed war bands.

In view of all this, anthropologically informed historians have reasonably tended to stress the fluid aspect of ethnic categories during the migration period.[12] A few of them, however, purporting to apply state-of-the-art tools in the theory of ethnicity, have adopted a hyper-skeptical approach: they have suggested that both the Germanic and Slavic ethnic designations were insubstantial constructs of the Greek and Roman imagination which imposed its definitions on the "Others." Among the strangest of arguments along these lines, made by a historian of the Slavs on the Eastern Roman Empire's Danube frontier, is the claim that the common Slavic language spoken by these people cannot be regarded as a marker of Slav identity because some Slavs are recorded to have learnt and been able to speak Latin or Greek.[13] Generally, such scholars seem to have been over-impressed by the fluid aspects of ethnicity and have lost sight of the other side of the coin: despite its shifting character and internal local variations, an ethnos such as the Germans or Slavs shared a common linguistic space, pantheon and cults, as well as other central features of culture.[14]

Historian Patrick Geary is another one of those who fall into this trap. Professing to be a liberal horrified by the new manifestations of European ethnonationalism, he sets out to debunk *The Myth of Nations: The Medieval Origins of Europe* (2002). In the process he ties himself in some strange knots. Forcefully advancing all the above-cited ethnoskeptic claims, he nonetheless concedes that peoples in effect existed on a clan-tribal (albeit shifting) basis during the barbaric migrations; that ethnic nationalism (although different from modern nationalism) is not a new phenomenon; and that even in early Medieval Europe ethno-national identities were very powerful (even if they were not the *only* form of identity).[15] Rather than refuting the medieval origins of European nations, his book implies, though does not expressly state, that modern European nations began to crystallize not during the migration period itself (effectively a straw man), but later in the first millennium. This is a proposition that the large majority of medieval historians tend to support and that traditionalists would happily embrace.

Some retreat from extreme forms of ethnoskepticism has also been registered. Scholars rightly point out that during their movements into and within the Roman Empire, the Germanic invaders were joined by opportunistic elements from various origins that augmented their ranks. As a historian of the Germanic Goths has confessed, the prevailing mood in the study of ethnicity first led him to the view that these ostensibly Germanic groups had in fact been multiethnic conglomerations assembled by enterprising leaders and elites. However, later on he came to the conclusion that the Gothic ethnic core was nonetheless significant.[16] Moreover, one should add that each of the Germanic ethnotribal conglomerations was far more homogeneous in its land of origin than some of them became after entering the Roman realm.

Indeed, the old Roman frontier turns out to have had a crucial and lasting effect on Europe's ethnonational map. In the first place, it has long been noted that despite the Germanic takeover of the Roman Empire the linguistic line between Germanic speakers and speakers of Latin languages moved only some 200 kilometers south of the Danube and about 100 kilometers west of the Rhine. Moreover, attention in the study of nationalism has tended to focus on the successor states established within the former Roman realm. These states mixed conquered and conquerors, which resulted in complex and protracted processes of ethnic and national consolidation and identity formation. Things were different, however, in Europe north of the old Roman frontier, where the spread and diversification of the Germans and the Slavs resulted in the early growth of national states, each possessing a strong ethnic identity from the start.[17]

We thus turn our attention to the relatively neglected northern parts of Europe. We shall trace the mushrooming of national states throughout the mostly Germanic and Slavic tribal spaces and observe how remarkably durable these incipient ethnopolitical consolidations would prove to be. Our survey begins with the British Isles and will proceed in a clockwise direction to eventually cover all parts of Europe. After this extensive survey of individual nation and national state formation, the chapter concludes with a comprehensive theoretical discussion and summation.

The British Isles: a history of four nations

English national identity holds a special place in the study of nationalism. Several theorists have credited the English with being the first European nation, which emerged by the sixteenth century, if not by the late Middle Ages.[18] This, however, was actually the *second* emergence of an English nation. It had been preceded by the formation of an Anglo-Saxon nation by the tenth century, which would be disrupted and transformed by the Norman Conquest in 1066.

The greater part of former Roman Britain was taken over from the fifth century on by Angles, Saxons, and Jutes, neighboring Germanic tribal conglomerations from the Frisian–Danish coast speaking closely related Germanic dialects ancestral to Low German. They arrived in Britain across the North Sea as traders, raiders, mercenaries, usurpers of local power, and, increasingly, immigrant settlers. The exact processes whereby they displaced the local Britons, whether physically replacing or merely subduing and assimilating them through elite dominance, has long been an open question shrouded in the mists of protohistory. Although both processes were involved, the latter appears to have been far more significant, as anthropological models suggest and genetic evidence seems to confirm.[19] According to the main historical source for the period, the monk Bede (672/3–735), describing the deeds of Ethelfrith (593–616), Angle king of Northumberland, he "more wasted the people of the Britons than any of the princes of the English … either driving the natives clear out of the country or subduing them, or making them tributary or planting the Angles in their places."[20] The Britons were able to avoid foreign rule and retain their language and identity only on the very margins of the country, in southwest Britain and Wales. The invaders' group leaders and war bands also violently competed with one another for domination over the conquered territories. By the seventh century these struggles had given rise to several petty-kingdoms, those of Kent, the West, South, and East Saxons, Mercia, East Angles, and Northumberland.[21] However, the close ethnic relatedness of the Angles, Saxons, and Jutes, who spoke mutually intelligible dialects, facilitated larger political unification among them. Intermittently, a ruler of one of the petty-kingdoms succeeded in establishing overlordship over the others, which usually collapsed and switched hands after his death.

Bede's *Ecclesiastical History of the English People* (in Latin), reflects this process and leaves no doubt as to how he viewed the ethnic realities in the British Isles and their political significance. While living in the kingdom of Northumberland, Bede took it for granted that the people of all the Anglo-Saxon petty-states comprised one people, the *gens Anglorum* of his book's title. Clearly, the repeated tentative formations of a single overlordship over the various states contributed to this sense of common identity. Yet this is precisely the nature of the process whereby common ethnicity and political unity progressively reinforce each other. Indeed, there is no question in Bede's narrative of who did *not* belong to the "English" people, was its main "Other": he chronicled the native (Christian) Britons' subjugation and displacement by the (then still pagan) Anglo-Saxons in a manner that hardly concealed that his sympathies lay with his own people. Regarding the above Ethelfrith's conquests of the Britons he writes: "he might be compared unto Saul, sometime king of the Israelite people, save only that he was ignorant of God's religion."[22] Clearly, even with a monk who laid great store on Britain's conversion to Christianity, ethnonational affiliation trumped religion in the allegedly primarily religious and non-national Middle Ages.[‡]

The same attitude characterized Bede's narrative of the Anglo-Saxons' conflicts throughout the country which was home to additional "Others" besides the Britons. He specifies the various languages of the British Isles: those of the English, Britons (P-Celtic, of which Welsh is the main survivor), Scots (Q-Celtic, or Gaelic, spreading with settlers from Ireland), and Picts (probably a P-Celtic language in Scotland, pushed northward and then going extinct with the spread of Gaelic), as well as literary Latin. And although social and political organization among these various linguistic populations varied, there is again little doubt on which side Bede was in any clash between the English and others.[23] Significantly, the above linguistic–ethnic distinctions (with the exception of Pictish and the inclusion of Gaelic-speaking Ireland) have exhibited remarkable resilience from Bede's

---

[‡] All this contradicts modernist theorist John Breuilly's attempts to cast doubt on the substance of Bede's account, his claim that Bede's "English" predominantly meant Christianity rather than ethnicity and his assertion that "one does not find cultural stereotyping in Bede (e.g., Britons against English, pagan against Christians, civilized against barbarian)": John Breuilly, "Dating the Nation: How Old is an Old Nation?," in A. Ichijo and G. Uzelac (eds.), *When is the Nation: Towards an Understanding of Theories of Nationalism*, London: Routledge, 2005, 15–39, esp. 19, 21. As we shall see, despite his allusions to the contrary, Breuilly's modernist views are contradicted by the overwhelming majority of the historians of the period. This is all the more evident in Breuilly's similar contribution, "Changes in the Political Uses of the Nation: Continuity or Discontinuity?," to L. Scales and O. Zimmer (eds.), *Power and the Nation in European History*, Cambridge University Press, 2005, 67–101, as opposed to the views of the historians in this superb volume.

time to the present. They have continued to underlie political borders in Britain through the ages. And they have survived in the form of Britain's various peoples, despite continuous historical transformations, centuries' long loss of independence, and even the adoption of the English language and decline of the other native tongues. Surely, these striking facts of ethnic identity and political history are anything but purely accidental.

As mentioned above, Bede regarded the people of Angle, Saxon, and Jute descent as one people even though at his time they were still divided among various petty-polities that only occasionally came under an overlordship of one of them. In the late eighth century the kings of Mercia formed a more stable union of all the southern and some of the northern petty-kingdoms. But a unified kingdom was only established by the kings of Wessex a century later, after Northumberland and Mercia had been destroyed by the Vikings. There was now a new and most threatening "Other" against which English national identity crystallized: the Vikings or Norsemen from Norway and Denmark, who had substituted conquest and settlement in England for mere raiding. King Alfred the Great (reigning 871–899), the first to call himself king of the Anglo-Saxons, emerged as the champion, savior, and sole monarch of this, now unified, people. He led defensive efforts throughout the realm, raised armies, built navies, established fortress towns, imposed taxation to finance all the above, and instituted a code of law.[24] During the tenth century his successors were able to regain control over the whole country all the way up to the Scottish border and crowned themselves kings of England. Moreover, from Alfred's time on England was one of several places in Europe where the spoken language, Old English, also became the language of writing. There was an explosion of literary output in the native tongue: administrative, legal, clerical, poetic, historical, scientific, and philosophical. As we shall see, the common view that writing in the local vernacular began to displace Latin in Europe only from the thirteenth century onward is based on a very selective choice of cases.

Alfred, himself a prolific writer in and translator into the English language, used the Church's widespread network as an effective channel of dissemination throughout the realm. As *The Cambridge History of the English Language* (1992) puts it:

> *Much of Old English prose writing was public and official,*
> *in a way that prose seldom was to be again after the*

conquest until the late fourteenth century. King Alfred presented his first work as a beginning of a considered scheme for national education, and made careful arrangements for its official dissemination and preservation.[25]

Abbot Ælfric of Eynsham (*c*. 950–*c*. 1010), one of the leaders of the Old English literary tide, "similarly offered his first work as a response to a national problem ... its immediate and widespread dissemination, probably from Canterbury, suggests again a deliberate and official activity."[26] The large ecclesiastical centers of the country also held copies of the Anglo-Saxon Chronicles, a national history in English compiled with royal encouragement from Alfred's time on by clerics and reflecting a "revival of English national awareness."[27] As medieval historian Susan Reynolds writes with respect to Europe in general: "one of the great achievements of the tenth and eleventh centuries was the vast proliferation of local churches, the formation of a vast patchwork of parishes that effectively brought the church to the people."[28] The grid of parishes and their priests planted in even the most remote reaches of the countryside is again a reminder of what Duara describes as the "complex relationship between the written and spoken word ... in agrarian civilizations," which "furnishes an extremely rich and subtle context for communication across the culture."[29] The messages from the texts at the centers of power and learning were echoed in a variety of popular forms throughout the realm.[30] The masses of peasantry could not read, but they were preached to. As already mentioned, this point has been entirely missed by modernists. Thus, the masses of peasantry were far from being entirely disconnected from and oblivious to anything beyond their allegedly isolated rural communities. Political unity, action by the state and the Church, and an ethnic common ground reinforced one another. Overall, it was the Anglo-Saxon and English-speaking parts of the British Isles, *and no other*, that were susceptible to both processes of political unification and identity consolidation as a people.

As Patrick Wormald, a leading authority on the period, writes: "In the tenth century England was permanently united, politically and administratively: much earlier than France, let alone Spain, Italy or Germany."[31] Furthermore, based on the content and context of the documents, Wormald rejects the modernist claim that Bede and Alfred represented no more than state- and nation-building propaganda by the political and clerical elite.[32] He concludes: "there *is* evidence of a remarkably precocious sense of common 'Englishness', and not just in politically interested circles."[33] James Campbell, another leading historian of the period, concurs. Describing the fundamental unity of the country before 1066, he writes: "It may seem extravagant to describe early England as a 'nation-state'. Nevertheless it is unavoidable."[34] Similarly, Chris Wickham, the author of the most comprehensive and authoritative recent history of the early Middle Ages, writes: "In the tenth century England's political structure would be unusually coherent for the period by European standards, and one can begin to talk about the English 'nation-state.'"[35] None of the above-cited historians seem to have been too impressed by the supposed absence and impossibility of nations and national states in the Middle Ages.

To be sure, neither should the Anglo-Saxon national state which had emerged by the tenth to eleventh centuries be viewed in overly unified terms; such a picture hardly fits modern national states, let alone premodern ones. Breuilly's conclusion that in medieval England "we are *not* dealing with national identity in anything like the forms it came to assume in modern times" reads more like a tacit concession than as an out-and-out rejection,[36] for who is denying that the modern national phenomenon was very different from the premodern one? Resistance to Wessex rule in the English north was occasionally manifested. Revolts and treachery by aristocrats and contenders to the throne were part and parcel of politics. The greater nobility dominated the provinces. Furthermore, Danish presence in the north, the "Danelaw," remained.[37] It left its mark on the local culture and precipitated the transformation of Old English that would intensify with the Norman Conquest and give rise to Middle English. Moreover, later in the tenth century the Danish threat revived, and in the early eleventh century the Danish King Knut conquered England, ushering in a generation of Danish rule. All the same, by the time of the Norman Conquest in 1066, England was thoroughly Anglo-Saxon in terms of culture, identity, and government.

The Norman Conquest profoundly transformed England. The conquerors ruled by force of arms, destroyed the Anglo-Saxon nobility, and introduced a French-speaking elite culture. And yet it is a remarkable testimony to both the endurance of the old Anglo-Saxon identity and the potency of national genesis processes that a new English national identity, mixing conquered and conquerors, had become an undisputed reality by the fourteenth, if not by the thirteenth century, or even earlier.[38] This must not be misunderstood as an "essentialist" proposition: I am not claiming that the new English culture and identity were the same as the old, though they were obviously greatly influenced by them. Cultures and identities exhibit both continuity and change, and the Norman Conquest was certainly a massive break that can be seen as the starting point of a new English national identity. Whatever classification one adopts in this matter, the point is that medieval England saw the formation of a national state in which culture and state overlapped both in the tenth and eleventh centuries and again in the thirteenth and fourteenth centuries.

The decline of French as the spoken language of the Norman elite was one element in the disappearance of the distinction between Normans and Anglo-Saxons, and the crystallization of a new English identity, people, and nation. In 1362, even the most ceremonial, and hence conservative, state functions reverted to English, including both the king's speech in Parliament and legal courts proceedings. English was now also the language taught in grammar schools.[39] The loss of England's possessions in France undoubtedly contributed to the Englishness of the English state by Tudor times. However, even where the empire survived within the British Isles themselves – in Wales, Scotland, and Ireland – this was an English-dominated empire. In this empire the other ethnonational identities "remained none the less defiantly conscious of being distinct peoples,"[40] and have survived all adversities. Indeed, as already recorded by Bede, Britain is famously the story of not one but four nations, *all* of which go back to medieval times.[41]

I shall only briefly sketch a picture which is very well known, or should be. Although divided among several petty-principalities and only occasionally coming together under the overlordship of one ruler, the people of Wales shared a language and culture that clearly set them apart from their powerful eastern neighbor. It was on the basis of this difference that the Welsh tenaciously defended their political separateness from both Anglo-Saxon and Norman England. King Edward I of England finally succeeded in conquering Wales in 1283, and henceforth the heir to the English crown was given the title Prince of Wales. Repeated rebellions against English rule in the fourteenth and fifteenth centuries failed, and Wales was formally incorporated into England, Great Britain, and the United Kingdom, successively, in the acts of

1535–1542, 1707, and 1801. It retained its separate language and culture well into the nineteenth and twentieth centuries, when modernization brought about a rapid decline of the Welsh language and the adoption of English. In the same period liberalization and democratization brought full and equal incorporation into the British state. However, they also spurred popular and political demands for the reassertion of a separate Welsh identity. There is a revival in the teaching of the Welsh language, and a separate Welsh Assembly was created in 1999, following a law of the British Parliament and a Welsh referendum. After 800 years of incorporation into England/Britain, and although English is the language of Wales and cultural differences with the rest of Britain are slight, a sense of kin–culture Welsh identity is still a distinct reality. Whether it would continue to be satisfied within a broader British national identity or increasingly opt out of it remains to be seen.

Scottish national identity is stronger. Like Wales, Scotland remained outside both Anglo-Saxon and Norman England simply because when the formative processes of ethnogenesis and state emergence took place the people of Scotland were not English *and* were able to defend their separateness. As Bede recorded, north of the Anglo-Saxon realm people spoke Scottish (Gaelic) and Pictish. By the beginning of the eleventh century the kingdom of Scotland had taken root, uniting earlier petty-kingdoms. In the process, Gaelic displaced Pictish and also became a written language, side by side with Latin. Clashes over territory with the English were endemic, but the famous "border" stabilized more or less in its present location, also in the eleventh century. Scotland was able to hold on to some districts which spoke northern dialects of Old English. This contributed to the fact that from the thirteenth century onward these dialects, now know as Scottish, became the main spoken language of the Lowlands. Gaelic survived mainly in the Highlands. Still, neither in Scotland nor in England was it ever felt that their respective peoples were the same people. Edward I of England, the conqueror of Wales, also succeeded in taking over Scotland in the 1290s. However, Scotland was stronger and farther away than Wales, so Scottish resistance succeeded whereas that in Wales failed.

As in most rebellions against a foreign rule, the popular element, discounted by modernists, played a decisive role in Scottish resistance. Whereas the Scottish baronial rebellion was crushed in 1296, the one led by William Wallace proved to be a far greater challenge:

"free landholders – lesser knights, freeholders and rich peasants – who had hitherto had no part in politics … now rose voluntarily and gathered without aristocratic leadership 'to defend ourselves and to free our kingdom.'"[42] Wallace "insisted upon the service in the army of every able-bodied adult male … enough is known to suggest that 1297–8 was a rising of peasants and therefore a sign of social change."[43]

Popular participation was not a sufficient condition of success, and Wallace was ultimately defeated and executed; it was, however, a necessary condition. As Robert the Bruce again raised the banner of rebellion, he managed to combine aristocratic and popular support:

> Reliable narratives of the years 1309–14 tell of Forfar
> castle taken by a small laird Philip Forrester of Platan,
> Linlithgow by William Bunnok a husbandman, Dumbarton
> by Oliver a carpenter, and the way into Edinburgh and
> Roxburgh shown by men of no social eminence; the
> foundation of this war was a capacity to by-pass the reluctant
> traditional leaders of the "community" and to appeal to
> and command the opinion of the other social ranks in the
> "nation" … the rise of nationality in this sense reflects the wide
> support and increased importance of the freeholders and
> husbandmen.[44]

The term nation here is not an invention of the modern historian. After the English defeat at Bannockburn (1314), Scotland's independence was reestablished, with its own monarchy and parliament of three estates. In a formal plea to the Pope, known as the Declaration of Arbroath (1320), the Scottish government asserted the right of the "*Scottorum nacio*" to independence from an alien English rule. Indeed, rather than the language of dynastic legitimacy, the signatory lords "and the other barons, and freeholders and the whole community of the realm of Scotland" invoked a right based on separate descent extending back over millennia to a (mythical) common origin, a long history of self-government and native kings, and surviving independence against foreign threats from all directions – all of which they recounted at great length.[45]

England and Scotland became dynastically united, though otherwise separate kingdoms, when King James VI of Scotland inherited the English crown as James I in 1603. The Stuarts' Catholic sympathies meant that most of Protestant Scotland supported the anti-Jacobite cause in both the 1648 and 1688 revolutions. But patriotic support for the Stuarts strengthened after the passing of the unpopular Act of Union which united England and Scotland (except the legal systems) in 1707. When the Stuarts landed in Scotland in both 1715 and 1745, making claims to the British crown, they were greeted with enthusiasm, especially by the Highland clansmen who rallied around their flag. As a result, after the Jacobite defeat at Culloden (1746) the Highlands were subjected to a bloody and brutal suppression specifically aimed at eradicating their distinctive culture and customs. Later in the eighteenth century, and increasingly in the nineteenth and early twentieth centuries, Scots shared in the benefits and glory of the British commercial and industrial empire, the mightiest in the world, forged in war against Catholic France (and Spain).[46] In this empire the Scots were full, albeit junior, partners; and were, indeed, among its leading exponents. However, as the balance of power and economic interests have changed – with industrial decline, the discovery of North Sea oil, the virtual disappearance of a foreign Great Power threat, and the creation of the European Union – the movement for Scottish independence has gained momentum. A devolved Scottish parliament was created in 1999, and was initially controlled by a minority government of the Scottish National Party (SNP) which supports full independence. However, although the SNP won an overall majority in the Scottish parliamentary elections of May 2011, opinion in Scotland on independence remains closely divided.

Historical circumstances made Irish distinct identity and separatism the strongest. As in Wales and in contrast to Scotland, there was no unified Irish state before the period of English domination. Although rich in Gaelic and Christian culture, including an extensive written corpus in both Latin and Gaelic, Ireland between the fifth and twelfth centuries was divided among local chiefs and petty-states.[47] Increasing Norman penetration and domination, involving aristocrats followed by the English crown, began in the twelfth century. Seeking to consolidate English control, King Henry VIII established the kingdom of Ireland in 1541 with its own parliament and himself as king. In view of his aim, this step makes it abundantly clear that Ireland was not England and could not be feasibly turned into an integral part of it politically.

As the Irish did not adopt Protestantism, their Catholicism became both a mark of their separate identity from the English and

Scottish settlers and a cause of their growing repression, the two elements reinforcing each other. Tudor conquest and repression were eclipsed by Oliver Cromwell's bloodbath and the carnage that followed the Glorious Revolution of 1688. Catholics were barred from the Irish Parliament. Political and religious repression was matched by economic exploitation, as land ownership passed into the hands of English and Scottish landlords. The Irish peasantry suffered from abject poverty and devastating famines which exceeded the "norm" in most European agrarian societies and which were not free from racial underpinning. The rebellion of 1798, again crushed mercilessly, led to the abolishment of the Irish Parliament and the incorporation of Ireland into the United Kingdom of Great Britain and Ireland (1801). Yet deepening liberalization and democratization in Britain by the late nineteenth century made Irish demands irresistible in a way that they had not been before. The Liberal government under Gladstone proposed a full-range liberal recipe: economic improvement, more equal citizenship, greater tolerance and "Home Rule." Nonetheless, as self-determination within the United Kingdom failed to satisfy the Irish, the process led within a generation to an independent Irish state (1922). The six counties of Northern Ireland which remained within the United Kingdom have been the scene of deep sectarian divisions and violence, which at present are more successfully contained.

So what does this history of ethne, peoples, and nations on the British Isles tell us? It clearly reveals the major significance of ethnicity and political ethnicity, and the long history and remarkable endurance of peoples and nations based upon them. As with respect to any other dominant people, the notion of English ethnicity is not common, and the term ethnicity is more naturally applied to the minority identities of Britain's other three peoples.[48] Yet there is no objective reason for such a difference. Present-day ethnonational distinctions in the British Isles, which trace their origins as far back as Bede's time, constituted the foundations of national states in England and Scotland shortly thereafter and survived many centuries of English domination. To be sure, identities have undergone constant transformations, and present-day realities are far from being preordained. For example, Pictish identity was assimilated into Scottish identity while contributing to determining the northern limits of England. Democratization and liberalization have elicited *both* greater incorporation into a joint British state and nation, and a resurgence of separate nationalisms. Indeed, a composite

British national supra-identity came into being in addition to Britain's four national identities. It has been facilitated by the triumph of the English language and the demise of the other national languages (even in Ireland, despite extensive state efforts to revive Gaelic after independence),[49] by the spread of a common British culture, and by the long tradition of mutual cooperation as a political community. Furthermore, although based on the above elements more than on a sense of kinship, the all-British identity is perceived by the peoples concerned as a *national* one, albeit composite and supra, rather than a supranational identity. In Britain there are four national identities which partake of a broader (English dominated) British national identity. Whether this British national identity splits into its constitutive national parts (as happened with the Irish) or survives depends on the strength of the national sentiments at each level and on how successfully these levels can be combined and kept in balance.

Scandinavian identity and national identities

Ethnic differences played a cardinal role in the formation of the English people and nation as distinct from the other three peoples/nations of the British Isles. However, the major role played by geography in the shaping of ethnic distinctions calls for special attention. As communities become separated by distance and major geographical obstacles, cease to interact extensively, and develop local differences, a historical dynamic of ethnic "speciation" occurs. This accounts for local variations and becomes all the more significant when geographical separation is sufficiently salient to create distinct social, cultural and political communities and identities. The English were thus separated within a few centuries from their Low German kin on the Continent. Likewise the prehistoric Celtic ethnos on the British Isles had much earlier separated into P speakers in Britain and Q speakers in Ireland. In turn, the P speakers then split into Welsh, Cornish, Breton, and so forth by the Germanic invasions, whereas Q speakers diversified by migration across the Irish Sea into Irish and Scottish Gaelic languages and identities. The Nordic countries to which we now turn are a prime example of the role of geography and territorial discontinuities in generating these dynamics, precisely because the ethnic differences between them were slight.

As previously mentioned, the process of ethnogenesis and nation-building in northwestern Europe is largely the story of the break up and diversification of a prehistoric Germanic ethnic space due to migration, distance, and ecology even before the invasions into the Roman Empire. By the late first millennium, speakers of North Germanic or Old Norse dialects in Scandinavia had already become quite distinct in speech and customs from other Germanic populations to their south, while being closely related to one another. According to the Byzantine author Jordanes' sixth-century *Getica* (III.23), the peoples on the "Island of Scandza" (Scandinavia) included the powerful Dani and the Suetidi of the same stock. When the West (proto-Low) Germanic-speaking Jutes and Angles migrated into Britain, the Norse-speaking Danes expanded into Jutland from the islands of today's Denmark and the province of Scania on the southern tip of today's Sweden. During the Viking era, as the Norsemen became famous for their devastating raids and daring oceanic voyages, state-building processes took off in Denmark, Norway, and Sweden. From around the year 1000, earlier petty-kingdoms crystallized into more or less permanent unified states in each of the three countries.[50]

Denmark, more populous, closer to the Frankish realm, and more developed, was the first to be unified, perhaps as early as the eighth century but definitely by the tenth. Its kings intermittently exercised suzerainty over parts of Norway. Yet Norway was more or less fully united under its own King Olaf Haraldsson (reigned 1015–1028). The newly formed realm proved vulnerable to centrifugal forces, as the Norwegian aristocracy fell out with the king and handed the kingdom over to King Knut the Great of Denmark, who also ruled England. However, this North Sea empire disintegrated after Knut's death, and, as in England, a local king (Olaf's son Magnus the Good) repossessed the throne (1035). So began 350 years of an independent Norwegian state. A Swedish kingdom similarly emerged in the late tenth century, consolidated more slowly and integrated the provinces of Götaland and Svealand during the eleventh to fourteenth centuries.

The main sources for these events are the Nordic sagas and chronicles written down on the basis of older traditions in the twelfth and thirteenth centuries. As with Bede in England, these are animated with an unmistakable patriotic spirit in each nation. There are endless debates as to how much the texts reflect the authors' own times rather than the past they describe, shrouded as it is in semi-legendary myths.

However, even if one is wholly inclined toward the former view, this still leaves us with a strong sense of native nationalism in these respective countries by the twelfth to thirteenth centuries. As Saxo Grammaticus states in his early thirteenth-century rendering of Danish history *Gesta Danorum*: "nations [*nationes*] are in the habit of vaunting the fame of their achievements, and joy in recollecting their ancestors." The project he undertook was "fired with a passionate zeal to glorify our fatherland (*patria*)."[51] Note that nation and patria are equated here as a matter of course, contrary to the modernist claim that such an identification was unknown before modernity. In view of the silence of the illiterate masses in the historical records, modernists also argue that the manifested national spirit in such texts merely reflects royal propaganda disseminated by the literati. Indeed, Saxo Grammaticus' work was supported by royal patronage. However, the various Norwegian sagas and chronicles were actually composed in the most free, almost anarchic, and unruly country of Europe, Iceland.

Iceland was discovered and settled by Norwegians in the ninth century, during the Viking era. Its distance, sparse population, and frontier mentality as the hub of the Vikings' oceanic explorations were likely responsible for both its anarchic freedom and role as the mainspring of Old Norse oral traditions and sagas, later written down in that vernacular. Hence, the special perspective Iceland offers on our subject. Dominated by powerful local chieftains, the country was a "Free State" or "Commonwealth" with the oldest parliament in Europe and only minimal ties with a distant Norwegian monarchy. And yet it was in Iceland that the chronicles of the earliest Norwegian kings were written down in the thirteenth century. Two points come across very powerfully from these narratives. First, they take the difference between Norwegians, Danes, Swedes, Russians, and English for granted. Second, in the chronicles this is not merely a difference between kings or kingdoms, nor between countries or territories alone, but clearly also between peoples. There is no question that the authors' sympathies and allegiance rest with Norway (and Iceland within it), and that the same attitude animates the people in each of the above countries. The popular aspects of native national patriotism repeatedly manifest themselves in the text.

The earliest surviving chronicle, *Morkinskinna* (c. 1220), begins significantly with the reestablishment of a Norwegian monarchy under Magnus (1035) after seven years of Danish rule. The rhetoric employed by all the sides involved is unmistakable:

> *King Magnus established his rule as far as his father's power had extended, and he subdued the land without a battle and with the consent and agreement of all the people, rich and poor. They all desired rather to be free under King Magnus than to suffer the tyranny of the Danes any longer.*[52]

The popular aspect of Norway's public life is attested to throughout; the "farmers" were a powerful estate with legally established rights. They constituted a concentration of political power side by side with the monarchy and the nobility, at times forcing their will on them.[53] The Norwegian national monarchy was far from being confined to the monarch and elite.

Things were not much different on the Danish side. As the tables turned a few years later and King Haraldr of Norway set out to become king of Denmark (1049–1064), "He bade the army prepare itself and declared that if they conquered the land, the Norwegians would forever after be the lords of the Danes."[54] In response to the Norwegian invasion, the Danish jarl Sveinn, who had earlier declared himself king, "convened the Vebjorg (Viborg) assembly. Here the royal title was conferred on him anew according to the wishes of the Danes."[55] Haraldr's bid for the Danish crown failed, as did his reach for the English crown which led to his death at Stamford Bridge (1066). Norway, Denmark (and Sweden) remained separate from one another.

It should be made absolutely clear that I mean no reified givens by using the terms Denmark, Norway, and Sweden. There is no such thing as natural countries supposedly waiting to be filled with a national content. The tribal Norsemen of Scandinavia could have ended up in completely different state, cultural, and national entities given other circumstances and historical trajectories.[56] And yet what happened in actuality in the late first and beginning of the second millennium was that geography played a decisive role in precipitating three distinct peoples and national states. In the cold Scandinavian landmass where people's livelihood and populations concentrated on the coastal plains and seashore, what became known as Norway was defined by the coast facing west, toward the North Sea and North Atlantic; Sweden emerged on the coast facing east, toward the Baltic

Sea, separated from Norway by great distance and high mountain ridges; whereas Denmark was defined by its archipelago location at the entrance to the Baltic, between the Skagerrak and Kattegat, including the provinces of Scania, Halland, and Blekinge, the southern – west and southern facing – tip of today's Sweden, far closer to Denmark than to early Sweden in terms of both distance and ethnicity. Denmark subsequently lost these provinces to Sweden in the seventeenth century.

The rest is history, although geography never ceased to be relevant. The early crystallization of the three distinct peoples with their protracted period of political unity, independent statehood, and increasing linguistic differentiation during the eleventh to fourteenth centuries would leave deep and enduring marks on future developments. On the other hand, these marks were not ineradicable by these developments. Thus, from 1397 to 1521, in the Kalmar Union, the three kingdoms of Denmark, Sweden, and Norway came together under the dynastic rule of the Danish royal house. At the same time, each of them remained formally distinct and retained separate institutions and systems of law. Moreover, frictions were soon to arise, especially with the Swedish nobility which objected to what it regarded as the subordination of Swedish interests to Denmark. Sweden gradually opted out of the Union even before leaving it formally in 1521 and electing the native Vasa as their royal house. The seventeenth century saw the creation of a Swedish empire in the Baltic and northern Germany. But the empire's collapse in the eighteenth century again limited Sweden to its native soil.

Norway remained dynastically united with Denmark, while retaining separate institutions. Connections with Copenhagen as the cultural center of the union and seat of university learning became strong in the eighteenth century, though resentment of this fact in Norway also grew.[57] Whether or not a united kingdom of Denmark and Norway would have survived voluntarily is an open question. It cannot be answered because in 1814 Norway was detached from Denmark, Napoleon's ally, by the European powers and put under Swedish rule. Again, the Swedish crown was able to secure its control only by guaranteeing Norway's constitution, autonomy, and separate institutions. Nevertheless, in 1905 Norway declared independence.[58] The map of peoples and states established around the year 1000 has prevailed with remarkably few changes, and at no time since has it been devoid of salient political significance.

One last debt remains before we leave Scandinavia. Finland is an often cited case for the modernity of nations, as a Finnish national consciousness did not emerge before the nineteenth century. However, Finland differed from Denmark, Sweden, and Norway precisely in that the Finns lacked even a rudimentary political organization when peoples, states, and nations formed in Scandinavia in the early second millennium. Like the Sami (Lapp) who still occupy the far north in all the Scandinavian countries, the Finns were a sparse tribal population. They spoke a Finno-Ugric language, entirely different from the rest of Scandinavia. Heavily colonized by Swedish settlers, incorporated into Sweden in the thirteenth century, and with Swedes constituting the urban elite and administration, Finland could have become a Swedish Wales. However, in 1809 Russia conquered it from Sweden and turned it into an autonomous Grand Duchy within the Russian Empire, and in 1917 Finland took the opportunity to declare independence.

The medieval German national empire

So far we have dealt with two territories on the expanding frontier of the Germanic ethnic space, Britain and Scandinavia, where due to geographical barriers and processes of historical divergence incipient peoples and nations constituted themselves separately. Germanic tribal conglomerations and war bands also migrated en masse to the territories of the Roman Empire, adopting Latin. Many of them, however, remained in old *Germania*. The ethnopolitical history of these people has been subjected to a great deal of tendentious interpretation, first by nineteenth- and early twentieth-century German nationalists, and culminating most perversely and horrifically with the Nazis. However, in an understandable reaction against them, there has been a tendency to deny that German political ethnicity and national identity played any role in history before modernity. And this view also is very far from reality.

We begin with the historical period when the Germanic tribal entities in *Germania* were brought within the fold of statehood. This occurred with the expansion of the most successful of the Germanic new states, that of the Franks under the Merovingians and Carolingians. It expanded to cover not only the former Roman province of Gaul with its Romanized populations and other Germanic successor states, but also central and eastern Germany. The process was completed in the late eighth century when Charlemagne subdued the Frisians, Saxons, and Bavarians. Having also conquered Italy, he revived the prestigious designation of the Roman Empire and had the pope crown him as emperor (800). However, for dynastic and administrative reasons the empire was divided among his successors, who fought incessantly over his inheritance. The Treaty of Verdun (843) partitioned the empire into three geographical strips from north to south: the Western, Central and Eastern Frankish realms. Yet other realities on the ground proved to be more potent. The year before, in the so-called Oath of Strasburg, the documents agreed upon by the kings were read to the opposing Frankish armies present in two different tongues: Gallo-Romance (descendant of Latin and ancestral to Old French) for the Western Franks and (Old High) German for the Eastern Franks. From this historians infer that the two halves of the Frankish realm were no longer using the same vernacular and thus unable to communicate. A generation after the Treaty of Verdun, the kings of Western and Eastern Francia signed the treaties of Meerssen (870) and Ribemont (880), which partitioned the third, central domain among them along lines which remarkably reflected the linguistic division between Romance and German speakers. From then on the two halves went their separate ways, developing into France and Germany, respectively.

This is not to say that medieval Germany was a national state or that Germany's future as one was preordained. Again, the real picture is more complex. A German national identity was under pressure from two opposing directions. First, there was the ambition of empire following the glorious Roman model. The title of emperor was passed among Charlemagne's successors and then lost for a while. It was resumed in Germany by Otto I of the Ottonian dynasty. Having been crowned king in Aachen (936) and having gained control over Italy through marriage, he was crowned emperor by the pope in Rome (962). In the eleventh century his successors officially assumed the title Emperors of the Holy Roman Empire. In the following centuries the emperors' ventures and entanglements in Italy famously weakened their position in Germany itself. Nevertheless, despite the Empire's universal guise and non-German periphery, which expanded as Germans spread eastward into Slav lands, there was no question that the Empire was fundamentally a German one. The emperors' power rested primarily on the German lands and their German subjects. Although the position of emperor was elective and the title passed from one dynasty to another, all but very few of the elected emperors were German. So were all the ecclesiastic and lay princes of the electoral college, except for the king of Bohemia (himself a German after 1310). Furthermore, the expansion eastward into Slav populated territories was carried out for the benefit of German princes, other German political entities, and German settlers, and it involved large-scale cultural Germanization of the Slav populations. By the twelfth century at the latest, the distinction between the *regnum Teutonicorum* and the rest of the Empire was clearly made.[59] When in 1512 the Empire officially changed its name to the Holy Roman Empire of the German Nation (*Heiliges Römisches Reich Deutscher Nation*), this was merely in recognition of a long-standing reality. Eight years later Martin Luther similarly wrote his "Address to the Christian Nobility of the German Nation."

As historian Leonard Krieger has put it:

> The Holy Roman Empire under its Saxon, Salian, and Hohenstaufen dynasties was regarded by its chroniclers as a German-based political order; it was popularly celebrated for its German base in the political lays of Walter von der Vogelweide and the Minnensingers; and authentic historians like Otto of Freising and Alexander von Roes identified imperial history with German history.[60]

Other recent historians have also extensively documented this strong sense of medieval German identity.[61] The same sentiment is evident in medieval German poetry, much of it popular and more indicative of popular feelings than the allegedly elite concepts of courtiers and clergymen. From early in the Middle Ages Germans regarded themselves in common kin terms. A shared language was increasingly emphasized during the High Middle Ages, despite strong differences in dialect and long before Luther produced a common popular literary language with his translation of the Bible.[62] Voltaire quipped that the Holy Roman Empire was neither holy, nor Roman, nor an empire. Yet it was German, *especially* during medieval times if not in Voltaire's own time.

The second and more significant challenge to the national character of the German Empire came from below. The legacy of distinct prestate German tribal entities and often mutually barely intelligible dialects persisted and was reinforced by the weakening of regal authority.[63] The elective nature of the German monarchy forced the rulers into ever greater concessions to the territorial princes. The emperors' preoccupation with Italy weakened them further. As a result, developments in Germany took a course opposite to other European monarchies wherein after a period of feudal fragmentation the crown was able to reassert its authority. In Germany, a more centralized state than France from the mid ninth to the mid twelfth century, the territorial princes were eventually able to become practically independent. Thus, early modern Germany became *less* of a national state than the medieval Reich.[64] The emperors' effective control became limited to their own hereditary domains long before the Empire was officially dissolved in 1806. The political fragmentation of the realm also facilitated the diversification of Old West Germanic into separate branches and a diversity of local dialects. Again, ethnicity and politics were mutually and reciprocally affecting.

Thus, the modern formation of a unified German state was not a foregone conclusion; yet nor was it a purely modern development unrelated to premodern historical ethnopolitical and national realities that go back to the beginning of state formation in Germany. Certainly, divergences occurred almost as much as convergences. The German-speaking population of Switzerland, organizing politically in opposition to the Empire in the late Middle Ages, underwent a separate process of national formation. So did the Dutch from the sixteenth century onward, having been detached from the Empire for reasons of dynastic inheritance by Charles V and having then won independence from Spain. Prussia's military victories during the 1860s played a decisive role in bringing about a union of diverse German states. But the union left the German population of the Austrian Empire out, a separation which ultimately survived both world wars. The partition of Germany into West and East after 1945 could have become entrenched over time had it not been for the economic and political bankruptcy of the Soviet system. None of these developments was preordained and others could have occurred in different places and settings. Still, while undergoing many changes, German identity, and *identities*, have been major factors with profound political significance from the very beginning.

The Czech lands

Similar to what took place in the Germanic ethnic space, processes of geographical expansion, ethnic diversification, and distinct national state consolidation also occurred among the Slavs further east. As we have already seen in Chapter 3, the prehistory and spread of the Slav tribal population is shrouded in the veil of illiteracy and is only dimly lit by Greek and Roman sources and by archaeology. Still, it seems sufficiently clear that the Slavs initially lived in a fairly limited area, probably around the upper-middle Dnieper; spoke a common Slavic language; shared a crude material culture, as well as aspects of a spiritual culture such as a pantheon; and spread in all directions from around the year 500, following the Germanic migrations into the Roman Empire.[65] As mentioned, Slavs moved westward into territories earlier inhabited and vacated by Germans; southward toward and across the Danube into the Balkan provinces of the Eastern Roman Empire; and eastward into thinly populated territories north and south of the Dnieper and the Pripet marshes. This extensive geographical spread caused the first linguistic diversification within common Slavic, giving rise to Western, Eastern, and Southern Slavic dialects during the second half of the first millennium. Further diversification was to follow as a result of the familiar interplay between geographical fragmentation and political consolidation.

We begin with the Western Slavs. Massive topographical barriers were responsible for a growing diversification among these originally closely related Slav tribal entities. Some of them settled along the open north European plain, all the way to the Elbe River. Others settled south of and in between the high Carpathian mountain ridges. The first more or less stable state to emerge in the Carpathian lands was the kingdom of Moravia, uniting the Slav tribes and petty-states in the Morava River basin around 830. Undergoing great expansion at its zenith, the kingdom was destroyed by Magyar-Hungarian raids (906). Its core territory and people were ultimately incorporated within the new state that emerged further west, in the Bohemian basin. This state was hammered together from related Slav tribes (including the eponymic Czech) by the native Přemyslid dynasty, which from a capital in Prague ruled the country continuously for more than 400 years, from the late ninth century to 1306. Squeezed between the Magyar threat and the German Holy Empire, the Přemyslid rulers recognized the suzerainty of the latter, while maneuvering to secure the practical autonomy and internal unity of their realm. In 1198 their *de facto* status became *de jure* when they gained the title of kings.

As the Přemyslid line ceased, the Czech nobility offered the Bohemian crown to a German prince from the House of Luxembourg. We shall devote some space to discussing the practice of foreign dynastic rule in the concluding theoretical part of this chapter. The cosmopolitan King Charles IV (1342–1378), also elected Holy Roman Emperor, further formalized the separate status of the kingdom of Bohemia within the Empire and cultivated the study of the Czech language, while also establishing a cosmopolitan university in the prosperous city of Prague. German settlement in Bohemia and Moravia, especially in the cities and towns, had long been very substantial. However, not long after Charles' reign the Hussite wars broke out in all their ferocity, with the national element constituting a significant aspect of them.

Influenced by the teachings of John Wycliffe in England, Jan Hus launched a Protestant reformation in Bohemia and Moravia more than a century before Martin Luther. His execution by the Catholic Council of Constance (1415) sparked a fully-fledged movement which engulfed the country and spectacularly defeated repeated invasions by the Imperial forces (1420–1434). The national character of the Hussite movement has long been stressed not only by Czech nationalists, but also by scholars. Certainly, the main issue was religious. At the same time, however, the movement was almost exclusively Czech, its enemies were predominantly non-Czechs, and it encompassed both the Czech nobility, and city and country people. Some scholars cautiously qualify all the above, pointing out that the movement had some influence among non-Czechs and that not all Czechs were Hussites.[66] Indeed, the Hussite wars were partly civil wars, waged not only against the German population of Bohemia and Moravia, but also against Czechs who opposed the movement. However, the same is also true of nearly any modern national movement. All in all, the Hussite movement was both Czech and popular, which is the very definition of national. This is clearly manifest in both its language and its deeds.

In their letters (in Czech) to the emperor and the Constance Council before and after Hus' execution, the Czech barons (ultimately 452 signatories) strongly protested "the dishonor of our nationality and of the Bohemian land."[67] As the conflict deteriorated, the Czech masters of the University of Prague denounced the execution of a Czech preacher by German townsmen, calling the killers "patent enemies of our nationality [*lingua*]," who tended "to the indelible besmirching of our Bohemian and Moravian race [*gens*] and of the whole Slavic nationality [*lingua*]."[68] In addition to their religious demands, the leaders of the brewing revolution requested, among other things (1419): that no foreigners were to be put in civil offices if capable Czechs were available; that the Czech language was to be used in judicial proceedings; and that Czechs were to have "first voice" everywhere in the realm.[69] Assembling in Prague Castle in 1420, the Czech nobles issued a proclamation in which they described Emperor Zikmund as "a great and brutal enemy of the Czech kingdom and language." To their religious demands they added "the common weal of the kingdom and our Czech language."[70] As late as 1469, long after the Hussite Wars ended, in response to a papal rejection of a Czech elected to the Bohemian crown, a call was issued "to all faithful Czechs and Moravians, genuine lovers of God's truth and disciples of your own Czech language." The pope and his allies were blamed for wishing "to destroy, wipe out, and utterly suppress the Czech language"; he "inflames and incites all the nations and languages of the surrounding lands against us."[71] As the modern historian who quotes this writes: "It is a remarkable passage; but one quite typical of its time and place. Virtually all Hussite manifestos since 1420 had struck the same notes." The passage, he goes on, is "rather disconcertingly modern – *or what we are accustomed, at any rate, to think of as modern* – in its identification of truth and virtue with a land, a people, and their language ... All this happened without the aid of the printing press."[72]

In addition to the concepts of *gens* (people in the ethnic sense) and *natio*, which we have already seen repeatedly used by the medieval sources, the frequent use of *lingua* in the above quotations merits special attention. Clearly, the Czech language was important because of its religious significance: the Bible was translated into the Czech vernacular as early as the 1370s and 1380s, 150 years before Luther's German translation, and, as during the Reformation, this was a most powerful device for reaching the masses in both written and oral forms. However, no less significantly, in the context of Bohemia and Moravia *lingua* was also used as synonymous to, but a clearer term than *gens* or *natio*, unambiguously referring to Czechs as opposed to the German population of the land. *Lingua* actually stood for ethnic nationality.

As already mentioned, in practice as much as in proclamations the Hussite rebellion was both Czech and socially inclusive, the hallmark of the modern definition of national. It began with the Czech intellectuals, was taken up by the Czech nobility, burghers, and urban masses, and then mobilized the Czech rural population. Founded as a cosmopolitan institution, the University of Prague soon became a battleground between its Czech academic staff, on the one hand, and its foreign, mostly German, staff, on the other. In 1409, in response to steps which limited their status, many of the foreign faculty members left, helping to found the universities of Leipzig and Erfurt. With the outbreak of violence after Hus' execution, Czech mobs in Prague and other urban centers attacked German residences and businesses. However, probably the most significant aspect of the Hussite Wars was the mass armies raised from among the Czech peasantry. Under the generalship of Jan Žižka they shocked Europe by repeatedly defeating the Imperial knightly forces and then carrying the war deep into the surrounding countries in punitive raids. The Czech masses were anything but politically unmobilized, and, as we have seen in the language of the movement, their religious and national zeal were inseparable.

To be sure, such a comprehensive case of national mobilization as occurred during the Hussite Wars constituted the far end of the spectrum in feudal Europe. Yet this and more ordinary manifestations of political nationalism were a far more common feature of medieval Europe than one could ever guess from the unhistorical modernist schema. The Hussite rebellion, split between extremists and moderates, was ultimately suppressed. But Czech separateness, autonomous institutions, and the supremacy of Czech as the language of deliberation in the country's estates, law courts, and culture at large were guaranteed.[73] Czech nationalism was broken and Czech independence was lost only in the bloody aftermath of the Czech defeat in the famous battle of the White Mountain (1620) at the beginning of the Thirty Years War. In reaction against the mythologizing of this event by Czech nationalists in the nineteenth and early twentieth centuries, some scholars have tended to downplay its significance.[74] Yet in reality the outcome of the Czech defeat was very significant indeed: the country lost its autonomous institutions and was placed under direct Habsburg rule; a large part of the Protestant aristocracy was expelled and its estates passed into the hands of foreigners; German presence increased and dominated the cities and cultural life; and the Czech language and identity receded, surviving mostly in the countryside. Given this historical trajectory, Gellner went badly astray in portraying premodern Bohemia and Moravia as quintessentially non-national. The truth of the matter was that the Czech lands had been distinctively national *before* losing their national independence and much of their national identity during the seventeenth and eighteenth centuries.[75]

The Polish national state and empire

Political consolidation also took place on the open plain north of the Carpathians. In the second half of the tenth century an enterprising leader, Mieszko, unified the ethnically related tribes (including the eponymic Polanie) and emerging petty-states of the area into the kingdom of Poland. Like the Přemyslids in Bohemia, his Piast dynasty ruled the country for 400 years. Remarkably, the ethnic distinctions which Mieszko had found and consolidated politically proved to be even more enduring than his dynasty, undergoing only limited changes. These changes concerned the westernmost territories settled by Slavs on the northern European plain, territories which would be taken over by the German expansion eastward from around the year 1000 on. The Polabian and Sorb Slav populations there slowly assimilated into German culture, a process that lasted until well into modernity. Next, along the west–east axis, the Slav provinces of Pomerania and Silesia, which Mieszko's immediate successors incorporated into Poland, were soon lost and underwent similar processes of Germanization. To the north of Poland, the Baltic-speaking Prussian tribal population experienced the same fate. At the same time, however, Poland's West Slav heartland remained little changed. Furthermore, as Poland came to possess a great empire in the east, the ethnic differences within that empire between what was Polish and what was not never disappeared despite many centuries of glorious rule. Indeed, they were always and everywhere very salient politically.

Not all of Poland's interethnic relations were hostile or unequal. After the end of the Piast line, Poland forged a close alliance with neighboring Lithuania in order to combat the serious threat from the German Teutonic Knights along the Baltic. The Lithuanian King

Jagiełło was also crowned king of Poland (1386), and his dynasty ruled for two centuries until 1572. In 1569, the dynastic union was replaced with the common consent of both sides by a joint state, the Polish–Lithuanian Commonwealth. Lithuanian is a Baltic language, so the Lithuanians were not even Slavs. Although the Lithuanian aristocracy underwent Polish acculturation over time, Lithuania retained its separate status, institutions, and identity within the union. All the same, the partnership between the two peoples was highly successful, and for very good reasons: in addition to defense against powerful common enemies, the Poles and the Lithuanians joined forces to rule over others. The Lithuanians brought to the union a large dowry, the lands of Rus in the east which they had conquered after their victories over the Tartars. Poland herself had incorporated the western Ukraine or Ruthenia in the fourteenth century. With the creation of the Commonwealth in 1569, the Rus lands were divided, their northern part remaining under Lithuania and their southern part coming under Poland. This was the background for the linguistic–ethnic diversification that occurred within the East Slavic-speaking population of these territories. The Byelorussian and Ukrainian languages evolved, respectively, in the Lithuanian- and Polish-dominated realms. The third and largest East Slavic language, Russian, developed further east, outside the Polish–Lithuanian Commonwealth.[76]

In their huge estates the Polish and Lithuanian magnates reduced the local peasant population of the east to serfdom and exploited them economically with an iron hand. Yet the same was also true of Poland and Lithuania proper. In no country of Europe did the nobility achieve such dominance. The Polish–Lithuanian Commonwealth was famously an aristocratic republic. The king was elected. The country's all-powerful parliament, the Sejm, excluded even the burghers, represented in most other European parliaments. The free peasantry of the early Polish state were progressively subjugated during the late Middle Ages, so that serfs constituted some 60 percent of the population in the middle of the sixteenth century, a European record (except for Russia).[77] In such extreme circumstances of aristocratic rule did anything like a comprehensive Polish nation exist? Did the Polish aristocracy regard the Polish peasants, whom they viewed with utter contempt, as part of a common collective? Did the illiterate peasants in Poland, whose voice is unheard in the records, view themselves as part of a Polish people and feel any affinity toward and solidarity with the nobles' "republic"? Many historians have been highly skeptical about this. They have argued that the concept of the nation in the Commonwealth was limited to the nobility alone, with little regard to ethnic categories.[78]

I am not disputing much of the above or downplaying the selfishness of the Polish and Lithuanian nobility as an estate and individuals. Ultimately, their conduct made the Commonwealth ungovernable and caused the demise of the once-mighty state, partitioned among its neighbors in the late eighteenth century. However, although the nobility's interests were the overriding principle of the Commonwealth, this was very far from being the *only* principle. The nobility's dominance in the Polish–Lithuanian Commonwealth overshadowed, but never eliminated the national factor. This was clear in relation to both outsiders and the local population. Indeed, recent trends in the historiography of Poland have turned the tables on the modernists, charging them with the anachronism they attribute to modern nationalists. A comprehensive study of sixteenth- and seventeenth-century Polish sources conclusively shows that the concept *naród szlchecki* – which modern historians have translated as "noble nation" and highlighted as signifying the aristocracy's self-perception as the exclusive members of the nation – was rarely used at all. Furthermore, on the rare instances in which it was used in early modern Poland it was always in the sense of a noble family origin or descent of the person involved (that is, noble descent rather than nation; the root *rod* has the broader meaning of kin in the Slavic languages).[79] Another study follows suit:

> The image of the Polish "noble nation" is indeed a creation of the modern era [in the nineteenth century] … sixteenth-century Poles imagined their nation (and nations in general) as linguistic and cultural entities, not political ones. Nor did they believe that only nobles were entitled to participate in the nation, or at least no such idea was formulated until modern times.[80]

Moreover, as yet another historian amply demonstrates, Polish national identity was actually clearer and more comprehensive *before* the late sixteenth century, during the late Middle Ages and Renaissance:

> *Up to the sixteenth century the Polish nation was still
> conceived as a community inhabiting the same territory and
> embracing population groups sharing the same customs,
> history, and language. It was only late in that century that
> substantial changes in the national consciousness among the
> nobility came about*

together with a great expansion of the Polish realm to include large
non-Polish populations.[81] The same historian continues:

> *During the Renaissance, the main feature that distinguished
> a nation was language. Thus no one, from Długosz to
> Andrzej Frycz Modrzewski, denied that peasants were an
> integral part of the nation, based on one common language.
> The eminent lexicographer Jan Maczyński, in his Polish–
> Latin dictionary, defined the word "natio" as a "nation
> using the same language ..." Advocates of the election of a
> Piast to the Polish throne also emphasized the need to
> protect the national language.[82]*

Indeed, one can go farther back, to the reunification of Poland at
the beginning of the fourteenth century. This followed a period of fragmentation during the twelfth and thirteenth centuries due to the practice
of multiple inheritances among the monarch's sons. In the face of deep
Czech and German involvement the nationalist aspect of the struggle was
unmistakable: "The Czechs were denounced as foreigners, servants of the
'German' Emperor, allies of the 'German' knights of Prussia, and of the
'German' Piasts of Silesia." Charges were made against dignitaries for
being the "enemy of the Polish people." "Investigations into the Craco-
vian revolt [by German residents of the city] were assisted by a simple
language test. Any suspect who could repeat and correctly pronounce
[four Polish words] was judged loyal; he who faltered was guilty."[83]

Evidence regarding the masses of peasantry must as usual be
inferred indirectly. Probably the best time to look for such evidence is
the era of the peasants' harshest subjugation in the middle of the
seventeenth century. This was also the time of the "Deluge," when
the Commonwealth was afflicted by unprecedented domestic upheavals and foreign invasions. The upheavals began in 1648 with the
Cossack revolt led by Bohdan Khmelnytsky. Joined by the masses of

171 / Premodern Europe and the national state

Ukrainian peasantry, the revolt turned into a massive conflagration in which the Commonwealth ultimately lost much of its Ukrainian domain. Indisputably, class, economic, and religious factors were all involved in the Ukrainian revolt: the Cossacks and the Ukrainian (Ruthenian) nobles (such as Khmelnytsky himself), with a long tradition of loyal service to the Commonwealth and of enjoying its benefits, felt dis-privileged; the Ukrainian peasantry were harshly exploited; the eastern parts of the Ukraine were Orthodox, as opposed to mainly Catholic Poland. Bu͟ all these elements were inseparable from the ethnonational factor. Ruthenian nobles who joined the revolt felt that their ethnic identity hindered their treatment as equal by the Polish and Lithuanian aristocracy. The Ukrainian peasantry felt that their oppressors were foreign. Indeed, although the Polish aristocracy viewed all peasants as barely human, they regarded their Ukrainian serfs as a particularly lowly breed and often treated them with a violence unheard of in Poland itself. The Orthodox faith contributed to the Ukraine's distinct ethnonational sense of identity. It was for these major ethnonational reasons that grievances which would commonly have resulted in disturbances and even a civil war created such a rupture and ended in secession.[84] A historian of early modern Ukrainian national consciousness has put in a simple, common-sense manner what should have been clear to everybody: "The nation as the primary identity of man is a nineteenth and twentieth century concept, but seventeenth century men viewed residence in a common fatherland or possession of a common descent, culture and historical tradition as important matters."[85]

Unable to defend their independence, the Ukrainian rebels reluctantly put their land under a Russian protectorate (1654), and the Ukraine would later be swallowed by the Czarist empire. Not having achieved statehood, the Ukraine's sense of nationhood was and remained tenuous. Still, their ethnic distinctiveness was a fact of life by late medieval times, was clear to both outsiders and insiders, and always carried political implications. We shall get back to this shortly.

The control case for the Ukrainian rebellion was Poland itself. Despite some attempts to arouse them, the Polish peasantry, themselves enserfed and exploited by the nobility, did not join the revolt even when Khmelnytsky's invasion of Poland brought it to their doorstep. Khmelnytsky himself well anticipated this. To the Polish envoys he

> *defined the western extent of his "land and principality"*
> *by the boundaries of ethnic Ruthenian territories ... He told*
> *the envoys that he was counting on the support of the*
> *peasantry all the way to Lublin and Cracow and that his*
> *goal was to liberate the whole Rus' nation from Polish*
> *captivity.*[86]

This goes to show that the Ukrainian revolt was not merely a class–economic affair within a multiethnic aristocratic empire, as some socially-minded scholars assure us. Moreover, on the heels of the Ukrainian revolt Poland was invaded and taken over by the Swedes (1655–1656). Some of the greatest Polish and Lithuanian magnates supported the Swedish monarch's claim to the crown of the Commonwealth and opened the doors to the invaders. Soon, however, a national revolt against the Swedes ensued, against which they had no chance of holding the country. Peasants were among the first to rise against the foreigners. As part of the nobility and regular army joined, the rebellion took the form of widespread guerrilla warfare enjoying massive popular support. Indeed, when the exiled King John Casimir returned to Poland, he was moved by this popular participation to declare in Lvov his support for improving the peasants' status.

Unsurprisingly, his declaration did not materialize. Yet the fact remains that in circumstances of a national emergency caused by an acute foreign threat the rulers and elite, which normally disenfranchised the people, did not recoil from relying on their assistance. And the people for their part responded in an unmistakable way. Furthermore, whereas parts of a national elite sometimes found it in their interest to collaborate with a foreign conqueror, one hardly hears of cases when the people of a premodern nation welcomed foreign occupiers as their liberators, as they widely did in relation to their own, albeit exploitative, kin. There was no question that the people preferred their often hated social superiors to "bloody foreigners." To be sure, peasants' main bonds were with their village and locality. Still, these were viewed as being part of a broader circle of belonging, as becomes clear when alien invaders enter the locality.[87] This was again demonstrated half a century after the first Swedish invasion, during the Great Northern War. In Charles XII's campaign in Poland and invasion of Russia (1708–1709), which ended in the Swedish crushing defeat at Poltava, "a conspicuous part was played ... by Polish peasants who harassed the Swedish columns."[88] In 1794, Tadeusz Kościuszko led a popular national uprising to revive partitioned Poland. In the spirit of the new age ushered in by the American and French revolutions, he issued a proclamation that promised the peasants freedom and civil rights. Still, the peasants' attitude and response had already manifested themselves unmistakably centuries before and under much less auspicious social conditions.

Finally, a few words about Lithuania, where the following quote from a study of medieval Lithuanian national identity portrays what should by now be a very familiar picture:

> The Lithuanian nation was formed during the thirteenth and fourteenth centuries, when the early feudal Lithuanian state came into being ... The Lithuanian ethnic group, divided among a number of "lands," i.e, tribal territories ... had long shared a common agricultural culture and been closely related linguistically; from the ninth to the eleventh centuries it had also been united culturally. Joined under one ruler, this group gradually started to lose its tribal diversity and to develop a common national consciousness.[89]

The Lithuanian empire created in the fourteenth century as the Lithuanians expanded over Rus only reinforced Lithuanian national pride as a dominant imperial people. This was so even though the conquered territories were culturally more developed and gave the Lithuanian state its official bureaucratic written language. Nor did the dynastic union with Poland weaken Lithuanian identity, jealously guarded during the late Middle Ages. Grand Duke Vytautas in 1420 defined the realm of Lithuania proper as "one language and one people," and chronicles of the Lithuanians' mythological origins and history proliferated in the late fifteenth to the early sixteenth centuries. Only after the closer union with Poland in 1569 and the participation of the Lithuanian magnates in the creation of the nobles' republic, did they also become increasingly Polanized.[90]

The example of Lithuania and other medieval and early modern nations of Eastern Europe portrayed in a special issue of *Harvard Ukrainian Studies* (1986) dedicated to the subject are instructive in many ways. Composed contemporaneously with the new surge of modernist publications on nations and nationalism during the

1980s, these collected studies are blissfully impervious to it.[S] Indeed, as we have seen with respect to Poland and shall see in other cases as well, they suggest that national identity was often stronger in medieval Eastern Europe, before the twin processes of deepening enserfment and imperial expansion unfolded during the early modern period. Rather than being the nineteenth-century nationalist fabrications that modernists claim them to be, medieval European nations turn out to be authentic and highly relevant to the subject of nationhood, more relevant in fact than the immediate premodern period postulated as the standard by modernists.

The Russian nation and the Russian Empire

The last national consolidation we examine in some detail took place among the Eastern Slavs, in the lands of Rus. It is an open secret of Russian history that the first organized polities in the country were established by outsiders. Rus is the Finnish and Estonian name for Swedes, who from around the year 750 sailed down the tributaries of the Volga and Dnieper rivers, trading with the Eastern Roman Empire, the Islamic Caliphate, and the Volga Kazars and Bulgars. From their fortified settlements they extended their rule over the surrounding countryside, thinly populated by Baltic- and Slavic-speaking tribes. Soon, however, the Scandinavian elite of warriors and traders adopted the East Slavic language of the locals, and a process of pagan syncretism took place before the adoption of Christianity in the late tenth century. By then the grand princes of Kiev had expanded their rule over the vast open plain land of Ukraine and the north, unifying earlier petty-polities. Notably, the Kievan state also had a strong tradition of citizen assemblies and civic institutions.[91] Because of the practice of dividing the inheritance among the princes of the ruling Rurik dynasty, the realm again fragmented into practically independent princedoms from the middle of the eleventh century. Still, the Rus lands retained a common language, a rich literary culture, the formal suzerainty of Kiev,

[S] One might claim that the authors, most of them of Eastern European descent, exhibit a nationalist bias for their respective countries, then part of the Soviet Empire. But in view of the diversity and high quality of the contributions, such a claim is on the whole insubstantial.

and a common Orthodox faith, with a metropolitan center in Kiev. Between the 1220s and 1240s, however, the Mongols swept through eastern Europe. Kiev was destroyed, and the principalities of Rus became tax-paying vassals of the Mongol/Tartar Golden Horde of the southern steppe.

After humble beginnings as a client of the Mongol overlord, the princedom of Moscow began its slow ascent in central Russia. As the power of the Golden Horde waned, Grand Prince Ivan III (reigned 1462–1505) ceased the payment of tribute to the Mongols, took over some of the major Russian principalities, and established overlordship over the others. The rulers of Muscovy also capitalized on the transfer of the Orthodox metropolitan seat to Moscow. They claimed to be the legitimate successors of Kiev, and after its fall in 1453 of Byzantium also.[92] To be sure, these were ideological claims which are by nature neither true nor false. Nor was Moscow's rise and unification of Russia preordained. Nonetheless, this successful unification and its survival in the following centuries in the face of the mightiest of challenges heavily depended on very tangible realities on the ground. The principalities taken over by Moscow in a vast open land which facilitated communication were all Russian, sharing language, religion, culture, and, indeed, a sense of kinship. From around 1200 on – before and after the destruction of Kiev and despite political fragmentation and foreign subjugation – epic poems and tales emotively used the term "the Russian land" as a designation for a beloved common motherland with a single people.[93] The neighbors all around – Mongols, German Teutonic Knights, Lithuanians, Poles, and later also Swedes and Ottoman Turks – were clearly foreigners, and their respective threats galvanized Russian identity. From the time of Ivan III Moscow's expansion was carried out under the legitimizing slogan of "the gathering of the Russian lands." Indeed, one can hardly claim that the rulers of Moscow trumpeted this slogan to advance their cause if they did not assess that it resonated powerfully with the people of the Russian princedoms. Again, when direct evidence from the people is scant, the actual behavior of rulers aimed at them is a sure sign of what they believe their attitude to be. To misquote Lenin, what counts with both leaders and peoples is what they say in connection with what they do.

Ivan IV, "the Terrible" (reigned 1547–1584), officially took the title czar of Russia. Under him despotism became the hallmark of the country, as he mercilessly crushed the power and independence of the boyar nobility. At the same time, the Russian peasantry was increasingly subjected to enserfment, becoming even more disenfranchised and destitute than their Polish counterparts. Indeed, both the Polish nobles' republic and Russian autocracy were extreme – and hence most illuminating – test cases wherein the mass of the population was devoid of freedom and rights. Similar to what we saw with respect to the Polish peasantry in times of national emergency, servitude did not mean that the Russian peasantry lacked a sense of Russianness or failed to identify with the Russian state when it was threatened by foreigners. The widely expressed love for their czar by ordinary Russians, attested to by contemporaries as early as the sixteenth century, was directly linked to his perception as the father and symbol of the Russian nation rather than a foreign despot.[94]

A most prominent instance of popular mobilization in the face of a foreign threat occurred during the Times of Troubles, a period of regime instability, civil wars, and foreign interventions that followed the death of Ivan IV. When the king of Poland, Sigismund III, took the Russian throne, a sweeping revolt, which scholars habitually and very naturally call national, erupted throughout the country against the foreign invaders (1612). Volunteer armies emerged almost spontaneously. They were composed of townsmen from Moscow and other cities, free warrior bands of Cossacks, and peasants, many of them serfs who ran away to join the insurrection despite the misgivings of their social superiors. For the benefit of those accustomed to dichotomist, binary thinking it should be stressed that while such serfs obviously sought personal freedom, this merged with rather than substituted for the cause of national freedom. A volunteer army led together by Kuzma Minin from the city of Nizhny Novgorod, "a butcher by trade, who combined exalted patriotism and the ability to inspire others with levelheadedness organizational and other practical talents,"[95] and by Prince Dmitry Pozharsky drove the Poles out of Moscow. An Assembly of the Land (zemsky sobor), which included free peasants, convened in Moscow to elect a czar (1613). After stipulating that the new ruler must be both Russian and Orthodox, the assembly chose Michael Romanov, ushering in the dynasty that would rule Russia until 1917.

Some historians of Russian national consciousness take the eighteenth century as their starting point, following Peter the Great and the penetration of modern Western concepts.[96] But as the popular insurrection that brought in the Romanovs strikingly demonstrates, *premodern* concepts of Russian consciousness, identity, and solidarity as a people and state had been clearly evident and very potent much earlier. Indeed, most of the resistance to Peter himself was directed against his alien Western imports which contradicted the traditional Russian outlook and customs. As early as the sixteenth century, Russians widely regarded themselves as the only true people, holy and pure from the moral corruption they attributed to all foreign nations.

Paul Bushkovitch, Professor of Early Modern Russian History at Yale, defines the scholarly misconception here most aptly:

> *Two methods are most common: to project into the past the modern forms of national consciousness (the approach of all nineteenth-century writers), or to despair at the distortion introduced by that approach and then deny the existence of any national consciousness in Russia at all before the eighteenth century. Neither position need be taken, however. Russians of the sixteenth and seventeenth century had a defined national consciousness, even if it did not take the same form as the national consciousness of Pushkin, Alexander III, or Lenin.*[97]

Bushkovitch goes on to write that Russian national consciousness in the sixteenth and seventeenth centuries was actually clearer than it later became because the Russian state was more clearly ethnically Russian. On the basis of an extensive reading of the contemporary texts he concludes that it was Russian identity rather than the notions of Russia as the Third Rome, autocracy, and empire – widely assumed by modern observers to be central to the Russian past – which dominated Russian chronicles of the time.[98] According to Geoffrey Hosking:

> *Russia appears to refute the modernist account of nationhood, since there modernization actually weakened national identity. In the sixteenth and seventeenth centuries the elites and arguably many of the people of Muscovite Rus had a lively sense of their ethnic identity and of their role in the world. Modernization, launched by Tsar Aleksei in the middle of the seventeenth century and intensified by Peter the Great in the early eighteenth, actually undermined that identity.*[99]

Two salient issues here need clarification. The first is religion. Was the revolt against the Poles national or was it an Orthodox reaction against the prospect of a Catholic ruler? After all, it was the patriarch of Moscow who raised the banner of revolt. Again, as the stipulation of the assembly that elected the czar indicates, the national and religious causes here were not mutually exclusive, but complementary. Church and state in Russia were inseparable, and the Orthodox faith was an integral part of Russian identity.[100] Indeed, to separate the effect of the two we need a control case that involves only a national and no religious distinction. This is provided by Russia's incorporation of the Ukraine after 1654. As mentioned earlier, Khmelnytsky's Ukrainian rebels fighting against Poland–Lithuania found it necessary to put themselves under a Russian protectorate. In doing so, Khmelnytsky emphasized the shared Orthodox faith of the Russians and Ukrainians as well as the brotherhood of the two East Slav peoples. Czarist Russia for its part was only too happy to underline these bonds. And yet Khmelnytsky's people were deeply apprehensive about losing *both* their national and personal freedom: the Russians and Ukrainians were two separate peoples, speaking two distinct East Slavic languages; autocratic Russia demonstrated little respects for individual rights and freedoms. For these reasons, Khmelnytsky and his men only conceded to a treaty that would guarantee their autonomy and freedom in relation to the Russian Empire.[101] In reality, neither survived for very long. During the second half of the seventeenth century there was a stream of Ukrainian chronicles, which "can only be described as 'national histories,'" celebrating "the Ukrainian narod (nation)."[102] However, after the Cossacks allied with king of Sweden, Charles XII, in the early eighteenth century in order to break loose from Russia, Czar Peter the Great crushed the rebels and sharply curtailed Ukrainian autonomy. Catherine II abolished the last vestiges of this autonomy later in the century, and while enserfment was expanded in the Ukraine, restrictions were imposed on the Ukrainian language and culture. As already mentioned, a Ukrainian national identity was unformed and weak until modern times because Ukrainians lacked a history of independence, because they were crushed under Russia's iron rule, and because the Ukrainian elite was successfully incorporated into the Russian imperial state apparatus.[103] Still, a distinct Ukrainian identity survived, and the question of whether it would be absorbed within an all-Russian identity or would take a separate national form was opened afresh during the nineteenth century.[104]

This brings us to a second salient issue, the empire. Both the Ukrainians and the Belarusians were Eastern Slavs and Orthodox. They were habitually referred to by the Great Russians as brothers in the all-Russian family. However, from as early as the sixteenth century the Russian Empire had incorporated non-Russian and non-Christian elements. Ivan IV conquered and annexed the Muslim Tartars of the middle Volga, and Russia continued to expand east toward the Urals and into Siberia and south and southeast into the Crimea, Kazakhstan, and the Caucasus during the seventeenth and eighteenth centuries. Some scholars regard the empire's multiethnic composition as a negation of Russian nationhood.[105] But as we have seen with respect to multiethnic empires in general, this was not the case. Then, as later, the Russian Empire was as much a manifestation and the pride of Russian nationalism as it was an expression of czarist expansionism.[106] Non-Russian peoples sometimes chose the protection of the empire against a greater menace, such as the Poles and, more widely, the Ottoman Turks. They could also be loyal subjects of the imperial state, and aspiring individuals from among them could serve this state and rise to the upper levels of its bureaucratic apparatus, as many did. As with the English-dominated Great Britain and United Kingdom of the early modern period a special terminology was introduced to denote the expanded multiethnic realm: the term *Russkii* means ethnic Russians, while *Rossiiskii* refers to all those belonging to Russia, whether ethnically Russian or not. As in the Ukraine, the latter variably came under subtle and not so subtle pressures to Russify (and adopt Orthodoxy), not that different in fact than those existing during the Soviet period. Imperial Russia earned a reputation of being "the prison house of nations." This assumed a distinction between the Russians in the empire, who may have wanted a change of regime and personal freedom, but were interested in the continued existence of the Russian state and possibly the empire, and the other peoples in the empire that above all aspired to collective freedom.

Clearly, there was a great deal of voluntary Russification, including among the foreign elite who came to settle in Russia. From as early as the sixteenth century, Lithuanian and Polish nobles found opportunity in Russia. From Peter's time and during the eighteenth century there was an influx of Western, mostly German, experts who were invited to serve the state. Although their arrival did not pass without resentment among the Russian elite, they were all Russified within a few generations. The same applied to the German consorts of the czars and to one czarina, Catherine II, "the Great," who did their utmost to adopt the Russian language and identify. All in all, much of Russia's confidence in its empire derived from the fact that in contrast to many other empires the Russians were by far the largest ethnic community in the realm and held a solid "controlling stake" in it. As Alex Yakobson puts it, coercive empires, which did not have to worry too much about dissenting national wills expressed in the ballots, could in some ways allow themselves to be more inclusive with respect to peoples and nations other than that of the dominant imperial people. Nonetheless, it helped that even within the Russian Empire's greatest extent toward the end of the czarist era, Great Russians constituted 43 percent of the population.[107] The empire was known as the *Russian* Empire – in comparison with its Habsburg and Ottoman neighbors – for a very good reason (officially *Rossiyskaya* = "Russiania"). Periodically after the national revolt against the Poles in the early seventeenth century, the state found it necessary to call upon the loyalty of the Russian people in times of severe foreign threat.

On the eve of the decisive battle of Poltava (1709) in which Charles XII's invading Swedish army was routed by Peter's new professional army of peasant conscripts, the czar's proclamation to the troops went as follows:

> *Warriors! Here is the hour that will decide the fate of the fatherland ... You should think that you are fighting not for Peter, but for the state, entrusted to Peter, for your kin, for fatherland [for faith and church ...] And know of Peter that he does not care about his life but only that Russia lives in bliss and glory for your well-being.*[108]

These words, carefully chosen for effect at a fateful moment, clearly indicate that the czar believed the notion of the holy fatherland of Russia resonated best with his peasant troops, rather than loyalty to the ruler as such or appealing to their professional pride as soldiers.

A century later, in 1812, Russia experienced an even graver trial, the invasion of Napoleon's great army. The most backward, premodern power in Europe faced the national forces raised by Revolutionary France with no lesser national fervor, much of it deliberately induced by the state and much spontaneous. In his preparatory memorandum of April 1812, Major-General Chuikevich stressed among Russia's greatest assets "the loyalty to him [the czar] of his people, who must be armed and inspired as in Spain, with the help of the clergy."[109] The Minister of War, Barclay de Tolly, corresponding with provincial governors, wrote that he knew that the loyal population would rise up to defend "the Holy Faith and the frontiers of the Fatherland."[110] Czar Alexander I expressed his position that "It was vital strongly to interest the people in the war, by waging it for the first time in over a hundred years on the territory of their motherland (*rodina*)."[111] He was obviously alluding to the earlier national crisis during the Swedish invasion in Peter's time. In his imperial manifesto to his subjects after the invasion, the czar invoked the yet earlier national mobilization against the Poles during the Times of Troubles. The manifesto stated: "We now appeal to all our loyal subjects, to all estates and conditions both spiritual and temporal, to rise up with us in a united and universal stand."[112] The Orthodox Church, which had already issued an anathema against Napoleon during an earlier war, responded fully: "On 27 July the Synod issued a blistering manifesto" stating it was "the duty of every priest to inspire unity, obedience and courage among the population in defense of the Orthodox religion, monarch and Fatherland."[113] Here, strikingly, were all the elements of *pre*modern nationalism. Indeed, it was largely through the dense network of village churches that the news of the national emergency and patriotic call reached even remote peasant communities in Russia.

There seem to have been unfulfilled expectations among the Russian serfs (58 percent of the population in 1812) that the French would free them, and some hopes that the czar would do so afterward. But in any case, widespread guerilla bands and local militias forming from among the peasants harassed the French to save Russia. The Cossack cavalry played the major role in bringing about the French disaster during their agonizing retreat, but everywhere they relied on the sympathy and support of the Russian peasantry. The Russian authorities, although calling on the people of Russia to oppose the invaders, were actually concerned about and tried to limit the spontaneous action of the peasant-serfs.[114] And yet in the Fatherland War of 1812, as the war is called in Russia and was already thus called at the time, the czarist regime found it necessary to rely on mass popular devotion to Russia. This, indeed, was not very different from the way the Soviet regime would find it necessary to beat the Russian nationalist drum (in an officially multinational Soviet Union) as its most effective weapon for arousing the masses in the Great Patriotic War, the Russian name for the Second World War.** As in the other cases we have surveyed, premodern Russian nationalism – the patriotic devotion of a particular people to its collective on a country scale – went back to the early consolidation of the unified Russian state and people themselves.

Conclusion

In his book *The Early Slavs* (2001), P. M. Barford dutifully cites modernist precepts, as any scholar must lest he or she be suspected of theoretical naiveté and lack of sophistication. Yet his conclusion is far from ambivalent. The Slav tribes consolidated even before the year 1000 into states that can only be described as national and that by and large have survived into the present:

> *The complex processes initiated by the Slav expansion and subsequent demographic and ethnic consolidation culminated in the formation of tribal groups, which later coalesced to create states which form the framework of the ethnic make-up of modern Eastern Europe.*[115]

Furthermore,

> *Most early modern rulers ... seemed to have recognized ... the importance of imposing some form of unity and promoting a "national feeling" among the people of their realms in order to discourage moves towards decentralization. In other words, like a giant roller the state*

** This indeed was no different than Nelson's arousing appeal on the morning of Trafalgar: "England expects that every man will do his duty." He chose these words even though he surely had Scots, Welsh, and Irish in his fleet, and his country was officially called the United Kingdom or at least Great Britain. The same was true of Churchill's carefully chosen invocation of England – intermittently with Britain, "these Isles," and the United Kingdom – when aiming to arouse the gut feelings of his audience during the Second World War. Again, Alex Yakobson called my attention to this point; cf. Kumar, *The Making of English National Identity*, 2, 7–8.

was to level out any local irregularities. These developments may have been imposed by force, encouraged by imposing a common ideology of some form (and propaganda), or may have developed naturally. These factors may have involved a common religion, linguistic unity, the invention of shared ideals and traditions, a common enemy or the establishment of a unified material culture.[116]

Nation-building was the norm long before modernity.

Even more significant than the summary of the modern historian is the contemporary account of one of the earliest medieval chroniclers of the Slavs, the twelfth-century German Helmold, priest of Bosau. He describes the states and prestate tribes around the Baltic and on the frontiers of the German realm as follows:

Many nations [naciones] are seated about this sea. The Danes and the Swedes, whom we call Northmen, occupy the northern coast and all the islands it contains. Along the southern shore dwell the Slavic nations [naciones] of whom, reckoning from the east, the Russians [Ruci] are the first, then the Poles who on the north have the Prussians,[††] on the south the Bohemians and those who are called Moravians and the Carinthians[‡‡] and the Sorbs.[§§][117]

This is how things were perceived and expressed in the authentic language *of the time* and without the benefit of hindsight.

We have covered ample ground to show that the national state was the most typical form of political consolidation in Europe north of the old Roman frontier soon after the beginning of state consolidation across these vast territories. From the British Isles to Russia ethnic realities formed the basis of the emergent states. To be sure, states subsequently had great effect in homogenizing the realm and instilling it with a common identity. And yet their success in assimilating alien ethnicities within their realm, especially large ethnicities occupying a distinct territory, while existing, was often surprisingly limited despite

---

[††] Baltic-speaking tribesmen later eliminated and assimilated by Germans.
[‡‡] Slovenes.
[§§] Slavic tribesmen later assimilated by the Germans.

many centuries of state rule. Furthermore, such ethnic differences within states were always politically significant. Nineteenth- and twentieth-century nationalist myth-making notwithstanding, ethno-national identities *did* exhibit remarkable endurance and resilience from early premodern times. Ironically, it is modernists who reveal an unhistorical anachronism about this. A number of interrelated biases have skewed their case selection and are responsible for their misperception:

- Modernists have ignored early national state consolidation common across northern Europe. Instead, they have invoked cases such as the Finns, Estonians, Latvians, and Slovaks who lacked a history of political independence until the twentieth century. They have thereby created the misleading impression that these cases represented the rule rather than the exception.
- As well as being geographically selective, modernists have chosen too short a historical time span for describing Europe's premodern conditions. Whereas in western Europe the early modern period saw a retreat of feudal fragmentation and the strengthening of national identity in some countries, in east-central Europe imperial expansion and deepening enserfment somewhat eroded the national cohesion of the states created during the Middle Ages.
- In central-eastern Europe modernists have been overly impressed by the multiethnic and multinational imperial model exemplified most extremely by the Habsburgs.

These and other misconceptions will be further examined as we turn now from the north to the territories south of Europe's old Roman frontier.

B SOUTHERN VERSUS NORTHERN EUROPE

Medieval national states and the clutches of empires in southeast Europe

As we turn to southeast Europe we shall spare the reader additional detailed expositions of medieval nation formation. The picture should be clear enough by now. Therefore, we shall make do with the briefest of outlines and move quickly to some general observations.

Slav tribal conglomerations and warrior bands that crossed the Roman frontier on the Danube into the Balkans from the sixth century on eventually settled down under the suzerainty of the Eastern Roman Empire in the mountainous province of Illyria. By the late first millennium they had been consolidating into a number of nascent national states speaking closely related South Slavic dialects. *The Royal Frankish Annals* (entry for the year 822) mentions the "Serbs, which nation (*natio*) is said to inhabit a large part of Dalmatia." In the ninth and tenth centuries, the various Serb principalities came together under one overlord in defense against the Bulgarians. The title of kings was accorded to the rulers of Serbia in the thirteenth century. The kingdom expanded into a Balkan empire in the fourteenth century, with a self-declared czar at its head, before undergoing feudal fragmentation. In the famous battle of Kosovo (1389), Serbia's ruler and army were disastrously defeated by the Ottomans, and in 1459 the country lost its independence and was incorporated into the Ottoman Empire. The Croats, settling in Illyria in the seventh century, were consolidated into a unified kingdom in the tenth century, also largely in response to Bulgarian pressure. From the early twelfth century, Croatia became dynastically united with and dominated by powerful Hungary, while retaining its autonomous institutions and laws. Following the crushing defeat of the Hungarian army at Mohács (1526), most of Hungary and Croatia fell into Ottoman hands. The remains of both countries had no alternative but to put themselves under the Habsburgs for protection. For centuries Croatia was a contested frontier land between the Habsburg and Ottoman empires. Closer to the Frankish and German domains, the most northwestern of the South Slavs, the Slovenes, Helmold's Carinthians, came under the suzerainty of the Holy Roman Empire very early and remained under the Habsburgs later on. Still, despite powerful German influences over 1,000 years, the country remained ethnically Slav.

The Bulgars were Turkic-speaking semi-nomadic equestrian tribes that created a large empire on the south Ukrainian steppe in the seventh century. After the empire was destroyed by the Khazars, some of the Bulgarian tribes joined their brethren who had migrated across the Danube into the Eastern Roman Empire. There they established a Bulgarian state in the late seventh century with a khan and later czar at its head, dominating the local South Slavic-speaking populations. During the following centuries they engaged in endemic wars with Byzantium. They constituted the greatest threat to its Balkan domains, and at times created an empire that ruled over much of them. Bulgaria also experienced military reversals, and the country was occupied by Byzantium during the eleventh and twelfth centuries. The kingdom regained independence and the empire was revived in the thirteenth and fourteenth centuries. Yet, defeated by the Ottomans in the late fourteenth century, Bulgaria became part of the Ottoman Empire for 500 years.

Interposed between the South Slavs in the Balkans and West Slavs in northern Europe, two non-Slavic-speaking populations consolidated politically north of the Danube. One was the Romance-speaking people of today's Romania. Although the Roman Empire ruled over former Dacia for less than 150 years, extensive Roman colonization was instrumental in changing the local language to Latin. This linguistic character survived the migration through, settlement in, and rule of the country by a string of steppe nomadic peoples, which continued until the early second millennium. By the late Middle Ages, three distinct Romance-speaking principalities had emerged: Wallachia, Moldavia, and Transylvania. The first two retained autonomy under Ottoman suzerainty, whereas the third came under Hungarian and later Habsburg rule and influence. The Magyars–Hungarians were Finno-Ugric nomadic tribes from the Urals region that crossed the Carpathians into the central European plain and were united by Árpád in the late ninth century. During the tenth century they terrorized west-central Europe with their raids. From around the year 1000 and during the Middle Ages the now Christian kingdom expanded into an empire. It ruled over its neighbors in Croatia, Transylvania, and Slovakia, and extended suzerainty further afield. The powerful Hungarian magnates exercised feudal control over the rural countryside in many of these lands. Having successfully withstood Ottoman pressure for centuries, Hungary finally collapsed and most of its territory was taken over by the Ottoman Empire toward the middle of the sixteenth century, following the battle of Mohács. The rump kingdom that survived had little alternative but to crown the Habsburgs over it.

From this brief historical outline we proceed to some wider observations and theory implications. First, one needs to pay attention to a major difference between early national state consolidation in the sparsely populated tribal lands of northern Europe and the processes which took place in the densely populated former provinces of the Roman Empire, where conquered and conquerors mixed. Fast advancing genetic studies show that in the north the Poles, for example, reveal clear genetic homogeneity. This is expected of a West Slav settlement in territories apparently vacated by their thin Germanic tribal population during the migrations. At the same time, the Poles reveal close genetic relatedness to other West and East Slav populations. As a recent extensive genetic study concludes: "Homogeneity of northern Slavic paternal lineages in Europe was shown to stretch from the Alps to the upper Volga and involve ethnicities speaking completely different branches of Slavic languages."[118] By comparison, genetic finds reveal that most of today's South Slavic-speaking populations (Macedonians, Serbs, Bosnians, and northern Croats, but not the Slovenes) are significantly different genetically from the Western and Eastern Slavs in the north.[119] The explanation researchers suggest for these finds accords with patterns of ethnogenesis we have already seen: in southeast Europe the barbarian invasions and constant wars decimated but hardly eliminated the dense local population of the former Roman provinces, which by and large went back as far as the Neolithic age. Yet, although the intruding Slavs were probably much fewer in number than the local population in the Balkan provinces in which they settled, the conquered population adopted the language and identity of the conquerors within a few centuries. Shared national identities were quick to emerge.

The same process took place in Hungary, where genetic evidence again suggests that the newcomers were a small minority that imparted their language and identity to the local population of the country through elite dominance. Thus, "Strong differences appear when the ancient Hungarian samples are analyzed according to apparent social status, as judged by grave goods. Commoners show a predominance of mtDNA haplotypes and haplogroups (H, R, T), common in west Eurasia, while high-status individuals, presumably conquering Hungarians, show" largely extinct Asian traits.[120] An opposite process was also possible, of course. The Turkic Bulgarians who settled in territories Slavonized only slightly earlier adopted a South Slavic language. A third trajectory is represented by the population of today's Romania, which continued to speak Romance dialects through countless upheavals. Needless to say, for our subject genetic history is important mainly for the light it sheds on the processes of ethnogenesis. What matters in these processes is not genetic maps *per se*, but the evolving subjective sense and tradition of kin–culture relatedness of the collectives in question.

That these ethnonational collectives have manifested remarkable endurance and survived the loss of political independence for many centuries is also clear. Again, neither the myth-making of nineteenth- and twentieth-century nationalists nor modernists' alleged demystification should obscure this reality. Far from being a modern invention, Serbs, Croats, Bulgarians, Hungarians, and, to a lesser degree, Slovenes and Romanians crystallized as distinctive ethnonational political identities during their early histories in the Middle Ages. Obviously, historical developments have continuously changed ethnicities and shifted ethnic boundaries. Some ethnic distinctions emerged as a result of later developments and never expressed themselves politically until recently (for example, Bosnia, Kosovo, and Macedonia). Furthermore, ethnicities have been proverbially mixed in many areas of the Balkans. This admixture, responsible for so many ethnic tensions and conflict, is due to a number of factors. First, mountainous landscape is well recognized as a variable that increases ethnic diversity (the Caucasus is another proverbial example). A second variable is national state action which tends to homogenize a realm, but has been absent in the Balkans since late medieval times. This in turn is related to a third factor, the effects of long imperial rule by either the Ottomans or the Habsburgs.

As we have already seen throughout the world, empires were the great juggernauts which by superior force eliminated early national states. Contrary to accepted wisdom, the latter were the primary module of large state formation. It was much easier to establish one's rule over one's own people or ethnos, on whose strength one could then strive to expand farther afield. In northeast Europe, the creation of Polish, Lithuanian, and Russian national states all preceded their respective empires. And in southeast Europe as well medieval national state formation preceded imperial expansion. However, in this part of Europe imperial expansion ultimately came from the outside and eliminated rather than built on the area's national states. The mighty Ottoman Empire was the major player in this process. However, its advance prompted the creation of the Habsburg Empire in central-east Europe, a very different animal, quite untypical of most empires, which has nevertheless been regarded as paradigmatic by students of the national phenomenon.

We usually view the Holy Roman Empire which the Habsburgs ruled from 1440 onward as one continuum, yet it had two very different historical phases. As we have seen, the medieval Empire was fundamentally a German state. It encompassed practically all the German-speaking population, and Germans constituted the core of its population, probably the majority, as the emperors' suzerainty over most of Italy was largely nominal. Indeed, although it possessed non-German domains and there was considerable diversity among its German principalities, the medieval Empire was the closest there would be to a German national state until the nineteenth century. Two parallel processes altered this course of development and changed the Empire's character completely, paradoxically shortly after it had been officially renamed the Holy Roman Empire of the German Nation. On the one hand, aristocratic fragmentation in Germany advanced more than in other countries, so that by the sixteenth and seventeenth centuries the German princedoms had turned themselves into virtually independent states with only nominal allegiance to what became an empty imperial structure. On the other hand, the Ottoman advance into southeast Europe forced the formerly independent states of that region, above all Great Hungary and its periphery in Croatia and Slovakia, to seek protection under the Habsburgs for their rump states. Through these dual processes the Holy Empire was transformed from a fundamentally German state into the multiethnic and multinational central-eastern

European Habsburg Empire that it continued to be even after the formal dissolution of the Holy Empire in 1806 and until 1918.

The Habsburg Empire was different from other empires not in its multiethnic and multinational character, but in what kept it together. We have seen that as a rule the mainstay of empires was their dominant imperial people or ethnic group. They were either numerically dominant or militarily superior, sometimes both. In the Habsburg Empire, however, the core German lands of Austria and its periphery did not really fulfill either of these conditions. In themselves they would not have enabled the Habsburgs to gain and hold their new southeast European domains had it not been for the greater menace posed to these Christian lands by Ottoman expansion. Thus, the Habsburg Empire came into being as a defensive force. The peoples of southeast Europe opted for it reluctantly as the lesser of two evils.

Under these conditions attitudes toward the Habsburg Empire were very ambivalent, especially among the Hungarians who now had the Habsburg monarch holding the crown of the formerly great kingdom of Hungary. As Habsburg absolutism deepened during the seventeenth century, the Hungarian magnates, resentful of the blatant royal disregard for the Hungarian constitution, customs, and privileges, even entertained the idea of switching their allegiance to the Ottomans. Religious conflicts between the Catholic Habsburgs and a largely Protestant Hungary contributed to the outbreak of periodic uprisings which encompassed the peasantry against the Habsburgs during the seventeenth century. But repeatedly it was the national sentiment that the aristocratic leaders of successive rebellions against the Habsburgs trumpeted. Istaván Bocskai, the leader of the 1604 insurrection, reached out to the peasants as the main potential source of troops. As his manifesto stated: "It should be demanded that every man who loves his country and fatherland stand up for his nation and hasten against our common enemy." The captains of the peasant armed bands (*haiduk*) who joined Bocskai issued similar manifestos: "We owe it to our dear country and nation ... to rise all together and live or die together."[121] The historian who cites this concludes:

> *The examples could be multiplied, but suffice these two to demonstrate that in the minds of the age, or at least the authors, there was a common fatherland of aristocrats, nobles, townsmen and* haiduk, *they were members of the*

> *same nation, and this solidarity obliged them to take up arms*
> *against the enemies of the people and the country. The*
> *Hungarian nobility had been promulgating the concept of*
> patria *and the concomitant duty of defense to all inhabitants*
> *of the country, regardless of their status, since the fifteenth*
> *century [when Hungary first faced the Ottoman threat to its*
> *survival. AG].*[122]

This is significant because in Hungary, nearly as much as in Poland, the nobility's power was supreme, and many scholars believe that it conceived the nation as its exclusive preserve.

The above was anything but an isolated episode or sentiment. Consider the proclamation of the leader of the nobles' opposition ring, István Petróczy, later in the century (1673). Its deeply emotional tone would have been readily recognized by any nineteenth-century nationalist:

> *Our eyes are full of tears when watching the sorrowful*
> *nightfall of our decaying dear fatherland and nation . . .*
> *Oh, Hungary! Hungary! Your empire comprised twelve*
> *countries . . . now you can mourn for twelve lost possessions,*
> *and you are driven back to only certain parts even of the*
> *twelfth . . . Understand, true Hungarians, make yourselves*
> *believe that the Germans hate the whole Hungarian nation* sine
> discretione religionis *[without any religious distinction] . . .*
>
> *The archbishops and the prelates have been deprived of their*
> *property, the chamberlains – although left in their offices –*
> *have become subservient to the Germans . . . In the frontier*
> *castles the Hungarians get neither payment, nor respect . . .*
> *The Germans use every means they can to get hold of,*
> *unheard of . . . [new kinds of taxes] to put the poor*
> *Hungarian nation's body and soul on the butcher's block*
> *and cut it into pieces . . . If, therefore, there is any Hungarian*
> *sensitivity, or any drop of Hungarian blood in you, my*
> *beloved nation, wake up, and love your brethren.*[123]

As another modern historian, who cites this document, points out, the proclamation made a conscious effort to appeal to all classes, including the peasants: it "opposed the new German taxes, this being the most serious grievance of the serfs. As the sources testify, that passage did not fail to arouse the sympathy of the peasantry."[124] The proclamation and similar texts repeatedly use the phrases "good Hungarians," "real Hungarian," "true Hungarian blood," "the stir of Hungarian blood," whereas the Germans were regularly referred to as the "alien nation." Such phrases "show unmistakably that it was the consciousness of ethnic unity that played the greater role in the national consciousness of the day."[125] As this historian concludes:

> *There is only a seeming contradiction in that this ideology, with its socially undifferentiated ethnic character, originated among the rank of the nobility ... in my opinion, there is an inevitable relationship between the two. In a situation in which the ruling class was in need of sympathy and support from the masses in its struggle with absolutism, national ideology was manipulated to be attractive and mobilizing.*[126]

Indeed, as we have repeatedly seen, in times of national emergency the elites did not hesitate to appeal to and arouse the masses' latent national sentiments, even if their socioeconomic interests differed and the nobles' token willingness to take up the peasants' cause scarcely survived the time of emergency. In summary:

> *Under the dual oppression of the country, Hungarian national consciousness in the sixteenth and seventeenth centuries in general, and in the late seventeenth century in particular, took on highly emphatic forms and penetrated deeply into the ranks of the unprivileged masses, as a defensive ideology.*[127]

In view of all the above, it is not surprising that as the Ottoman threat receded, the Ottoman Empire was rolled back, and Hungarian territory was liberated from the end of the seventeenth century onward, Hungarian unrest grew. When Ferenc II Rákóczi led a war of independence against the Habsburgs (1703–1711) he also appealed to "All true Hungarian patriots, all laymen and clergy, noble or commoner, armiger or untitled, who seek the former glorious liberty of our dear country."[128] Despite the deep misgivings of the Hungarian aristocracy, he followed words with deeds, exempting serfs who joined the rebellion from feudal duties. The result was one of the greatest popular guerrilla wars of the early modern period. It was, as yet another modern historian puts it, "a broadly based, national rebellion ... Though it is not fashionable to speak of 'national' feeling in Europe before 1789, the xenophobic reaction brewing before the Kuruc War was stocked with many of the same ingredients as the modern world's national and colonial wars of liberation."[129] The pronounced national character of the rebellion is heightened by the fact that the Serb, Croat, German, and Romanian populations in the kingdom of Hungary remained out of it.[130] Another scholar concludes: "As the struggle evolved, national unity emerged of a degree unprecedented in Europe outside Revolutionary France. Political and economic considerations played a great role in the war, but the fight for national independence was the predominant factor after the nobility joined in."[131]

The rebellion ultimately failed and Hungary was kept within the empire by a combination of coercion and cooptation. Under constant pressure, its status in the empire was progressively equaled with that of the German element. During the War of the Austrian Succession (1740–1745) it was Empress Maria Theresa's appeal to the Hungarian diat and the response of the Hungarian nobility that took up her cause that saved her crown. Thereafter the incorporation of the Hungarian nobility into the Vienna court and assimilation into German culture increased. There was a division of spoils whereby German landlords dominated the Czech and various other Slav countryside, while Hungarian landlords did the same in Slovakia, Transylvania, and much of Croatia. The nineteenth century brought widespread bourgeois nationalism and a recognition of Hungarian as the exclusive official language in all the lands of the crown of Hungary. However, the restructuring of the Habsburg Empire as the Dual Monarchy of Austro-Hungary in 1867 was only the final step in a process that had begun long before the Age of Nationalism. Once the Ottoman threat subsided, the Habsburg Empire could survive only by basing itself on the dominant joint power of two imperial peoples, the Germans and the Hungarians. Ethnonational realities and ethnonational power relations, rather than dynastic, absolutist, and aristocratic factors alone, underpinned the Habsburg Empire from the very beginning.

We shall return to discuss some of these issues in the concluding theoretical part of this chapter, after rounding up our clockwise survey of Europe with the southwest.

States, geography, and national consolidation in Romance southwest Europe

The Italian and Iberian peninsulas and Gaul were the most thoroughly Romanized provinces of the Roman Empire in terms of language and culture. The barbarian invaders into these territories invariably adopted both the *lingua romana* and Christianity, and eventually merged with the locals to form common identities. However, the political break up of the Western Roman Empire resulted in linguistic–cultural fragmentation, with a great number of increasingly differentiated Romance languages and dialects evolving within a few centuries.[132] In each of the above territories developments followed a different course. Yet in all of them the relationship between ethnic and political formations was a very close one, and in all of them geographical configuration played a major, though not an exclusive, role. In the first place, the much abused concept of "natural frontiers" helps to explain why, divided by high mountain ridges and seas, this Romance-speaking space broke into three distinct political–cultural blocs, despite countless invasions, interventions, and cultural influences among them.

The Italian peninsula remained politically divided until the nineteenth century. Dominance by the Frankish and later German emperors is an often cited cause. So is the role of the popes who, as Machiavelli complained, being unable to unify Italy themselves, prevented anybody else from doing so. The stupendous wealth and splendor of the leading Italian city-states during the late Middle Ages and Renaissance also strengthened their distinct identities and accentuated their rivalries. But there was a deeper, geopolitical cause behind the city-states' emergence and Italy's political fragmentation. As we have seen, the city-state was the typical form of incipient political organization in ancient Greece and Italy, Europe's most rugged peninsulas. This course of development was in contrast to the formative national states that emerged everywhere in the more open north.***

*** Again, peninsular and rugged Norway was too sparsely populated and devoid of a habitable inland territory for a significant city-state system to emerge.

Medieval Greece remained within the fold of empire, first the Byzantine and then the Ottoman. But in the Italian peninsula after the Roman Empire had gone the rugged landscape again proved most conducive to the rise of smaller polities which were able to assert their independence and cultivate a distinct identity. This recurring rise of the city-state in the very same theater was far from being a pure coincidence.

We have seen in Chapter 4 that city-state systems were not unrelated to ethnic realities. Political cooperation among the people of each local polity was underpinned by their sense of being a kin–culture community. Furthermore, with political multiplicity came linguistic diversification. A large number of distinct and often mutually unintelligible local dialects, in effect separate languages, emerged throughout the Italian peninsula. Local and regional identities dominated the political scene. At the same time, there is no reason to doubt Machiavelli's earlier cited testimony that a pan-Italian identity also existed.[133] As always, this was stimulated by a perceived foreign threat, be it German, French, or Spanish. Moreover, even though there was no unified Italian state, as in France, the dialect of Florence was adopted throughout the peninsula during the Renaissance as the literary Italian standard, both reflecting and reinforcing a distinct Italian identity. In foreign countries, too, people from Italy were regarded as Italians in more than a geographical sense. Obviously, it is not at all necessary for my argument that a pan-Italian identity existed; nothing prescribes that a single ethnopolitical identity should prevail throughout the geographical concept Italy. Yet the simple historical fact is that, secondary and ineffectual as they were, some supraregional Italian identity and sentiment did exist.

The Iberian peninsula became politically both more unified and more divided along ethnonational lines than Italy. During the second half of the first millennium the Germanic invasions were followed by the Moorish-Muslim conquest of most of the peninsula and the reemergence of a number of Christian polities in the north. A plurality of Romance dialects developing into several separate languages, together with distinct identities, increasingly evolved in these polities. They included from west to east: Galician-Portuguese, Leónese, Castilian, Aragonese, Catalan, and the non-Romance, non-Indo-European Basque. Although the emergent Christian-Hispanic states often fought each other, the cleavage between them and the Moors of *Al Andalus* was far more salient. It fueled the centuries-long *Reconquista*, which ended with the fall of the last Moorish state,

Granada, in 1492. The most conspicuous "Others," the Jews and the Moriscos, were expelled from Iberia, for religious reasons to be sure, as well as for economic reasons in the case of the Jews, but also because they were perceived as being ethnically alien. The concept of *limpieza de sangre*, "cleanliness of blood," was coined and codified in law even with respect to Jews and Muslims who had converted to Christianity. The racist concept of purity of blood was not invented in the late nineteenth and early twentieth centuries.

The *Reconquista* also reinforced the process of political conglomeration among the Christian kingdoms. This included the takeover of León by Castile and the union of Aragon with Catalonia, both in the eleventh to thirteenth centuries. In 1469, with the marriage of Isabella of Castile to Ferdinand of Aragon, the two crowns were united, creating the kingdom of Spain. Irrespective of whether or not violence was used in this process, and it often was, all the above cases were dynastic unions in which the separate systems of government, law, and coinage in the various principalities were guaranteed. Nonetheless, Castile was the largest and strongest component of the union and it soon dominated it. Its role in the shaping of a Spanish national identity is somewhat akin to the role of England in Britain or the United Kingdom. For centuries the expectation among both the Castilians and the English was that all the others in their respective countries would eventually become like them.

The successes and failures of Spanish integration are revealing. Long before modernity the Galician, Leónese, and Aragonese languages contracted with the spread of Castilian, which earned the status of Spanish. Absorption within a joint (Castilian-dominated) Spanish identity has been the most successful in these parts. Things went differently, however, in the west, east, and north. Portugal and Catalonia are strikingly similar in this respect despite the marked differences between them. Portugal emerged as a separate state in the eleventh to twelfth centuries from Galician-speaking provinces which opted out of Castile–León. As the kingdom expanded southward at the expense of the Moors, its language and identity became increasingly distinctive. In 1580, following a succession mayhem, Philip II of Spain took over the crown of Portugal, joining the two countries with their large overseas empires. However, in the face of a Spanish attempt to turn this dynastic union into a unified realm and raise the taxes levied in Portugal to the level of Castile, a popular national rebellion broke out in Portugal (1640), "where the union with Castile had always been abhorrent to the mass of the population."[134] The rebellion reestablished and successfully defended Portuguese independence, which as we have seen goes back almost uninterrupted close to a full millennium, to the early beginnings of statehood in Iberia. Portugal has been a national state, exhibiting a clear, non-accidental congruence of culture and statehood, from the very start.

As noted, Spain was not similarly construed, and the project of Castilian integration has never been fully completed. Most notably, the separate status of Castile and Catalonia within the Spanish realm was not merely formal. For example, it meant that Catalonians were barred from the Spanish Empire in America, which was exclusively Castilian. It also meant that Catalonians carried a lighter burden of taxation. When Spain's reforming chief minister Count-Duke of Olivares tried to thoroughly integrate the Spanish realm and level the burden of taxation among its constitutive parts, Catalonia, like Portugal, rebelled. Unlike in Castile, both the peasants and townsmen in Catalonia had long enjoyed freedoms and rights;[135] and this helped to turn the Reapers' War (1640–1652) into a popular national uprising involving both these classes and the nobility. Incidentally, the flaring up of the insurgency serves as a striking lesson to those who underestimate the traditional means of cross-country communication in premodern societies:

> It took little time for the news of trouble to spread from one village to the next, especially as it was common practice in Catalonia for villages to ring their church bells whenever help was needed. The bells were ringing in all the valleys from Sant Feliu to Tordera during the first week of May. The countryside stood armed and ready.[136]

An independent Catalan republic was declared and put itself under French protection. However, unlike in Portugal, Castilian troops conquered Catalonia, seized Barcelona (1652) and put down the rebellion. Half a century later, during the War of the Spanish Succession, Catalonia once more opposed Castile and was again defeated. After the fall of Barcelona (1714), Catalonia's autonomous constitutions and institutions were abolished and it was forcibly incorporated into Spain. The Catalan language was prohibited in the administration, universities, and later in all schools. Thus, it remained for centuries, long before Generalissimo Franco again crushed Catalan resistance and prohibited any manifestation of Catalan identity. In short, ethnonational identity and allegiances can hardly be described as politically insignificant in the premodern Spanish monarchy.

As these lines are written the question of Catalonia's future, within or outside Spain, remains open. The same applies to the Basques in the north. Far less powerful and less troublesome to Spain than the Catalans before modern times, they have retained a distinctive non-Romance, pre-Indo-European language and a distinct identity. These have survived for close to a millennium after the Basques lost the separate political existence they had exercised in the medieval kingdoms of Pamplona and Navarre.

The French paradigmatic case

It is only appropriate that we should conclude our survey of premodern European national consolidation with France. Its nation-building project has been the most successful in assimilating diverse populations with various identities and speaking a mosaic of languages and dialects. Involving many centuries of state influence mixing brute force, subtler coercion, successful cooptation, and the proverbial prestige and charm of French culture, the French case has become paradigmatic in the study of nations and nationalism. Indeed, France is the country in which the concept of the nation is supposed to have been inaugurated with the French Revolution. However, scholars who have turned the French nation-building process into a descriptive model and the French supposedly "civic" rather "ethnic" concept of nationhood into a prescriptive one have often overlooked two cardinal points: they have failed to notice that historically French national development was in some crucial ways the exception rather than the rule; and they have tended to disregard major normative aspects and implications of the French model. For these reasons the French case calls for a somewhat extended analysis.

What makes France unique is the remarkable success of the French in what other dominant nations in ethnically heterogeneous states – such as the English in the United Kingdom and the Castilians in Spain – have never fully managed to do; that is, bring all the other ethnic groups within the realm to adopt French culture and identity.

The French state has never recognized other ethnicities or nationalities in France except for French. More importantly, remarkably few such claims have been advanced by groups who in similar circumstances usually aspire to a distinct status.

Central to this historical development was the formation of a French ethnopolitical core identity in the north of France. Although there were countless partitions of the Frankish realm between multiple heirs to the throne both before and after Charlemagne, practically none of them endured, and the realm was repeatedly reunited, except for one telling instance: the division of Charlemagne's empire into the Germanic-speaking part, which would become the Roman/German Holy Empire; and the Romance-speaking part, Western Francia/France. Reflecting the linguistic division that had been well established by the ninth century, this split has survived more than 1,000 years of mighty conflicts and border alterations with remarkably minor changes. While certainly not preordained, this conspicuous stability of the linguistic split was clearly not purely accidental either.

Western Francia/France itself was a highly fragmented realm. Linguistically, there was a major geographical division between two emergent Romance languages: the *langue d'oïl* or Old French in the north and the *langue d'oc* or Occitan of the former Visigothic realm in the south. Each of these linguistic spaces was further divided among dialects and regional identities, a diversification process enhanced by West Francia's feudal fragmentation. During the tenth to twelfth centuries the later Carolingians and the Capetians who replaced them as kings of France lost authority to the provincial dukes, becoming in effect weaker than the most powerful of them. Only between the late twelfth and early fourteenth centuries did a string of French monarchs from Philip II, "Augustus", to Philip IV, "the Fair," reunify the realm under central authority. They made the kingdom of France one of Europe's most powerful and prosperous states, and elevated the status of the *langue d'oïl* dialect of the region around Paris into the prestigious language of the French state.

Again, this process, while not predetermined, relied on very tangible realities and forces. These help account for the French monarchy's success in warding off the three main challenges to the integrity of its realm: feudal fragmentation, Angevin–Norman England, and the French–Occitan divide. There were many factors, relating to socioeconomic development and to the intricate balance of power between central authority and periphery, which explain why the monarchs in the large majority of the European kingdoms succeeded in rolling back the high tide of feudal fragmentation. But one of these factors was a fundamental sense of common identity among the peoples in the various countries concerned. The popular Song of Roland, written around 1100 when feudal fragmentation was at its most extreme, emotionally celebrates the memory of "sweet France" as the fallen hero's last thought. It indicates that a popular notion of France as an entity and identity, the tradition of its being a single political realm from Roman-Frankish times and emotional attachment to it transcended the monarchy's momentary fortunes and facilitated its recovery. The ideas expressed by the abbot and historian Sugar, writing before the middle of the twelfth century, still during the nadir of French royal authority, are paraphrased as follows:

> France is "our land" ... the mother of us all, of the king and of the commoner. The land gives us life and everything associated with it. We are all born French of France, all "from the same womb," part of one and the same flesh, protected by this earth and sky. We all owe it therefore our love and support.[137]

One princely house posed a particularly hard challenge to the unity of France: the Angevins–Plantagenets, who from the reign of Henry II (1154–1189) joined through dynastic inheritance the kingdom of England and its duchy of Normandy together with the county of Anjou and duchy of Aquitaine. The territories of the so-called Angevin empire in France alone, encompassing all her western parts, were larger than the kings of France's own domains. King Philip II (1180–1223) was determined to break up the Angevin empire in France and gain control of its territories, which he succeeded in doing by the end of his reign. There were many reasons for his success, including the death of the English warrior King Richard I, "Lionheart," and his replacement by John I, "Lackland." But the leverage of his position as king of France in terms of legitimacy and power should not be underestimated, and this encompassed more than a purely dynastic element. Even if one recoils from the term national as applied to these places and times, which I do not, Philip was the *native* king of France. This fact surely did not carry all before it – other factors counted no less – but it did matter a great deal.[138] Certainly, the Plantagenets were themselves French, and their kingdom of England was ruled by a French-speaking Norman elite. Nonetheless, England was not only a separate kingdom, but also a foreign country, whose large possessions in France and threat to that country's political integrity created a problem of legitimacy that went beyond lord–vassal relations. This was so around 1200 and became even more the case with the rise and fall of the second English empire in France in the mid fourteenth to mid fifteenth centuries.

Before turning to this episode and the Hundred Years War, we need to look at the third potential challenge to the unity of the French realm, the north–south linguistic–cultural split between French in the north and Occitan in the south. In the eleventh and twelfth centuries the Mediterranean-facing south, mostly encompassed within the county of Toulouse, was as prosperous, if not more so, than the north. It experienced a cultural and literary renaissance, with written Occitan being the medium of this rich outflow. It is anybody's guess whether or not the Occitan south would have gone its own way, either outside France altogether or retaining a separate identity and an uneasy coexistence within it. This would have been similar to the position of the Catalans in relation to Spain or the Irish or Scots in Britain. In fact, Languedoc and Catalonia were close linguistically, geographically, and historically, and might have conceivably developed into one state and nation. However, it so happened that between 1209 and 1229 Languedoc was subjected to a papal-declared crusade against the Cathar–Albigensian heresy deeply entrenched in the south. This turned into a genocidal bloodbath, which decimated the population of the south, brought massive destruction on its urban centers, and inflicted a fatal blow to its independent literary culture. Initially apathetic toward the pope's urgings, Philip II soon became aware of the political opportunity, and he and his successors joined the fray to tighten royal French control over Languedoc. In a process that would continue until the twentieth century, the south would be progressively drawn into France and the French nation by much subtler and more attractive means. Nonetheless, the legacy of the gruesome events of the early thirteenth century may very well have been a historical crossroad.

To avoid misunderstanding it is important to emphasize that it was not inevitable that Languedoc would become part of the French nation. Rather, it was a prerequisite of such a process that Occitan culture, tradition, and identity would yield to the advancing French, first, mostly among the elite and, then, at the grassroots level. This is not to take any value position on whether this outcome was good or bad. This book is descriptive, not normative. It merely suggests that without such a process a separate national identity would in all probability have survived in the south.

Much the same applies to the Angevin empire. The Plantagenets could have conceivably retained their French possessions and affected a partition of France. But in the first place, this would have had to overcome the prevailing perception in France that the country was one and French. Second, in the absence of a French acculturation of England (which did not happen under the Normans) or English acculturation in Angevin France (highly unlikely) the Angevin empire would have remained multiethnic and multinational, with its French part, by virtue of its size, weight, and overseas location, far more difficult to keep within the realm in the longer run than Wales, Ireland, or Scotland. There was, third, the prospect of the French parts of the Angevin empire eventually developing into a national state or states west of France, separate from both England and France. After all, French-speaking Flanders in the north ultimately remained outside France, and Burgundy's course to independence in the east was nearly successful. The point is that populations speaking a similar native language and bordering on each other can sometimes develop within separate states and into separate nations, as the German-speaking Swiss and Austrians, among others, demonstrate. It is rarer for populations of different tongues and cultures to constitute a nation. Although both cases exist, the power of shared kin–culture attachments of solidarity and mutual cooperation, while not exclusive, has always been a highly potent force, including most emphatically in the Middle Ages.

The gravest challenge which the French state and incipient nation faced again came from England, during the Hundred Years War (1337–1453). There were a number of differences between this and the prior conflict with England, and these differences are instructive for our subject. First, the kings of England now aspired not merely to virtual independence from the French crown for their French possessions, but to the crown of France itself. In terms of medieval codes of legitimacy this made them dynastic claimants to the crown rather than rebellious vassals. As the Capetian dynasty died out without an apparent heir in 1328, the English king's claim to the throne of France on dynastic principles of family relatedness was the strongest. Still, the

French nobility responded to the inheritance crisis by electing the closest related French candidate, ushering in the new House of Valois. They twisted the legal dynastic procedure because they did not want a foreign candidate who was also the king of England.

The same principle was reasserted a century later, during the nadir of the French cause in the protracted struggle. After crushing military victories the English monarch extracted a settlement that brought him very close to realizing his ambition to the crown of France. In response, the uncrowned French dauphin and his remaining loyalists issued a manifesto (1421) elaborating the dynasty's unalienable rights. However, it went on to emphasize that the honor and crown of France belonged not only to the dynasty but "more generally to all three estates of France according to various grades and obligations."[139] This was a concept of a common will residing in all the estates of France taken together: nobility, clergy, and commoners. Existing side by side with the dynastic and social hierarchy codes of legitimacy, it was not the sole or predominant principle and was far from applying equally to all subjects of the French crown. Nonetheless, the people as the ultimate source of the ruler's authority, however nominally, was widely recognized by the later Middle Ages, *inter alia* buttressed by the authority of Roman law.[140] Formally asserted in times of national crisis, it played a major role in practice, far more central than dynastic parlance reveals. We shall return to discuss this point more generally later on.

Indeed, a major reason for the ultimate defeat of the English despite their military superiority, crushing victories, and large conquests in France was that they were *English*, that is, they were perceived as foreigners far more distinctly than they had been around 1200. Although the English elite were still largely fluent in French, there was no question about the alien national character of the English rank and file. Colette Beaune, author of the learned and much-cited *Naissance de la nation France* (1985), translated as *The Birth of an Ideology: Myths and Symbols of Nation in Late-Medieval France*, explains the success of the French propaganda of nationhood very well:

> *Any form of effective propaganda certainly has* a deep-seated link to shared sentiments, *and the success of this French propaganda has long since been demonstrated. Although the English won the Hundred Years War militarily*

in 1338–1360 and in 1415, they never won the hearts and minds of their enemy.[141]

Beaune adds:

> *The term propaganda should not be interpreted pejoratively here. Medieval governments were all too aware of how to manipulate opinion. But I have chosen to use propaganda in reference to all those projections France made of itself, whether or not they rang with truth and sincerity and whether or not people were paid to create them. In some cases these were unconscious projections, in some they were shared beliefs.* Such beliefs did more during the fourteenth and fifteenth centuries to shore up the unsteady trusses of the state than any institutions.[142]

Although the French elite was on the whole loyal to the French crown, on occasion parts of it allied with the English. The most significant case is the bloody conflict that erupted between two branches of the French royal house. As a result, the Burgundian branch allied with the English between 1419 and 1435, a development which turned the war with England simultaneously into a French civil war and marked the darkest hour for the French. Yet, while elites everywhere had interests, ambitions, and connections that were sometimes at odds with the national cause, making them "treacherous," this was far less the case with regard to popular sentiments. In the French case as well echoes from the illiterate masses, while extremely rare, are not non-existent. For example, the bloody peasant uprising against the nobility known as the *Jacquerie* (1358) was partly motivated by popular anger at the French nobility's crushing defeat at the battle of Poitiers (1356) and subsequent failure to defend the peasants. Furthermore, the bands of rampaging peasants raised the banner of and loudly expressed their allegiance to the king of France. This widely recurring phenomenon in peasant rebellions has usually been interpreted solely in socioeconomic terms, and this aspect was indeed the most significant. But the appeal to the monarch – always loftily perceived as "good" – for protection from exploitative nobility rested on the perception of him not only as the country's ruler, but also as the father of the people. Significantly, it was very common in national states, sometimes also among privileged minorities or minority peoples that found protection within a larger state from greater external threats, but hardly ever in relation to a conquering foreign ruler. This did not mean that the peasants' hopes were not regularly dashed, as monarchs joined the nobility to quash their rebellions, in France as elsewhere. And yet the widely manifested sentiments of love for and devotion to the ruler as the head of the nation family and symbol of the motherland were there. They could not be more strikingly manifested than with Jeanne d'Arc.

What was so special about Jeanne d'Arc was the fact that such a barely literate peasant and a woman was given the opportunity to stamp her mark on high politics and lift France up from its lowest point. Obviously, this otherwise quite ordinary peasant girl, about nineteen at her death, had some very remarkable personal traits. Obviously, too, it was only in a most desperate situation that she could have conceivably been given a chance. All these were very special. By contrast, there is no reason to think that the sentiments Jeanne d'Arc expressed were anything out of the ordinary among the people. They wanted the devastating ravaging of their settlements and property to cease, yet they were not indifferent to the question of how this was to be achieved. They wished to see the English gone. Unlike any other peasant, Jeanne d'Arc is clearly recorded in her own voice in the protocol and documents of her trial by the English for heresy (1431). Her letter to the king of England and his subordinates, dispatched barely two years earlier, before she set out to free Orléans, repeatedly stated: "I am sent by God, the King of the Heaven, to chase you one and all from France."[143] In her trial,

> *Asked whether God hates the English, she said she knows nothing about the love that God has for the English, nor what he will do with their souls; but she knows for certain they will be driven from France, except for those who stay and die ...* [144]

The role of religion, God, and the saints who talked to Jeanne in his name is central here. France and its monarchy had been surrounded with a Christian holy aura carefully cultivated over the centuries, ever since the baptism of Clovis and the role played by the Frankish kings as defenders of the Catholic Church and papacy. Clovis was elevated to sainthood; St. Dennis was the patron of the kingdom and monarchy; St. Michael was its defender; the Lily of France expressed Christian purity; thirteenth-century King Louis IX became another king-saint. The French king and monarchy were "the most Christian," and the French were God's second chosen people.[145] If so, however, were the sentiments expressed by Jeanne d'Arc really national or actually religious and quintessentially premodern? It should be quite obvious by now that this is an utterly false dichotomy: as a premodern phenomenon, the medieval French national sentiment, like any other, was steeped in a religious worldview and partly expressed in religious idioms. There was compatibility rather than contradiction here. Indeed, the fact that Christianity is supposed to be universal only accentuates the point, as Beaune again perceptively points out:

> *Nations are particularistic; Christianity is universal. One might have expected that Christianity itself would have tempered the growth of nationalism. But this did not happen. Most European nations in the Middle Ages had little difficulty projecting their sense of nationhood in religious terms. This was especially true with France, which emerged into nationhood particularly early.*[146]

Moreover, the central role of religion explains the mystery of how the sense of nationhood spread out in the countryside. What we have already seen in other premodern national states also holds true for France. All such states were sustained by the most powerful propaganda organ of the times: the dense network of parishes planted in the countryside, reaching the most remote villages, and served in a perpetual cycle of rite and sermon by the lower clergy. Like the high nobility, the higher echelons of the priesthood had various interests and calculations, which in the case of Christianity in particular could on some occasions cut across national boundaries. But the lower clergy, close to the people in background and at the same time linked to the wider world through education and Church channels of information, were as a rule the most effective popular amplifiers of the national sentiment heavily loaded with religious significance.

As Beaune wryly comments: "The origins of the Nation is a subject that has blessed us with much theorizing but little information."[147] Indeed, in contrast to modernist theorists who have made little effort to test their concepts against the realities of premodern times, historians of late medieval France tend to have few doubts about the crystallization of French national consciousness in that period. This includes not only nineteenth- and early-twentieth-century nationalist historians, but also recent historians, schooled in critical skepticism toward the excesses of the nation and nationalist ideology. For example, leading historian Emmanuel Le Roy Ladurie, famous for his studies of the French rural community, has no hesitation in pointing out the widespread existence of French national consciousness in the late Middle Ages and early modern period: "Consciousness of the state, as well as of national identity, was becoming widespread, both in the elites of the French kingdom and (to some extent) among the people in general, including the rural population."[148] His book chapter "National Identity" is in total agreement with Beaune. Although national sentiments were more evident among the elite and middle classes, Ladurie draws attention to "the anti-English resistance in Normandy at the end of the Hundred Years War; it is clear from their actions that many villagers displayed 'national' sentiments at this period."[149] Indeed, in view of the scarcity of written evidence, it is the *actions* of the peasants that constitute our main sources of evidence for their attitudes.

Beaune's study concludes:

> What was the France of the late Middle Ages? What were the sources of the "incomprehensible and natural love" its inhabitants held for it? It was the awareness its people had of being a particular human community, unique in its origins and history, a people who imagined themselves linked to this specific valued land for all time. Its difference was imagined to be superiority, for it was willingly xenophobic. In order to see itself as good, it had to project an evil outside itself. The English played this role. French national sentiment was both ethnic and territorial; it rose from a conjunction of a given people and a given countryside.[150]

The use of the term the French nation was rare before the late fifteenth century. The Latin *patria* had been used since the end of the twelfth century, and its French form *patrie* was introduced in the mid sixteenth century. People mostly referred to France, the kingdom, or the country, as in *amour du pays*, love for one's country.[151] Yet all these essentially meant the same thing. Identification with, allegiance to, and love for one's country, patriotism on a country scale that reached down to the grassroots, have no different meaning other than a sense of national belonging and solidarity.

Certainly, the fact that a very distinct and deep-rooted French national identity had come into being by the late Middle Ages does not mean that it has not gone through constant historical transformations, some of them truly massive, in response to changing circumstances. Orest Ranum's edited volume *National Consciousness, History and Political Culture in Early-Modern Europe* (1975), a title which appears as an oxymoron in the wake of the modernist surge of the 1980s, brought together some of the leading historians of the time. William Church wrote the chapter on France, and his summary of the changes of perception during the early modern period could not be improved upon. He indicates that French identity was in some aspects more broadly based in the sixteenth than in the seventeenth century:

> *A survey of the relationship between the French monarchy and patriotic sentiment demonstrates that the latter fluctuated significantly according to the fortunes, policies, and repute of the monarchy itself. During the sixteenth century, French patriotism assumed the form of a broadly based idealization of many elements of the life of the nation, the monarchy included. But in the seventeenth century, as part of the massive swing towards absolutism, this sentiment was more and more centered in the crown, even in the person of the king. With the triumph of absolutism, both in theory and in fact, it was in the nature of things that the sovereign should symbolize the nation and become the focal point of patriotic sentiment. In the years of Louis XIV's reign, however, a revulsion began to be expressed toward the equation of patriotism with loyalty to the Bourbon dynasty, and the way was opened for the much more comprehensive views of the Enlightenment which grounded patriotism in the life of the people and eventually led to the massive, virile nationalism of the French Revolution.*[152]

Given historical change, some of it revolutionary, it is not surprising that historians of different periods have tended to trace the emergence of French national identity to their own particular period of study. This has been a recurring phenomenon in the historiography, already evident among an older generation of historians, who nonetheless agreed that French national sentiment had gone back a very long way: did this sentiment

> *exist all through the middle ages, as claimed by J. Huizinga? Did it originate only at the end of the Hundred Years War, in the second half of the fifteenth century, as suggested by H. Hauser? Or was it only later still, in the sixteenth century, that it can be unmistakably be recognized as such, as is the view of F. Chabod?*[153]

The same ambivalence prevails among more recent historians. We have already seen the medievalists' tracing of French national identity to the Middle Ages. In her book on national consciousness in France during the Wars of Religion (1559–1598), Myriam Yardeni emphatically identifies this consciousness as "a major and independent phenomenon" based on four pillars: the monarch and monarchy; the country and the people; the French language; and a sense of a common French history.[154] In his *The Cult of the Nation in France: Inventing Nationalism 1680–1800* (2001), David Bell richly documents how French national identity was "constructed" in various sectors of French society during the ages of absolutism and Enlightenment. But then, the birth of the nation is widely identified with the French Revolution and its introduction of popular sovereignty. And then again, it is almost as generally accepted that peasants turned into Frenchmen, as in the title of Eugen Weber's superb book, only in the late nineteenth century.[155] Only that late did the school and the railway reach the depths of the French countryside, while peasants moved to the cities. As a result, the French language, still not spoken by the majority of the French people during the Revolution, became standard. Thus, was the French nation inaugurated during the late nineteenth century or in the Revolution? Or perhaps earlier? Can all these seemingly contradictory positions be right?

Quite obviously they are. This does not mean that French national identity is a constant, "essentialist" reality. It simply means that a very distinct identity, which had become entrenched by the late Middle Ages, continued to evolve and expand. Far from bringing the

French nation into being, the French Revolution's concept of popular sovereignty invested this nation's source of legitimacy in the people rather than in the monarch. That this, as well as the equality of all people before the law, enhanced the popular sense of participation in France and contributed to the Revolution's ability to mobilize the masses for military service is undisputed. Similarly, the rise of mass urban society and leveling of local differences from the late nineteenth century further solidified French national identity. Among other things, it completed the amalgamation of the originally non-French speaking elements in France within the French nation. This applied to the distinction between French and Occitan, and the many significantly different spoken dialects of each. The Gascons, for example, in the southwest of France, England's allies during the Hundred Years War, were incorporated into the French nation only in the early modern period and increasingly adopted the French language in lieu of their own during the twentieth century. The Celtic-speaking Bretons, German-speaking Alsatians, the Basques, and the Flemish underwent similar processes.

As stated at the outset, France has been unique in its success in completely incorporating into French national identity what in other countries would have been considered distinct ethnonational identities. Although both the United Kingdom and Spain have succeeded in creating supra, British and Spanish, national identities, there remain within both of them other, distinct, and in many ways stronger national identities and, as a result, considerable tensions and an ever-looming prospect of secession. The actions of the French state and the prestige and charms of French culture were responsible for the highly unusual fact that all the potentially distinct communities of identity within France accepted their incorporation into French culture and the French nation. The German-speaking people of Alsace, annexed to France in the wars of Louis XIV, are a well-known example of that success. Ceded to the new German Reich after the French defeat in 1871, they protested and professed their undying love for and devotion to France. They continued to resist their incorporation into Germany until their return to France after the First World War. It was in view of this rather unusual phenomenon that Ernest Renan articulated his concept of the nation as an act of volition.[156] In today's France only in one region, Corsica, do sentiments of separate identity and aspirations to independence exist.

Large, successful, and confident national cultures that exercise hegemonic influence genuinely tend to perceive their culture in universalistic terms. This has been pointed out with respect to the English in the United Kingdom and, formerly, the empire and, indeed, the world.[157] It equally applied to France, and all the more so to French culture within France. France is often credited with a "civic" as opposed to an "ethnic" concept of the nation. This is true only as far as "ethnic" is defined by descent alone. Far from being limited to the acceptance of common civic institutions of government and law, joining the family nation in France explicitly means the forsaking of not only any other national identity, but also any different cultural identity, and complete assimilation into French culture.[158] As France has been so successful in this process, its reality has been elevated to the status of a desired model. However, those who prescribe this "civic" model to others, especially in ethnically heterogeneous, nationally unformed parts of the world, tend to forget what this model actually involved in France: the eradication of all other cultures within the state except for the dominant culture by means of massive state action. This process is unlikely to be pretty. Indeed, whoever attempts to carry it out nowadays generally attracts the sharpest condemnation on normative grounds as being profoundly oppressive. Furthermore, nor in the vast majority of cases is such an effort likely to be as successful as it has been in France. This is where Karl Deutsch's nation-building as state-building concept, largely based on the French paradigm, has been so misleading.[159] Whether or not multiethnic nations which retain their cultural heterogeneity can be formed in countries – some old and many new – that lack a clearly dominant ethnic core or *Staatsvolk* is another question. There are precious few such cases, and France is certainly not one of them.

Needless to say, France itself is now facing a challenge that has little parallel in its recent history: large immigrant communities from Arab-Muslim North Africa which prove resistant to assimilation into French culture and forsake neither their native identity nor their culture. Whether or not they eventually will do so, or force changes on the French concept of nationhood and citizenship, only the future will tell. We shall return to this subject in the following chapters.

C WAS THE PREMODERN EUROPEAN NATION IMPOSSIBLE DUE TO RELIGION, EMPIRE, DYNASTIC RULE, INEQUALITY, AND DIALECT FRAGMENTATION?

Following our survey of states, ethnicity, and national states in premodern Europe, a more general theoretical conclusion looking into some of the major issues involved is in order. As we have seen, national states, building on *and*, in turn, homogenizing existing ethnic formations, emerged throughout the continent close on the heels of the process of state consolidation itself. Indeed, the national state was the dominant form of state consolidation, albeit not the exclusive one, as some ethne remained divided among a multiplicity of petty-states, while in other cases national states expanded their rule over other ethne and peoples to create empires. It was only natural that primary state consolidation tended to coincide with ethnic realities and give rise to incipient national states. Simply put, it was immeasurably easier to create and sustain a state where bonds and affinities of a common culture and a collective sense of shared kinship existed and could be potently invoked and harnessed. Furthermore, antagonistic tribal populations of close ethnicity often gained their sense of common identity and crystallized into nascent nations and states only as a result of the challenge and pressure from foreign neighbors, who sometimes even gave them their communal names.

In all this Europe was no different from other parts of the world. Indeed, in Europe as elsewhere the national state was almost as old as the state itself. The reason why even the traditionalist discourse on the national phenomenon largely begins with medieval times, that is, late in universal history, is that Europe north of the old Roman frontier only entered the fold of civilization and saw the rise of states at that relatively late stage in history. The Eurocentric perspective on the world creates a highly misleading optical illusion, because European civilization, states, and nations were *all* late arrivals in terms of universal history. As we have seen in Chapter 4, in other parts of the world states and with them national states had emerged millennia earlier.

Europe differed from some other parts of the world only in that its geopolitical contours were more favorable to the consolidation and *survival* of the middle-size, national state. A partial exception to this pattern of survival was central-eastern Europe, where a process of empire-building was well advanced by the early modern period, swallowing up earlier national states that had emerged throughout that space in medieval times. Thus, contrary to accepted wisdom, the national state as a primary form of incipient state consolidation was a stronger reality in earlier times than during (early) modernity, at least in central-eastern Europe.

All this has been ignored by modernists, who have scarcely tested their abstract schema of historical evolution against the actual experience of premodern times. Yet the above developments are affirmed by the overwhelming majority of historians of the societies concerned who have applied themselves to this question. I refer not to nationalist historians of earlier generations, but to more recent historians of our liberal and skeptical age who have become aware of the modernist thesis and have responded to it. Obviously, their first-hand knowledge of the subject is of paramount significance for deciding the issue, especially as they have no special stake in the question one way or the other. Like all historians, they stress the need to understand their chosen period and society in their own particular terms. They rightly point out the great differences between premodern and modern forms of nationhood and nationalism. Still, as we have seen, the overwhelming majority of these historians do not hesitate to intentionally speak of national identities, national affinities, and national states as a salient element of the medieval and early modern world. This is evident in the first-rate collections of studies by leading historians cited above, including Ranum, *National Consciousness, History and Political Culture in Early-Modern Europe* (1975),[160] Forde, Johnson, and Murray, *Concepts of National Identity in the Middle Ages* (1995), and Scales and Zimmer, *Power and the Nation in European History* (2005). As the editors of the last of these, a superb volume derived from a conference dedicated to the subject, have stressed: "A deep rift still separates 'modernist' perspectives, which view the political nation as a phenomenon limited to modern societies, from the view of scholars concerned with the pre-industrial world who insist, often vehemently, that nations were central to pre-modern national life also."[161] Needless to say, the authority of the two sides in this matter on the societies in question is not the same. Scales and Zimmer have gone on to note that the debate "often resembled a dialogue of the deaf," while concluding, perhaps too optimistically, that the conference produced a modest change among some modernists.[162]

The evidence for premodern national realities comes from the premodern sources themselves. Throughout this chapter we have repeatedly cited the prominent uses of the concept of the nation in highly relevant contexts in the contemporary texts, both in the Latin forms *gens* and *natio/nacio* and in their vernacular derivatives. In the order of their appearance in this chapter, these references include: Bede's *gens anglorum* in the seventh century; the Scottish official plea to the pope in the Declaration of Arbroath (1320), asserting the right of the *Scottorum nacio* to independence from England, based on separate descent and a separate history of self-government; Saxo Grammaticus' thirteenth-century Danes, who like all "nations [*nationes*] are in the habit of vaunting the fame of their achievements, and joy in recollecting their ancestors"; the German *Nation* in the official title of the Reich and in Luther's address in the early sixteenth century; the prominence of the Czech *gens* in a pronouncedly ethnonational sense in the extensive fifteenth-century Hussite written records, accentuated to remove any doubt by the synonymous use of *lingua* so as to distinguish between Czech and German inhabitants of Bohemia and Moravia; the Polish fifteenth- and sixteenth-centuries definition of the nation in comprehensive cultural terms, encompassing all speakers of the common language; Helmold's twelfth-century account of the "many nations [*naciones*]" around the Baltic, "the Danes and the Swedes," to the north and "the Slavic nations [*naciones*]" to the south; the Serb nation (*natio*) of *The Royal Frankish Annals* for the year 822; and the fervent rhetoric of a Hungarian ethnic nation (*natio*) in the seventeenth century. While this is only a small sample of citations, the context, meaning, and significance of the concept of the nation in all these cases is abundantly clear.

This should be sufficient to finally discard the strange quirk in the literature on the national phenomenon: the notion that the word nation itself is a new one and that its earlier Latin-medieval forms actually meant something different. It has been claimed and widely accepted among non-medievalists that *natio* in the Middle Ages referred to little more than students' subdivisions according to their various countries of origin, most notably at the University of Paris.[163] Obviously, concepts can change meaning and assume new significance over time; there is nothing fixed about terminology. However, in the main this hardly happens to be the case with the concept of *natio*. This fact has recently been pointed out by Susan Reynolds, the medievalist historian who has long challenged the modernist thesis, and not only in specific cases as historians of premodern societies have often done with respect to the particular society they study. As she writes:

> *There is no foundation at all for the belief, common among students of modern nationalism, that the word* natio *was seldom used in the Middle Ages except to describe the* nationes *into which university students were divided. It was used much more widely than that, and often as a synonym for* gens ... *Like a* gens *or* natio, *a* populus *was thought of as a community of custom, descent, and government – a people.*[164]

> *In the nineteenth century, as in the middle ages, the groups which medieval writers called* gentes, nationes, *or* populi *were actually thought of as units of common biological descent ... as well as of common culture.*[165]

Medieval historian Julia Smith basically writes the same thing:

> *central to Latin and the various local languages of the early Middle Ages were words that denoted in undifferentiated fashion a group whose members shared one or more of the following: putative descent from a common ancestor; common cultural attributes; organization into a single polity ... Writing between 906 and 913, Regino of Prüm echoed a millennium-long tradition and encapsulated the assumptions inherent in this vocabulary when he declared: "the various nations and peoples are distinguished from each other by descent, customs, language and laws."*[166]

There is nothing new in any of this. Towering medieval historian Johan Huizinga made the same point as far back as 1940:

> *The word* natio *has always remained much more current than* patria. *Actually it had changed very little in connotation since classical times. Closely linked with* natus

and natura, *it vaguely indicated a larger context than* gens
or populus, *but without being any fixed distinction between
the three terms. The Vulgate used* gentes, populos, *and*
nationes *interchangeably for the nations of the Old
Testament, and that biblical usage determined the
significance of* natio *for the time being.*[167]

Huizinga adds:

> *Gradually, over a period of a good six centuries, Latin
> Christendom arranged itself in a number of kingdoms
> corresponding, though still very roughly, to national lines ...
> France, England, and Scotland, the three Scandinavian
> kingdoms, Aragon, Castile, and Portugal, Sicily, Hungary,
> and Poland had all of them taken their places as units of
> Latin Christendom by around 1150.*[168]

Nor, incidentally, did Huizinga have any doubt as to the deeper roots of
all these sentiments: a "primitive instinct in human society."[169]

Finally, the fact that the Latin *gens* and *natio* as near synonyms
go back to Roman times and have barely changed their meaning is
elucidated in an unmatched scholarly summary in David Althoen's
superb article on early modern Polish national identity. It merits quotation at some length:

> *Ever since the two terms [*gens, natio*] began to take on the
> general meaning of "nation" during Romans times, they
> have been almost identical in meaning. The origins of the
> terms help clarify the early subtle difference in their
> meanings. The term "gens", for example, originally meant
> "clan", but soon expanded to include such meanings as
> "family", "descendants", and also "race", "nation", and
> "people". During the height of the Roman empire, the term
> "gens" was mainly used in the plural in its meaning of
> "nations" or "peoples" and primarily signified any foreign
> peoples – in opposition to the* populus Romanus. *The term
> "natio" had similar origins. In the very early Roman period
> it meant "birth", and in the common language it came to
> mean "litter" when referring to a brood of animals born to*

the same mother. It was in this sense that it expanded to its meaning close to "nation", signifying those individuals born in the same place with a common ancestor. By the 1st century AD the meaning of "natio" had become very similar to that of "gens". In the language of the Roman Church the term "nationes" served, as did "gentes" to translate "the pagan nations", in opposition to the "people of God" ... By the 8th century Isidor of Seville's influential "Etymology" was claiming that "natio" and "gens" were synonyms. This merging of meaning continued well into the early modern period ...

An examination of the subtle differences between "gens" and "natio" shows that "natio" carried the more narrow, restrictive meaning – closer to the meaning of "tribe". "Natio" referred to a nation or people who trace their descent to one ancestor, and who lived on the land where their mythological origins began, while "gens" referred to the larger sense of "people" or "nation" – independent of homeland or common ancestor ... Tacitus spoke of all the Germans as one "gens", and then broke them up into their various nati] nationes, and Cicero chose the term "natio" when emphasizing common descent ...

By no means, however, did all writers understand such a difference or consistently maintained clarity in their terminology ... Moreover, there was no hierarchy understood when the terms "natio" and "gens" were used together; rather, the terms were usually used together for the rhetorical effect.[170]

Clearly, the medieval references cited in this chapter tally perfectly with these general observations.

The most amazing medieval document I have come across relating to the question of the nation – scarcely noted in the modern debate – is the deliberations on the national question in the ecclesiastic Council of Constance (1416). The Catholic Church's ecumenical councils supposedly embodied the indivisible unity of the Church. But in practice they introduced representation by nations and national bloc voting from the thirteenth century on, as the European national kingdoms increasingly took shape. At the Council of Vienne (1311–1312), there was a separate vote by the following "nations": Italians, Spaniards, Germans, Danes, English, Scots, Irish, and French. At the Council of Pisa (1409), aiming to end the great schism, the weight of the great powers increased. Representation and voting clustered around the delegations from Italy, France, Germany, and England (the Spaniards were absent). This arrangement was carried onto and formally adopted a few years later, at the beginning of the deliberations at the Council of Constance (1415). Hungarians, Czechs, Poles, Danes, and Swedes were included in the German "nation"; the Mediterranean periphery (except Spain which joined later) in the Italian "nation"; the French periphery in the French "nation"; and the British Isles in the English "nation". Soon, however, claims for separate representation for the smaller nations were made on the basis of language and sovereignty.

Unsurprisingly, the realities of power politics helped to determine which claim was accorded recognition. The Hungarian claim was not heeded, but that of the Aragonese, who refused to be included in a joint Spanish delegation, was championed by the French as a weapon against the English mandate. With England and France entering the most bitter phase of the Hundred Years War, the head of the French delegation argued that England, by virtue of its smaller population and territory compared with the others, should not be treated as a "general nation" encompassing the British Isles and periphery. Instead, it should be included in the German nation, in accordance with an old ecclesiastical administrative division. Alternatively, if the principle of individual national representation was universally applied, all the other claims by European nations should be accepted. In that case, the English delegation itself should be divided into its constitutive national parts, including the Scots, Welsh, and Irish, all of which were barely represented in, but were claimed to be represented by, the English delegation.[171]

Predictably, the English delegation defended the opposite position: that England constituted not only a separate "nation," but, indeed, a general one that encompassed all its periphery. In the process of what looks like a strikingly modern debate on nations and national representation in the most general council of medieval Europe, seemingly most modern definitions of what constituted a nation were put forward by the delegations. According to the English delegation, England satisfied all the characteristics of a nation,

*whether nation (*natio*) be understood as a people (*gens*)
marked off from others by blood relationship and habit of
unity or by peculiarities of language, the most sure and
positive sign and essence of a nation (*natio*) is divine and
human law ... or whether nation (*natio*) be understood, as it
should be, as a territory equal to that of the French nation
(*natio*).[172]*

Furthermore, the English delegation put forward as a general truism a
seemingly strikingly modern concept of the nation as transcending the
boundaries of dynastic rule:

*Everyone knows that it matters not whether a nation obeys
one prince only or several. Are there not many kingdoms in
the Spanish nation that pay no tribute to the king of Castile,
the chief ruler of Spain? But it does not follow that they are
not parts of the Spanish nation. Are not Provence,
Dauphiny, Savoy, Burgundy, Lorraine, and many other
regions that have nothing to do with our adversary of France
included nevertheless in the French or Gallican nation?[173]*

It is difficult to imagine more impressive evidence for the
national question in medieval Europe. Here were delegations from
all over the Continent struggling for recognition of their independent national status, voting in national blocs of interest and debating
the meaning of the national concept. In this debate they invoked
blood relations, language, common customs, and shared history, on
the one hand, as well as territory, systems of government. and law
and voluntary participation, on the other. The English delegation
even insisted that: "Nations in a general council should be considered equals and each should have the same rights."[174] Compare
the Council of Constance's musing over alternative concepts of the
nation with the remarkably similar Recommendation by the Parliamentary Assembly of the Council of Europe regarding "The Concept of the Nation" (2006):

*The Assembly has acknowledged that in some Council of
Europe member states, the concept of "nation" is used to
indicate citizenship, which is a legal link (relation) between a*

*state and an individual, irrespective of the latter's ethno-
cultural origins, while in some other member states the same
term is used in order to indicate an organic community
speaking a certain language and characterized by a set of
similar cultural and historical traditions, by similar
perceptions of its past, similar aspiration for its present and
similar visions of its future.*[†††]

Quite obviously, the claim that the concept of the nation was unknown, unimportant, or devoid of political significance to the people of premodern, indeed, medieval Europe is one of the greatest missteps taken by modern social theory. This does not imply an opposite simplistic error. The world of the ecclesiastic Council of Constance was very different from that of the twenty-first-century Council of Europe. We shall now proceed to examine several major features of premodern society which have been widely claimed to make the nation impossible and seek to establish more closely what their true interrelationship with the national phenomenon actually was. These features include: religion, empire, the dynastic principle, sociopolitical inequality, and dialect fragmentation.

Religion and the nation

The debate on the nation in the Council of Constance is a good reason to begin with the factor of religion. Religion is claimed to have been the principal form of broader common identity and attachment in pre-modern societies. In the case of universal religions in particular, such as Christianity and Islam, religion has been widely regarded as directly competing with and impeding the growth of particular national iden-tities. There is some truth to these claims. In addition to its powerful promise of deliverance and salvation, religion confers on its believers a sense of spiritual brotherhood somewhat akin to biological kinship.

[†††] Recommendation 1735 (2006), "The Concept of the 'Nation,'" Parliamentary Assembly, Council of Europe at http://assembly.coe.int/main.asp?Link=/documents/adoptedtext/ta06/erec1735.htm. It does not matter here if there is an actual basis in reality to the concept of the nation as synonymous with citizenship without reference to a common culture and sense of collective belonging.

It also constitutes a major, though seldom the chief, element of a shared culture that serves as a basis for mutual cooperation. In the case of universal religions, both the sense of brotherhood and shared culture far transcend national boundaries. This, however, is only one side of the relationship between religion and the nation. As we have seen on many occasions throughout this chapter, religion, even an ostensibly universal one, was as much if not more of a force for the nation and a leading element in its consolidation.

This was patently true for national religions *per se*. As we saw with respect to ancient Egypt, for example, any distinction between Egyptian religion, civilization, statehood, and national identity is entirely artificial. All of them were one and were so perceived by Egyptians who participated in the perpetual cycle of rite, ceremony, and festival, as people habitually did even in the remotest of rural communities. Indeed, religious syncretism on a country scale and temple-based propaganda were among the most powerful instruments of Egyptian state- and nation-building. Obviously, there were often tensions of various sorts, sometimes severe, between state leaders and religious authorities. But both of them purported to speak in the name of Egypt. The same was true of other national religions. Even where the same pantheon was shared by a civilization larger than its individual polities, as, for example, in ancient Mesopotamia or in the Greek-Classical world, each of these polities had its patron god, and its clergy demonstrated zealous devotion to the patriotic cause. In time of war the gods were universally enlisted in support of the native polity. More general spiritual systems like Confucianism, although profoundly Chinese, were inherently adaptable to serve any state, as Confucianism did in national states throughout east Asia. It helped to consolidate the notion of a national state community in China, Korea, Japan, and Vietnam. Buddhism, although entirely non-worldly in doctrine, had the same effect in practice in all these countries. Fashionable claims that Jews constituted a religion rather than a people during Diasporic times have no meaning at all before modernity. Alex Yakobson puts this most tellingly: as becomes immediately obvious to anybody who has ever opened the Jewish Holy Scriptures, the idea that the Jews constituted a single people – indeed, a chosen and holy one – is absolutely central to that religion.[175]

The strong connection between religion and the nation applied even to universal religions. In Christianity this was true almost irrespective of the question of whether or not a central religious authority existed. In Eastern Christianity, even before and more strongly after the fall of the Byzantium center, national churches of the Orthodox faith – Bulgarian, Serb, Greek, Russian – became a reality of the utmost ethnocultural *cum* political (together making national) significance. Notwithstanding its official doctrine, the universal faith patently expressed itself in terms of national culture (and often language), identity, and solidarity. Indeed, here as elsewhere religion served as a major instrument of state and national consolidation, with rulers and clergy cooperating in this venture. Moreover, when Greek, Bulgarian, and Serb statehood ceased to exist as a result of the Ottoman conquests, it was the national churches above all that preserved, zealously protected, and came to embody the national identity for centuries. Much the same held true outside Greek Orthodoxy, as with the Armenian national church, the oldest Christian national church, and the Georgian national church which broke away from the Armenian Church on national grounds. In both Kievan and Muscovite Russia Orthodox Christianity was a crucial element in the consolidation of Russian national identity, a reality further reinforced after the fall of Byzantium by Moscow's assumption of the role of the Third Rome. The Russian nation was most profoundly a *holy* nation. Catholic–Orthodox antagonism within the Polish–Lithuanian Commonwealth was inseparable from the formation of Ukrainian national identity. As Michael Petrovich has put it in a comprehensive and penetrating survey of religion and nationalism in eastern Europe since medieval times:

> *Most of the people of Eastern Europe achieved a sense of identity and some political expression of that identity in medieval times, long before the Age of Nationalism ... Religion in Eastern Europe served a nation-building role and it acted as a surrogate state for people who had lost political independence ... The Church has been literally militantly involved in movements for ethnic survival and wars for national independence in Eastern Europe from medieval times to the present.*[176]

The rule in all this is two-directional: in view of the strong sense of kin–culture identity, affinity, and solidarity within peoples, even a universal faith expressed itself in partisan national churches; and given the central role of religion in premodern society, premodern nationalism was profoundly and intrinsically religious. It was couched in religious idioms, as Petrovich, Connor Cruise O'Brien, Adrian Hastings, Steven Grosby, Philip Gorski, Anthony Smith, and Anthony Marx have all suggested in critique of the modernists.[177] Rather than a fundamental contradiction existing between the national and religious sources of identity, the two more often than not complemented and reinforced each other.‡‡‡ And the more central to identity religion was, the more an intrinsic element of culture and, therefore, of ethnicity and nationalism it was. We have already cited Colette Beaune, another prominent student of this interrelationship: "Nations are particularistic; Christianity is universal. One might have expected that Christianity itself would have tempered the growth of nationalism. But this did not happen. Most European nations in the Middle Ages had little difficulty projecting their sense of nationhood in religious terms."[178] Moreover, religion was the most potent form of a broader culture which penetrated to the grassroots level and spread out into the most remote parts of the countryside. Precisely for this reason its network of village clergy and perpetual cycle of rite and sermon were the most powerful transmitters of cross-cultural messages, which were almost invariably also national. The use of church bells as a means of intra- and intervillage communication in times of emergency is a vivid demonstration of the point. Here was the framework of the premodern "imagined

---

‡‡‡ Despite their important contributions in demonstrating this, Anthony Marx and Anthony Smith err in a similar way. Marx assumes that religion was the only widespread popular sentiment in medieval and early modern Western Europe, which functioned as the binder and primer of early nationalism. This was more true with respect to Spanish nationalism (but not Spain's particular constitutive nationalities) whose "Other" was non-Christian; but it was hardly the case with England, or even France, Marx's other main examples, or indeed most other early European national states we have surveyed. In his *Chosen Peoples*, vii–viii, 5, Anthony Smith also presents religion as the original emotional primer and source of national consciousness. However, as already pointed out in the Introduction, shared religion in and of itself has rarely trumped linguistic differences to create a common ethnic or national identity. More than creating ethnic and national communities, religion's greater effect has been in either reinforcing them, if it was shared, or sometimes undermining them, if it was not. Smith himself, of course, has played a leading role in emphasizing *The Ethnic Origins of Nations*, but has lacked an explanation for the deep roots and potency of the ethnonational sentiment, explained in Chapter 2 above.

community" which Anderson has missed completely. In fact, the nation was widely imagined – and as holy and God's chosen one. Modern nationalism is often described as a religion; but in premodern times it was thoroughly religious in a non-metaphoric way. Indeed, everywhere the network of country clergy served as chief agents of nation-building, which they continued to pursue even where the state itself collapsed.

As O'Brien, Hastings, Marx, and Beaune suggest, this was as true of the western, Catholic part of medieval Europe as it was of the Orthodox (and Catholic) east. Again, we have seen this throughout this chapter. Contrary to Breuilly's claims, the Venerable Bede cared not only about the Christianization of Britain but, indeed, about the Christianization of the *gens anglorum* and its conquest of Britain. His was a sacred *national* history. He showed absolutely no sympathy for the Christian Britons assailed and dispossessed by his own still pagan people. Similarly, the joint nation-building effort by Alfred and the clergy is widely recognized by scholars. The same applied to the Scottish struggle against subordination to England around 1300. As a historian of the period writes: "The attitude of the Scottish Church was also significant at this time. Most of the Bishops were staunch nationalists, who had stocked their dioceses with like-minded relatives and dependants."[179] To get a proper idea of what this meant in terms of the cross-country penetration of the Church here are some telling figures: by the late Middle Ages Scotland had over 1,000 parishes for a population of about 1 million, one parish to less than 1,000 people. It also had thirty abbeys, twenty-seven priories, nine nunneries and some twenty friaries.[180] As we have seen, things were no different in every other country: the Scandinavian countries; Germany; the Czech lands; Poland, and all the more so after its loss of independence and partition among mostly non-Catholic powers; the key role played by the Russian Orthodox Church and its extensive network of village priests during both the Polish and French invasions; the Iberian nations (including the Catalans); and the holy kingdom of Francia/France, whose village churches the peasant girl Jeanne d'Arc attended like everybody else. In the majority of these cases, both sides to the conflict were Catholic, and yet the Church in each country almost invariably championed the national cause.

Miroslav Hroch has performed an important service by analyzing the occupational composition and background of national activists in some of Europe's small nations during the nineteenth century. Early in the century the clergy dominated the ranks of the national activists in most of the countries surveyed. They figured as the largest group – a third or more – before students, officials, the free professions, and burghers in general in Bohemia, Slovakia, Finland, and among the Flemish community in Belgium. They were prominent (10–20 percent), not dominant, in Norway and Lithuania (and less significant among the Danes in Schleswig-Holstein and Estonia). As the nineteenth century progressed, their share declined somewhat while that of the other social groups increased.[181] Indeed, this dynamic amply reflects the transformation from premodern/preindustrial society, as still existed in the early nineteenth century, toward an increasingly modernized/industrial society later in that century. Clearly, in the premodern phase the clergy, with its massive spread throughout the countryside, were chief proponents of the national cause. Naturally, the figures show that peasants were barely represented in the national-literary associations of the early nineteenth century; but the priests and pastors whose sermons and preaching they regularly heard were vastly over-represented.

I have seen no figures for Italy. But as Machiavelli complained, Italy was the exception (at least with respect to the highest echelons of the clergy) in being the seat of the popes, who did not desire a unified national state which would compromise their autonomy. Feudal fragmentation in France and disastrous German Imperial entanglements in Italy weakened both the French and German states in the eleventh and twelfth centuries to a degree that gave the popes an image of universal temporal power they never possessed either before or after. However, rather than being an alternative and competing reality that dominated the Middle Ages, as much of the literature has made it to be, universal papal authority was a mirage. It only briefly appeared in ecclesiastical documents during a blip in the growth of the European national monarchies.

The Islamic *ummah* (Arabic for nation) of believers has a better claim than Christianity to being a source of competing identification with particularistic national states. However, as we have seen in Chapter 4 and shall only briefly repeat here, other factors were more responsible for the differences in national state formation between Christendom and the lands of Islam.[182] In the first place, the landscape of southwest Asia was more open. Thus, unlike in Europe, it favored imperial expansion which from Assyrian times on destroyed the early national states of the region and prevented new ones from taking root up until the collapse of the Ottoman Empire in the early twentieth century. Second, there was the Arabic language and identity which spread on the heels of imperial conquest and did not branch out into separate languages and national identities as happened in Europe with Latin after the fall of the Roman Empire. Pan-Arab identity thereby competed with potential local national identities. Third, as empire and Arab identity undercut national state growth in the Middle East, loyalty remained invested in small-scale kin circles: the extended family and the tribe. This was reinforced by the fact that the pastoralist tribe, absent in temperate west-central Europe, was a central feature of the semi-arid lands of Islam. It was above all these differences, sanctioned rather than determined by religion, which accounted for Europe's special path as compared with the lands of Islam. Tellingly, in Iran, where most of the above conditions, except the last, did not exist, national consciousness has been present and potent. Indeed, it has been closely identified with Shia Islam in a way that is not very different from the role played by, say, Orthodox Christianity in Russian nationalism.

Empire

In tandem with universal religion the ideal of universal empire on the Roman model has long been claimed to have dominated the Middle Ages and worked against the rise of particularistic national identities. In actuality, however, this ideal lost any real potency not with the weakening of the Holy German emperors in the late Middle Ages, but with the disintegration of Charlemagne's empire in western Europe in the ninth century and the collapse of Byzantine power in the Balkans even earlier. In contrast to Asia, the geopolitics of Europe north of the Mediterranean proved to be conducive to the growth and survival of national states as the primary form of state formation. As we have seen, except for the prestige of the imperial title and imperial ambitions in politically fragmented Italy, the Holy Roman Empire was essentially German and was regarded as just another European power by its neighbors. As Susan Reynolds puts it: "Forget the old textbook idea of universal empire, which was used in polemics between pope and emperor but was never a serious threat to the supremacy of kings as the archetype of rulers and kingdoms as the archetype of political communities."[183]

We have discussed empires around the world at some length in Chapter 4, and shall return to them only briefly in the European context and in relation to the ethnic and national factor. As already pointed out, there was an imperial people or ethnos at the center of almost every empire, which identified itself and was identified by all others with the empire. This imperial people was the empire's mainstay upon whose prowess and loyalty above all the empire depended for its survival. This was true of nearly all empires, mini-empires, and short-lived empires reviewed in this chapter: Danish, German, Polish–Lithuanian, Russian, Bulgarian, Serb, Hungarian, Castilian–Spanish, and English.

It was above all the elite of the imperial people/ethnos that reaped most of the benefits and held the majority and highest of the empire's offices. But the common people also sometimes benefited materially. A major example is the citizens of Rome, who after 167 BC, with the influx of wealth from the empire, were no longer liable to direct taxation (*tributum*). In all the colonial-trading empires, Spain–Castile, Portugal, Holland, England, the people of the mother country benefited in various ways and degrees from the prosperity. This helps to account for the fact that the imperial people quite often also carried the burden of empire more than all the others, and not only the burden of military service but also that of taxation. It was normal for the empire's national core to be taxed more heavily than its periphery. Castile carried the burden of taxation (and soldiering) far more heavily than the Spanish crown's other domains, both inside or outside Spain. Indeed, the attempt to distribute the tax burden throughout the empire precipitated rebellions in the Low Countries, Catalonia, Naples, Sicily, and Portugal, and lost the empire the first and last of these. This echoes the yet more famous case of the British Empire in the eighteenth century in its attempt to level the burden of imperial defense by taxing its North American colonies. (The same problem preoccupied the British Empire in the early twentieth century.) In the Russian Empire as well, the Russian core was more heavily taxed than the non-Russian periphery, as was the case in the Ottoman Empire, where the burden of taxation (and military service) fell more heavily on Anatolia.[184]

Other factors also accounted for the greater burden shouldered by the core imperial people. In Castile, for example, monarchic authority was more absolute and less liable to be checked by representative assemblies and local privileges than in the other Spanish domains, which actively resisted increased taxation.[185] Still, the exercise of power was also stronger among the empire's core people because rulers could rely on far greater legitimacy among their own people and on that people's strong identification with an empire they perceived as the nation's own. This logic endured even when the empire turned into a financial drain or never benefited the imperial people writ large, as with the wretched and heavily oppressed Russian peasantry. Historians have pointed out that in comparison with the Russian peasantry, non-Russians at the outskirts of the empire "always paid smaller taxes and enjoyed various exemptions. The logic behind this was that from the government's point of view non-Russians could cause troubles more easily than Russians." However, the question of *why* the Russian government could so confidently assume and act for centuries has been left unanswered.[186] Indeed, if this defiance of the economic rationale seems implausible, it should be recalled that Imperial France under Napoleon in the so-called Age of Nationalism was barely any different. Even though Napoleon perfected the art of spreading the cost of empire over the whole of French-dominated Europe, France still carried most of the empire's burden. And it was said that while the marshals of the French army won both tremendous wealth and glory, and the quartermasters great wealth, the rank and file had to do with glory alone – that of France.

The great majority of empires were *both* national and multinational, and there was no necessary contradiction between the two. Empire's multinationalism was inclusive but also graduated and hierarchic, with an imperial people/ethnos at its center. All the other peoples collaborated with and were coopted into the empire in recognition of this fact and its underlying balance of power. To be sure, while military superiority was the *ultima ratio* of empire, it was not its only one. Local elites often shared in the benefits of the empire, made careers in its service and were its loyal subjects. The empire had every interest to project an all-inclusive image and ideology. Moreover, small and weak peoples sometimes took shelter within the empire as their best option in a violent world and against overbearing threats. This was true, for example, of Christian peoples of the Caucasus that much preferred the Russian empire to the Ottoman. And as we have seen, it is this factor that explains the formation of the Habsburg Empire in central-eastern Europe during the sixteenth and seventeenth centuries, even though this empire scarcely possessed a truly dominant imperial people.[§§§] Furthermore, the customs, laws, and institutions of the various regions and peoples were often guaranteed and respected by the imperial authorities. In such ways the imperial framework accommodated and contained different ethnonational identities.

And yet the political salience of the ethnonational factor meant that benign means were far from being sufficient. Depending on the circumstances and prospects of success, empires vacillated between tolerance for other ethnonational identities within the realm and official and unofficial pressure on them to assimilate into the hegemonic national culture. Either way, the assumption was that loyalty was far less secure among those who did not belong to the imperial people/ethnos. For this reason, when ethnonational resistance and secessionist pressures were strong, the local culture became the target of harsh repression because it was regarded as the root cause of the troubles. The Castilian ban on the local language and culture in the Catalonian public sphere after the violent crushing of the rebellious province was not very different from what the English did in Wales, Ireland, and the Scottish Highlands, or the Habsburgs in the Czech domains. Realities in France were only somewhat more benign. As all this indicates, the notion that ethnonational identities scarcely mattered politically in premodern Europe – including its occasional, mostly nationally dominated, empires – is an incredible myth.

The dynastic national kingdom

The dynastic kingdom has also often been presented as incompatible with the national idea. If provinces and whole realms switched hands on the basis of rulers' inheritance, what substance and permanence

[§§§] In his study, "Justifying Political Power in 19th Century Europe: The Habsburg Monarchy and Beyond," in Miller and Rieber (eds.), *Imperial Rule*, 69–82, historian Maciej Janowski has discovered, contrary to his initial expectation, that the Habsburg Empire was not unique in shying away from the national principle. All European empires, he writes, had large minorities and were therefore obliged to carefully balance the national and imperial sources of their legitimacy. But, indeed, while this balancing act and a combination of principles was the norm in all empires, the Habsburgs were unique in lacking a truly dominant national people on which to rely.

could national states have? In reality, however, many if not the majority of Europe's dynastic monarchies were *national* monarchies. The concept has long been employed by scholars in recognition of this fact. In these monarchies political boundaries were roughly congruent with kin–culture identities. Indeed, the monarchies drew communal support and legitimacy from this sense of common identity, which in turn they reinforced. The exceptions, above all the Habsburg Empire in the unusual form it took from the sixteenth century on, as well as its Spanish cousin during its heyday, also in the sixteenth century, have distorted scholarly perceptions as they have been wrongly taken to represent the general pattern.

This is not to say that the dynastic principle was not cardinal and pervasive. It certainly was, and there were two main reasons for this, relating respectively to rulers and ruled. We shall begin with the latter because their perspective is less recognized and not well understood. For a large state in premodern times single rule was the only available option. Neither democracy nor a purely aristocratic regime, both existing in some small-scale polities, ever survived in large ones because of the insurmountable obstacles that distance placed on political communication and representation. Therefore, as single rule was the only available regime option, it was crucial that the inheritance process be as smooth as possible. Experience taught that without a strict order of inheritance every change of ruler would spawn a ruinous anarchy, as contending heirs to the throne fought each other. A rigid inheritance procedure was thus primarily in the interest of the political community itself, for a ruler might sometimes wish to pass on the inheritance to one son rather than to another. The price of a less gifted heir was reckoned to be less than that of the uncertainty of inheritance and specter of anarchy and civil war.

Certainly, monarchs could also be elected by the higher aristocracy or the nobility as a whole. This was an ancient custom, and later it proved stable enough when instituted in the Holy German Empire and Polish–Lithuanian Commonwealth. In both these cases elected monarchy was a tremendous achievement that the nobility extracted in its continuous power struggle with the sovereign. For the same reason, however, monarchs had a paramount interest in retaining the dynastic principle that guaranteed the bequest of power to their direct descendants. It was therefore natural that the language of dynastic legitimacy dominated royal and hence state rhetoric, as well as medieval legal language that emanated from court circles. And yet, while highly significant politically and paramount officially, the dynastic principle was far from being alone in the game. Nationality was always there, in practice and often also formally.

In the first place, the monarchs in the majority of kingdoms and times were native, and they derived legitimacy from this fact. Certainly, foreign conquerors could make themselves kings, but they sat on bayonets far more than a native ruler did. Knut made himself king of England by force of arms, but Danish rule did not last because it was perceived as foreign. The Norman Conquest proved to be far more effective in its use of violence to force itself on the country for a century or two, until it was no longer foreign. In France we have seen that the native factor favored the monarchs in their struggle against the Plantagenet empire around 1200. Later, when the Capetian direct line ceased (1328), the French nobility manipulated the inheritance laws to block the accession of the king of England to the crown of France, electing a native Valois instead and triggering the Hundred Years War. In 1421, side by side with the dynastic principle, the supporters of the French dauphin stressed the stake in the inheritance question of "all three estates of France according to various grades and obligations." As noted above, this notion of a communal national will distinct from the dynastic principle, which the monarchs were naturally less quick to invoke in normal times, was formally asserted in times of a national emergency. It fitted with the central tenet of Roman law regarding the people as the ultimate source of the ruler's authority, however formally. We have seen the same reliance on the communal national will with the Scottish struggle for independence from a foreign English sovereign in the early fourteenth century. The Declaration of Arbroath asserted the right of the "*Scottorum nacio*" to independence based not on dynastic legitimacy (which gave the king of England a strong claim), but on communal descent and a separate history of self-government. The Declaration spoke for the signatory lords, "other barons, and freeholders and the whole community of the realm of Scotland."

Native monarchs ruled the early Scandinavian kingdoms, and national sentiments were responsible for the disintegration of the dynastic Kalmar Union and the election of the native Vasa in Sweden. In the Holy German Empire, nearly all the emperors were German, even though the Imperial office was elective. In Russia, in the wake of a sweeping national struggle to remove a Polish monarch, the Assembly of the Land stipulated that the new sovereign must be both Russian and Orthodox, and elected the native Michael Romanov (1613). Native dynasties ruled Hungary and the south Slav kingdoms of Bulgaria and Serbia until the Ottoman conquest. The same held true for the Iberian Peninsula before Castilian ascendancy, and for those able to reestablish independence from Castile, such as Portugal.

The simple fact that most European dynastic monarchies were national and were ruled by native dynasties has been obscured by exceptions that were taken to represent the rule. True, quite apart from the Habsburg domains and from cases of foreign conquest, foreigners sometimes became monarchs on the principle of dynastic inheritance. Furthermore, a foreign dynasty was sometimes invited to the crown of a national kingdom by that kingdom's own elite. However, where, when, and under what conditions this occurred should be carefully analyzed. In the first place, foreign rulers and dynasties from strong and prestigious countries were mostly invited to the throne of small countries which existed tenuously on the frontier of mighty neighbors and desperately felt the need for foreign connections, alliances, and prestige. This general maxim, exemplified by fourteenth-century Bohemia and Moravia and by sixteenth-century rump Hungary, again demonstrated itself in the Balkan states which regained independence in the nineteenth century with the disintegration of Ottoman rule: Greece, Bulgaria, and Romania.

Larger countries also sometimes accepted foreign rulers in order to cement coalitions against major threats. Poland's alliance with Lithuania in the late fourteenth century and with Saxony in the early eighteenth century involved personal dynastic unions under a foreign sovereign for this very purpose. However, Poland accepted foreign rulers not only in the face of mighty foreign challenges during the periods of its rise and decline, but also during its heyday. As the monarchy became elective from 1573 on, foreign candidates, most notably from the Swedish House of Vasa, were elected by the nobility to the Polish crown. Indeed, it was the nobility's dominant power in the "Republic" that was largely responsible for this. In the first place, the nobility was reluctant to see any of their number, one of the aristocratic grandees, gaining the advantage by rising above the rest. A foreign monarch was a good compromise which did not upset the delicate balance of power among them. By the same token, a foreign monarch, who lacked a local power base, was also less able to threaten the nobility's freedoms, privileges, and dominance. That this also resulted in the gradual weakening of the Commonwealth was another matter.

Furthermore, even in cases of sovereigns of foreign origin it was abundantly clear that the country itself retained its indigenous national character, whose customs and laws the sovereign vowed to respect and protect. Indeed, the sovereigns themselves quickly ceased to be foreign, often as a condition of their accession. They were sometimes required to adopt the religion or brand of Christianity common in their kingdom, and they and their descendants and heirs went through a process of local acculturation. When the Lithuanian Jagiełło became king of Poland, he converted to Christianity, and the kings from his dynasty who ruled the country for nearly 200 years were unquestionably Polish. In the same way, the later Vasa kings of Poland in the first half of the seventeenth century, despite their Swedish origins and ties, became above all Polish. In eighteenth-century Russia the German wife of the czar became herself the ruler as Czarina Catherine II, following a coup by the imperial guard and court circles. Crucial to this remarkable accession was the fact that she had converted to Orthodoxy upon her arrival in Russia, had become fluent in Russian (a language in which she also wrote prolifically), identified herself passionately with the interests of her adopted country, and made this known in every possible way. On the other side of Europe, in England, one reason for the weakness of the Stuarts was their Scottish origins. When a Hanoverian became King George I of Britain in 1714 through the laws of dynastic inheritance, suspicion of and loathing for his German identity and ties were very strong. By that time, however, the Parliamentary regime in Britain had already been well established and it became more deeply entrenched because of the weakness of the foreign sovereigns. Needless to say, the German identity barely survived the first two monarchs of the House of Hanover. Their descendants and heirs became thoroughly English long before the reigning house officially changed its name to Windsor.

Modernist theorist John Breuilly has argued that nations and nationalism are absent from medieval political thought, regarding this a proof that they did not exist.[187] But given the primacy of dynastic legitimacy and the dominance of court circles in shaping political and legal doctrine, the secondary role played by the nationalist discourse is not surprising. As political philosopher Michael Walzer has written:

Most political theorists, from the time of the Greeks onward, have assumed the national or ethnic homogeneity of the communities about which they wrote. Prior to the work of Rousseau, theory was never explicitly nationalist, but the assumption of a common language, history, or religion underlay most of what was said about political practices and institutions.[188]

Medievalist historian Susan Reynolds has summarized the point as follows in her *Kingdoms and Communities*:

A kingdom was never thought of merely as the territory which happened to be ruled by a king. It comprised and corresponded to a "people" (gens, natio, populus) ... So much was this taken for granted that learned writers seldom argued about this directly when they discussed political subjects: they merely made remarks which suggested that it was an unreasoned premise of their political arguments ... The trouble about all this [modern theorizing about the nation] for the medieval historian is not that the idea of the permanent and objective real nation is foreign to the middle ages, as so many historians of nationalism assume, but that it closely resembles the medieval idea of the kingdom ... [189]

Sociopolitical inequality

Aristocratic dominance, legal inequality, and subjugation and political disenfranchisement of the masses of peasantry prevailed in the great majority of premodern societies. Modernists have claimed that this was one of the reasons why a sense of national identity, affinity, and solidarity were non-existent in such societies. According to this claim, neither the elite nor the peasantry felt themselves part of a common collective. This chapter has shown that this was not the case. First, not all premodern state societies were *equally* polarized in terms of status, rights, and the sociopolitical distribution of power. There was great diversity which has been overlooked by modernists, and this diversity mattered. As we have seen, in the ancient national state of Macedonia reliance on mass infantry armies empowered the common people and their assemblies vis-à-vis both the monarchy and the aristocracy. Scottish rebellion against English rule around 1300 could succeed only because of its broad popular base which involved all estates. In medieval Norway and Sweden, although dominated by the aristocracy, the farmer estate held its ground and made its voice heard in the affairs of state far more than in most other European countries of the time. The same was true of Catalonia in comparison with Castile. The Hussite movement that engulfed the Czech lands was a mass popular affair. Generally, many state societies, especially those in eastern Europe, experienced advancing peasant enserfment and became more oppressive and socially polarized in the early modern period than they had been during medieval times.

Second, although the illiterate masses in premodern societies are mute in the written records, we have suggested ways of overcoming this seemingly insurmountable obstacle to determining their feelings and attitudes: one should look at what they did in lieu of what they said, surely an even better indication of where they stood. The results of such a test are unmistakable: even in the most despotic and/or oppressive of state societies the masses of peasantry identified with their native country and kinsmen, most notably in time of national crisis due to a grave foreign threat. In such extreme circumstances the state authorities, which normally disenfranchised and ignored the masses, appealed to them with arousing invocations of common brotherhood, culture, and motherland. Obviously, they expected such appeals to have an effect on their people. And, indeed, the masses for their part responded, often by risking their lives and much else. Throughout history whole peoples habitually rose in arms to defend or restore their freedom. Since the overwhelming majority of their societies were not democratic and recognized little personal freedom, the collective freedom they desperately aspired to and were willing to pay for with their blood and property was obviously freedom from *foreign* rule. It mattered to people greatly whether or not their rulers – and often their oppressors – were their own.

In Chapter 4, we saw this happening, for example, in ancient Egypt under the Hyksos and in China facing the Jurchen and Mongols. Much the same occurred even in the most oppressive national states of Europe. Russia, for example, could always rely on the deeply rooted devotion of its people to the holy Russian motherland. In time of emergency, against the Polish, Swedish, and French threats in the early seventeenth, eighteenth, and nineteenth centuries, respectively, particularly the first and last cases, mass popular participation played a central role in defeating the foreign invaders. Indeed, in both these cases, as in Sung China, popular mobilization was more spontaneous than state-induced, because the authorities were somewhat apprehensive about the release of popular national sentiments lest they threaten the existing social order. Either way, such popular nationalist sentiments were most evidently there. Things were no different in Poland during the "Deluge," when popular resistance against the Swedes manifested itself in the middle of the seventeenth century and again in the early eighteenth century. Here, too, in a country that subjugated the peasants more harshly than most others, the king and nobility were uneasy about how to respond to such popular actions whose contribution to the defeat of the foreign invaders they could not afford to lose. In yet another proverbial *Herren* country, Hungary, the nobility most emphatically and emotively appealed to popular nationalist sentiments as their grievances against Habsburg rule reached boiling point in the second half of the seventeenth century.

Thus, contrary to the modernist schema and in line with the common-sense cliché, people always loved and identified with their native people and country, even to the point of risking their lives and much else for them. Great sociopolitical inequality and oppression surely hindered such sentiments and often left them little room in the public sphere. Yet even in the most polarized national state societies popular ethnopatriotism on a country scale – alias nationalism – spontaneously and powerfully surfaced in times of national crisis. The peasants of old, barely less so than the European proletarians of 1914, did have a motherland after all.

How deep was dialect fragmentation?

Granted that in premodern national monarchies national sentiments were limited rather than negated by the dynastic principle and sociopolitical stratification, were such kingdoms not hopelessly fragmented by deep dialect differences that prevented any real sense of a common culture and common collective? Once again, the modernist claim here, superficially persuasive, has been very selective in its choice of cases and highly misleading.

To be sure, linguistic diversity was very considerable in some countries. In Germany, it created genuine barriers to mutual understanding between regions. In Italy, it gave rise to what were in effect different languages. The same was true of medieval Iberia. In France, there was a diversity of local dialects within two separate language spaces, those of *langue d'oïl* and *langue d'oc*. Clearly, there was an interplay between political and linguistic unity. The disintegration of the medieval German Empire and the absence of a unified Italian state reinforced the process of linguistic fragmentation. Spain moved in the opposite direction as its separate small medieval states, each with its own Romance language, were increasingly subsumed within expanding Castile and the Castilian language. Similarly, in France political unity led to the expansion of French and its imposition at the elite level. Notably, however, shared literary languages in both Germany and Italy reinforced in each of them a sense of common identity as *Kultur Nationen*. And as we have seen, the interface between the High Culture of the literate classes and the Low Culture of the illiterate masses was considerably more significant than Gellner imagined. Moreover, in France, for example, with its long tradition and strong sense of political oneness, linguistic diversity did not prevent the consolidation of French national identity during the Middle Ages.

However, the main flaw in the modernist argument is the assumption that the above cases, which have been elevated to paradigmatic status, reflected the *norm* in premodern state societies, whereas in reality they represented only one pole on a spectrum. In some countries dialect diversity was very mild and inconsequential. In others it was somewhat more pronounced and yet far from resembling the above-cited cases, and from being a significant obstacle to mutual understanding or to a shared sense of a national collective. We have already seen, for instance, that despite significant local accents and idioms, spoken Arabic has been intelligible throughout the great expanse of the Middle East (except for the Maghreb). Latin, with slight local variations, mainly of accent, was spoken throughout the Western Roman Empire, completely displacing the older local languages in Italy, Spain, and Gaul. And things were not very different in some parts of premodern Europe.

The term dialect is famously fraught with hidden assumptions and ambiguity, as the line between different dialects and separate languages is sometimes blurred and determined by politics. In extreme cases dialects in ostensibly the same linguistic space can be mutually incomprehensible. Thus, the quip that "a language is a dialect with an army and navy" is a clever exaggeration intended to make a point. Even professional linguists use the term dialect loosely, as it covers either greater or smaller variation in accent (phonology), vocabulary (lexicon), or grammar (morphology), or any combination of these. Scholarly linguistic studies in this field are almost entirely devoted to minute recording of such variations. They are seldom concerned with questions that interest historians, social scientists, and ordinary people, such as what these variations meant in terms of mutual understanding, let alone how they affected social communication. All the same, it occasionally becomes apparent from such works that "dialect" differences in some cases, including a number of very large state societies, were in reality very slight.

Both open plain land which facilitates movement (as opposed to rugged, mountainous terrain) and unified state control (as opposed to political fragmentation) decrease linguistic variation. The effect of both factors is aptly demonstrated by Europe's most open plain lands that have also been the home of some of Europe's largest and oldest national states: Poland and Russia. We begin with Poland. Apart from very small populations in the north (Kashubians) and in the Carpathian south, Poles speak the Polish language and have been closely identified with it. In the past there were speakers of other languages in the realm ruled by Poland – Ukrainians, Belarusians, Jews, Germans – but they were never considered Poles, and in any case our concern is with Polish speakers. Linguists distinguish between four major dialect areas of Polish speakers, those of Greater Poland, Lesser Poland, Mazovia, and Polish Silesia. However, what is meant by dialects in this context is very slight differences indeed. As far back as the late Middle Ages and early modern period, "the dialect variation in Poland was weak and a large number of features common to all regions dominated over a few differences."[190] This applied even to the most basic distinction in premodern societies between the common language of the peasantry and the "refined" parlance of the elite: "The pronunciation of the nobility even in the sixteenth (and possibly even in the seventeenth) century was no different from that of the peasants."[191] The elite adopted a more "refined" pronunciation only later. There had been a Polish literary style ever since the eleventh or twelfth centuries and a high, formal literary language from the sixteenth century. But all these were clearly recognizable as Polish by any Polish speaker. We have already cited the following passage regarding the relationship between a common language and national identity during the Renaissance:

> the main feature that distinguished a nation was language. Thus no one, from Długosz to Andrzej Frycz Modrzewski, denied that peasants were an integral part of the nation, based on one common language. The eminent lexicographer Jan Maczyński, in his Polish–Latin dictionary, defined the word "natio" as a "nation using the same language."[192]

To be sure, a major process of linguistic standardization and weakening of local variation took place in Poland after 1945 with mass migration from the east, industrialization, urbanization, and universal education.[193] But such local variations as prevailed before 1945 are nothing like the dialect differences that existed and still exist in Germany, for example, whose case is regarded as paradigmatic. Covering far too much, the term dialect is a real obstacle here. The testimonies of both my father and father-in-law, who were both born in Poland before the Second World War and survived the Holocaust while moving around the country, may be regarded as anecdotal but are fully in line with what we have seen: both maintain that they never met a Polish speaker in any village community or part of Poland whom they had any difficulty in understanding.

One hears the very same testimony from any Russian speaker. What linguists map as northern, central, and southern Russian "dialects" are small and superficial variations in pronunciation and vocabulary. A common Russian language has existed since the days of Kiev, and the linguistic unity of the country was maintained by the unification under Moscow. Church Slavonic was augmented from the sixteenth century by chanceries' Russian as a written language, and a literary Russian style took shape in the eighteenth century.[194] But, plainly put, Russian was Russian. Again, standardization increased with modernization during the twentieth century and especially from the 1930s on, but it was anything but created by it. Compare this with Germany, wherein a much earlier and more thorough process of modernization, including a near universal system of primary education from the early nineteenth century on, has not eliminated preexisting deep-rooted regional and local dialects.

Dialect variation in other European countries covered a whole range. In medieval Bohemia the Prague vernacular became the literary standard, but language variations in Bohemia and Moravia were fairly slight.[195] The extensive documentation of the Hussite period referring to the Czech language in the Czech lands denoted something clear and specific. By comparison, in neighboring Slovakia, lacking political unity and independence and more mountainous, dialect variation has been considerably more pronounced. The Hungarian of the medieval kingdom on the central European plain was pretty homogeneous. Whatever variations that later emerged, and they were fairly slight, resulted from the disintegration of the empire and the division of its former realm and Hungarian-speaking communities among several countries. Dialect variation within Croatian, Serbian, Bulgarian, and Romanian was somewhat more significant, exacerbated by the loss of independence and political unity. In Scandinavia, dialect differences in mountainous Norway were considerably more distinctive than in either Sweden or Denmark (except for southwestern Sweden whose speech is closer to Danish). Although Iberia was divided among various Romance languages, variations *within* Castilian were slight. Despite Castile's large size, such variations were far less significant than those within Catalan. In European Portuguese local variations were also slight. There were local variations in the English of both Anglo-Saxon and late medieval England, with a particularly strong Danish influence in the north. Nonetheless, as with all the above cases and in contrast to the strong dialect/linguistic diversity in Germany, Italy, or France, such variations never came close to mutual unintelligibility. Nor did they hinder a sense of common peoplehood, most notably when a unified state existed. The blanket concept of dialect fragmentation in the study of nations and nationalism has been very misleading. Gellner's claim that landlords and peasants often spoke different languages, mostly referring to some Habsburg and eastern Baltic lands, has been wholly unrepresentative. The difference between premodern and modern linguistic diversity and its significance in relation to the contrast between premodern and modern nations, although considerable, was far from being as uniform and dichotomous as Gellner and others have claimed.

Conclusion

There is no argument between modernists and traditionalists that modernization brought about a sweeping transformation of every aspect of human society, whose far-reaching effect on the national phenomenon is denied by no one. The question in dispute is whether or not a sense of common identity and solidarity on a country-state scale existed in the premodern world on the basis of a collective sense of kinship and shared culture; whether or not such a collective sentiment extended down into the grassroots level and across the countryside and played a major political role. Contrary to modernist theorizing, we have seen that the congruence between an ethnos or a people and early states was very strong indeed, precisely because formative states built on shared kin–culture affinities and solidarity. Because of its geopolitical contours, Europe north of the old Roman frontier proved particularly conducive to the rise and survival of such states. Hence, the long history and resilience of most of Europe's peoples and nations, what Seton-Watson has called Europe's old nations. After all the necessary debunking of nationalist myths, it turns out that the great majority of the European peoples and nations do go back to incipient medieval consolidation of state societies on the basis of earlier ethnic formations. What Anthony Smith claimed for modern nations was also true for the premodern world. Indeed, the Middle Ages, especially in central-eastern Europe before the growth of empires and deepening peasant enserfment, were in some respects *more* national in character than the early modern period.

Obviously, not all premodern European states were national states. There were a large number of petty-states that incorporated only part of a larger ethnic space, while some other states were ruled by a foreign conquering warrior class at least for a while. There were also full-blown empires, which in reality were national empires wherein one ethnos or people dominated. Obviously, too, not all nascent national states survived. Many early ethnonational identities disappeared or have been transformed beyond recognition, while others have emerged in later centuries. And still, a look at Europe's ethnonational map strikingly reveals how resilient such identities have been for many centuries, often for over a millennium, ever since they were first formed during the Middle Ages. It has been pointed out that the number of political units in Europe has shrunk since 1500 from some 500 to around 25.[196] It should be added, however, that practically all the "victims" in this process were semi-independent magnatic domains, petty-states of all sorts, and a few multiethnic empires. National states, great or small, exhibited remarkable resilience.

This is not to say that there were no significant differences between the nation and nationalism in premodern and modern Europe; far from it. Premodern forms of the nation carried all the attributes of the premodern world; for example, they were deeply imbedded in a religious worldview. Indeed, religion was a major vehicle of ethno-national sentiments on a country scale and a major instrument of state- and nation-building. To claim that such premodern features of national identity were not truly national because they were different from modern forms of nationhood is to beg the question. Admittedly, premodern national sentiments were less dominant in politics than they would become during modernity. They were at least formally over-shadowed by the monarchic-dynastic principle as a source of legitimacy, competed with strong local identities, and were compromised by sociopolitical inequality. And yet it is the fundamental error of modernist dichotomist theorizing to claim that all this meant that national sentiments of affinity, identity, and solidarity were not there, and as a very significant political force that shaped borders and the frontiers of loyalty and political legitimacy.

Susan Reynolds has made the very same point:

> *Some modern scholars, perhaps influenced by Rousseau's belief that solidarity with one group ruled out any other, have believed that medieval people can have felt no loyalty except to their lord or local community. Anyone who belongs at the same time to a family, a town, a university, and a nation-state ... ought to find this idea implausible ... government consisted of layers of authority, and loyalties were attracted to each layer accordingly. Kingdoms were the units of government which were perceived as peoples. The government and the solidarity were both essential.*[197]

It is perhaps not redundant to repeat the simple, common-sense truths already cited in this chapter. As a historian of early modern Ukraine writes: "The nation as the primary identity of man is a nineteenth- and

twentieth-century concept, but seventeenth-century men viewed residence in a common fatherland or possession of a common descent,
culture and historical tradition as important matters."[198] According to
another historian, of early modern Russia:

> *Two methods are most common: to project into the past the
> modern forms of national consciousness (the approach of all
> nineteenth-century writers), or to despair at the distortion
> introduced by that approach and then deny the existence of
> any national consciousness in Russia at all before the
> eighteenth century. Neither position need be taken, however.
> Russians of the sixteenth and seventeenth century had a
> defined national consciousness, even if it did not take the
> same form as the national consciousness of Pushkin,
> Alexander III, or Lenin.*[199]

As many have noted, what greatly empowered the national
phenomenon and turned it from a significant to a dominant political
factor at the center of the Age of Nationalism were the doctrine of
popular sovereignty, citizenship, civil–legal equality, democratization,
and the erosion of local identities. All of them were closely bound up
with the process of modernization, to which we now turn.

6 MODERNITY: NATIONALISM RELEASED, TRANSFORMED, AND ENHANCED

Modernization has been the most profound transformation that human societies have undergone since the adoption of agriculture, and has deeply affected the national phenomenon. Europe and the West pioneered and led the modernization process for centuries, but other parts of the world have been catching up. Several major developments enhanced nationalism during the early modern period. Print technology greatly reinforced linguistic–national "imagined communities," which shared in a continuously expanding medium of books, journals, and newspapers.[1] Rising commercial capitalism created economies on a national and international scale and diminished local autarky. Absolutism strengthened central state control over the realm; but government by representatives on a country-state scale – progressively emerging by the eighteenth century in Holland, Britain, the United States, and Revolutionary France – had an even greater leveling and integrative effect. Fully-fledged, explosive modernity began around 1800, as commercial capitalism gave rise to industrialization and its multifarious upshots. Societies have become overwhelmingly urban rather than rural. The expansion of communication and exchange networks has accelerated exponentially. Populations have become fully literate, as large-scale education systems became standard. Modernists have variably stressed intensified communication, industrialization, and popular government as the prime factors behind the age of nationalism. But *all* of the above had an effect and all were mutually related and mutually reinforcing.

Indeed, there is scarcely a dispute between traditionalists and modernists about any of these changes or about the fact that every aspect of life has been radically transformed by the process of modernization, including the national phenomenon. However, were nations and nationalism transformed and greatly enhanced by modernity, or did they actually originate with it? As we have seen so far in this book, sentiments of kin–culture identity, affinity, and solidarity on a country-state scale very much existed before modernity. Moreover, they were highly potent politically, largely underpinning the frontiers of loyalty and thus borders among, and power relations within, political communities. The politicization of ethnic difference goes as far back as the beginning of politics itself. We now turn to examine the modernity transformation more closely.

A THE WILL OF THE PEOPLE AND THE NATION: WHAT ENABLED WHAT?

A lot hinges on the concept of popular sovereignty. Many modernists regard it as a constitutive element of the nation, without which it has no existence. Earlier confined to some city-states and other small political communities, popular sovereignty was only introduced on a country-state scale with modernity and became the norm, empowering the people and turning it into a fully-fledged political player. This was a profound change, firmly rooted in the above-mentioned processes of modernization. During the early modern period, the pressures for active political participation came mainly from country gentlemen and urban burghers. They were the exponents of the new capitalist economy and the main beneficiaries of the greatly enhanced flow of information made possible by print. It was these people who spearheaded the English, American, and French revolutions. The expansion of the cities during that period also had some effect, most notably in the proverbial case of Paris, where, despite the ambivalence of Enlightenment liberals toward the "mob," it nonetheless played a decisive role in toppling the Old Regime. Still, a far more sweeping change took place during the nineteenth century, with the growth of mass society.

The term "mass" connotes popular concentration, interaction, and mobilization rather than numbers, because multitudes of peasants had always existed in premodern large states, typically comprising 85–95 percent of the population. Their problem, however, was that they were impotently dispersed throughout the countryside, like potatoes in a sack, in Marx's phrase, and therefore were little capable of pulling their weight. As we have seen, peasants were not equally subservient and disenfranchised in all premodern large states as many historical sociologists assume. Furthermore, their ethnonational identity and allegiance mattered a great deal. All the same, the change generated by industrialization and urbanization was nothing short of revolutionary. There was an exodus to the cities, which turned societies from being overwhelmingly rural to overwhelmingly urban. Different countries modernized at different times: Britain, for example, crossed the 50 percent point around 1850; Germany around 1900; and China in 2008.[2] The middle class, the vanguard of the national cause, grew momentously in both numbers and significance. Moreover, as the populace crowded into the cities, they became located near the centers of power and political authority which could no longer ignore them. The people now constituted concentrated masses rather than large dispersed numbers, and could always barricade the main streets of the capital or march on the palace. Thus, henceforth any regime had to be "popular" in the sense that it had to derive legitimacy from one form or another of mass consent: old liberal parliamentarianism became democratic as the franchise was progressively expanded during the nineteenth century; popular plebiscitean autocracy on a national scale was pioneered by Napoleon I and Napoleon III, and labeled Bonapartism or Caesarism; totalitarian regimes of both the right and the left emerged in the first decades of the twentieth century, galvanizing the masses with a popular creed, while brutally suppressing all opposition.

Additional developments played a role in enhancing popularly-based regimes. Parallel to the exodus to the cities, the spread of railways worked in the other direction, connecting rural populations that had rarely, if ever, left their native villages to the wider world.[3] The spreading school system and compulsory military service, where it existed, served as major agents of national socialization and promoted the national ethos. (Notably, however, both institutions had this effect only in national states and barely at all in multiethnic and multinational empires.) Widespread literacy gave rise to the popular press, which tapped the new mass market and was, indeed, almost invariably nationalistic. The electric telegraph of the nineteenth century was followed during the twentieth century by other breakthroughs in communication technology, which further enhanced mass society even in countries that lagged behind in urbanization. These included cinema and newsreels, which joined the popular press in reaching into the remote corners of a country, as did the radio from around 1920 and television from around 1950. The automobile, augmenting the railway, had the same effect.

All this meant far-reaching integration and politicization of the masses, unprecedented in large countries before modernity.

Popular sovereignty and the Age of Nationalism went hand in hand. Still, what was the exact relationship between the two? Many modernists postulate popular sovereignty as inseparable from the concept of the nation, but this conflation may mean that they are in fact defining the former rather than the latter. The connection and interaction between the two phenomena needs to be elucidated.

We begin with the direction of causation. Nobody denies that nationalism became predominant during modernity as both a principle and a reality. The question is why. Clearly, the transformative effect of industrialization and urbanization played a decisive role. Ethnically related populations were thrown together, with much of the old local diversity in dialect and customs eradicated in the process. Gone, too, were the close-knit, small-scale village communities, which were replaced by a new mobile, "atomistic," mass society. As *Gemeinschaft* gave way to *Gesellschaft*, intermediate – provincial and in some places tribal – foci of primary identity were either weakened or disappeared altogether. Thus, in a far more integrated and homogenized society, the nation became the principal object of kin–culture identification beyond the nuclear family. Furthermore, to some degree the surge of nationalism can be regarded as a traumatized response to the dislocation, disorientation, and alienation the people experienced during the massive modern transition. Yet is this all? Much of the above can be true, *is* in my opinion very true, without excluding an additional thread of causation: the politicization of the masses, the empowerment of the people, and popular sovereignty meant that the people, who had very often harbored national sentiments of identity and solidarity, were now able to express their preferences politically. *Two* complementary processes were at work fueling the age of nationalism: mass society and popular sovereignty greatly enhanced national cohesion and the people's stake in the nation; and *by the same token* they opened the door and enabled the expression of long-held popular nationalistic sentiments.

I emphasize that this by no means implies that nationalism was either a given, an unchanging quantity, or otherwise immutable. Premodern nationalism, although sometimes very potent politically, was both less cohesive and weaker than the modern phenomenon. Furthermore, while in actuality the premodern dynastic state was often a national monarchy and encompassed an entire ethnopolitical community, nationalism became the predominant *language* of statehood only when older principles of legitimacy, above all dynastic, receded. Rather than creating the French nation, the Revolution substituted the people for the monarch as the nation's sovereign, and by that act it *also* charged the nation with popular energies and allegiance. This was a truly massive change, yet less drastic than modernists construe it to be. Modernists have been overly impressed by the highly impressive modern transformation. According to the more complex picture suggested here, the sweeping processes of modernization, rather than inaugurating nationalism, simultaneously *released, transformed, and enhanced it, while greatly increasing its legitimacy.*

Thus, popular sovereignty gave expression to nationalism as much as it contributed to it. Yet there was another, often forgotten, aspect of the relationship between the two phenomena: national identity, in most cases historically rooted, was a *precondition* of popular rule in a country, much more than the other way around. J. S. Mill pointed this out as far back as 1861: "Free institutions are next to impossible in a country made up of different nationalities."[4] Famously, in nineteenth-century Europe the liberal and nationalist causes were almost inseparable. And American president Woodrow Wilson championed both democracy and national self-determination for the post-First World War world. The reason why free government in a country depends on the existence of a shared national sentiment should be obvious: once people, rather than being coerced by force, are given the freedom to express and enact their will, they almost invariably elect to live in their own national state. The people's will, once spoken, has been revealed to be unmistakably nationalistic. Notably, while there have been many national states without free government, free government has scarcely existed in the absence of a national community.

The resounding break up of multiethnic empires, first in Europe and then elsewhere, speaks volumes. As we have seen, premodern empires very much rested on ethnonational foundations: they relied on the power and loyalty of a core imperial ethnos or people to enforce their rule on others; and these others usually acquiesced to foreign rule only because of the realities of power. Widespread resistance and mass rebellions by subject peoples were ever to be expected within empires and were often drowned in rivers of blood. It is impossible to deny the occurrence and popular scale of many such struggles for independence, as it is awkward to describe a people's urge for collective freedom as anything other than national. And it mattered little that the people were subservient and often lacked personal freedom in their own societies. While most empires denied their own people personal freedom, they denied other peoples *both* personal and collective freedom. The two forms of freedom should not be confused. The question, then, is why did the Ottoman, Habsburg, and Russian empires begin to suffer the pressure of nationalism from their subject peoples only from the nineteenth century onward and not before? Clearly this was not because such pressures for independence by subject peoples had not existed earlier. What happened with modernization was not only an enhancement of nationalism, but also a decline in imperial coercion for a variety of reasons, only some of them having to do with nationalism. This gave dependent peoples greater ability to break away. Modern nationalism and freedom of political choice due to the decline of imperial coercion were intimately connected. Yet they did not correlate perfectly, showing the latter to be as significant in accounting for the surge of nationalist secessionism.

We begin with the least modern of the three empires, the Ottoman. Gellner has well recognized the Greek War of Independence from the Empire (1821–1833), and those by other Balkan peoples, as major challenges to his thesis regarding the birth of nationalism as a consequence of industrialization.[5] To be sure, Greece was not entirely unaffected by some of modernity's incipient developments. A small nucleus of intellectuals, influenced by Western ideas and by the American and French revolutions, championed the national cause in books and pamphlets, and educated merchants played a significant role in precipitating the insurgency. At the same time, however, Greek society was on the whole highly traditional and entirely preindustrial. Levels of urbanization and literacy were extremely low. Although Greeks, scattered throughout the Empire, were among its more commercial and enterprising elements, there was scarcely a commercial-capitalist economy connecting Greece proper on a country scale, nor was there a unifying central state. Secret nationalist societies (most notably the *Filiki Eteria*) comprised a network of conspirators throughout the country. But the uprising relied on the local groups of rough rural brigands (*klefts, armatoli, kapi*), some of which had acquired the status of semi-official militias, and it hinged on the enthusiastic volunteering of the masses of illiterate peasants incited and often led by the clergy.[6] An authoritative study of the Greek struggle, while giving due weight to modern influences, has no doubt about "the intense feeling of nation-hood among the Greeks of all classes, a feeling which derived from their common language, from the traditions of their church ... and from a consciousness of being under alien rule."[7] As we have seen, rather than suggesting that the revolt was religiously and not nationally moti-vated, the strongly religious character of Greek nationalism simply meant that Greek Orthodoxy was central to and inseparable from Greek national identity. The lower clergy in particular, nestled across the country and far removed from the high politics of the patriarchy in Istanbul (whose hapless leaders were lynched there on the outbreak of the revolt), was full of nationalist zeal. The Greek War of Independence was not significantly different from any other premodern popular national revolt against foreign rule (whether it was of the same or different religion), some of them crushed by force and some of them successful, depending on the strength of the empire vis-à-vis the insur-gents. The revolt succeeded where earlier Greek insurgencies had failed not because modernization inaugurated Greek nationalism, but because Ottoman power had greatly declined.

Indeed, although the Ottomans and their Egyptian allies were still stronger than the Greeks and did not recoil from the violence needed to crush the rebellion, intervention by Britain, France, and Russia tipped the scales and eventually decided the issue. The Concert of Europe during the post-Revolutionary, post-1815 Reaction opposed the dangerous idea of national self-determination, but philhellenic (and Christian) sentiments were strong enough to bring about the interven-tion. Thus, while facilitated by rudimentarily modern developments among parts of the elite, the Greeks succeeded in winning independence primarily because the aspirations of a fundamentally premodern people in an empire which remained wholly unreceptive to the popular will were supported from outside. As Gellner has conceded: "Bandit rebels in Balkan mountains, knowing themselves to be culturally distinct from those they were fighting, and moreover linked, by faith or loss-of-faith, to new uniquely powerful civilization, thereby became ideological ban-dits: in other words, nationalists."[8] In the words of another historian: "it was not from the ashes of the Enlightenment that the Greek revolt was to emerge but more directly from a pan-Hellenic dream inspired by the Russians and based on traditional peasant movements."[9]

Things were not very different elsewhere in the Balkans. As Gellner has come to recognize: "not merely Greeks, but also the other

Balkan Nationalisms can be seen as constituting a major problem for the theory, given the backwardness of the Balkans by the standards of industrialization and modernity."[10] Serb popular rebellions against the Ottomans hardly began in the nineteenth century. The Serb nobility had been practically wiped out with the Ottoman conquest. Nonetheless, in the Banat uprising of 1594, for example, in the words of a popular song: "The whole land has rebelled, six hundred villages arose," led by the clergy and the local notables in a holy national war.[11] The uprising was crushed, as were all other attempts until Ottoman power declined in the eighteenth century. In the failed uprising of 1727, the rebel force reportedly numbered 20,000, a large number out of a total Serb population estimated at about half a million.[12] Together with the Church's influence, the highly popular patriotic songs (*Pesmes*) of the bards played a central role in spurring mass peasant mobilization in this predominantly illiterate society.[13] The Kočina Krajina revolt (1788), aided by the Habsburgs, also preceded the French Revolution and its inciting message of popular sovereignty.

When the Serb struggle against the Ottomans resumed between 1804 and 1815, it again engulfed the masses of peasantry, which in the spirit of the new revolutionary age were promised the abolishment of feudalism and serfdom (which occurred only in 1835). Certainly, economic exploitation was central to the uprising. Yet, rather than contrasting with the national cause, it combined with and reinforced it, as any comparison with the core of the Ottoman Empire demonstrates. As Gellner has honestly admitted: "Balkan rebels – unlike, say, Berber rebels within another Muslim empire – were not just rebels, but nationalists as well."[14] The success of the Serbs in winning formal autonomy and practical independence from the empire under their own prince was mainly due to Ottoman weakness and fear of intervention by Russia, otherwise the guarantor of the reactionary order. In short, echoes of Western ideas of freedom and secularism resonated with, more than they enabled, Serb national freedom.

It took another half a century, until the 1870s, for much of the rest of the Balkans to be detached from the Ottoman Empire, including the establishment of two more national states, in Romania and Bulgaria. Although still the most backward part of Europe by every measure of modernization, the Balkans had advanced on most of these criteria during that period.[15] In addition, the various ethnicities and peoples of the region had also become more exposed to Western European national ideas. Furthermore, they benefited from growing foreign sympathy toward their national aspirations as an expression of the popular will, as these interrelated principles grew in legitimacy in Western public opinion. This in turn swayed the Great Powers' policy in their favor. Russia's military intervention was motivated by its old imperial designs and Orthodox–Slavic solidarity. But Britain's abstention from fully pursuing its long-held policy of preventing the disintegration of the Ottoman Empire as a bulwark against Russian expansion was greatly affected by the new public sensibilities.[16] Here again, national liberation in Romania and Bulgaria would not have succeeded without Great Power military intervention made possible by the weakening of the Ottoman Empire.

The point of all this is not that incipient processes of modernization in the Balkans did not leave their mark, greatly affect, and enhance national consciousness among the region's various ethnicities and peoples, as well as facilitate national independence; it is just that in the majority of the countries in question, modernization released as much as it transformed premodern national identities and aspirations previously suppressed by Ottoman might. What incipient modernization introduced into many of these countries was *modern* nationalism, rather than nationalism. Old premodern national states and peoples, which had desperately defended their independence in the face of the Ottoman advance and survived Ottoman rule despite many failed rebellions, reemerged when Ottoman power declined. This applies to Serbia and Bulgaria, earlier to Hungary, and in different ways also to Greece and Romania. The popular Bulgarian brigand groups which harassed the Ottomans during the fifteenth to eighteenth centuries, known as the *haiduk* movement, were celebrated in epics and enjoyed the sympathy of the rural population and the Bulgarian clergy. A meticulous study of the sources on the *haiduk* concludes: "Ottoman documents may be scattered and prejudiced, but they give the lie to any claim that the haiduk and similar movements in Ottoman Europe had no national content or intent ... "[17]

As mentioned in Chapter 5, ethnic identities and boundaries were transformed continuously, in the Balkans as elsewhere. Some ethnic identities, most notably in Bosnia, Kosovo, and Macedonia emerged late, and minority ethnic communities were, and largely remain, scattered throughout the Balkans. Furthermore, once each of the Balkan states became independent, processes of nation-building were vigorously pursued by their respective governments, and a nationalist ideology was propagated and became dominant. Yet these intense forms of modern nationalism could barely succeed – indeed, hardly ever succeeded – in the absence of deep sentiments of *premodern* ethnic and national identity, affinity, and solidarity. The myth-making of nineteenth-century nationalists acknowledged, the prevalence and strength of the modernist fiction in the study of nations and nationalism is almost as mystifying.

We have dwelt on the creation of independent Balkan national states because more than other cases they allow us to disengage the effects of modernization from those of the popular will when the people were freed from imperial coercion and suppression. Adding to our study of the premodern world, early-nineteenth-century Serbia and Greece in particular demonstrate that popular aspirations are a sufficient condition for a life-and-death struggle for national independence even when modernization had scarcely occurred. The Russian Empire, followed by the Soviet, reveals a similar picture from the opposite direction: despite far-reaching modernization, popular aspirations for national self-determination were not allowed to materialize before the system of imperial suppression had been broken.

The Russian Empire combined forceful coercion with elite cooptation to keep diverse ethnicities and peoples under its rule. Recurring Polish rebellions (1831–1832, 1863–1864) were crushed, the ban on the Ukrainian and Belarusian languages in the public sphere was intensified, and a policy of Russification was vigorously pursued wherever possible.[18] From the late nineteenth century on, the empire went through a process of industrialization and modernization, which enhanced national sentiments and unrest and gave the empire its reputation as "the prison house of nations." Still, these national aspirations had no chance of materializing until the First World War broke the empire's back and allowed some of the inmates in the prison house – Finland, the Baltic countries, Poland – to make their escape. Others, most notably the Ukraine and the peoples of the Caucasus, tried but failed, as Soviet rule established itself through massive violence.

Although the Soviet Union was supposedly based on the supranational solidarity of the workers, it recognized the national principle and ostensibly allowed its various peoples and ethnic groups an autonomous cultural and political self-determination within a federative framework.[19] All the same, when the Soviet Union was threatened with destruction during the Second World War the (recently occupied) peoples of the Baltic states and many in the Ukraine and elsewhere again saw it as an opportunity for national liberation. Certainly, they also wished to escape the highly unpopular communist system and collectivization. However, the Russian people, who were also very ambivalent about the system, demonstrated steadfast patriotic heroism. Indeed, it was to the mobilizing force of nationalism that the leadership of the Soviet Union resorted in desperation as by far its most effective rallying cry. This applied first and foremost to the Russian people, called, as earlier in history, to save the fatherland, the sacred land of Russia, from invaders. But it also included the other peoples of the Soviet Union, especially as Nazi Germany's murderous racial policy toward the Slavs diminished the attraction of the alternative. With the end of the war came a thorough and brutal Soviet repression of national aspirations in the Ukraine, the Baltics, and the countries of the new empire in eastern Europe, including those with the longest and most fervent tradition of nationalism, such as Poland and Hungary. Repression continued throughout the life of the Soviet Empire, and it made no difference that levels of modernization – industrialization, urbanization, and literacy – were fairly high in all these societies. True, within the Soviet Union itself continued processes of Russification facilitated the emergence of a *Soviet* national supra-identity. Similarly to British identity in English-dominated Britain, it built on the older interplay between the concepts of *Russkii*, ethnic Russians, and *Rossiiskii*, all those belonging to Russia. Still, as the coercive Soviet system was dismantled in the late 1980s, for economic rather than nationalist reasons, not only the countries of eastern Europe, but also the peoples of the Soviet Union invariably opted for national independence.

Whereas the nineteenth-century Balkans demonstrate the potency of nationalism even in the absence of modernization, when imperial coercion waned, the Russian–Soviet Empire revealed the impotency of nationalism even after modernization, as long as imperial coercion remains in place. The two cases thus serve as a controlled experiment that shows that it was the release of national aspirations even more than modernization that accounted for the success of nationalism and national independence. In the Habsburg Empire the various factors were more closely intertwined and less separable empirically, with modernization advancing freedom, and nationalism released and enhanced by both. As early as 1830 the Austrian dramatist Franz Grillpalzer noted the interplay between modernization and the decline of imperial coercion in the rise of nationalism in the Habsburg realm. He likened the various nationalities of the Empire to "horses absurdly harnessed together ... [who] will scatter in all directions as soon as the advancing spirit of the times will weaken and break the bonds."[20] During the later part of the nineteenth century the Habsburg Empire experienced industrialization, urbanization, intensifying communications, and growing literacy. All these both increased the popular pressures for political participation by way of democratization and enhanced nationalism among the empire's many peoples and ethnicities. As we have seen in Chapter 5, the Habsburg Empire, unlike the Russian, had no dominant people, or *Staatsvolk*, with a "controlling stake." The settlement of 1867, according to which control of the empire was divided between the German and Hungarian elements, turning the Habsburg Empire into Austro-Hungary, could not stem the tide for long. With the introduction of universal male suffrage in the Austrian realm (but not in the Hungarian) in 1907, the Austrian parliament became divided along ethnonational lines, with sectarian parties voted in by each of the main nationalities. Even the socialists were divided along such lines.[21] Despite some existing sympathy for the old Habsburg ruler and the imperial tradition, democratization immediately revealed that the popular will was invariably nationalistic.

Most of the nationalist movements started out by demanding autonomy and equality within the imperial framework, rather than fully-fledged independence. But to a large degree this was so because demands for independence would have put them beyond the pale of political legitimacy and legality, were tantamount to disloyalty to the emperor, were initially unrealistic and, indeed, would have been countered by robust force by the still very powerful and oppressive imperial authorities. Moreover, in view of the many obvious complications inherent in a partition of a multiethnic realm and supposedly alleviated by the imperial framework, nationalists sometimes made virtue out of necessity in their political statements and programs. Indeed, in theory, the empire could have been transformed into a democratic federation of nationalities, each having its own linguistic, cultural, and educational autonomy. This solution was ostensibly appealing in view of central-eastern Europe's proverbial minority problem, with ethnic enclaves existing within ethnic enclaves almost *ad infinitum*. In his remarkably fresh *The Question of Nationalities and Social Democracy* (1907), Social Democrat Otto Bauer suggested that, irrespective of his place of residence, each individual would be allowed to freely choose the national community with which he wished to associate, most notably for educational and cultural purposes. In this manner, Bauer's scheme intended to combine individual choice with national and minority rights. How truly realistic such visions were remains an open question, as the First World War dealt the empire a final death blow and made it possible for its various nationalities to declare independent states, each rife with its own national minority problems.

The near universal process of imperial disintegration belies the so-called instrumentalist thesis, according to which manipulation of the masses by the elite is the cause of nationalism. Although all the major instruments of manipulation and nation-building – schools, universal military service, and, in totalitarian empires, also the media – were tightly controlled by the imperial state, a single *imperial* nation scarcely emerged even after centuries of imperial rule. It appeared barely at all in the Habsburg domain and very weakly in the Russian–Soviet state. By contrast, the slightest crack in the imperial wall of suppression was sufficient to spark nationalist eruptions and political secessionism, even though the leaders of the national movements lacked all the above instruments of state power. True, in the post-communist collapse of the Soviet Union and Yugoslavia, the local party bosses and state apparatus of the Soviet and Yugoslav republics played a decisive role in steering their respective ethnonational territories toward separatism and independence. This brought about a renewed surge of the manipulation thesis.[22] However, its proponents fail to notice how easily the new ethnonational successor states were created despite generations and sometimes centuries of state indoctrination to the contrary. They equally fail to recognize how surprisingly stable the successor states have proven to be despite a lack of national state tradition and countless other problems, not least those of national minorities. Certainly, manipulation of national, as all other popular sentiments by political leaders is central to politics. And yet, simply put, leaders can manipulate only what is *manipulatable*. They can and do play on sentiments they know to be strong among their constituencies, and are hardly ever able to do so on something that is not there. Moreover, a failure to play on sentiments that resonate powerfully with their constituencies is likely to result in the loss of power to other political leaders who do. This included the Communist Party bosses in many of the Soviet republics who had to work hard to convince their peoples that they were good nationalists. In fact, instrumentalism is at odds with the modernist thesis that nationalism is intimately connected with popular sovereignty and the popular will. Although cynicism and manipulation always exist, the reality is that leaders tend to share the national sentiments prevalent among their peoples, and indeed become and remain leaders for being the exponents of these sentiments.

Not only the three east European empires, but also the British and French overseas empires disintegrated when imperial coercion broke down. Liberalization and democratization of the imperial center itself played a much greater role in bringing this about in their cases: economic liberalism prescribed that imperialism did not pay; political liberalization and democratization undermined the legitimacy of foreign rule without indigenous consent, while also making ruthless suppression and the threat of wholesale massacre, the *sine quo non* of imperial rule throughout history, no longer acceptable. And it did not matter how affected by modernization the imperial territories that broke into independence were, something that varied considerably, from the barely touched to the lightly so, transforming mainly the colonial elites. Thus, at least as much as being the outcome of modernization processes in the formerly colonial territories themselves, the great proliferation of the independent nation-state throughout the globe after 1945 resulted from the increasing liberalization of the democratic imperial powers, a process which undermined and delegitimized their empires.* What broke the liberal empires was fundamentally not a loss of power, but a change in the economic

---

* This is the real interpretation of the statistical findings presented by Andreas Wimmer and Yuval Feinstein, "The Rise of the Nation-State across the World, 1816–2001," *American Sociological Review*, 75 (2010), 764–790. The authors "find no evidence for the effects of industrialization, the advent of mass literacy, or increasingly direct rule, which are associated with the modernization theories of Gellner, Anderson, Tilly, and Hechter." They also correctly emphasize the centrality of imperial disintegration: the Spanish in Latin America, the Habsburg and Russian in the First World War, and the massive post-1945 Western liberal decolonization. But their connection of all these points is less successful.

rationale and a loss of legitimacy to use power, especially in the old effective ruthlessness. Again, authoritarian and totalitarian empires, which retained the old methods of brutal suppression, serve as control cases for the effect of imperial coercion. Both the German and Japanese empires were dismantled after the First and Second World Wars by defeat at the hands of other Great Powers, rather than by indigenous struggles for independence. To judge by these empires' ruthless conduct during their imperial period, by the Soviet experience during most of the twentieth century, and by today's authoritarian China vis-à-vis secessionist nationalism in Tibet and Xinxiang, there is no reason to believe that such struggles would have been successful against *them*. We will return to this key subject later in the chapter.

Many modernists may regard my discussion of the relative weight of modernization vis-à-vis the break up of imperial coercion in the surge of modern nationalism as irrelevant. In contrast to the founders and leading exponents of the modernist school – Hayes, Kohn, Deutsch, Gellner, Anderson, Hobsbawm – who emphasized the revolutionary transformations generated by communication technology, urbanization, and industrialization, the recent trend among modernists has been to concentrate almost exclusively on popular sovereignty as the hallmark of the nation. It is somewhat curious that social scientists should so focus on the ideological or ideaic element, highly significant as it is, to the neglect of tangible realities that made possible the triumph of the new ideology. More importantly, this conflation of the concepts of popular sovereignty and the nation blurs the main issues: whether or not the popular will before modernity was very significantly ethnonational; whether or not this factor heavily affected the political frontiers of loyalty between and within states, while maintaining a dynamic balance with other forces and principles, most notably imperial coercion and dynastic rule.

To repeat, there is no question that the triumph of the principle of popular sovereignty over competing principles of legitimization and political rule owed a great deal to modern developments and was closely related to the triumph of nationalism as an ideology and reality. But did popular sovereignty beget nationalism or did it set it free, turning it from a major force in determining state configuration during premodern times to the predominant one during the modern era? As the evidence here suggests, modernization, rather than inaugurating nationalism, at one and the same time released, transformed, and enhanced it, while greatly increasing its legitimacy.

B CIVIC NATIONS OR ETHNIC NATIONS? EUROPE, THE ENGLISH-SPEAKING IMMIGRANT COUNTRIES, LATIN AMERICA, AFRICA, AND ASIA

The distinction between civic and ethnic nationalism was made by Hans Kohn on the basis of earlier ideas by Ernest Renan and Friedrich Meinecke, and has been in common use ever since. Ostensibly, civic nationalism is defined as belonging to a political community, state, and territory, whereas ethnic nationalism is based on a perception of blood relation and common descent. The civic nation has been identified with a benign Western European liberal model epitomized by Britain and France, whereas xenophobic ethnic nationalism supposedly character-ized Central and Eastern Europe. It has been further suggested that the difference was rooted in the fact that in Central-Eastern Europe emer-gent nations preceded and created their states, rather than the other way around as in the West. Lacking a political definition, the nations of Central-Eastern Europe were obliged to define themselves in ethnic terms.[23] As pointed out earlier in the book, this picture is largely misleading, both with respect to Europe and elsewhere. In what follows, we examine the shaping of national identity during the nine-teenth and twentieth centuries in Europe, the Anglo-Saxon immigrant countries, Latin America, Africa, and south-southeast Asia. This survey demonstrates that, whatever their civic features, national identities are hardly ever divorced from shared ethnic realities.

The European national templates

We begin with the historically paradigmatic cases of civic nationalism in Europe: Britain and France. As we have seen in Chapter 5, both are simply cases wherein a state based on a strong ethnic nucleus, the English people and the *langue d'oïl*-speaking population of northern France, from very early on and over centuries successfully spread their rule and culture through a combination of coercion and dominance.

In Britain, this process has created an English-speaking British national identity on top of the four national identities of the British Isles. France, for its part, has been uniquely successful in that French acculturation and national identity have been accepted by all other ethnic and national identities within the French state. French culture and nationality are inseparable. Indeed, contrary to the cliché regarding civic tolerance and openness, France, the paradigmatic "civic" nation, has been entirely intolerant toward all other ethnic identities and cultures within the country. By contrast, many "ethnic" nations grant their national minorities, which they are less reluctant to recognize as such, extensive cultural and even political autonomy.[24] Moreover, the kin element of ethnicity, in addition to the cultural component, is far from absent in French national identity. The famous *patrie*, patria, is literally the land of the fathers, or fatherland. The Revolution, which inaugurated the modern concept of the French nation based on the popular will and a common law, also proclaimed, most famously in the Abbé Sieyès' "What is the Third Estate," that the French people had a common origin, descending from the Gauls and Romans (as opposed to the aristocracy's alleged descent from the Frankish conquerors). This idea has since been taught to generations of French schoolchildren. After the provinces of Alsace and Lorraine were stripped from France against their people's will, Renan advanced a voluntarist concept of nationality as a "daily plebiscite." Nonetheless, the constitution of the Fifth Republic, like its predecessors, proclaims the indivisibility of France, allowing no secession.[25]

France and Britain are different from other cases in that like any hegemonic people, with a long and successful tradition of dominating various ethnic populations, the French and British have become accustomed to regarding their identity as unchallenged and, indeed, universal, rather than as particularly ethnic. They were cavalierly confident of their ability to absorb outsiders, who could not possibly desire anything more than the privilege of being admitted into their respective spheres. With the French, acculturation became a state ideology and constitutional principle, whereas for the British assimilation was more an unspoken and unreflective assumption. Consequently, the two states were somewhat more open to accepting foreigners into the family of the nation as "adopted sons," the French proudly and gloriously, while the British with far greater disdain.[26] In both cases, however, either the formal requirement (France) or the tacit assumption

(Britain) was that newcomers would sooner or later become "like us."
When large waves of immigrants deemed particularly alien arrived, this
general attitude came under pressure, with the public mood becoming
hostile and immigration policy becoming more rigid. Ultimately, all the
waves of immigration into the two countries were fully assimilated.
However, a greater influx of immigrants from Muslim countries, who
have failed to integrate and who retain their separate identity, has
created an acute threat perception among the public and the traditional
posture has come under great strain.

A number of points need clarifying. I am not prejudging
whether or not and to what degree Muslim communities in Europe
would be successfully integrated within their adopted countries like
earlier waves of immigration. Very substantial processes of integration
and assimilation evidently take place, *inter alia* with respect to language,
but much else and future developments are a matter of speculation. Nor
am I judging who is to be "blamed" for the shortcomings of integration,
the host countries or the immigrants. Moreover, I am not suggesting
that the newcomers *should* assimilate into Europe's national cultures. In
the first place, processes of cultural integration tend to involve fusion
and variably affect the native culture and not only the newcomers.
Culture is neither a given nor immutable. Second, this is a descriptive
not a normative book. My purpose is to point out how ethnic and
national sentiments and categories, being the highly potent forces that
they are, manifest themselves in reality. Certainly, rather than a monolith, culture is a diverse and rich mosaic, and tolerance and respect for
other cultures and minority rights are the foundations of life in liberal
democratic societies. At the same time, in the overwhelming majority
of cases, national identity rests on a thick shared cultural matrix, which
sustains only a limited level of challenge to its core.

Thus, given the challenge to their cultural identity acutely felt
by the public in Europe's various national states in relation to mainly
Muslim immigration and difficulties of integration, reactions have been
fairly similar in countries supposedly possessing different concepts of
nationalism. Both David Cameron, Prime Minister of "civic" Britain,
and Angela Merkel, Chancellor of traditionally "ethnic" Germany,
have separately stated that multiculturalism has not worked. The
French state, which never recognized multiculturalism, legislates
against cultural customs that violate the republic's "secular character,"
in effect its culture as an officially secular nation with a predominantly

Christian cultural–historical heritage. Holland has made a language and values test a condition for immigration. Although the stringent new requirements formally test "civic compatibility," language has long been posited as the main objective characteristic of ethnonational identity, while values are also quintessential cultural artifacts. Denmark, a civic nation whose people happen to have a very specific ethnic character, has passed even more restrictive immigration laws which make the right to become a citizen conditional on cultural affinity. And Switzerland, the quintessential multilingual civic state, has always regarded the naturalization of foreign residents with great disdain and has the most restrictive immigration policy. The naive ideological fiction that civic nations rest purely on citizenship and shared political institutions has been just that: at best an ideological expression of a desire for tolerance and a rejection of bigotry, and at worst a deep state of "false consciousness." Undoubtedly, all nations have a strong civic element, and there are various mixes and balances here, but very few nations do not rely on a sense of shared kin–culture identity as the basis for civic cooperation.[27]

The catalog of supposedly civic as opposed to ethnic nations includes a number of other paradigmatic cases which call for a closer examination. For example, after a short-lived union with Protestant Holland and subsequent independence in 1830–1831, Catholic Belgium was home to two different ethnic populations, the French-speaking Walloons in the south and Dutch-speaking Flemings in the north. In reality, however, the Walloons dominated the Belgian state. Once the Flemish population became more organized politically, it increasingly pressed for linguistic equality and then for a practical division of the country between the two ethnic populations.[28] In consecutive "state reforms" since 1970, real power has been devolved from the central government to the two provinces. The supposedly civic state is actually divided and dominated politically by intensely ethnic categories and institutions. Belgium has thus become a very rare case of a democratic binational state, with its future hanging in the balance as its constitutive ethnic nationalities (particularly the Flemish) would have evidently preferred to part ways. They are constrained from doing so by practical problems, above all what to do with the ethnically divided capital, Brussels, located as an enclave within Flanders.

Switzerland has gained an even more prominent paradigmatic status in the literature on civic nationalism. It demonstrates that a long-standing, stable, and otherwise successful nation can be multi-ethnic/multilingual, as Switzerland is. However, while the Swiss case may be considered enviable and desirable, its paradigmatic status is highly questionable given its extreme rarity and the special circumstances which brought it into being. Again, as so often in the study of nations and nationalism, the exception – the Habsburg Empire, France, Switzerland – has been regarded as typical. The Swiss Confederation was created in the Middle Ages as a military alliance between German-speaking mountain cantons and city-states of the plain. During the early modern period it was loosely joined by French-speaking city-states and cantons further west. The alliance was struck in the interest of freedom, on a sociopolitical rather than a national basis, to defend peasant and civic liberty against feudal and regal subjugation by the German aristocracy and empire, Burgundy, and France. It succeeded largely because of Switzerland's geography as a mountain fortress, while practically lacking a central government. Political authority remained in the cantons, whose character was clearly ethnic. Some Italian-speaking districts were added to Switzerland by way of conquest and were ruled by the German cantons until the nineteenth century. The modern reorganization and fuller democratization of the Swiss Confederation occurred in 1848, including the creation of a central government.[29]

Swiss national identity rests on a long tradition of both independence in defense of liberty from outside and successful democratic cooperation within the two levels of the cantons and the confederation. These have been fostered by Switzerland's aloofness from and stability amid the turmoil and great wars which engulfed the Continent during the twentieth century. (Notably, though, Switzerland was polarized along linguistic lines between German and French sympathizers during the First World War.) Another major factor has been the country's economic prosperity. All these made Swiss national identity more attractive than any secessionist alternative in conjunction with national states across the border – Germany, France, or Italy. More recently there have been concerns that some of these factors no longer apply and that Switzerland's linguistic groups are drifting apart. The European Union has created a new challenge to Swiss national identity, with French speakers more favorable to the idea of joining, while German speakers have been largely opposed.[30]

The European Union

The European Union has become a focal point for the discussion on nationalism, because it is purported to both transcend the national principle and rest on civic rather than ethnic categories of citizenship and political incorporation. Indeed, Europe's transformation from a continent ridden by interstate war into a peaceful economic and political union is one of the most signal developments of the post-Second World War world. Enthusiasm about this change has been understandable and justified. Europe's prosperous and peaceful cooperation is only the most striking manifestation of a more general phenomenon in the affluent world, resulting from a combination of economic development, economic interdependence, and an interdemocratic peace.[31] Contrary to the fears of the European community's founders, these effects have been achieved within the developed and democratic world even without political unity. All the same, it is Europe's political union that makes the continent special. As these lines are written, the European Union faces its greatest challenge ever, generated by the European debt problem, the crisis of the common currency, and the resulting tensions among the Union's member states. As the period of euphoria is replaced by the trials of bad times, commentators advance conflicting opinions regarding the Union's condition and desired course of development. Because Europe has been proclaimed a principle, an ideal, and a model for others, it is necessary to spell out what this model actually involves and what it does not, as well as what parts of it are relevant for others.

Undoubtedly, the partial transfer of authority and sovereignty from the states to the European Union has created something new and unprecedented. And yet the European Union remains a union of states, and, indeed, of national states. Not only do these nation-states remain the chief agents in every sphere, but in some ways they are more ethnically defined than before. The so-called ethnic revival in Europe is closely associated with the Union's framework. Small peoples and territorially concentrated ethnic populations, which were previously sheltered within larger states, are now attracted by the option of breaking away and establishing national independence within the Union's wider political and economic framework. Scotland, Flanders, the Basque country, Catalonia, and perhaps also Wales, Corsica, and Lombard Italy entertain this option, or as a minimum seek to achieve extended political autonomy.[32] Processes of ethnic fragmentation previously attributed to eastern Europe are also evident in "civic" Western Europe.

Moreover, the European Union itself, although often described in purely civic terms, has in reality a distinctive cultural–civilizational identity which constitutes the basis of a shared sense of affinity and solidarity among its peoples. This sense of a common European civilization goes back to the Middle Ages and has its roots in an even earlier classical heritage. It is practically identical with what was used to be known as Christendom, which now exists mainly as a secular, cultural–historical identity.[33] This shared identity is not national but supranational, and at present it is much weaker as a focus of affinity and solidarity than the various particular national identities in Europe. Nonetheless, it is a broader familial-civilizational identity which underlies attitudes concerning who is a natural member of the Union and who is not.

Turkey has been the most prominent case in point. Partly captive to their own rhetoric of Europe as a purely civic idea and partly disbelieving that Turkey would be able to transform, the members of the European Union in the years after 1999 presented Turkey with a list of reforms it had to implement as a condition for being allowed to join the Union. Surprising by the scope of its reforms, Turkey still found the gates of the Union closed. Its case contrasted markedly with those of Romania and Bulgaria, whose still dubious standards of government and economic conduct did not prevent them from being accepted into the Union in 2007. Some European leaders have begun to cite the difference in cultural identity as the cause of Turkey's exclusion. But others have found it more convenient to talk about the geography of what constitutes Europe as the natural boundary of the European Union. This supposedly applies not only to Turkey (which lies partly in Europe) but also to the Arab-Muslim countries of North Africa, across the Mediterranean. Conveniently, the geography of Europe and the boundaries of European Christendom converge pretty neatly, with the only open frontier in the Balkans. To be sure, religion is only one, albeit major, aspect of the overall cleavage in culture and identity: in the Balkans the Muslim populations of Bosnia, Kosovo and Albania are probably considered both European enough and small enough to qualify for future absorption into the Union, together with Christian Croatia and Serbia. In practice, the European Union has moved toward offering Turkey and the countries of North Africa every form of economic and other cooperation short of actually joining the Union and exercising the right of free immigration into its national states.

Thus, in contrast to Europe's past of expansionist and warlike nationalism, today's Europe is an example of a peaceful and mostly defensive nationalism, yet nationalism nevertheless. People are barely aware of it in their daily life and are scarcely called upon to sacrifice for it as in olden times or when the Soviet threat was still present. For this reason it is transparent to most of them and may appear as transparent to some scholars. This condition of unrecognized pervasive nationalism has been aptly called "banal" nationalism.[34] In actuality, people's main allegiance and sense of solidarity still lies with their own people and national state rather than with the Union at large. The sovereign debt crisis has brought this to the surface, while also demonstrating how interconnected the fate of the Union's various peoples is. Indeed, it is sovereignty more than nationalism that has been eroding. When acutely challenged in their home countries, for example by dense immigrant communities which fail to integrate, people's reaction, expressed politically, is unmistakable.

Will the European Union grow from a supranational identity into a national one, supplanting or more realistically incorporating the old, particularistic European national identities? Will it develop a graduated, composite structure of identity in which that of Europe will become politically supreme? Some of the European Union's advocates hope so, believing that over time the Union can in this sense become a United States of Europe. Rather than attempting to predict the future, I would like to offer a few thoughts on the processes involved. First, if the European identity is to become dominant, this would rely as much on the sense of a shared European cultural and historical tradition and familial affinity becoming yet more deeply entrenched as on the Union's economic and political success. While this sentiment can be actively cultivated, it is real rather than merely "manipulated." Second, the European Union is a long way from becoming the United States of Europe because its constitutive national states are very far from being akin to the states of the United States. Whereas the latter share a language and, by and large, a culture, while lacking separate histories and a tradition of separate independence, the states of Europe are very distinct from one another in all of the above. In its linguistic and ethnic fragmentation the European Union is more akin to India, with the difference that the states of India were united under the British Raj for nearly two centuries and had earlier also had a much weaker tradition of separate independence. We shall discuss both the United States and India as we proceed with our review of so-called civic nations.

The English-speaking immigrant states: purely civic nations?

Some of the largest and most significant states in today's world are almost entirely populated by immigrants and their descendants. The United States, Canada, Australia, and New Zealand, for example, were created by immigrants who arrived during recent centuries. Immigration remains central to their experience, ethos, and identity. The people of each of these countries (with the partial exception of Canada, discussed below) view themselves and are viewed by others as one nation. But what sort of nations are they? Many theorists postulate that they are quintessentially civic because their people have clearly arrived from different countries of origin and diverse cultures, and are supposedly multiethnic and united only by allegiance to their new country and adherence to its laws and institutions. In actuality, however, the immigrant countries' common national identity is far more substantial than that.[35] While retaining a distinct sense of their origin and culture, especially during the first generations after immigration, the various immigrant communities take on a great deal more in terms of cultural baggage, replacing most notably their language and much else. They increasingly merge into a shared, amalgamated new culture, to which they also variably contribute. Typically, from the third generation onward intermarriages among the immigrant ethnic groups rise steeply, as differences of culture and identity become thin and the common denominators become a much stronger reality. The new people's self-perception as a community of culture and, to some degree, also kinship (intermarried, adopted) becomes very recognizable. It is at least as potent as the people's perception of their state as a framework for mutual cooperation (which it reinforces). Except for habits of speech which identify ethnicity with minorities, there are plausible reasons for referring to these new kin–culture national communities in ethnic terms; in any case, they are widely and properly referred to as new and very distinctive peoples.

The United States is the most prominent case in point. Certainly, the United States is as civic as can be, based on its constitution and the eagerness of immigrants over the centuries to be admitted into this highly successful society. However, this is only part of a much wider picture. Before writing these pages on the United States, I read Michael Lind's *The Next American Nation* (1995) and was struck by how closely my views on the development of American national identity parallel his.[†] As he and a few other scholars point out, the United States began as a country of Englishmen who found themselves obliged to declare their independence from the motherland when they felt that their liberties as Englishmen were being infringed upon. According to the Declaration of Independence (1776):

> *Nor have We been wanting in attentions to our British brethren. We have warned them from time to time of attempts by their legislature to extend an unwarrantable jurisdiction over us. We have reminded them of the circumstances of our emigration and settlement here. We have appealed to their native justice and magnanimity, and we have conjured them by the ties of our common kindred to disavow these usurpations, which, would inevitably interrupt our connections and correspondence. They too have been deaf to the voice of justice and of consanguinity.*

British rights and the ties of brotherhood, descent, kinship, and, indeed, consanguinity (shared blood) between the motherland and the colonies were inseparable in the Declaration.

The political ties with Britain were severed during independence, but the part of the common stock that became the new nation in the new land remained tied together by the strong bonds of a common descent, kinship, and culture, including the English language and a Protestant religion. As John Jay put it in the second of *The Federalist Papers* (1787), a work he composed with Alexander Hamilton and James Madison:

> *Providence has been pleased to give this one connected country to one united people – a people descended from the same ancestors, speaking the same language, professing the same religion, attached to the same principles of*

[†] I refer to Lind's historical reconstruction rather than to his panacea for the future, which is more normative than descriptive.

*government, very similar in their manners and customs, and
who, by their joint counsels, arms, and efforts, fighting side
by side throughout a long and bloody war, have nobly
established general liberty and independence.*

Here was "a band of brethren, united to each other by the strongest ties," which far outweighed the separate identities and institutions of the thirteen colonies. Even the Jeffersonian Republicans, the Federalists' protagonists, who advocated a looser confederate structure for the United States, shared the perception of it as an Anglo-Saxon Protestant nation.

Certainly, there were also people of non-British descent in the young republic, and there would be more arriving during the first 100 years of its existence, mainly from various countries of western and northern Europe (to say nothing of the Native Americans and black slave population). And yet the new and very distinctive American nation, culture, and identity were clearly Anglo-Saxon, English-speaking, and Protestant, with other immigrant groups largely assimilating into it and partly remaining outside its core. The arrival of Irish Catholics around the middle of the nineteenth century elicited negative reactions. But the most significant challenge to American national identity was the split and mutual alienation which developed between the plantation, slave-owning Southern society and culture, and the Yankee North, industrial and a magnet for non-Anglo-Saxon immigrants. Had the South succeeded in its bid to secede, there could have emerged two separate national communities, as distinct from each other as Britain and the United States are despite a common language.

The next significant change came during the late nineteenth and early twentieth centuries, as new waves of immigrants arrived from the countries of southern and eastern Europe, and were Catholic, Orthodox, or Jewish. More threatening still in the eyes of many Americans, some of the immigration was non-white, coming from east Asia. A Chinese Exclusion Act was passed as early as 1882, and broader stringent immigration laws were enacted in 1921 and 1924, putting an end to a history of practically unrestricted immigration (for whites). In an attempt to perpetuate the ethnic composition of the United States, these laws set quotas that allowed in people from each country of origin in proportion to its then existing share in the American population. Nonetheless, as people of Anglo-Saxon descent had lost the status of majority in the American population, declining from 60 to 40 percent between 1900 and 1920,[36] American identity was transformed. It was broadened, in Lind's apt phrase, from Anglo-American and Protestant to Euro-American and "Judeo"-Christian. Correspondingly, the ideology and policy of a "melting pot" dominated, whereby all immigrants were to be assimilated into an English-speaking American culture. On the whole, the immigrants themselves aspired to "become American," which meant integrating into American culture.

With the increasing liberalization of the United States and the civil rights movement of the 1950s and 1960s came another transformation and broadening of American national identity. In 1965, immigration quotas by country of origin were abolished so as not to discriminate on the basis of ethnicity. The ideology of the "melting pot" has similarly fallen into disrepute, and ethnic and racial diversity of cultures and origins is celebrated. A new surge in immigration has followed, unparalleled in scale since the turn of the twentieth century, with immigrants arriving mainly from Latin America and east Asia rather than from Europe. However, while all these changes have been far-reaching and highly significant, their exact meaning needs to be closely understood. Certainly, the United States is no longer white, let alone Anglo-Saxon, and in the public sphere its predominately Christian identity has been giving way to a kind of generalized religiosity (Lind: indifferentist theism[37]). Yet the rhetoric of multiculturalism and multiethnicity, justified and commendable as it may be in expressing new norms of respect for diverse group heritages in the public sphere, should not obscure the more fundamental reality: there exists a very distinct American culture, widely shared by the large majority of Americans, and characterized by a common American-English language and all-pervasive folkways. These encompass mores, symbols, social practices, and public knowledge; popular tastes, images, and heroes; music, sports, cuisine, public holidays, and social rituals. Epitomized by the nineteenth-century Yankee, the distinctive American culture has been powerfully shaped from the twentieth century on by the media and entertainment industry, most notably the press, Hollywood, and television.[38]

That this has been a fusion culture, drawing from many immigrant sources and traditions is uncontestable and is much celebrated as a wellspring of richness and creativity. The point, however, is that this fusion, ever-changing like any culture, is quintessentially American, widely shared by the American people, and projected beyond the United States' borders as distinctively American. Indeed, the Americanism of American culture is deeply felt around the world, regarded either with approval or disapproval, and Americans become very conscious of it whenever they encounter the outside world. This common American culture far transcends the political-civic culture that many theorists have posited, naively, as the exclusive binding element of the American nation. Also questionable is the claim that immigrant ethnicities should not be labeled "minorities" because there is no majority ethnicity in the United States, given that people of British descent constitute only a small part of the American people (15 percent in 1981 and falling). It can be argued that the majority identity in America is actually *American*.[39] Ascribing ethnicity to the immigrant communities, but not to the common creation of the majority of Americans, brings to mind a person from Minnesota who in reply to an inquiry what the accent there was responded that in Minnesota there was no accent. One's own culture, especially a great and dominant one, appears transparent. Only the others are ethnic.

Certainly, many immigrants and their descendants in the United States have a distinct sense of origin and tradition, sometimes a strong one. In the first generations after immigration this has regularly given rise to a mosaic of close-knit ethnic communities. Where religious identity has been involved, these communities have been all the more entrenched. They largely account for the American "anomaly" in the developed world: the relatively large number of people attending institutions of worship, which double as ethnocommunal centers. Furthermore, throughout American history ethnic communities have maintained ties with the old country and people. Some of them have also carried out lobbying activity in Washington for them, especially when they felt their kin needed their help.[40] Moreover, since the 1970s a surge in the quest for roots in terms of origin and tradition has been very noticeable and much celebrated even, indeed, most typically, among people three generations or more in the United States.

Still, the cultural identity of the so-called "hyphenated Americans" past the first one or two generations after immigration is overwhelmingly American, with the search for origins and tradition playing a symbolically important but mostly secondary role.[41] American history and tradition becomes theirs at least as much as their consciousness of distinctive roots, in most cases much more so, with some strong variations such as the experience of slavery for African-Americans. Americans would say as a matter of course that they won the War of Independence, or the Second World War, even if their forefathers had not yet arrived in the United States when these historical events took place. Indeed, not only linguistic distinctions disappear as the second and third generations after immigration speak English as their primary and then only native language; this language replacement is merely the most conspicuous element of a wider integration into a generalized American culture, tradition, and identity.[42] Was singer and actor Frank Sinatra, American-born to Italian immigrants, who retained some life-long ties to the Italian community, including reputedly to the Mafia, ethnically more Italian than American? And what about actress Jennifer Aniston of the hit television drama series *Friends*, who is American-born to a father of Greek descent and a mother of Scottish and Italian descent?

Rates of intermarriage among the original ethnic communities are the most tangible and robust indicator of these processes. While intermarriages are still marginal in the first and second generations after immigration, they rise steeply thereafter. Studies mostly concentrate on two categories: interracial and interreligious marriages. Interracial marriage among whites, Asians, Latinos, African-Americans, and Native Americans, where differences in physical appearance variably remain after the cultural differences diminish, are nonetheless steadily rising in all categories. More than half of the Native Americans marry outside their group, as do between one-third and one-half of American-born Asians and Latinos (marrying mostly whites).[43] Interreligious marriages also range around 50 percent. This is a huge change from the endogenous marriage patterns within Protestants, Catholics, and Jews still observable in the 1950s, which gave rise to the theory of three distinct melting pots.[44] Moreover, the focus on interracial and interreligious marriages is partly misleading. This is so because the barriers among the genuinely original ethnic communities, those by native country and people of origin, for example, among people of European descent, have been collapsing even more sweepingly through intermarriage and American acculturation.[‡]

[‡] Richard Alba, *Ethnic Identity: The Transformation of White America*, New Haven, CT: Yale University Press, 1990, extensively documenting these processes, suggests that they have created a new European–American joint ethnic identity that largely replaces

Thus, the more generations one's family has been in the United States, the more "fourth," "eighth," or "sixteenth" parts of descent from different countries and communities of origin one is likely to have and the more ethnically all-American one becomes. This has contributed to a growing sense of kinship among old-time Americans, which reinforces common culture and mutual social cooperation in American national identity. As one study has put it: "These connections between assimilation and intermarriage may be said to describe how once-distinct peoples become one stock, literally members of one family."[45] In a relatively young nation and with an ongoing immigration project, the shared kin element is weaker than in other nations, yet it is there. To remove any unnecessary quibbles, it does not at all matter whether or not one accepts my definition of ethnicity and agrees that to a large degree it applies to the people of the United States, especially old-time Americans; the point is that far more than civic allegiance to a constitution and political society, a common dense national culture, as well as increasing interracial and interethnic mixing, underlie American sense of nationhood.[§]

It is probably not superfluous to stress that all the above means neither homogeneity nor harmony, but a dynamic and highly variable process. Among other things, some ethnic groups and categories are

the old country-of-origin ethnic identity. Alba agrees that there is a large convergence between European–American and what may simply be regarded as American ethnic identity (pp. 203, 312, 315). Indeed, this is how it is described by Kaufmann, *The Rise and Fall of Anglo-America*. Kaufmann holds that this American core ethnos, originally Anglo-Protestant and from 1960 simply white, has been losing its dominance because of the recent arrival of non-white immigrants. However, in my view, both Alba and Kaufmann miss one step. Americans of European descent happen to be the older waves of immigration, but continuing similar processes of intermarriage and cultural integration within American society and into an all-American identity seem to be occurring also with the newer waves of arrival from east Asia and Latin America.

§ In response to Will Kymlicka's critique (p. 279), Michael Walzer, retracting from his earlier position, has effectively conceded that the United States is not ethnically neutral, most conspicuously with respect to the English language. He claims, however (and Kymlicka agrees), that this ethnic element is thin in comparison with non-immigrant countries: Michael Walzer, "Nation-States and Immigrant Societies," in Kymlicka and Opalski (eds.), *Can Liberal Pluralism be Exported?*, 150–153. Although this view is obviously true to a large degree, I believe it still overestimates the sometimes marked, yet mostly symbolic, significance of the ancestral ethnic identities in the United States; generalizes from particularly strong cases of such identity; and underestimates the depth of American culture and the degree of cultural integration and intermarriage over the generations.

less successfully incorporated into the American nation, as reflected in both social realities and perceptions, including self-perception.[46] For example, despite high levels of intermarriage, Native Americans remain somewhat outside American national identity and, indeed, have recognized rights as distinct "nations" in their reservations. Also, although major strides have been made in the past decades, both the intermarriage rates and social integration of African-Americans lags behind those of other groups. Moreover, since the 1960s there have been some trends among African-Americans to define themselves as not only ethnically, but also nationally distinct. One dares predict that such trends will remain marginal to the more general process of integration into American society and identity. In this respect, Barack Obama's 2008 election to the presidency of the United States is a historical landmark. With both Kenyan and Irish descent and some African-American self-identification, his identity is surely, above all, American.

As immigration remains a major feature of the United States, the issue of immigrants' American acculturation and social integration continues to be ever-present and the focus of attention. Although even during the peaks of immigration immigrants consisted of less than 15 percent of the American population, together with their children (second generation) they periodically reached about double that figure. Furthermore, new waves of immigration replace older ones which have been absorbed into the American mainstream.** Today's large-scale Latino immigration is at the center of debate. While there are various aspects to this debate, including the effects of immigration on the economy and the welfare services, we shall restrict ourselves to the significance of this immigration in terms of American ethnic and national identity.

** Will Kymlicka claims that immigrant communities are growing, rather than shrinking or disappearing through cultural integration: "Liberal Multiculturalism: Western Models, Global Trends, and Asian Debates," in W. Kymlicka and B. He (eds.), *Multiculturalism in Asia*, Oxford University Press, 2005, 31–32. However, in reality, and contrary to Kymlicka's fundamental thesis, although the immigrant population worldwide is indeed growing due to the continuing influx of new immigrants, *earlier* generations of immigrants, in the United States but also in many other places, do integrate culturally and otherwise into the absorbing societies over time. There is a "conveyor belt" process, whereby immigrants are being continuously integrated in most places.

Samuel Huntington's *Who Are We? The Challenges to America's National Identity* (2005) has voiced widespread concerns. The book claims that the current wave of immigrants from Latin America, especially Mexico, is in some crucial ways different from earlier waves of immigration to the United States. Not only are immigrant numbers large, but they also arrive from countries adjacent to the United States and settle mostly in states along the United States' southern border. They thus create dense concentrations that have close proximity to and territorial contiguity with the Latin American countries and cultural sphere. Earlier immigrant communities in the United States were practically cut off by distance from their native countries. By contrast, according to Huntington, the Latino communities are more likely to retain their close links with their native countries across the border, as well as their distinct culture, language, and identity. In extreme scenarios this could ultimately lead to irredentism, the demand of new Latino majorities in some southwestern states to join Mexico (to which most of their territories belonged before the 1848 peace settlement that ended the American–Mexican War). More realistically, but as problematically in Huntington's view, the large numbers of Latino immigrants, territorial concentration, and strong ties with their native countries may split the United States in two in terms of language, culture, and identity. Such a threat to its national integrity has never occurred in American history except during the Civil War.

Huntington's critics cite data which reveal that Latino immigrants overwhelmingly profess pride in and identification with the United States, adopt American core values, and exhibit a clear generational switch to English only, albeit a little slower than with earlier immigrations.[47] If so, the Latino immigration is not fundamentally different from earlier waves of immigration in its gradual American acculturation. It is not our business to decide who is right on this issue, which involves both major empirical questions and speculations about future trends. Nor are we concerned with normative–ideological questions of multiculturalism and the nation. Rather, it is the more general theoretical questions of culture, ethnicity, and nationhood which are the subject of this book. Even if Huntington's predictions regarding the Latino immigrants' American acculturation or lack thereof are proven wrong, he touches on questions of central significance for the study of the national phenomenon. He makes the point missed by so many: that American national identity has rested on a common language adopted by the immigrants and a shared culture into which they integrated.[††] Although English has never been formally declared the official language of the United States, there has been no need for this as it has anyway held this position in practice virtually unchallenged. Only during the past decades have quite a number of US states promulgated English as the official language.

In the eighteenth century dense German settlement raised the prospect of the German language becoming entrenched in Pennsylvania (and in the nineteenth century, Wisconsin). This prospect alarmed Benjamin Franklin, who for cultural and racial reasons wanted German immigration to the United States to be terminated.[48] As it happened, it did not take long for Americans of German origin to trade their language for English and merge into Yankee identity, as did later waves of German and other immigrants. However, what if they had not? What if there had been in the United States territorially continuous stretches of immigrant communities which retained their linguistic and cultural identity? What if these had been more substantial, continuous, and resistant to American acculturation than, say, the Scandinavian settlers of the northern states of the Midwest, or the urban concentrations of Italian, Polish, Ukrainian, or Jewish immigrants? Might the United States then have become *truly* multiethnic and perhaps also multinational, or fragmented into separate national states? As Huntington suggests, become a Canada?

Indeed, Canada serves as an instructive contrast to the United States in terms of nation-building and national identity, at least in one crucial respect. (This gives new meaning to the half-whimsical observation that Canadian identity has been shaped as being not the United States.) The processes taking place in Canada's English-speaking parts have been not unlike those occurring in the United States. Diverse immigrant communities have transformed an originally Anglo-Saxon, British-dominated society. They have introduced a rich variety of cultural traditions and have maintained strong ethnocommunal ties within themselves, especially in the first generations after immigration. At the same time, and increasingly with every generation after

---

[††] It is of the utmost importance to Huntington that this culture remains predominantly Anglo-Saxon and Protestant. Yet for the existence of a common sense of national identity it matters little what the content of the shared culture is, however important this question may otherwise be.

immigration, immigrants and their descendants have integrated into an English-speaking Canadian national identity, fusing a joint Canadian culture.[49] These processes reoccur continuously as Canada remains an immigration country. There are, however, two exceptions to this general picture. There is the small Inuit population of the north, which like the Native Americans in the United States has been very imperfectly integrated into Canadian society and identity, and has in the past decades been accorded great attention in the discourse over multiculturalism and minority rights. Far more significant in terms of numbers, socioeconomic development, and power, and hence politically, has been the Francophone population of Quebec. Descendants of the French settlers in the French colony conquered by Britain in 1759, they have retained their language and identity for centuries. As the dominance of English-speaking Canada weakened with increasing liberalization, the Québécois have reasserted their identity from the 1960s on, claiming to be a separate people and nation. They have legislated the dominance of the French language and culture in the province, and in 2006 won official recognition in the Canadian House of Commons as a nation within Canada, transforming Canada into a binational state of sorts. Although two referenda in Quebec on secession from Canada were defeated in 1980 and (on the narrowest of margins) in 1995, the prospect of Quebec leaving Canada continues to loom on the horizon.

Canada is thus different from the United States on precisely this point: a substantial part of its population, the Québécois, has not merged into the prevailing language and culture, which together with their territorial concentration and strong feeling of identity results in a distinct sense of peoplehood and nationhood. This is not to suggest that either the American or Canadian experience is superior. Again, this is not a normative book. The Quebec issue in Canada merely accentuates the factual claim we have been making: rather than resting on civic foundations alone, American nationhood is based on a deep-rooted, widely shared, and proudly manifested American culture, in effect a genuine American ethnic identity. This common identity is forged from and enriched by, but over time is far deeper as a living reality than, the United States' multiethnic/ multicultural character.

On a smaller scale, Australia and New Zealand are quite similar to the United States in this regard and different from Canada.

With the exception of a much stronger British connection, their immigration and ethnic history resembles that of the United States and shall be compressed here into the briefest of abstracts. Both Australia and New Zealand were settled in the late eighteenth and nineteenth centuries by immigrants from the British Isles who gave both countries their language and cultural template. Both also absorbed some immigration from northwestern Europe in the nineteenth century and from other parts of Europe by the twentieth century. Both countries kept a white-only policy, barring immigrants from Asia until the second half of the twentieth century. At that time racial discrimination was abolished and a multicultural ideology became hegemonic. Yet in both countries immigrants have integrated into the society, changing their language to English, and adopting (while also contributing to) what are very recognizably Australian and New Zealander national cultures and historical traditions. Australians and New Zealanders celebrate the colonial settlement, as well as the ANZAC participation in the First World War and the Gallipoli campaign, as their national historical landmarks. This is so irrespective of the fact that the ancestors of most of the people living in these countries had not yet arrived in the country even during the later events. Interracial, interreligious, and interethnic marriages, rising dramatically by the second and third generations after immigration, both facilitate and are a strong indicator of the process of integration. The native elements, the Aborigines in Australia and Maori in New Zealand, remain on the margins of the common culture and national identity in each country. Yet here also growing social inclusion has gone hand in hand with rising intermarriage, which encompasses about half of the native population in both countries.[50] As in the United States, a shared culture and an expanding sense of kinship, from the core people to the newcomers, rather than civic allegiances alone, has always underpinned both Australian and New Zealander nationhood.

Liberal philosopher of multiculturalism and citizen of Canada Will Kymlicka, has made this important point in response to widely held misconceptions regarding a supposedly ethnic neutrality of the liberal state: all the liberal states do in fact give preference to a particular ethnicity, their own, as reflected most notably in their standard language; all are engaged in nation-building.[51]

Ethnicity and nation-building in Latin America

Nation-building and its relation to ethnic realities is all the more intriguing in the case of the Latin American countries. While they have been largely shaped by immigration, mostly Spanish (and Portuguese in Brazil) but also from other sources, a few of them have or had a large native (Indian) population (presently the majority in Bolivia and the largest category in Peru); most have native minorities and a large mixed-race, European–Indian, Spanish-speaking majorities; and a few have a large black (formerly slave) and mixed white–black–Indian population (Brazil, the Caribbean). Pan-Latin American identity, that of the individual states, and local Indian identities have all been around in Latin America, competing over and challenging the concept of the nation. Thus, more than in Europe, the English-speaking immigrant countries, and much of east Asia, nation-building in Latin America is still an ongoing project. Like any other part of the world, the Latin American countries are widely diverse and far from being a monolith. The following seeks to highlight both common patterns and major differences among them.

There were densely populated agricultural civilizations in both Mesoamerica (Mexico and periphery) and the Andes before the European conquest. The native population plummeted in the first century after the conquest perhaps by as much as 90 percent due to the importation of Old World diseases against which the natives had no natural immunity. But thereafter the native population recovered and constituted more than half of the people in both Mexico and Peru around 1800.[52] There were two reasons as to why it did not take a national form in the countries where the native population was large in number. First and foremost, Latin America was a mosaic of native ethnicities and languages, with some 400 native languages still in existence today. More than sixty languages are spoken by small ethnic communities in both Mexico and Colombia, and about half as many in Bolivia.[53] There was little to connect these diverse groups, and in most places they lacked any sense of common identity or the makings of such, except for their position vis-à-vis the Spanish colonizers. The empires of pre-Columbian America, most notably those of the (Nahuatl-speaking) Aztecs in Mesoamerica and the Incas in the Andes (Quechua speakers), were potentially capable of generating processes of large-scale ethnic leveling as had taken place in ancient states and empires of the Old World. There was a similar potential in major city-state systems such as that of the Maya. Yet, with the partial exception of the Quechua speakers in Peru who have survived as a large-scale linguistic group, these native trajectories were cut short by the conquest. Indeed, the order imposed by the conquerors was the second reason why the native populations of Latin America failed to express themselves nationally even where they were in the majority. The Spanish colonial possessions, which would later become the basis for independent states, were dominated by the elite and people of Spanish descent (*Criollos* = Creole) who harshly subjugated and economically exploited the natives in agricultural, mining, and industrial estates (*haciendas*).

As the Creole elite and people found their interests increasingly divergent from those of Spain and their perspective very much that of their new American homelands, they opted for and won independence. The struggle with Spain (*c.* 1808 to the mid 1820s) was mostly carried out locally in each province, but there was also some cooperation among the rebels. Continental military campaigns were led by Simón Bolívar and José de San Martín, who also championed a political unity of Spanish Latin America. However, there was not to be a Hispanic United States of America, with Bolívar as its Washington, if only because the territories of Spanish America were seven times larger than that of the United States at the time of US independence (and thirty times larger than Spain itself), and they were yet more dispersed geographically. Even regional federations established in newly liberated Latin America during the 1820s proved to be short-lived. In what were former vice-royalties, captaincies, and provinces of the Spanish empire, the local Creole elite took over and declared independent states.[‡‡]

The commercial and cultural interaction of the elite in each of the new states with Europe (and later with the United States) would quickly grow more significant than among these countries, further eroding pan-Latin American identity. On the other hand, state control

---

[‡‡] Benedict Anderson, *Imagined Communities: Reflections on the Origins and Spread of Nationalism*, London: Verso, 1983, ch. 4, 50–65, has rightly stressed the effect of local newspapers in shaping a distinct identity in each of the former provinces of the Spanish empire. But this was only one among the constraints of communication, government, and diversity imposed by Latin America's great size and geographical dispersion.

and identity were also weak, as provincial landlords and warlords (*caudillos*) in each country secured practical autonomy from the capital.[54] Some sense of individual state patriotism was cultivated among the Creoles, especially in the urban centers. It can be referred to as nationalism as far as this element was concerned (and was so regarded by them). However, such a designation would be problematic in the majority of the Latin American states because the divisions between Creoles and Indians, with people of mixed race (*mestizos*) in the middle, were not merely social, economic, and political but also ethnic. Bolívar and San Martín realized that the eradication of these deeply entrenched divisions would be a necessary precondition for nation creation, because Creoles and Indians did not regard themselves as belonging to the same people. Modernist Benedict Anderson has turned reality on its head by claiming that the new Latin American countries were among the first nations, preceding Europe. But in actuality, the much older European nations served as a model and an ideal to be pursued by Latin American nationalists, who acutely felt that their own countries fell far short.[55]

In fact, early-nineteenth-century Latin America is where Gellner's model of the premodern world is at last valid: there was a land-owning and urban upper stratum, on the one hand, and a lower stratum of agricultural producers, on the other, with the latter being ethnically different not only from the former but also among themselves, constituting a mosaic of native ethnicities and local cultures. The various Indian ethnic groups in each country lacked both common attributes of culture (above all language) and a sense of shared kinship. This was radically different from the situation between nobility and peasants in Castile, Portugal, England, the Scandinavian countries, Poland, or Russia (about which Gellner is so misleading). It was also significantly different from the Bohemian or Baltic peasants under their German landlords, the Ukrainian peasants under their Polish landlords, or the Chinese under the Mongol or Manchu yoke, in all of which two distinct ethnic communities or peoples were superimposed on each other in a relationship of political subjugation and economic exploitation. Native communities in the Latin American countries resisted and often rebelled against their oppressors. Yet peasant rebellions, anywhere tending to be local/provincial in scope, were all the more so in the Latin American countries, being confined as most of them were to a particular ethnic space. The large-scale Tupac Amaru rebellion of Quechua speakers in Peru during late colonial times (1780), raising the banner of the Inca, was a telling exception, as were some large-scale peasant uprisings in Mayan Yucatan.

Thus, the great majority of the new Latin American countries during the nineteenth century were weak states and even weaker nations, with these two features being significantly interrelated. For them to become national states both the state had to gain power and a common kin–culture identity had to emerge and engulf European and the various Indian ethnic groups (and blacks). Central to this process has been the increasing prevalence and symbolic role of the *mestizo*, the people of mixed Spanish–Indian race. This in turn was inseparable from the spread of the Spanish language among the Indians, and their even earlier conversion to Catholic Christianity. Finally, there was the fusion of the Spanish and Indian grand traditions into collective national histories.

Sexual relations and marriages between the Spanish and natives in Latin America have been common since the conquest and carried a lesser social stigma than they did in British North America. The high proportion of single men among the Spanish newcomers and the dense Indian population in much of Spanish America help to account for this, contrasting as they did with the more common family immigration to, and much thinner native population in, the British colonies. A strict, legally codified hierarchy of races, from Spaniards to mixed Spanish–Indians to Indians and blacks, prevailed in colonial Spanish America. Nonetheless, people of mixed race have become very much the norm in the countries of Mesoamerica and the Andes, particularly around the main centers of Spanish settlement, though barely in the more remote rural areas. Present-day genetic studies corroborate this long-held notion.[56] The spread of the Spanish language has contributed to the blurring of interracial boundaries. By the twentieth century, mixed-race, Spanish-speaking *mestizos* had become the majority of the population in nearly half of the Latin American countries.

Modernization greatly accelerated the dual process of state- and nation-building. Again, the modernist model of nation creation fits the countries of Latin America much better than other places. Urbanization, the railway and the road, elementary education, and compulsory military service vastly increased connectivity, state penetration, political mobilization, and cultural integration.[57] The limited representative systems and old oligarchies of estate-owners and urban notables increasingly gave way to regimes of popular legitimacy, including the populist authoritarianism that became synonymous with Latin America. The native population has been progressively, if variably, brought into and integrated within the nation.

Mexico very much led this process.[58] The 1910–1917 Revolution that inaugurated the modern Mexican state turned the *mestizo* into the idealized Mexican identity. Mexicans have been perceived and projected as a people and nation of mixed blood. The spread of the Spanish language and the receding of the Indian languages with modernization reinforced the fusion of identities. Only 10–15 percent of Mexico's population is still categorized as Indian, and less than half of them speak one of the sixty-two Indian languages. Most of them live in the remote and least modernized provinces of southern Mexico, such as Yucatán, Oaxaca, and Chiapas, wherein, indeed, centrifugal pressures and separatist uprisings are still a reality. Ethnic mixing also involved a merging of historical traditions. The glory of the pre-Columbian Mexican civilizations, castigated after the conquest as heathen and bloodthirsty, has been fully brought into the national story, where they peacefully coexist with the *conquistadores* who destroyed them as the common past, heritage, and pride of Mexicans. Similar processes of ethnic and national fusion have taken place in other countries of Spanish Latin America, such as Venezuela, Colombia, Ecuador, and Paraguay. In Peru and Bolivia, where these processes have been less advanced, large rural Indian populations remain, still weakly integrated into the national body, or indeed, politically mobilized to take it over.

In Argentina and Uruguay, the native population was much thinner in the first place, and both Indians and *mestizos* together constitute less than 10 percent of the population. These countries' development in terms of nationality resembles that of the English-speaking immigrant countries. Both Argentina and Uruguay (and also Chile, with a white majority and a large *mestizo* population) have absorbed large-scale non-Spanish immigration, particularly from Italy and other European and Mediterranean countries, as well as from east Asia. However, the immigrants have adopted Spanish and much of the local culture, enriching it with their own and fusing a Spanish-speaking national identity in each country.

Brazil represents a special variation on the same themes. Large numbers of black Africans were brought to the country as slaves to work in plantations owned by the Portuguese. Slavery existed in Brazil until 1888, but widespread interracial sexual relations have created both a reality and perception of a mixed-race and multiracial society. According to the 2010 census, whites constitute a little less than a half of the population in Brazil (47.7 percent), followed closely as the second largest category (43 percent) by mixed white–black–Indian people (*pardos*). About 7.5 percent of the population identify as blacks, and around 0.5 percent as Indians.[59] No less significantly, both blacks and non-Portuguese immigrants, mostly from Europe, have adopted the Portuguese language and fused a distinct cultural and national Brazilian identity. Obviously, none of this implies social and racial harmony. That is not the point. The extreme class and wealth differences in Brazil closely correspond to race. Still, the reason why Brazilians of all descents view themselves as one people and nation is the distinctive culture, including a common language, they share and the salience of "mixed-blood." Again, this is an ongoing project. Those who have not been touched by it so far, most notably the thin Indian tribal population isolated in the depths of the Amazon rainforest, remain very much outside the frame of the nation, in both the view of Brazilians and these groups' own self-perception. In the Caribbean countries an even larger part of the population, the majority, came from an ethnically diverse African origin and, as in Brazil, lacked a common language. Each of these mixed-race island societies adopted the language of the ruling elite – Spanish, English, or French-Creole – and fused a common Creole culture and identity.

In conclusion, the project of nation-building has advanced almost irresistibly in Latin America. It has involved the spread of the Spanish language (except in Brazil and some of the Caribbean); the fusion of a common national culture and tradition, which in addition to the whites encompasses the natives and blacks (wherever either exist in large numbers); and the reality and perception of a racially-mixed people. Some of these processes work against and some reinforce a pan-Latin American identity. It is recognized that a common Latino identity in the United States has only weakly been created with immigration, partly through official classification, because the newcomers from different countries of Latin America possess strong distinct identities. Whether, with growing economic integration and tightening communication, the countries of Latin America will retain and deepen their distinct national identities or move to fulfill Bolívar's dream of a single Latin American nation, or opt for something in between, only the future will tell. Our task is merely to point out the kin–culture bonds that make any of these options possible. Latin America is much more closely tied together in these respects than the multinational European Union (while being dispersed over three to four times its area). It more resembles the Arab world with its mixture of local, state, and pan-Arab identities.

Ethnicity and nation-building in sub-Saharan Africa

There are very good reasons for the prevailing reluctance to associate nationalism with ethnicity. Traditionally, states have been apprehensive about secessionist claims by ethnonational minorities within their borders. Indeed, both the chauvinism of ethnonational majorities or dominant peoples and secessionist pressures by peripheral ethnonationalities have been responsible for some of the worst human calamities of the past two centuries. Eastern Europe, wherein relatively small and geographically mixed ethnonational populations asserted their national identity, has been plagued by strife. The Balkans in particular have become proverbial in this respect. Where ethnic enclaves exist within ethnic enclaves almost *ad infinitum*, no drawing of the political borders can neatly separate ethno-national communities into distinct states without the massive dislocation and horrors of ethnic cleansing. This has often occurred, during the nineteenth and early twentieth centuries, in the wake of the Second World War, and with the disintegration of Yugoslavia. Theorists have coined the concept of civic nationalism, supposedly associated with Western Europe and contrasting with Central-Eastern European ethnic nationalism. They have postulated that when democracy, liberalism, and equal treatment of all ethnicities prevail, the nation could, and should, be construed irrespective of ethnic identities. But as we have seen, national identity in model "civic" cases has in fact been shaped by centuries of successful domination. Indeed, as liberalism deepened, secessionist pressures along ethnonational lines divided the United Kingdom and might divide it even further, as they could also do in the case of Spain. In reality, Switzerland is the only nation in Europe which has a strong claim to being multiethnic.

If central-eastern Europe and the Balkans sparked theorists' conceptualization of civic as opposed to ethnic nationalism, concerns over the new states of Africa and south-southeast Asia have made this distinction all the more pivotal in the scholarly and political discourse. In view of these states' circumstances, civic nationalism has been upheld as a model because the alternatives have been too horrible to contemplate. Africa in particular suggests a potentially nightmarish scenario. As we have seen earlier in this book and some scholars have noted, precolonial African polities, like their counterparts around the world, were ethnically constituted. City-states and confederations of city-states formed along ethnic lines, while empires were dominated by an imperial people or ethnos.[60] However, the new African states that emerged after independence in the 1950s and 1960s inherited the colonial boundaries drawn in the nineteenth century by the European powers with little regard for ethnic realities. As a result, in nearly all of Africa's sub-Saharan states, political boundaries both encompass a mosaic of different ethnicities and cut across existing ethne, separating them among neighboring countries. Very few states roughly center on a single ethnic group. These include Swaziland, Lesotho, Botswana (all descended from precolonial ethnic-tribal states), and Somalia (currently torn by tribal-based civil war).[61]

There are about 3,000 different linguistic ethne in sub-Saharan Africa, divided among forty-seven states. The majority of the states are home to several major ethne, each numbering in the millions or tens of millions and together comprising the lion's share of the population. In addition, there are scores, sometimes hundreds, of very small ethnic communities in each country (Nigeria holds the record with 250–400 languages). Africa's ethne are often referred to as "tribes," reflecting the common confusion between the two very different social entities already discussed in the Introduction. The Zulu or Maasai, for example, are each an ethnos that may be tribal in composition, but they are not *a* tribe.[62] Ethne share a culture (above all a language) and sometimes also a sense of kinship and common identity. In prestate societies they are divided into socially more significant but still loose tribal formations which may linger on in formative states, as they do in most African states.[§§] Indeed, this is very much a living reality:

[§§] As we have seen in Chapter 3, pp. 48 and 58, the anthropological notion of the 1960s and 1970s that the colonial powers invented the tribe in Africa is much overblown.

*In sub-Saharan Africa, there is a strong emotional
attachment to language and ethnicity. Language is seen as
the storehouse of ethnicity: each ethnic group expresses and
identifies itself by the language it speaks, and its cultural
paraphernalia is shaped by its language. Sameness of
language and ethnicity creates a bond of acceptance and
provides a basis for togetherness, for identity, for
separateness, for solidarity, and for brotherhood and
kinship.[63]*

According to a major recent book on the subject: "It is, thus, the
durability of kinship as the most fundamental unit of social trust that
ultimately grounds the vitality of ethnicity as the idiom of political
identity and competition in post-colonial Africa."***

Given their deep ethnic and tribal cleavages, there is little by
way of a common identity to weld individual African states together,
nor is there greater substance to the pan-African idea voiced here and
there before and after decolonization.[64] Africa is similar to Latin
America in the diversity of its native ethnicities, but different in lacking
a unifying supra-culture at the state and continental levels. As the great
majority of the African countries each lack a common native language,
they often use the language of the former colonial power as the state's
lingua franca and in their educational system. This is one of colonialism's most significant legacies to African nationalism, somewhat

What they did was invest local tribal chiefs with authority that they previously
lacked and turned tribal areas into administrative units, making them much more
formal and binding. If by tribe what is really meant is ethnos, then it is true that the
colonial administrators tended to regard defused tribal populations that shared
cultural traits (most notably language) but had little sense of a common identity as
one unit; i.e., they turned unconscious ethne into conscious ones. See also the next
footnote.

*** Bruce Berman, Dickson Eyoh, and Will Kymlicka (eds.), "Introduction," *Ethnicity
and Democracy in Africa*, Athens, OH: Ohio University Press, 2004, 11.
Unfortunately, having so stressed the durability of ethnicity, the authors go on to
proclaim in the book's Conclusion (p. 317) that "contemporary African ethnicities
are modern, not primordial survivors of some primitive tribal past." This
categorical statement conforms to the shibboleths of the past decades. It fails to
realize that ethnicities can be *both* very old (as many are in Africa, as elsewhere) *and*
subject to great historical transformation, fusion, fission, and change of identity,
including those "linked to the processes of colonial and post-colonial state
formation and the development of capitalist market economies" (*ibid.*).

offsetting the absurdity of the colonial boundaries. Still, in the absence of a large and dominant colonial population as in Latin America (except for South Africa, and in a different way the Arab legacy of the Swahili Creole lingua franca in east Africa), no process of assimilation into an elite culture and language, facilitating the fusion of a common identity, has occurred. Divided as many of Africa's countries are between Christianity and Islam (and a host of animistic cults), they do not even have religion as a unifying element, as Catholicism is in Latin America. Leaders of independence movements during decolonization built on the general otherness of the foreign Western rule and most often also on the loyalty of a core ethnic group, rather than on anything like a general national sentiment.[65] Indeed, in some African countries there is a dominant people or ethnos that pretty much dominates the state. These include the Amhara and Tigre in Ethiopia (around one-third of the population), the Kikuyu in Kenya (about one-fifth), and the Hausa-Fulani in Nigeria (perhaps one-eighth). Still, none of these dominant ethne comprises a majority of the population (some are not even the largest group), and none is powerful enough to generate processes of ethnic assimilation. On the other hand, their superior position arouses resentment among the other ethnicities within the state. Times have changed since the French state managed to enforce ethnic leveling throughout France, and even then the French case was unique. Karl Deutsch's formula of state-*cum*-nation-building for the new countries of Africa and Asia, modeled on France, has been highly simplistic, as even he would partly come to recognize.[66]

Under these circumstances, Africa has been rife with intra- and interstate wars of an ethnic character or at least a strong ethnic background. About half of the states in sub-Saharan Africa, twenty-two out of forty-seven, have together experienced thirty-six civil wars between 1960 and 2002.[67] There have been secessionist and irredentist challenges to the integrity of states;[†††] and there has been widespread ethnic

---

[†††] A short list includes: attempted secession in Sudan from the Arab and Muslim north by both the non-Arab, animist, and Christian south (successful in 2011) and the non-Arab province of Darfur in the west; Eritrean secession from Ethiopia, followed by an ethnically based civil war in Eritrea; war between Ethiopia and Somalia over the Ogaden, populated by Somali ethnics but part of Ethiopia; Tuareg rebellions in the north of Mali and Niger; failed Ibo secession from Nigeria with the establishment of Biafra.

strife and ethnically-based competition over control of the state.[‡‡‡] Millions of lives have been lost in ethnic conflicts, massacres, and genocide, and many millions of refugees have fled war or have been victims of ethnic cleansing. The causes of war in economically undeveloped Africa are many, but ethnicity has been central among them.[68]

It is widely hoped that a democratic and liberal path, which does not favor one ethnic identity over others and institutes political power-sharing, might succeed in sustaining multiethnic states and even multiethnic *national* states in Africa. Federalism and devolution of power to the provinces and their ethnic-linguistic communities are other means for containing ethnic tensions. However, advancing democracy and liberalism could equally mean that individual ethne within existing states might decide to go their own separate way, sometimes in conjunction with their ethnic kin across the border. Federalism has had a similarly mixed, if not negative, record in preserving multiethnic states.[69] The collapse of the Soviet Union and Yugoslavia and, indeed, the secession of Ireland from the United Kingdom, as well as current secessionist pressures in, for example, the United Kingdom, Spain, and Canada, testify to this. In the conclusion of one scholar of the subject, democratic multinational federations which lack a dominant *Staatsvolk* are extremely prone to disintegrate.[§§§] This conclusion seems to apply to all multiethnic democratic countries whose ethnic populations are territorially concentrated and distinct, but a federal subdivision may make secession yet easier. Both the state and democracy are weak in

---

[‡‡‡] Ethnic disturbances in Kenya following the 2007 elections; civil wars with ethnic background in Uganda; civil war between the Issa and Afar in Djibouti; genocidal civil war between the Hutu and Tutsi in Ruanda and Burundi, spilling over into and sparking a massive conflagration in Congo (formerly Zaire); conflict between the Arab-Muslim north and the black-Christian south in Chad; civil war flamed by large-scale cross-border immigration into the north of Côte d'Ivoire; tensions and civil war in Liberia over the dominance of the Afro-Americans; protracted conflicts between white minority rule and the black majority in Rhodesia (Zimbabwe) and South Africa.

[§§§] O'Leary, "An Iron Law of Nationalism and Federation?" I am not sure that even a clear ethnic majority in a democratic system is any guarantee for the survival of multiethnic federations when the minority is large enough and territorially concentrated and distinct. In cases such as Spain and Canada the outcome is still open; and, while I agree with O'Leary that India has an ethnic majority, its democratic regime is not liberal enough to allow secession (see below).

sub-Saharan Africa, and there are many reasons for this dual weakness which have to do with the continent's overall level of socioeconomic development. Yet one of these reasons is the absence of nations. Africa's postcolonial history of dictatorship is partly explained by the problems of holding together states of diverse ethnic composition.

True, the global wave of democratization of the 1990s has had a sweeping effect on Africa, with more than half of its countries now classified as free or partly free.[70] Still, while democracy in Africa has many shortcomings, some of the most significant are divisions and sectarianism along ethnic lines.[71] Indeed, as studies have found, democracy tends to be more successful in the smaller African countries, which are also more ethnically homogeneous.[72] Furthermore, although the democratic peace theory reveals an extreme rarity of wars among modern democracies, newly established democracies have proven to be a partial exception. This appears to be so largely because previously suppressed ethnic identities and antagonisms often express themselves in secessionist and irredentist pressures once the people are given a choice. Thus:

> In the 1990s, political violence has broken out after the adoption of democracy in Côte d'Ivoire, Togo, Ghana, Sierra Leone, Kenya, Chad, and Nigeria. Similarly, the onset of democracy has not put an end to violent conflict in the Democratic Republic of Congo, Uganda, or Burundi. From these examples, it is apparent that new democracies will not necessarily be less prone to violence.[73]

For all its other merits, democracy may not be a better guarantee than authoritarianism against the disintegration of multiethnic states.

Modernization in Africa might intensify centrifugal ethnonational pressures, for, indeed, the modernist thesis is not without foundation. As people of completely different ethne, who are presently spread out in the countryside, increase their contact with the world outside their village and town, and become more educated and politically mobilized, particularistic nationalist sentiments and aspirations are likely to gain in strength. Furthermore, with urbanization, people of different ethnicities come in touch with each other in large cities, with each ethnic population tending to flock together in ethnic enclaves, as they do in Africa's metropolises. As leading scholars of the subject have pointed out, ethnic tensions often rise in such circumstances, as occurred in Austro-Hungary in the late nineteenth and early twentieth century.[74]

Where ethnic boundaries are more or less distinct, as between the two peoples of the former Czechoslovakia, there is no reason why a redrawing of the political map to account for national aspirations should not take place without much disturbance. But where ethnicities are small, numerous, and mixed together and state boundaries are hopelessly divorced from ethnic realities, as in Africa, any attempt to bring the two into line is likely to open a Pandora's box and lead to untold horrors. This is what has made the colonial boundaries, as opposed to colonialism itself, so sacrosanct in Africa ever since independence. Given this unhappy choice between often forced ethnic cohabitation and mayhem, what is the best direction to take? There is an expectation among social scientists that their inquiries should highlight solutions. However, clear practical solutions do not always arise to bridge over complex and difficult circumstances.[75] The glaring discrepancy between states and ethne in Africa and the problems this entails are far from being unrecognized. Yet a lack of good political options coupled with the proprieties of political correctness result in widespread denial that multiethnic states, nation-building in such states, and purely civic nationalism are truly extraordinary. One hopes that each of these will have at least a measure of success in the states of Africa, but they are unlikely to be successful everywhere across the continent. Of course, different African countries have different circumstances and developmental paths, and may fare differently. Still, nation-building in the majority of the colonial-territories-turned-states was and remains an open-ended and uncertain project. The problem of state and nation in Africa has yet to unravel, and, one suspects, it will occur over a very long period of time and with much turbulence.

Ethnicity and nation-building in the southeast Asian archipelago

Southern Asia, including the southeast archipelago, constitutes another major test for postcolonial projects of nation-building out of multiple and highly diverse ethnicities. In this the region is in many ways similar to sub-Saharan Africa and different from east Asia and Indochina, but also from the countries of central Asia or the Middle East. Studies titled Asian nationalism conflate very different categories. As we have seen, China, Korea, Japan, Vietnam, Thailand, Cambodia, and to a somewhat lesser degree Burma-Myanmar and Laos all have long histories of premodern nationhood, a rough and non-accidental congruence of ethnicity and statehood extending over centuries or even millennia. Central Asia and the Arab Middle East constitute intermediate categories. In central Asia the collapse of the Soviet Union immediately led to the secession and independence of the former Soviet republics, which had lacked a well-defined history of statehood but each bore a clear ethnic character. There are 90 percent Azeri in Azerbaijan, around 80 percent Tajiks in Tajikistan, more than 75 percent Turkmen in Turkmenistan, more than 70 percent Uzbeks in Uzbekistan and Kyrgyz in Kyrgyzstan, respectively, and more than 60 percent Kazakhs in Kazakhstan. In the Arab Middle East the link between ethnicity and statehood is Janus-faced, making the national project tenuous. Both the predominant Arabic language and religion and culture of Islam underpin each of the individual Arab states, yet also challenge them with the visions of pan-Arabism and pan-Islam. In addition, millennia of imperial rule have left many of these new states with little in the way of a common collective tradition. From the opposite direction, from below, the states are undercut by tribalism and by ethnic and religious cleavages.

In comparison with all the above regional types, both the great archipelago of southeast Asia and the Indian subcontinent have had little by way of either a shared national history or a common ethnic substratum. Hence, the great ethnic diversity of the modern states there, created, like those of Africa and unlike those of east Asia and Indochina, within colonial boundaries. Clifford Geertz's original formulation of the contrast between what he termed "primordial" identities and modern "civil" nation-building arose from his observations in Indonesia and Malaysia, the scene of his anthropological studies, and India.[76] And Benedict Anderson was led astray by the very same geographical field of specialty into positing the general absence of premodern Asian nations.

Indonesia is one of the world's largest and ethnically most diverse states. Stretched over 4,000 kilometers of islands and seas, it comprises a population of nearly 240 million to-date and more than 700 linguistic–ethnic groups. The vast majority of these groups number only in the thousands; less than twenty groups have a population of 1 million or more; only three of them comprise 10 million and more; and one, Javanese, heads the list by a wide margin with 86 million speakers and about 40 percent of the population of Indonesia. Occupying the larger part of the island of Java, the Javanese are also the only ones among the ethnicities of present-day Indonesia to have had a precolonial history and identity of peoplehood and statehood. And yet a long period of Dutch colonial dominance, over 300 years, as opposed to the 100 years of French rule in Indochina, has led to a different development than that in Indochina. The Dutch adopted Malay as the lingua franca of their East Indies Empire because of its significance as the language of trade and despite its being a minority language. Malay is the native tongue of less than 10 million or 4–5 percent of the population of Indonesia. The Dutch also turned Malay into the written vernacular, in contrast to the multiple written vernaculars the French introduced along ethnonational lines in Indochina. Thus, independent Indonesia came into being (1945–1949) with the dual colonial inheritance of boundaries and official language, which the leaders of the independence movement and new state chose to adopt and reinforce rather than tamper with and cause total mayhem.[77] In the vigorous nation-building project that has been going on since independence, the Malay dialect used in Indonesia has been termed Indonesian and promoted as the official language of the country. State affairs, the educational system, and the national media are all conducted in Indonesian, and practically the entire population of the country is able to use it while mostly speaking other languages at home.

Thus, although Indonesia is as multiethnic as can be, it is far from being based on civic principles alone, for the state has successfully created a shared supra-culture, above all a common language. Furthermore, although there is no official state religion in Indonesia, the public–cultural significance of Islam, professed (in a generally moderate version) by 85 percent of the population, is paramount in consolidating a common Indonesian identity. In its nation-building project Indonesia is probably the postcolonial nation closest to historical France. This is so even if the uncompromising means employed by the French state to instill the French language and culture as the only officially recognized ones throughout France are no longer deemed permissible or practiced in most countries, including Indonesia. It remains to be seen how successful the Indonesian nation-building project will continue to be in spreading the common language (maybe even to the level of first language) and common culture, and how able it will be to withstand centrifugal pressures by splinter ethnic groups. The independence (since 1999–2002) of the former Portuguese colony of East Timor, unilaterally annexed by Indonesia in 1975, testifies to the power of the colonial heritage and borders: in East Timor the supra-language is Portuguese and the prevailing religion is Catholicism. By contrast, the absence of a similar linguistic, religious, and historical rift may account for the failure of the secessionist insurgency (1976–2005) by the Acehnese people, the most conservative Muslim element in Indonesia, who objected to the government's cultural unification policies.[78] Ongoing modernization, as well as advancing democratization since 1998, can both be double-edged processes in multiethnic, socioeconomically developing societies. They are capable of either tightening or loosening evolving pan-Indonesian national bonds.

The Philippines is similar to Indonesia in some important respects. Although smaller than Indonesia, the Philippines is one of the largest and ethnically most diverse countries on earth. The archipelago's population is fast approaching 100 million, speaking 120–175 languages. Thirteen of these languages have more than 1 million speakers, and together they encompass around 90 percent of the population of the Philippines. The archipelago was never united before the Spanish established their rule in the early sixteenth century. Spanish rule gave the Philippines not only unity but also a shared official language, Spanish, and a shared religion, Catholicism. About 90 percent of the population to-date is Christian, and more than 80 percent are Catholic. With American rule replacing Spain in 1898, English became the official language of the Philippines. As steps toward independence were taken before and completed after the Second World War, the Philippine government declared Tagalog a second official language. Renamed Pilipino, Tagalog is the largest native language and that of the capital Manila, yet it is the native tongue of only about 25 percent of the people of the Philippines. Successive government and legislative acts have been enforced to promote the adoption of Pilipino in official use, the educational system, and the media. Although not as prevalent as Indonesian has become in Indonesia and sharing a place with English, Pilipino is nonetheless gaining status as a common national language in the Philippines. Here as well, a shared and deepening cultural matrix has been integral to the crystallization of Philippine civic identity and sense of nationhood.

Malaysia is different from both Indonesia and the Philippines. It was formed from the colonies and semi-independent sultanates of the British imperial realm of Malaya unified in the late 1950s and early 1960s. Although home to 137 linguistic groups, the vast majority of them minuscule, Malaysia has a clear ethnic core: Malayans comprise slightly over 50 percent of the population and their identity dominates the official definitions of both the state and the nation. These definitions have been deeply affected by Malayan threat perception vis-à-vis the large and successful ethnic minorities of non-native descent in Malaysia, above all the Chinese (close to 25 percent of the population) and to a lesser degree the Indians (7 percent).[79] Arriving in Malaya as laborers in the nineteenth and early twentieth centuries, both communities have thrived economically, and the Chinese in particular have grown to dominate business and trade. With the Malayans initially apprehensive of becoming a minority in their own country and later increasingly resentful of the leading economic position of the Chinese, intercommunal relations in Malaya–Malaysia have been tense. Alienation and at times animosity have manifested themselves in the isolation of the Chinese insurgents against the British in the 1950s, in party politics after independence, in occasional rioting, and also in the state of Malaysia's constitution and policies. The government has enacted affirmative action in education, the public sector, and the economy on behalf of what it regards as native Malaysians (*Bumiputras* = roughly 50 percent Malayans plus 10 percent other indigenous groups). The Chinese population in particular regards these acts as discriminatory. The Malayan–Malaysian language is the country's only official language (with English holding a major position in practice). Islam is the country's state religion, and despite religious tolerance this also signals the otherness of the Confucian and Buddhist Chinese and mostly Hindu Indians.

So far the Chinese in Malaysia have more or less acquiesced to this state of affairs, and future developments have yet to be seen. With respect to our subject, however, one notes that the sense of common nationhood in Malaysia mostly encompasses the Malayan and other indigenous groups. By contrast, the Chinese and Indian position within the "nation of intent," as Prime Minister Mahathir Mohamad (1981–2003) called it, is highly ambivalent both in the eyes of Malayans and in their own self-perception. They are not regarded as distinct, minority nations within Malaysia, primarily because they

lack territorial contiguity (other than urban concentration) and therefore a claim for separate statehood. Yet their conception as ethnically
alien deeply affects their status as largely outsiders to the Malaysian
nation.

Singapore is the other side of the Malaysian coin. Immigrating
into the newly established British port and naval base from the early
nineteenth century on, Chinese constitute about 75 percent of Singapore's population today, with the rest being mostly Malay and Indians
(each of these ethnic categories is itself highly diverse). A city-state
more than a country-size state, Singapore separated from Malaysia
after a short union (1963–1965) and became independent because of
the tensions between its predominantly Chinese population and the
Malay. Under such circumstances, the government of Singapore went
to great lengths to cement the vulnerable new creation against interethnic implosion. Although Chinese dominate the country in every
practical way, the state is officially and very strictly multiethnic. It
has four official languages, English, Malay, Chinese, and Tamil,
with state affairs and the educational system conducted in English.
If Indonesia comes closest to the French model of cultural integration,
Singapore is in some respects the Switzerland of the east: it is a
genuinely multiethnic and civic *national* project, whose consolidation,
like Switzerland's, owes a great deal to the small polity's staggering
economic success. This success reinforces Singapore's sense of being
a fortress threatened by powerful neighbors, and it renders Singaporean
nationality superior in the eyes of its various ethnic communities
(the Malays in particular) to any alternative across the border.
However, unlike Switzerland, Singapore's regime since independence
has been authoritarian–paternalistic–meritocratic. The regime's "de-
politicization" of the ethnic question has blended well with its professed
ideological "de-politicization" of the running of the state, supposedly
reduced to sound administration.[80]

Ethnicity and nation-building in India and Pakistan

The model and great hope of postcolonial, multiethnic "civic" nationalism is India. Its population of more than 1.2 billion comprises one-
sixth of the world's population. They are divided among some 1,650
officially counted linguistic groups (thirty of them with over 1 million

speakers) and several major religions. Still, with the exception of the partition of the subcontinent between India and Pakistan upon independence (1947), and despite some deep cleavages and strong tensions, India has remained united as one nation. This achievement is compounded by the fact that India has been democratic since independence, a unique example of stable democracy in a poor country and an achievement as surprising and unforeseen in its robustness as India's unity. Thus, a clear understanding of what makes Indian nationhood possible is imperative.

There was no premodern unified Indian national state, as there was in China, Japan, or the other east Asian and Indochinese cases. Like Europe, the Indian subcontinent was a mosaic of states and ethnicities, a geographical and civilizational concept rather than a political one. India's early city-states (*Mahajanapadas*) and many of its regional states bore a distinct ethnic character and could have become the basis for enduring national states. Yet, unlike Europe, large parts of the subcontinent, especially the north, occasionally became subsumed under imperial domination. Empires included most notably the native Maurya (322–185 BC) and Gupta (*c.* AD 320–550), and the last three imperial rulers arriving from outside: the Afghans of the Delhi Sultanate (1206–1526), the Mughals (1526 to the eighteenth century; officially abolished in 1858), and the British (mid eighteenth century to 1947). Imperial rule in Indian history was sufficiently salient to destroy incipient national states, yet was neither enduring nor indigenous enough to bring about grassroots' cultural leveling. The British Raj was the first ever to unify the entire subcontinent, and it also left a deep cultural imprint.

By the late nineteenth century, members of the modern native elite that had emerged in British India wished to become proud citizens of the glorious British Empire. These were the lawyers, administrators of all sorts and levels, journalists, and other professionals educated in English and with Western acculturation. For many reasons, including, but not limited to, the attitude of the British themselves, such a re-creation of the ancient Roman model was not to be. As equality was central to the Western liberal creed assimilated by the new native elite, its members were stung by their rebuttal and by British superiority. In a pattern archetypal in colonial settings, the local elite's adoption of native nationalism was very much a wounded reaction to their frustration.[81] Indian national identity was created from native materials vis-à-vis the British "Other." Anthony Smith's thesis that modern nations have been construed from premodern ethno-symbolic materials is too modest in that it overlooks the existence in many places of premodern nations and national states. But in India, where no unified premodern national state existed, it fits perfectly.

The artificiality of the process of building a national identity out of traditional local materials, in India as in other colonial cases, has been the subject of debate. Critics have been all too aware of the novelty of many of the new forms of consciousness, of the anachronisms and the "invention of tradition" involved, sincere or deliberately fabricated. Thus, they have regarded the process as little more than cynical elite "manipulation," a modern "instrumentalist" act. Obviously, in different countries, depending on the local history, there is different depth and authenticity to the historical traditions that have gone into the forging of the nation. Some of the new postcolonial countries have little to show for it except for the otherness of the Western "Other." However, India was after all one of the world's most ancient civilizations. How contrived then was the construction of Indian national identity from the late nineteenth century on, when Indian intellectuals and professionals, connected by print and railway technology, established the Indian National Congress (1885) to represent the Indian cause? This move was counteracted by political self-organization and mobilization by Muslims and by Sikhs. These two major religious populations felt threatened by the predominantly Hindu character of the Congress, which reflected India's Hindu majority.

Paul Brass launched the scholarly debate concerning Indian nationalism. He suggested that all the above identities – Hindu-pan-Indian, Muslim, and Sikh – were modern creations, as the respective elites mobilized the masses around religious symbols. The modern ethnonational identities allegedly had little in common with the great diversity of India's past religious communities or with the fundamentally non-ethnic character of its premodern politics.[82] Brass' views have provoked criticism from quite a number of authors, with the result that Brass himself has somewhat reformulated his position, adopting more of a middle ground between "primordialism" and "modernism."[83] Thus, something close to a scholarly consensus has tacitly emerged from the heat of the debate. No one is denying that Indian nationalism was a new creation and that the cultural forms on which it was built have been radically transformed by modernity. Although they had already been strongly challenged by Islam, the highly diverse, poly-theistic, and caste-fragmented Hindu traditions – religious, cultural, and communal – were consolidated into a self-conscious, comprehensive, and distinctive creed only in the nineteenth century. Much of this was a response to the classification standards of the Europeans, which called for something comparable to Christianity and Islam. On the other hand, it is agreed that modern reconstruction could not be carried out by the elite just at will, *ex nihilo*. This would not have been possible had Hindu traditions not had the longest and deepest roots in India's history and culture, and among its people, including, most emphatically, the elite itself. Scholars have revealed how, long before print technology, a Hindu spiritual world was propagated through pre-modern media. It was rooted in the ancient epic scriptures, transmitted through oral recitation, ceremony, and drama, and reinforced by popular pilgrimage to holy places and the prevalence and public role of holy men.[84] Duara has already been cited regarding the effect of these premodern forms of imagined communities in China and India, as well as in other traditional societies.[85] The following is a similar citation, from another leading scholar, on the growth of Indian nationalism in the late nineteenth century:

> *Nationalists and communalists alike used newspapers and books to spread their ideas. But there were equally important methods, which find no place in Anderson's theory. The visual aids of drama, public spectacles and religious displays were necessary to reach out to a largely non-literate society. Both modern and traditional forms of communication played a crucial role in the transformation of customary culture into community of consciousness.*[86]

In Chapter 4 we saw that ethnicity and religion were clearly significant in India's historical empires. They were intrinsic in the system of imperial coercion, but were also subdued by it. This was true of the zealous Muslim-Afghan Delhi Sultanate, but also of the pro-verbially tolerant Muslim Mughals.[87] The British are sometimes accused of dealing with Indian society during the nineteenth century through religion and caste, thereby objectifying and politicizing these categories, and also in order to divide and rule. But the real problem lay elsewhere. The replacement of Mughal rule by the British broke

Muslim dominance in India, and the introduction of universal male suffrage by the British in the early twentieth century alarmed the Muslim elite even further, because it meant inevitable Hindu dominance. Again, rather than being a modern invention, political ethnicity was released, transformed, and greatly reinforced by democratization, taking a national form, which in India's particular case was indeed new.

The Congress leaders made great efforts to allay the fears of Muslims, Sikhs, and other minorities over Hindu dominance, lest they compromise the independence movement and the unity of India. They emphasized the comprehensive character of the movement, and, as the rift with the Muslim League deepened toward independence, they proclaimed the secular nature of the Indian nation. This principle became central to India's state ideology and constitution. However, what exactly it has meant requires closer scrutiny. While Jawaharlal Nehru, India's first prime minister (1947–1964) was the most secular among the Congress leaders, the others, including Mahatma Gandhi, were far more steeped in Hinduism. Rather than a religion *per se*, Hindu for them was a cultural identity and a message of deep spirituality. It was India's contribution to the world and a counterpoise to Western culture, which should be merged with it to form India's modern national identity.[88] This was very much the essence of Gandhi's powerful appeal to India's masses, which he mobilized for the national cause, turning the Congress from an elite club into a mass popular movement. There was scarcely a difference here between the manipulative leader of the "instrumentalist" cliché and the people: both were as sincere and deeply committed in their attachment to the world of beliefs, symbols, and sentiments which Gandhi made the cornerstone of Indian national identity.

To be sure, Gandhi and the other Congress leaders stood for the utmost tolerance toward all religious and ethnic groups, for state neutrality in such matters, and for the all-encompassing character of the Indian nation and national identity. Still, that identity was perceived by them, as well as by their mass constituency, as an extended version of Hindu identity. The rise of a Hindu nationalist party, the Bharatiya Janata Party (BJP), from the 1980s on, which broke the long-held hegemony of the Congress Party over Indian politics and held power from 1998 to 2004, has alarmed many commentators. *Inter alia*, the BJP wants India to become more formally and pronouncedly Hindu.[89] This vision stands in contrast to the Congress' traditional line and the ideology of the Indian state. All the same, it is easy to get confused by this crucial difference and lose sight of the actual content of the Congress' nationalism from its inception. Pluralistic, comprehensive, and secular as it was in the quest for Indian national unity, Indian identity for both its leaders and constituency was very much stamped in the image of Hindu tradition and culture. This outlook was genuine and deep enough to win mass popular appeal, while being sufficiently pluralistic to keep some weary non-Hindu minorities within India. At the same time, however, it was not inconspicuous and insignificant enough to prevent a break up with the largest of these minorities, the Muslims, who comprised 25–30 percent of British India's population. The provinces with a Muslim majority in former British India separated upon independence (1947) and established the state of Pakistan. The trauma involved a massive human tragedy. An exodus of Muslims from India to Pakistan and Hindus in the other direction took place, accompanied by widespread sectarian violence. Hundreds of thousands died and an estimated 12 million became refugees. Kashmir, with a Muslim majority but joined by its Hindu ruler to India, remains a bleeding wound in the relations between the two countries and the scene of a local Muslim insurgency. Otherwise, despite periodic eruptions of interreligious rioting, the roughly 140 million Muslims living throughout India are fairly successfully integrated into the nation.

Other large and small ethnic minorities have been similarly integrated within the Indian national state, though the relations of some of them with it have not been free from ambivalence, tensions, and occasional eruptions of sectarian violence. As Alex Yakobson puts it in Chapter 7 below, where there are ethnic minorities there is also an ethnic majority. And the balancing act between a majority ethnic identity and an inclusive, pluralistic, civic definition of Indian nationalism has never ceased. We now turn to look more closely at India's ethnic core and the patterns of inclusion and exclusion it creates. This ethnic core is dual, Hindi–Hindu, with one circle encompassed within a wider one. The first, smaller and weaker core is linguistic; the second, broader and more significant is religious–cultural.

Hindi is by far the most widely spoken of India's many languages, the language of most of northern India, the seat of government of the subcontinent's major historical empires. However, despite being the native language of more than 40 percent of India's population, with the next most prevalent languages (Bengali, Telugu, and Marathi) spoken by only around 8 percent each, Hindi is not a majority language. Furthermore, while most of India's other languages belong, like Hindi, to the Indic branch of the Indo-European family of languages and are similarly derived from ancient Sanskrit, they are no more mutually comprehensible than the modern Latin languages are to one another. Finally, languages of a completely different family, Dravidian, are spoken in the south, while languages of the Austro-Asiatic and Tibeto-Burman families are spoken by small ethnic communities in the northeast. This linguistic divide matters politically. For example, in non-Hindi British Bengal a distinct national consciousness emerged as early as the second half of the nineteenth century, and resistance to Hindi dominance has been strong there, as it has been in other non-Hindi states.[90] The Dravidian-speaking Tamil south was historically independent from the empires of the north and manifested strong secessionist pressures at the time of and immediately following India's independence. These pressures have been successfully checked and substituted by local state self-rule and the cultivation of the indigenous culture.[91]

Thus, the founders of India, who sought to make Hindi the national language, encountered intense resistance and had to compromise in order not to alienate non-Hindi speakers.[92] In view of the salience of the language question, the States Reorganisation Act of 1956 made state boundaries in India conform to and reflect linguistic boundaries. Furthermore, the limited acceptance of Hindi and the widespread resistance to its status as a national language have been reinforced by the role of English. Although the creators of India wanted to phase out English in favor of Hindi in official use and the educational system, English survived as a second and in many respects primary official language. Like many other postcolonial countries, India benefits from a linguistic legacy which is both universal and, paradoxically, once the colonial master was gone, perceived as neutral vis-à-vis the country's many linguistic–ethnic communities. All in all, the language issue in India, and the country's linguistic divides which could easily (and still might) become the markers of separate peoples and national states, have been accommodated within a compromise composite linguistic structure. India has a trilingual educational policy, whereby English, Hindi, and the local language of each state are taught at school.

The wider and stronger core of majority Indian identity, which holds together India's many distinct linguistic communities, is Hindu.

More than 80 percent of India's population is Hindu. A comparison with predominantly Christian Europe is called for, and often made. As mentioned earlier, Hinduism, not unlike Christianity in Europe, is as much a cultural–civilizational identity as it is a religious one. But its political–historical trajectory has been somewhat different. Christianity was a self-conscious creed in medieval Europe, monotheistic and strongly defined vis-à-vis the pagan, Jewish, and Muslim "Others." It also carried an idealistic vision of political community as Christendom, a vision weakened by the rise of Europe's national states, but returning in a tacit cultural–identity form with the European Union. By comparison, not even Islam but only the challenge of the West and modernity was powerful enough to shake the Indian subcontinent from its relative isolation and spur it to consolidate its religious–cultural polytheistic heritage into the unified concept of Hinduism. As Hindu religion and culture are more indigenously and exclusively Indian than Christianity is European, and as India lacks a history of premodern national states, Hindu has become the most signal element of Indian national identity.

While the Hindi linguistic component of Indian national identity has caused some alienation among non-Hindi speakers, the more significant Hindu element of Indian national identity has been the cause of deeper cleavages. The rupture with British India's second largest religious community, Islam, and the creation of Pakistan has already been mentioned. But the cleavage with another of India's religious community, the Sikhs, has also been deep and has not resulted in secession mainly because of the balance of power between the sides. Numbering around 19 million, mostly concentrated in India's northwestern state of Punjab and speaking Punjabi, the Sikhs arguably have had a better claim to nationhood and statehood than the multiethnic Muslims of the subcontinent.[93] Politically organizing close on the heels of the Congress and Muslim League, their leadership aspired to a separate state in the Punjab in 1947. They were turned down by the British, who made it clear that the Muslim was the only secessionist claim they were prepared to concede. Since then the Sikhs' integration within India has been a mixed story. Intercommunal tensions have occasionally erupted into sectarian violence, especially during the 1984 rioting surrounding the Golden Temple affair. This caused the death of thousands and led to the assassination of India's Prime Minister Indira Gandhi by her Sikh bodyguards. A Sikh uprising took place in the Punjab between 1987 and 1993 and was only suppressed by robust force. On the other hand, from 2004 on, and as these lines are written, India has had a Sikh prime minister from the Congress Party, the first non-Hindu since independence. In addition to the Muslims and Sikhs, dissention vis-à-vis the Indian nation-state has been widespread in the non-Hindi and largely non-Hindu ethnically diverse northeast, where secessionist movements and insurgency groups have been very active.[94]

The tension of balancing national inclusiveness and core Hindu identity has been intrinsic to India since independence and, with the exception of Pakistan's secession, has been managed quite successfully thus far. In part, this success is attributed to India's political pluralism, which has been no less important than its ideological and constitutional pluralism. Here also the founders and leaders of independent India struggled with an inherent strain and ended up with a delicate balancing act. Although the Congress and India's first prime minister Nehru wanted a strong centralized state and were highly suspicious of local states' power, they nonetheless pragmatically conceded to the devolution of a great deal of political power to the state level. India is a federal state, and, as we have seen, in practice its constitutive states give expression to its diverse linguistic–ethnic identities. Federalism is not a panacea for multiethnic states, as it might reinforce rather than allay secessionist tendencies. But in India it has worked, so far.[95] In addition, the Congress Party has been very adept in cementing broad coalitions at the local level across the country, coopting various groups into the political system. Pluralist, "consociational" democracy theorist Arend Lijphart has highlighted this aspect of the Indian political system.[96]

Indeed, democracy has been rightly credited with much of India's success, yet, like federalism, it might be double-edged. While allowing pluralistic political self-expression to diverse ethnic identities, Indian democracy does not recognize the right to secede and actively suppresses secessionist attempts by military force. It is similar in this respect to the United States at the time of the Civil War. However, although the right to secede remains highly disfavored by states worldwide, the norms in advanced liberal democracies increasingly allow for this option when a majority in a distinct ethnonational community occupying a certain territory opts for independence. The same norms rule out suppression by force. As India modernizes, increasing liberalization concerning the right of secession may follow. Furthermore, as we have seen with respect to other developing countries, the process of modernization itself may either reinforce or undermine India's national unity. Currently, two-thirds of India's population still lives in rural areas and is scattered throughout the countryside. It remains to be seen what sort of national identity formation and mobilization, whether pan-Indian or local, the people will undergo when concentrated in cities after urbanization. India is a successful, yet an ongoing project. Rather than a complete break up, which India's Hindu identity and modern political history makes less likely, the main challenge to Indian unity seems to be more specific secessionist pressures. These could come from any of the aforementioned ethnic groups – Kashmiri Muslims, Sikhs, Tamils, or the small ethnicities of the northeast – all of which lie at the periphery or outside of Indian national identity.

All the above does not mean that India is not a civic and highly pluralistic nation. But the naive false dichotomy of civic versus ethnic nationalism assumes the former to be based solely on allegiance to the state and its constitution, and wholly overlooks the role of kin–culture communal identity, which in India centers on a broadly defined Hindu identity. This core identity has been essential to the consolidation and survival of India's sense of nationhood, though it is by no means a sufficient condition for it. Pakistan, in many ways India's "Other," may serve to highlight additional conditions for the success of multiethnic nationalism, or lack thereof.

Separating from India upon independence because of a deep, identity-constituting religious cleavage, Pakistan's story is often contrasted to India's. Muhammad Ali Jinnah, the leader of the Muslim League in British India, who steered the Muslims away from a unified India and became Pakistan's first head of state from 1947 until his death the following year, was not very different from his Congress counterparts in his vision of statehood. He regarded Islam primarily as a historical–cultural identity and aspired to create a fundamentally secular modern state. In reality, however, Pakistan took a different course from that of India. Because of the circumstances of its creation and perhaps also because of Islam's greater monotheistic zeal, not yet tempered, like Christianity, by modernity and liberalism, Pakistan has been constitutionally and publicly more Islamic than India has been Hindu. Furthermore, the salience and influence of Islam in Pakistani society and politics has grown considerably over time. This is often criticized by commentators. However, as far as our subject is concerned and in view of the role we have attributed to Hindu identity in consolidating India's sense of nationhood, one would have expected an even stronger Islamic identity in Pakistan to be at least as successful in crystallizing a Pakistani sense of nationhood. And yet this is not the case. Certainly, Islam has been the main identity binding the various ethnicities of Pakistan together. Nonetheless, the sense of a common national identity has been weaker in Pakistan than it has been in India, and the distance among Pakistan's main ethnic building blocs has been more significant.

Muslim Bengal in the east, geographically separated by India from western Pakistan, seceded and created independent Bangladesh following a civil war and an Indian military intervention (1971). The Punjabis, Seraikis, and Sindhis (each with its own Indic language), together with the Pashtuns and Baluchis (each speaking an Iranian language and with kin across the border in both Afghanistan and Iran) remain Pakistan's major linguistic–ethnic populations. Although these ethnic populations are geographically mixed in some areas and in large cities, each of them has a separate territory and distinct identity, which is often stronger than their sense of common nationhood as Pakistani. In addition, there are scores of other linguistic communities, the vast majority of which are very small. Urdu, with its glorious literary tradition and historical role during the struggle for separation from India, is Pakistan's official language while being the native language of only 7–8 percent of its population. Even more than in India, English serves as the true national language in the central state's administration.[97]

What, then, are the sources of the difference between Pakistani and Indian nationhood? One factor may be religion. This does not refer to Pakistan's more religious constitution and public sphere, but to Islam's status as a universal religion that transcends Pakistan's national borders. Although the percentage of Indians who are Hindu is less than that of Pakistanis who are Muslim (divided, however, between a large Sunni majority and a small Shia minority), Hinduism is more specific to India and makes for a more distinct national marker. A second possible factor is democracy. In contrast to the vibrancy and endurance of Indian democracy, Pakistan has alternated since independence between unstable democracy and military-authoritarian regimes. As mentioned previously, democracy or the lack thereof is a double-edged tool as far as multiethnic nationalism is concerned. An authoritarian regime may suppress secessionist pressures and enforce policies of ethnic leveling, but it can also hinder the process of political power-sharing, compromise, and cooptation more typical of democracy. Thus, in addition to the crucial language question involving official Urdu versus Bengali, a major reason for the secession of Bangladesh was the dominance of the

Punjabi and Sindhi elite in the governing of Pakistan. Despite being the largest ethnic population before secession, the Bengali felt discriminated against and neglected within the Pakistani state.

A third, less recognized factor may be as significant in explaining the limited success of the Pakistani nation-building project as compared with India's. Obviously, the lack of geographical contiguity mattered in the case of Bengal, which was separated by 1,500–2,000 kilometers from western Pakistan. But also in western Pakistan the existence of four or five major ethnic communities appears to be more destabilizing for national unity than the presence of dozens of such communities under one national roof as in India.[98] It is easier to imagine and carry out a division of the country along ethnic lines in the former circumstances than when the alternative to unity is a much greater array of ethnic units. The latter circumstances are not immune to secession by larger or smaller ethnonational communities, or to more extensive disintegration, but perhaps less easily so.

The difficulties encountered by the United States and its allies in their state- and nation-building projects in Afghanistan and Iraq at the outset of the twenty-first century are further demonstrations of the problems of multiethnic countries. Across the border from Pakistan, Afghanistan is home to a large number of distinct ethnicities, of which by far the largest one, the Pashtuns, comprise only about 40 percent of the population. In Iraq, the three major ethnic populations, the Shia, Sunnis, and Kurds, were only held together in a single state by political coercion (and Sunni dominance). This was imposed first by the British, who drew Iraq's boundaries with little regard for ethnic realities, and later by successive despotic governments in Baghdad. In addition, tribal affiliations are still very much alive in both Afghanistan and Iraq, and take precedence over national affinities. Given the political alternatives, the notion that either of these countries should be regarded as a nation is an understandable long-term aspiration at best; at worst, it is naive and costly wishful thinking.

Conclusion: civic versus ethnic nations?

The new, postcolonial states of Africa, southern Asia, and the southeast Asian archipelago have been central to the concept of civic nationalism and partly responsible for the increasingly prominent role it has played in the political and scholarly discourse. In a multiethnic reality, wherein the disintegration of existing states is likely to bring about cata-strophic upheavals, massive communal violence, and the horrors of ethnic cleansing, civic nationalism has been posited as a benign anti-thesis to ethnic nationalism. The new states have not only been expected to keep their unity and find a way to peacefully accommo-date their diverse ethnic groups, but also to develop a sense of common nationhood (and the two goals are indeed connected). This common nationhood has been assumed to be based on civic allegiance to a state and its constitution. However, the notion that the various ethnic groups within the state would regard themselves as a single political community of solidarity and fate even when lacking closer kin–culture bonds has been based on a profound misinterpretation. This misinterpretation concerns the meaning of civic nationalism in Western history and derives from a false dichotomy between the civic and ethnic elements of nationhood.

Nation-building in the above-described states of Africa and Asia is still an ongoing project, which is likely to have different results in different countries. Although the sanctity of the colonial borders has been a guiding principle since independence so as to avoid opening a Pandora's box of ethnic mayhem, ethnonational secession has occasionally occurred. Most notably, Eritrea seceded from Ethiopia, and South Sudan from Sudan. A similar attempt by the Ibo people in Nigeria to create an independent Biafra was crushed only by a murderous civil war. In the long run it is unlikely that postcolonial Africa and Asia will be entirely immune to partitions along ethnonational fault lines, such as those that occurred in post-communist Eastern Europe and the Balkans. Indeed, the main chal-lenges facing countries in Africa and Asia still lie ahead. They have all yet to undergo the massive transformation of modernization, and some also the process of democratization. Both these developments deeply affect nationalism and may result in either national consoli-dation or political disintegration along enhanced ethnonational lines, depending on each country's particular circumstances.

Some possible reasons for the success or failure of national projects have already been touched upon above. Nations are easiest to build when the state has a large ethnic majority core, or *Staatsvolk*. Depending on the sides involved in each particular case, such an ethnic majority may engulf the others to create a broader common identity which largely carries the majority's stamp. Alternatively, the minority ethnic groups, while citizens of the state, may remain on the margins or altogether outside the main national identity, while enjoying a greater or lesser right to cultivate their own ethnonational identity. A Switzerland or a Singapore is very rare and depends on highly exceptional circumstances. Be that as it may, most countries of post-colonial Africa and Asia do not have a core ethnic majority. As we have seen, in such cases it may be more desirable for the purpose of nation-building for the state to have a greater rather than lesser plurality of ethnic groups. This decreases both the prospects of one group's dominance, with the resentment that it creates among the others, and reduces the viability of complete disintegration along ethnic lines. Alex Yakobson comes to a similar conclusion in Chapter 7, and this observation may also explain some of the findings regarding the conditions for ethnic violence.[99] Most importantly, however, nation-building in multiethnic states depends – is almost conditional upon – the creation of pan-cultural bonds which facilitate the transformation of diverse ethnic groups into a national community. Such cultural bonds are the strongest cement of national communities in the absence of a shared sense of kinship. Moreover, the forging of a common culture also fuels processes of intermarriage among populations living in the same territory, which over time may produce a growing sense of shared kinship. Thus, rather than being a sufficient condition for nationhood, the acceptance of life in a common state, allegiance to it, and obedience to its laws are very much the *result* of such processes of kin–culture national consolidation.

A shared language has been documented to be by far a nation's most common unifying bond.[100] As we saw in Chapter 2, this is quite obvious in view of the role of language as the medium of shared social communication, group cooperation, and symbolic projection. In multi-ethnic states pursuing a nation-building project, either the former colonial language or one of the native languages, sometimes with a history of being a lingua franca, is turned into the national language. Spread by means of the education system and the media, it becomes the second language of the people side by side with their particular native tongue, and may or may not become their first language over time and with increasing modernization and urbanization. Similar processes took place in some countries of Europe (achieving their greatest success in France, to a lesser degree in Britain and Spain, and in a way also in Germany and Italy); in the English-speaking immigrant countries; and in Latin America. At the same time, it should be borne in mind that many of the practices which historically states have used to impose linguistic leveling and assimilation are no longer deemed legitimate nor practiced.

Far less powerful than language, common religion is nonetheless a significant cultural resource of shared identity consolidation.[101] This has been very noticeable in the countries of southern Asia and the southeast Asian archipelago, as it has been in Latin America. The same also holds true for much of Africa, and constitutes a major problem in those countries where the large-scale presence of both Islam and Christianity is the cause of a deep cleavage. To be sure, religious tolerance can facilitate national consolidation, and all the more so in a religiously divided society. And yet such tolerance is often difficult to achieve in traditional societies experiencing the early stages of modernization in which religion plays a prominent role in spirituality, culture, and identity-formation. It took Europe centuries to adopt the principle of religious tolerance; and the fact of the matter is that the great majority of the people in most European countries are overwhelmingly either Catholic or Protestant, at least in terms of cultural background if not actual religiosity. In any case, as already noted in the Introduction, religion *per se* rarely serves as a basis for nationhood, unless it is a national religion, that is, unique to a people and therefore far more defining of its identity. Even then, a common language remains a top priority for national consolidation. It is for these reasons that Belgian and Pakistani national identity has proven to be so shaky, whereas Jewish-Israeli and Indian identities have been quite robust. Religious cleavages may split an ethnos or a people speaking the same language more than a common religion can unite speakers of different languages into one people.

To be sure, shared cultural features do not guarantee a sense of common nationhood. This is certainly not the case with religion, or even with language. Separate historical traditions and distinct geography may still keep communities apart in terms of national identity. Nonetheless, much-cited exceptions should not obscure the more common realities: in the vast majority of nations there are strong ties of common culture; and over time these ties also produce a perception of the nation as an extended family, if a sense of kinship did not exist from the outset. Conversely, in the absence of such unifying bonds, or if the state fails to create them, states find it extraordinarily difficult to keep their unity and form a national community. Democracy, liberal rights, and respect for ethnic diversity, all very important in their own right, may assist in preventing ethnonational dissent and disintegration, or they may set them loose. Whether a state's concept of the nation and citizenship leans toward territory and culture or more toward descent and culture, hardly any nation exists based solely or even mainly on political allegiance to state and constitution.

C NATIONAL CONFLICT AND SOLIDARITY IN A GLOBALIZING WORLD

We live in a fast globalizing world in terms of communication, culture, and the economy. Concomitantly, liberal values of individualism, multiculturalism, and universalism deepen in the West and other parts of the world, arguably globally. Like the state, nationalism is reputed to be eroded from both above and below, by the forces of the international system, as well as by group and individual rights domestically. Voices heralding the demise of the nation and nationalism as anachronistic (as well as dangerous and morally problematic), a relic from a bygone age, have sparked a counter-reaction which points out that nations and nationalism are alive and kicking everywhere, including the supposedly postnational Europe.[102] Of course, nationalism is not a given quantity which obeys a law of preservation. The forces underlying it transform and fluctuate in their manifestations and power. In what follows we look at the potency of nationalism in today's world, most notably in reference to the two major, classical spheres of state activity, in which national affinity and solidarity have been the most prominent and reached their apogee during the twentieth century. These spheres are war and the welfare state, relating to the outside world and domestic society, respectively.

The audit of war: willingly killing and dying for one's nation

War has a reputation for being the ultimate expression of national affinity and solidarity, of the sharp distinction between "us" and "them." Societies have mobilized and have been galvanized by war, in which people kill and get killed not merely by compulsion, but with inner commitment, with desperate determination, or even enthusiasm. Indeed, this highly charged emotional willingness to sacrifice life and limb for people and country, so patently clear to any observer, has been the weakest, unexplained point in any "instrumentalist" or "manipulation" theorizing regarding the national phenomenon, both premodern and modern. As we have seen, pan-national mobilization for war variably existed during premodern times as well. Even in highly exploitative societies (and not all societies were equally exploitative) rulers could usually count on their people's patriotic sentiments, as they did in times of emergency. Undoubtedly, however, national mobilization and popular commitment for war became much more significant with modernity and the age of popular sovereignty, as the people far more closely identified the wars with their own interests.

Two major trends call for attention in examining the relationship between nationalism and war in the modern globalizing international system: the number of wars has declined sharply since 1815, and those subsequent have overwhelmingly been caused by ethnic and nationalist motives. We begin with the former trend. In the century after 1815, wars among the Great Powers and other economically advanced countries declined in frequency to about one-third of what they had been in the eighteenth century, and even less compared with earlier times. The same low frequency continued during the twentieth century, although resource and manpower mobilization in the major wars that did occur, most notably in the two world wars, increased.[103] Many assume that there is an inverse relationship here, with the frequency of war declining because wars have become too expensive and lethal. However, *relative to population and wealth*, wars have not become more lethal and costly than earlier in history.[104] In nineteenth-century Europe (1815–1914), the most pacific century in European history, the frequency of war sharply declined even though the wars that did occur were far less devastating compared with both earlier and later times. Conversely, in the twentieth century, the mere twenty-one years that separated the two world wars – the most intense and devastating wars in modern European history – do not support an inverse relationship between war intensity and frequency either. The Second World War has been followed by the so-called Long Peace among the Great Powers and other economically developed countries. Although this is widely attributed to the nuclear factor – a decisive factor to be sure – the trend became evident long before the advent of nuclear weapons. The three longest periods of peace by far in the modern Great Power system have all occurred since the beginning of the nineteenth century: thirty-nine years of peace between 1815 and 1854; forty-three years between 1871 and 1914; and more than sixty-five years to date since 1945.

Even before the middle of the nineteenth century, thinkers such as Saint-Simon, Auguste Comte, J. S. Mill, and the Manchester school were quick to note the change and realized that it was caused by the advent of the industrial–technological–commercial revolution, the most profound transformation of human society since the Neolithic adoption of agriculture. Since that sweeping change, wealth has been growing steeply and continuously, a dramatic break from the "Malthusian trap" that characterized earlier human history. Per capita production in developed countries has increased in comparison with preindustrial times by a factor of 30–50, so far.[105] This revolutionary change has worked against war in several ways. First, wealth no longer constitutes a fundamentally finite quantity, its acquisition having progressively shifted from a zero-sum game where one participant's gain could only be achieved at others' expense. Second (and this is the most widely recognized factor), as production has been intended for sale in the marketplace rather than directly consumed by the family producers themselves, economies have become increasingly interconnected in an intensifying and spreading network of specialization, scale, and exchange, the much celebrated globalization of the markets.[106] In consequence, prosperity abroad became interrelated with one's own, to the extent that foreign devastation potentially depressed the entire system and was thus detrimental to a state's own well-being. This reality, already noted by J. S. Mill,[107] starkly manifested itself after the First World War, as J. M. Keynes had anticipated in his *The Economic Consequences of the Peace* (1920). Third, greater economic openness has decreased the likelihood of war by disassociating economic access and opportunity from the confines of political borders and sovereignty. It is no longer necessary to politically possess a territory in order to benefit from it. In conclusion, rather than war becoming more costly, as is widely believed, the reason for the decline of war has in fact been peace growing more profitable.

Side by side with the decline of war in the developed world, studies show that the main cause of the post-1815 wars has been ethnic–nationalist. According to Andreas Wimmer's computations, for example, this factor, accounting for around 30 percent of all wars in 1820, had risen to 68 percent in 2000.[108] Consider, for example, the wars involving the Great Powers that disturbed the nineteenth-century's relative peacefulness. Apart from the Crimean War (1854–1856), these were the war of 1859 which led to Italy's unification, the

American Civil War (1861–1865), and the Wars of German Unification (1864, 1866, 1870–1871). It was above all issues of national unity and national independence that constituted the deepest and most inflammable motives for these major wars. The same held true for violent conflict in general throughout Europe. The hotspots of such conflict were nationalistic: conquered and partitioned Poland; fragmented and foreign-dominated Italy; disunited Germany; the territories of the future Belgium briefly stitched to Holland; suppressed Ireland; the Habsburg-incorporated Hungary; the Ottoman-held Balkans; and Alsace-Lorraine, annexed to Germany but retaining their affinity of national sentiment to France. Thus, the rising tide of modern nationalism often overrode the logic of the new economic realities.

Furthermore, in line with the teachings of the school of national economists, from Alexander Hamilton and Friedrich List on, and following the highpoint of free trade in the mid nineteenth century, the United States, Germany, France, Russia, and Japan all adopted strong protectionist policies against British manufacturing during their period of industrial takeoff. Moreover, by the late nineteenth and early twentieth centuries, with the new imperialism, the Great Powers expanded their protectionist policies to the undeveloped parts of the world. It thus appeared that the emergent global economy might become partitioned rather than remaining open for all, with each national-imperial bloc becoming closed to everybody else, as in fact occurred during the 1930s. A snowball effect ensued, generating a runaway grab for territory. For the territorially confined Germany and Japan the need to break away into imperial *Lebensraum* or "co-prosperity sphere" seemed particularly pressing. Here lay the seeds of the two world wars.

After 1945, the wave of decolonization triggered numerous wars of national independence in Asia and Africa. Among the Great Powers nuclear weapons have concentrated the minds of all concerned wonderfully, but no less important have been the institutionalization of free trade and the closely related process of rapid and sustained economic growth. As a result, the modernized, economically developed parts of the world constitute a "zone of peace." War now seems to be confined to the less developed parts of the globe, or "zone of war," where countries that have so far failed to embrace modernization continue to be engaged in wars among and within themselves, as well as with developed countries.

All this indicates that there has indeed been a clear correlation between economic modernization coupled with commercial globalization, on the one hand, and the decline of national economic autarky, war, and national mobilization for war, on the other. Globalization does have the effect of eroding nationalism, as the system of economic benefits strides across national borders. Growing connectivity and global cultural leveling work in the same direction. Finally, the liberal economic system is supplemented by the spread of liberal values, which promote individualism and universalism while viewing particularistic group identities very ambivalently. Although tolerant of or even celebrating the diversity of group identifications, liberalism is concerned about those group allegiances that threaten individual rights and the idea of liberal humanity, and is especially suspicious of national chauvinism. At the same time, however, liberalism also upholds the right of peoples to political self-determination according to their own free choice, and this choice has almost invariably turned out to be nationalist.

The particular historical development of liberalism sometimes obscures this point, yet may also serve to clarify it. Late-seventeenth- and eighteenth-century English-dominated Britain, wherein the principles of liberalism were formulated, was a grand hegemonic nation that, like all grand hegemonic nations, regarded its nationhood as self-evident and universalistic. Having overcome external threats from Spain and France, Britain was secure and superior in its identity, while discounting Irish and Scottish national aspirations. Under these circumstances, British liberals concentrated on the domestic element of the doctrine – the people's rights versus the crown – and had little to say about the national question vis-à-vis other countries. Although they were proud, ardent British themselves, they looked through the national phenomenon as if it were transparent. In the nineteenth century, J. S. Mill, for example, tended to believe (as did Marx) that small ethnicities should assimilate into the great historical nations, because this was their most promising way by which to gain the blessings of progress and liberal liberties. Things were different, however, for liberals in the smaller countries of Europe.

Famously, liberalism and nationalism were widely regarded as closely intertwined from the French Revolution on and during the nineteenth century. Both worked against the old order in the name of the people's rights. For the leaders of national liberation movements, such as Giuseppe Mazzini and Thomas Masaryk, as well as for American President Woodrow Wilson, popular sovereignty, liberal rights, and national self-determination free from foreign rule were inseparable from one another. However, by the late nineteenth and early twentieth centuries anti-liberal nationalistic doctrines had emerged, and chauvinistic and aggressive nationalism had widely demonstrated its horrendous potential. In the wake of the two world wars and Nazism, liberal attitudes toward nationalism have taken a sharp negative turn. Although liberal opinion has grown even more supportive of national self-determination, most notably in the case of the formerly colonial countries, mainstream national identity and sentiments in the developed liberal democratic countries themselves have been increasingly regarded with distaste. Not without reason, they have been suspected of being chauvinistic, detrimental to individual and minority rights, and an obstacle to growing cosmopolitanism. Only a few recent liberal theorists have had good things to say about nationalism or underlined its liberal justification.[109]

Paradoxically, however, a crucial development of our times has been overlooked in this context, barely recognized precisely because it has so comprehensively materialized: national self-determination in the liberal democratic world has been all but secured on the principle of the people's choice. Therefore, with few exceptions, there has been little need to fight for it. When national rights are secured domestically while genuine foreign threat has practically disappeared with the collapse of the Soviet system, it is hardly surprising that national sentiments are viewed lightly or even disparagingly in the liberal democratic countries. As it is said about good health, it is only when something is lacking that its absence is felt.

Thus, secure and widely available like the air one breathes, national identity and sentiments appear transparent to many in the liberal democratic world, even though they are anything but non-existent and can be triggered when challenged.[110] In Europe, for example, they are presently most conspicuously manifested, sometimes chauvinistically, with respect to the question of the integration of Muslim immigrants into Europe's national state societies. All in all, in contrast to the aggressive nationalism of the past, national identity and sentiments in the liberal democratic countries have become liberal, largely implicit, and predominantly defensive. While this is a huge change, its scope and contours should be clearly understood: liberalism and globalization have decreased protectionist national economy, war, and national mobilization for it; but only by also securing national self-determination, in the absence of which conflict still simmers and sometimes erupts. While aggressive nationalism has declined sharply in the liberal world, defensive nationalism is very much alive. Nationalist sentiments seem to be in decline in the developed world precisely because the national principle has so thoroughly materialized and is peacefully secured.

Side by side with globalization, growing connectivity, and cultural leveling – and partly because of them – there is also widespread concern among peoples for their national culture and identity.[111] Finally, it may not be redundant to add that in contrast to predictions made after the end of the Cold War, the worldwide triumph of liberalism, and with it liberal nationalism, are not yet secured. China is poised to become the twenty-first-century's rising superpower, and it is an open question whether or not it will retain its current authoritarianism or embrace democracy and liberalism as it modernizes.[112] At present China is ardently nationalistic, while harshly suppressing non-Han national aspirations in both Tibet and Xinxiang.

China's suppression of non-Han nationalism is yet another reminder that the global victory of nationalism is at least as much a result of the defeat of the authoritarian and totalitarian imperial powers as it is the product of modernization. As we have seen earlier in this chapter (pp. 258–259), it has scarcely been noticed that the massive wave of decolonization after 1945 took place *only* vis-à-vis the liberal democratic empires (most notably Britain and France), and was sweepingly successful precisely because they were liberal and democratic. The non-democratic empires, far from being made to withdraw by indigenous resistance, were either crushed in the two world wars (Germany and Japan) or dismantled peacefully when the totalitarian system disintegrated (the Soviet Union). As Sherlock Holmes has noted, it is "the dog that didn't bark" – the imperial domains kept down under the totalitarian iron fist – that is the most conspicuous, and most telling.

Throughout history imperial conquest necessitated ruthless pressure on the conquered peoples, which generally resisted foreign rule, often desperately so. Premodern powers, as well as modern authoritarian and totalitarian ones, rarely had a problem with such measures, and overall they have proved quite successful in suppression. All empires worked this way, including democratic and republican ones, such as ancient Athens and Rome. They could *only* work this way. However, as liberalization deepened from the late nineteenth century onward, the days of formal democratic empires became numbered, even while outwardly they were reaching their greatest extent. At the turn of the twentieth century, the British setbacks and eventual compromise settlement in South Africa and withdrawal from Ireland were the signs of things to come for other liberal democratic empires as well.[113]

Undeniably, liberal democratic countries during the twentieth century could be quite ruthless. However, the question should be posed in relative, comparative terms. Did French conduct during the Algerian war of independence, ruthless as it undoubtedly was, match Marshal Bugeaud's tactics a century earlier in that same country? Did British methods during the twentieth century come anywhere close to the methods used during the suppression of the Indian Mutiny of 1857, let alone in the Scottish Highlands after 1746, or in Ireland up until and as late as 1798? Has there ever been a successful Gandhi or Nkrumah, or, indeed, *any* instance of successful decolonization from the authoritarian and totalitarian Great Powers? It is not necessary to invoke Nazi Germany. Imperial Germany's genocidal methods in crushing the Herero revolt in southwest Africa (Namibia) (1904–1907) and that of the Maji-Maji in east Africa (Tanzania) (1905–1907) provide horrific demonstrations of the sword that hung over the heads of the subject peoples in all non-liberal empires.

Certainly, winning over at least the elites of conquered societies – through benefits, cooptation, and the amenities of "soft power," the "winning of hearts and minds" – has always played a central role in imperial "pacification." Tacitus described this memorably with respect to the taming of the barbarian Britons by Rome. Still, that velvet glove always covered an iron fist that had crushed local resistance mercilessly in the first place and remained unmistakably in place as the *ultima ratio* of foreign control. Once the liberal democratic powers no longer regarded such means as legitimate, their empires disintegrated and the national principle triumphed even in the still barely modernized countries of Asia and Africa. Liberal economics, politics, and morals reinforced one another in the dismantling of liberal democracies' imperial domains. Rather than liberalism and nationalism being mutually contradictory or conflicting, liberalism and democracy in the imperial core countries have been vehicles for the release and proliferation of national self-determination worldwide. Instead of nationalism being something new and modern, it took the center stage as democratization gave free expression to the popular will among subject peoples and as the liberalization of imperial powers de-legitimized foreign coercive rule.

In today's liberal democracies wars are sanctioned only as a last resort, after all other options have failed. Yet a feeling that there may be another way, that there *must* be another way, always lingers on. Under these circumstances and in the absence of a direct and acute threat to life and national independence, people in affluent liberal democratic countries exhibit a dramatically heightened "casualty sensitivity," a sharp decline in their willingness to die for the nation, at least when the ends of a war seem remote and dimly connected to their daily lives.[114] More in line with the modern world, however, are people willing to *pay* for their national kin?

The nation and the welfare state: for whom are people willing to pay?

During the twentieth century government expenditure in the industrial and affluent countries rose unabated from less than 10 percent to around 30–50 percent of GDP. Military expenditure, historically the largest item on states' budgets, has pretty much retained its share of up to 5 percent of GDP (except during the two world wars). The quadrupling of government expenditure thus reflected a steep increase in spending on social services – education, health, and welfare – which for the first time grew far larger than military expenditure.[115] This change mirrors both the growth of wealth and the decline of war outlined above. In a way, the question of for whom are people willing to pay has replaced the traditional question of for whom they are willing to die as a test of collective affinity and solidarity. Three indicators seem most relevant in this context: the scale of societies' redistribution of wealth from the affluent to the poor by way of taxation and welfare policies; the degree to which societies' ethnic homogeneity affects these policies; and the resources societies dedicate to foreign aid.

To be sure, social welfare policies and the redistribution of resources from the affluent to the poor are not entirely attributable to genuine solidarity and altruism. In large part they are an expression of what people perceive as their self-interest, because helping to pull the poor of one's society out of their condition may be regarded as an investment intended to increase social wealth, lower crime, and so forth. Still, might differences among states in the scale of their redistributive policies point to differences in social solidarity and to the causes of these differences? This has recently been the subject of research and debate centering on the ethnic and national factor. Some social critics have claimed that the growth of alien ethnic immigrant communities and the erosion in the sense and legitimacy of a homogeneous national community have resulted in a rolling back of the welfare state. Both the public and governments have become less willing to pay for ethnically alien poor, with whom they feel little solidarity because they barely view them as part of the national collective.[116]

This claim has been empirically substantiated by leading economists Alberto Alesina and Edward Glaeser. They have systematically analyzed the data pertaining to the well-known differences in wealth redistribution policies between the United States and the European countries. Government expenditure averages 30 percent of GDP in the United States, as opposed to a European average of around 45 percent. Expenditure on social programs totals 14.6 percent of GDP in the United States, as opposed to a European average of 25.5 percent.[117] The authors recognize that these differences, which go back a long way historically, have a variety of causes. They calculate that about half of the difference is attributable to differences in the political system and geopolitical size between the United States and the European countries. The other half they demonstrate to be rooted in the United States' ethnic and racial heterogeneity.[118] Throughout American history there has been little sense of solidarity with new immigrant communities, which have always constituted a large part of the poor population. Today this attitude mostly applies to the Latino immigrant population. Predominantly, however, the sense of ethnic alienation has applied to the black population of the United States, which figures disproportionally among the poor. Many white Americans view the black population as being outside the core of the American national community, feel little solidarity with it, and are very reluctant to contribute to it financially. Among the various states of the United States, social redistribution policies appear to vary in proportion to the size of the black population.[119] By contrast, the authors highlight the relative ethnic homogeneity of the European states as a major factor underlying their

welfare policies. The ethnically homogeneous and most socially redistributive Nordic countries head the list. The authors suggest that
growing immigrant communities may change social policies in Europe
as well. Finally, they show that by various indicators, including the Gini
coefficient of income inequality, immigrant countries Canada,
Australia, and New Zealand, but according to the authors also Japan,
stand somewhere in between the United States and Europe.[120] Other
researchers make similar claims in different contexts.[121]

Many variables and local idiosyncrasies combine in determining each country's redistributive policies. Therefore, the relationship
between such policies and the degree of ethnic homogeneity is far from
being simple, non-ambivalent, or undisputed.[122] The global data seems
to be the most conclusive with respect to new immigrant communities
negatively affecting redistributive policies.[123] As for native ethnic and
national minorities, there is the question of whether or not they are
viewed as entitled to special compensations and affirmative action
because of past wrongs or dispossession. Most significant, however, is
the question of whether or not there are marked differences in the levels
of affluence among the ethnic communities in a country. Only if such
differences exist does the ethnic factor become a major obstacle to
redistributive policies. Thus, binational Belgium, for example, is very
high on the redistributive scale because its two ethnic communities are
not very different in wealth. In such circumstances welfare policies do
not appear as channeling resources from one community to the
other.[124] In the study by Alesina and Glaeser, Japan appears as an
outlier in being one of the most ethnically homogeneous countries in
the world, while ranking only on the middle of the scale in terms of
government expenditure and income inequality. However, in the UN
Human Development Report for 2009, Japan ranks with the Scandinavian countries among the most equal societies in the world, with a
Gini coefficient of 25.[125] This fits Japanese's self-perception of their
people as being both close kin and middle class. It is clearly not an easy
task to devise a formula that will encompass all the major variables
affecting the relationship between ethnicity and wealth redistributive
policies worldwide (for obvious reasons, only affluent countries have
been compared here). Still, with all the reservations mentioned above,
such a relationship appears to exist.

The difference between "us" and the "other" is starkly revealed
in the data on foreign aid from rich to poor countries. In contrast to

their lavish domestic programs, affluent countries' foreign aid amounts to no more than 1 percent of the GNI at most (Sweden), according to OECD data for 2008 and 2009. That of the United States, the greatest donor in absolute terms, amounts to 0.2 percent. To be sure, in foreign aid as well, utilitarian considerations play a significant role in addition to altruism. Foreign aid is often a tool for achieving political influence in the beneficiary countries. In addition, the gap between domestic and international aid spending is partly accounted for by the fact that it is clearly more in people's self-interest to invest in their own poor rather than in those of far-away countries, even if the latter are much needier. All the same, the notion that altruism toward one's own people takes precedence is very deeply ingrained. In a globalizing world of spreading cosmopolitan culture and individualistic capitalist gain, genuine feelings of national affinity and solidarity remain one of the main buttresses of the welfare state.

Jürgen Habermas has tied together the ethnic and civic elements of nationhood, the role of the former in securing social solidarity, and the danger to that solidarity once the national sense of cohesion declines:

> The cultural symbolism of a "people" secures its own particular character, its "spirit of the people", in the presumed commonalities of descent, language, and history, and in this way generates a unity, if only an imaginary one ... Constructed through the medium of the modern law, the modern territorial state thus depends on the development of a national consciousness to provide it with the cultural substance for a civic solidarity ... members of the same "nation" feel responsible enough for one another that they are prepared to make "sacrifices" – as in military service or the burden of redistributive taxation.[126]

Hence, in Habermas' view, "the fears of the disempowering effects of globalization are, if still vague, far from unjustified."[127]

And yet, despite the above, Habermas has advocated "constitutional patriotism" as the proper form of nationalism.[128] Given his native Germany's horrendous twentieth-century history, this concept is an understandable ideological construct, reflecting and stimulating the change in German public norms. In reality, however, as the quotation from Habermas himself reveals, such *purely* civic national identity and solidarity, disassociated from kin–culture affinities hardly ever exists, in Germany or elsewhere. Indeed, it is with the constitution of the German people and state – surely liberal, inclusive, respectful toward ethnic minorities, and cooperative with their European neighbors and the rest of the world, but nonetheless their *own* people and state – that Germans identify, and are likely to identify.

Conclusion: are the nation and nationalism here to stay?

The reader who has gotten so far may think that my answer to this question is resoundingly affirmative, but it is actually more qualified. In the historically ever-unfolding interaction between the biologically evolved human propensity for kin–culture solidarity and human cultural transformation, neither the state nor the nation is in principle more than a particular and transient reality. Both have had far longer longevity than is recognized by some social science orthodoxies, and their future trajectories may prove to be far longer than cosmopolitan enthusiasts predict. However, this latter point, the future of the nation, the state, and the national state is a matter of assessment, as none of them are necessarily destined to retain their present form, or survive at all, with future historical transformation. They are no different in this respect than the tribe. I do not attempt to predict any of these future developments or venture to hypothesize about them in any detail. Yet one thing that might be learnt from this book about the future is the following: transformed as they might turn out to be and fluctuating in their manifestations and significance, kin–culture bonds of identity, affinity, and solidarity – which lie at the root of tribalism, ethnicity, and nationalism – will remain a potent social force. They will continue to deeply affect people's choices and collective action as long as kin–culture communal heterogeneity itself remains. Furthermore, the various particular ethnic and national identities are a powerful self-perpetuating force, and as of now there is little indication that the difference among them is about to be eradicated any time soon.

It is revealing to find Eric Hobsbawm arriving at very similar conclusions. As we have seen in the Introduction, this is not the only point where Hobsbawm hedges significantly against what his followers have come to identify and embrace as his own. In the last chapter of his

Nations and Nationalism since 1780 (1990), he outlined the decline in the role and prominence of the national state with globalization and suggested that the world might be moving beyond nationalism. Yet in a 2010 newspaper interview Hobsbawm denies that such a process is occurring:[129]

> *The enormous and, since the 1960s, accelerating process of technical and economic globalization is undeniable. But it is so far dramatically stopped short at the borders of politics and, in spite of the establishment of English as a single global lingua franca, shows little sign of penetrating the diversity of linguistic/confessional cultures. To this day, territorial nation-states remain the only effective decision-makers, as tensions within the European Union are demonstrating at present.*

Addressing the causes and effects of nationalism's resilience, Hobsbawm continues:

> *Nothing in the spontaneous operations of the global economy has so far been able to replace the social, redistributive and welfare functions of the territorial state, nor of the desire of human groups to establish specific collective identities. Politics remains central. State and world continue to coexist in conflict and symbiosis. Thus, unlike the 100 percent global mobility of other factors of production required by the prophets of capitalist turbo-globalization, no state, however committed to the universal "free market," has been able to establish the unlimited and uncontrolled cross-border movement of labor against the resistance of its citizens.*

Finally, in response to a question concerning the danger of xenophobia, Hobsbawm replies:

> *Xenophobia, whether a form of defense of national jobs against competition or of traditional national identity, is a profoundly troubling phenomenon for many who believe in the values of the 18th century Enlightenment. However, it is*

probably the only global (negative) mass ideology, and its force and growth are not to be underestimated.

Xenophobia, the hostility toward the foreign on account of its foreignness, and the often horrendous aggressive and violent expressions of this hostility, are undoubtedly the dark side of the ethnic and national phenomenon for those who believe in the values of the eighteenth-century Enlightenment. However, it is all too easily forgotten that the philosophers of Enlightenment liberalism were patriots of their nations as much as they were cosmopolitan. Like Aristotle, the great majority of them regarded attachment and devotion to one's people and country as a natural sentiment, a further extension of the attachment and devotion to one's close family and broader kin circle. They saw no fundamental contradiction between these sentiments and the love of humanity in general, provided that ethnic and national sentiments were kept liberal and enlightened. Herderian romantics similarly stressed the liberating, humanitarian, and universalistic virtues of peacefully prospering ethnonational cultures.

As mentioned above, the horrendous manifestations of chauvinistic and aggressive nationalism have made liberals much more suspicious of and ambivalent about the phenomenon as a whole. In the last chapter before the Conclusion, Alex Yakobson offers a close scrutiny of the ideological and constitutional norms adopted in today's world to accommodate liberal views and concerns with respect to the relationship between states, nationhood, and ethnicity.

7 STATE, NATIONAL IDENTITY, ETHNICITY: NORMATIVE AND CONSTITUTIONAL ASPECTS

ALEXANDER YAKOBSON

This chapter addresses the subject of the book from a specific angle: it examines the manner in which ethnic and national identities, and the connection between them, find expression in constitutional definitions and norms of contemporary states. Modern constitutional texts, reflecting the pivotal importance of the principle of equality in modern democratic doctrine, strongly emphasize the universal rather than the particular. There is an inevitable tension between this universalism and any kind of official connection between the state and a specific national identity, culture, and language, unless these are regarded as common to all the state's citizens. Nevertheless, the importance of national and cultural identity to the people (or peoples) in question is such that these factors do regularly find expression not merely in actual official and societal practice, but in the country's credo – its constitution. While modern states commit themselves solemnly to civic equality, they neither practice nor pretend to practice cultural neutrality in their constitutional texts. Of course, the question of neutrality or lack of it arises only if there are significant cultural differences within the citizen body; but such differences are very much the rule. The usual way to protect a cultural minority group (whether or not it is officially defined as a national minority) from discrimination and cultural oppression on the part of the majority is to safeguard its civic and cultural rights in the constitution. This is often done. However, where there is a minority there is also, by definition, a majority. It is often forgotten in the scholarly discourse that the very existence, and acknowledged distinctness, of a cultural minority also indicates the existence of a cultural majority. And its significance – more or less inevitable in a democracy based on the popular will – strongly impacts on the identity of the state as a whole.

National identity and state

When discussing the relations between statehood, nationhood, and ethnicity in today's world, few things – including the very terms used – are straightforward and uncontroversial. Still, despite "postnational" rhetoric, a modern state typically defines itself in national terms. The meaning of these terms, however, varies greatly. There are different ways in which nationhood and statehood are connected, and national identity itself is conceived differently in different cases. The following is the conceptual framework suggested in this chapter. If, as happens in the great majority of cases, a state defines itself in terms of a single national identity, however conceived, then such a state is a national state or nation-state. This term, it should be stressed, does not necessarily imply cultural homogeneity, for a considerable degree of ethnocultural pluralism may exist within what is regarded as a shared national identity. If a significant group of citizens is regarded as having a national identity that is different from that of the majority, they constitute a national minority. If, on the other hand, the state is based on giving expression to more than one national identity, it should be defined as binational or multinational. Needless to say, both the definitions and boundaries of national identity, and the political arrangements based on them, are often contested.

A precise definition of the connection between the nation and the state in a nation-state may in itself prove controversial. If the national identity in terms of which a nation-state defines itself is regarded as comprising the entire citizen body, the connection between the nation and the state is straightforward: there is no difficulty in saying that the state "belongs" to the nation. If, however, a substantial minority of citizens is regarded as having a distinct national identity of their own, it may be debated whether and in what sense the state can be regarded a state "of" the (majority) nation. Certainly, a democratic state, in which political sovereignty lies with "the people" as a civic community (regardless of any differences of national or cultural identity among citizens), cannot be regarded as "belonging" to the majority nation exclusively. Nevertheless, it is obvious that the majority nation and the nation-state are connected in such a case in a significant way. This is typically – though not invariably – expressed by the fact that the same adjective is used in ordinary parlance and in constitutional texts to designate the nation, the state, and the state's official (national) language. Such a state can be regarded as a nation-state "of" the majority people in the sense that it gives official expression to this people's national identity and realizes their right to national independence. By the same token, a binational or multinational state gives official expression to the two – or several – main national identities that exist in it, even though it cannot properly be said to "belong" solely to them, to the exclusion of other groups of citizens. Similarly, national movements struggle for independence in the name of their people's right to a nation-state "of their own," even if such a state, once established, can be expected to include people from other national groups.

Civic and ethnic nationalism

A modern national identity is usually classified as either "civic" or "ethnic." The former means that citizenship and national identity are congruent, just as "nationality" and citizenship are often synonymous in (west) European languages. All the citizens of a civic nation-state are regarded as sharing the same national identity. What makes a national identity "ethnic" is far less easy to agree upon, since ethnicity itself is, of course, a far more elusive and controversial concept than citizenship, and, moreover, a far less prestigious one in our world. The ethnic label is carefully eschewed by nation-states, by autonomous national entities within a larger state, and even by separatist national movements. In scholarly debates, many prefer to speak of "ethnocultural" or even simply "cultural" nationalism when referring to a type of national identity that, avowedly, is confined to only a part of the whole citizen body of a state, characterized by a certain culture. In the broad and flexible sense in which ethnicity is understood in this book, subgroups within the citizen body sharing a common culture and a sense of peoplehood, whether they are a minority or a majority, are indeed ethnic.

"Civic" and "ethnic" are both loaded terms. "Ethnic nationalism" is widely used in a sense that is at least mildly pejorative. Citizenship is thought to provide a much better definition than ethnicity of national identity in a modern state, especially a democracy. As we have seen in Chapter 6, there is a long tradition describing civic nationalism as democratic, liberal, and inclusive, and ascribing the opposite qualities to ethnic nationalism. The former is said to be characteristic of "civic" West European democracies, the French Republic being a sort of "ideal type"; the latter has usually been associated with nineteenth-century German nationalism and with the troubled history of rival – and often oppressive – nationalisms in Eastern Europe. All in all, anything designated as "civic" is bound to enjoy greater prestige in modern liberal-democratic parlance than anything called "ethnic." There have been quite a few scholarly criticisms of this common classification. They challenge the very dichotomy between "civic" and "ethnic" nationalism, pointing out the significant ethnocultural characteristics of even the most exemplary "civic" national identities. Moreover, they dispute the assumption that civic nationalism is inherently more liberal than ethnic nationalism, stressing its tendency to deny or even suppress ethnocultural differences within the civic nation.[1]

This chapter suggests that from the viewpoint of the need to ensure the rights of minorities, both civic and ethnic nationalism have their inherent advantages, yet each comes at a price. The balance varies from case to case, depending in large measure on whether and in what sense the different groups of citizens in a state do in fact consider themselves as sharing the same national identity. Civic nationalism that insists on the full congruence between nationhood and citizenship means that all those, regardless of ethnic identity, who wish to be included in the nation are indeed included; those who may waiver (including immigrants) are strongly encouraged to integrate fully; while those who regard themselves as belonging to a distinct national group cannot receive any official acknowledgment of their identity; moreover, the state may be tempted to realize its ideal of nationhood by subjecting them to various pressures to assimilate. On the other hand, a distinction between national identity and citizenship (characteristic of what is usually defined as ethnic nationalism) gives legitimacy, at least in principle, to the existence of national minorities alongside the (majority) nation. At the same time, it creates the potential for undermining the minority's status as fully-fledged and equal members of the civic community. Even if the civic equality of the minority is fully respected and its distinct identity fully acknowledged, this very acknowledgment means that the national identity of the nation-state itself reflects that of the majority rather than of the whole citizenry, as under civic nationalism. The state may accept the legitimate existence of two or more national identities within it, either expressly or implicitly, by employing some other term to signify the minority's distinctness, but conceding the substance of a national minority status. Yet it cannot be neutral between them, unless the status of the minority in question is "upgraded" so as to make it one of the constituent components of a binational or multinational state, which is indeed based on giving roughly equal expression to these components. We shall examine the particular problems raised by this latter configuration later in the chapter.

"The nation together with national minorities and ethnic groups"

Thus, the constitution of Slovakia speaks in its preamble in the name of "we, the Slovak nation (*národ slovenský*)." This nation adopts the constitution

> *mindful of the political and cultural heritage of our forefathers and of the centuries of experience from the struggle for national existence and our own statehood, in the sense of the spiritual heritage of Cyril and Methodius ... proceeding from the natural right of nations to self-determination, together with members of national minorities and ethnic groups living on the territory of the Slovak Republic.*[2]

This definition of the Slovak nation is unambiguously ethnic, according to the usual classification, though Slovakia, naturally, does not officially adopt this label. It regards itself simply as a Slovak nation-state with a large (*c.* 10 percent) Hungarian national minority, expressly recognized as such, as well as several smaller minority groups. The "nation" is not the whole body of citizens, but the Slovak-speaking majority, whose cultural identity and historical memory are expressed in the preamble and on whose right to national self-determination the legitimacy of the state is based. This very fact enables the state to recognize the Hungarian-speaking minority as having a distinct national identity of its own. In this framework, "Everyone has the right to freely decide on his nationality. Any influence on this decision and any form of pressure aimed at assimilation are forbidden" (Article 12.3). The democratic principles are assured by providing that "State power is derived from the citizens," rather than from the "nation," since the latter, as defined in this text, comprises the majority of citizens rather than all of them (Article 2.1). Full equality of civil rights is guaranteed regardless of, *inter alia*, "affiliation to a nation or ethnic group" (Article 12.2).

Both in the constitution (Articles 33 and 34) and in practice, considerable cultural rights are granted to the Hungarian minority, allowing it to preserve its distinct national identity, first and foremost its language. However – indeed, for this very reason, since two national identities are recognized but only one of them is "Slovak" – it is obvious that it is the majority Slovak, rather than the minority Hungarian national identity that is given expression by the state. Thus, in addition to the state's very name, "Slovak is the state language." Moreover, "the Slovak Republic shall support national awareness and cultural identity of Slovaks living abroad … as well as their relations with their homeland."

The question of language is, of course, crucial. Language is widely considered as the main cultural feature of a typical modern national identity. Designating a particular language as "official" is the usual way for a constitution to express the national character of the state.* Binational states signify their binational character by conferring an equal status on both their main languages. Conceding language rights to a minority community is – at any rate, in Europe – the typical way for a state to recognize, explicitly or implicitly, the existence of a national minority. On the other hand, some states explicitly deny a national status to linguistic minorities; not all linguistic minorities consider themselves as nationally distinct; and different nations may speak the same language. In many postcolonial countries, the prevailing concept of nationhood and the process of nation-building are based, with various degrees of success, on linguistic pluralism. Not even language, for all its importance, is "the essence" of a national identity. Rather, it is the will on the part of the people in question to be

---

* In Ireland, where English is in practice the main language but Irish is considered an important element of national identity, the constitution states that "the Irish language, as the national language, is the first official language," while "the English language is recognized as a second official language" (Article 8).

a nation, or a national group – a somewhat circular, but still the least unsatisfactory definition of an elusive but powerful phenomenon. All the same, the link between sharing a distinct language and the sense of belonging to a shared national community is, in practice, strong and far from accidental.

This is one of the chief reasons why national identity can hardly be separated from politics in the same way that religion can be. A state can be neutral between all religions, but it cannot be neutral between all languages in the public sphere. This is technically unfeasible, quite apart from the fact that most voters in a democracy will not stand for it.[3] As we shall see, even India, which is a multilingual nation *par excellence*, with a huge diversity of languages, is anything but neutral and indifferent when it comes to language, despite its being inclusive and pluralistic. Some local languages are recognized as official at the state level – which inevitably means that many others are not thus privileged. And at the federal level, the official status of both Hindi and English results from political decisions that are of high ideological and cultural significance.

In both "ethnic" Slovakia and "civic" France, the centrality of language to national identity is stressed by the constitution using a stronger expression than the usual "official language": "state language" in Slovakia, "the language of the Republic" in France. For a minority group wishing to preserve its distinct language – an issue of vital importance to many minorities – the Slovak arrangements in this field are certainly preferable to the French ones. But this advantage comes at a price, and the price is not inconsiderable. Members of the Hungarian minority may enjoy equal rights as citizens, but the state language of the country where they live is not their national language, and the heritage of Cyril and Methodius in whose spirit the constitution is proclaimed is not their national heritage. Fundamentally, the state in the Slovak nation-state is their state, since they are its citizens, but the nation is not their nation.

It should be noted that what is crucial here is not the use of the term "nation" (or what is considered as its equivalent in the various languages) as referring to the majority rather than to all the citizens. This term, notoriously, may mean different things in different contexts, as is recognized, *inter alia*, in a Council of Europe document dealing with this issue and quoted in Chapter 5.[4] Even when it is clearly recognized that there is more than one national identity within the borders of the state, one may still speak of the nation in the sense of the civic community, the entire citizen body. The same applies to the term "people" in an avowedly multinational setting: one can speak of different peoples in a country, but the electorate choosing the country's parliament will still be defined as "the people." Moreover, sometimes (quite often, actually) "nation" refers to the state itself, as in the expression United Nations, which does not purport to tell us anything about how questions of identity are dealt with within each of the member states. What is crucial is whether or not it is recognized that there exists a minority of citizens with a distinct national identity of its own. If so, there inevitably exists a national identity that is shared by the majority, but that is not congruent with state citizenship. It should be obvious that where there is in this sense a national minority (or minorities) to which some of the citizens belong, there is also a *national majority*, as distinct from the whole body of citizens. Such a majority may or may not define itself explicitly as a "nation," yet it is the national identity of the majority that is expressed by the state (unless the state is binational or multinational).

When the distinct minority in question is large enough to comprise a significant part of the citizen body, the majority is more likely to perceive and define itself, formally or informally, as distinct from the civic community as a whole. This is the case, formally, in Slovakia. When, on the other hand, the majority comprises nearly all of the country's population, it naturally tends to identify itself with the whole, even if the distinct identity of the minority or minorities is fully acknowledged. This is in fact the case in most West European countries, where national minorities, explicitly or implicitly acknowledged as such, are simply too small to give rise to a notion of majority nationhood. For example, some 20,000 Germans in Denmark are not numerous enough to create an awareness of a distinction between Danish national identity and Danish citizenship, though their right to a German national identity, as distinguished from their Danish citizenship, has been explicitly recognized by the Danish state. At the same time, as part of the Bonn–Copenhagen Declarations of 1955, Germany recognized the right of the small Danish minority on the German side of the border to a Danish national identity.[5] Danish national identity thus includes, officially, people who are not Danish citizens (but are Danes ethnically), whereas some Danish citizens do not share it (because they are ethnically related to a neighboring state). Analytically, this makes the Danish national identity doubly non-congruous with the citizenship of the Danish state, and, thus, "ethnic" rather than "civic" according to the usual classification. But most Danes will surely be surprised to hear this. When they think of a Danish citizen who is not quite a Dane, they presumably think of an immigrant who has failed to integrate successfully.

The German speakers of South Tyrol, an area that was once part of Austria, numbering some 300,000, are the largest national minority in Italy. They regard Austria as their "kin-state,"[6] and their distinct peoplehood is fully acknowledged by the Italian Republic. Italy has repeatedly agreed to involve Austria in negotiations pertaining to their cultural rights (as it has also done in the case of Slovenia and the smaller Slovenian minority). Following these talks, Italy conferred on the German-speaking people of the Tyrol a substantial measure of territorial autonomy in the province of Bozen-South Tyrol where they constitute a majority. German, alongside Italian, is recognized as one of the two official languages of the province. However, this group comprises only some 0.5 percent of Italy's population. This, as well as the existence of several other small minority groups, is naturally far from sufficient to give rise to any notion of an Italian majority nation or identity as distinct from the civic "people of Italy." And yet the distinction between the Italian national–cultural identity and the citizenship of the Italian Republic is very real within the autonomous province of Bozen-South Tyrol itself, where the Italian-speaking population constitutes a large minority and, thus, one of the two main distinct ethno-national communities in the area.[†] Further non-congruence between Italian national identity and Italian citizenship is provided by Italy regarding itself as a "kin-state" for the small Italian minorities in Croatia and Slovenia. Nonetheless, all these are relatively minor issues as far as Italy as a whole is concerned. When the question of possible non-congruence between Italian citizenship and Italian national and

---

[†] The Italian constitution (Article 6) speaks of "linguistic" (rather than national) minorities, and this is also the language of the various laws dealing with those groups' status and rights. However, Italy treats these groups, as regards their cultural rights and their ties with their "kin-states," in a way that is compatible with their self-perception as fully-fledged national minorities. It also accepts that their rights are protected under the European Convention for the Protection of National Minorities. This should be distinguished from those countries that explicitly deny, as a matter of principle, the status of a national minority to cultural minority groups (like Greece or Bulgaria regarding their Turkish communities; see below).

cultural identity arises, what is usually referred to (similarly to what happens in Denmark and Germany) are the difficulties in integrating immigrants and thus, at least according to some, making them fully Italian. There is no attempt on the part of the Italian state to make the German-speaking Italian citizens of South Tyrol "Italian" in this sense (though this was certainly its policy under Mussolini). Indeed, there is a widely accepted traditional distinction between "native" national minorities and immigrants as far as the right to preserve one's distinct national identity is concerned. This distinction has been weakened – but not removed – by the multicultural attitudes of the recent decades. Later in the chapter we shall return to this question, which is central to many of today's debates on citizenship and identity.

Civic nationalism: the French model

On the other hand, civic nationalism, French-style, based on the notion that all the citizens share a common national identity, means that a national minority within the citizenry cannot in principle exist. In practice, this means that should such a minority exist in the opinion of those who regard themselves as belonging to it, it cannot be officially acknowledged. This, indeed, is the explicit official position of the French Republic, according to which there are no national minorities in France (nor "ethnic" ones, usually implying a lesser degree of distinctness), but only the French people. The national identity of every French citizen is held to be French and French only. One of the pillars of this identity is the French language, defined in the constitution as "the language of the Republic" (Article 2). It is quite wrong to assume, as some do, that the pure version of "civic nationalism," as practiced in France, means that citizenship, as a legal concept entailing a list of rights and duties, is all there is to nationalism. On the contrary, it means that all the citizens are presumed to share the same national identity which is endowed with a significant cultural content.

The idea is, of course, that this cultural content is something that all citizens can be reasonably expected to share, or to adopt. Yet what is reasonable in this context may well be a matter of controversy. This cultural content is indeed indifferent to ethnic descent but not to ethnic identity, if one's ethnic identity includes a language other than French. Furthermore, because the republic is secular, it is avowedly indifferent to one's religion. However, as the controversy over the Muslim veil in French state schools has demonstrated, it is far more in tune with the modern secularized version of Christian (or post-Christian) culture than with that of many of France's citizens who originated in Muslim countries. The reality behind the secular republic's official neutrality on matters of religion is that some religions (as contemporary social phenomena, to be sure, not in any essentialist sense) are more secular than others.

This unadulterated civic model, which was once widely influential and is still regularly held up in scholarly discussions as the ideal type of civic nationalism, has in recent decades become rather exceptional among developed democracies because of increasing emphasis on minority rights. This tendency has since the 1980s influenced the policy of many democracies and found expression in numerous international and European normative and quasi-normative documents. Will Kymlicka describes the process:

> Throughout much of the twentieth century, the most influential example of a normal state was France – i.e., a highly centralised state with an undifferentiated conception of republican citizenship and a single official language. In this model, there is no room for minority rights ... In recent years, however, international organisations have revised their views on what a "normal" and "modern" state looks like ... In contemporary international discourse, [this model] is increasingly described as an anachronism, a throwback to the nineteenth century.[7]

In accordance with its concept of nationhood, France has refused to sign the international and European conventions on the protection of the rights of national minorities. It has rejected criticism on this score from both UN and European bodies, pointing out that the fundamental character of the republic, set out by its constitution, precludes it from acknowledging any "minorities" within the French nation. This nation consists of equal individuals, not collective subgroups with special rights.[8] In 1991, the French Parliament, as part of an attempt to ease tensions in Corsica, passed an Act on the Status of the Territorial Unit of Corsica referring to "the historical and cultural community which constitutes the Corsican people, a component of the French people." The Act guaranteed this community's right to preserve its culture, subject to the overall French "national unity." However, France's Constitutional Council quashed the law, holding that the "*unicité*" of the French people was a binding constitutional norm and no other "people" could be recognized in France. In another ruling, the Constitutional Council held that the government's signing of the European Charter for Regional or Minority Languages was unconstitutional on the grounds that the French Republic cannot officially recognize any language other than French, which, according to the Constitution, is "the language of the Republic."[9] The official explanation of France's refusal to sign the European Framework Convention for the Protection of National Minorities sets out the principles of pure civic nationalism as practiced in France: "the principle of the unity and indivisibility of the nation [in the Constitution] ... relates both to territory and to population"; French, and French only, is "the language of the Republic"; "France cannot accede to international legal instruments which recognize the existence of a group, or make it identifiable, on the grounds of its race, religion, sex, ethnic background etc."[10]

It should be noted that the term "national minority" in the Convention is left undefined. European normative documents use it in a very broad sense, "encompass[ing] a wide range of minority groups, including religious, linguistic and cultural as well as ethnic minorities, regardless of whether these groups are recognized as such by the States where they reside and irrespective of the denomination under which they are recognized."[11] In this pragmatic way, obviously intended to mobilize maximum support among European states, the Convention attempts to gloss over the contradiction between two discourses that enjoy wide legitimacy: that of inclusive civic nationalism, and that of the protection of the rights of national minorities (a term that logically implies that there are *national* differences within the citizen body).[‡] France could therefore have agreed to sign the Convention without

---

[‡] State declarations added to the ratification of the Convention reflect the variety of ways in which this delicate question is dealt with in different countries. The German declaration, for example, states that "national minorities in the Federal Republic of Germany are the Danes of German citizenship and the members of the Sorbian people with German citizenship." But it adds that the Convention "will also be applied to members of the ethnic groups traditionally resident in Germany, the Frisians of German citizenship and the Sinti and Roma of German citizenship." The latter are not being accorded a "national" status. See: http://conventions.coe.int/Treaty/Commun/ ListeDeclarations.asp?NT=157&CM=&DF=&CL=ENG&VL=1.

giving up the notion of a French national identity shared by all the citizens of the republic. Instead, it chose to make a stand on this issue as a matter of principle. There are, indeed, as we shall see, various versions of civic nationalism that are more flexible than the French "ideal type." They combine the principle of a single national identity with the acknowledgment of a considerable measure of cultural (including linguistic) diversity within the citizen body. The distinct identity of the minority is thus recognized, though not accorded a fully-fledged "national" status.

By contrast, the French model insists on what Kymlicka disparagingly calls the "older ideology" of "one state, one nation, one language."[12] The cultural cost of this model for any minority group wishing to preserve its distinct identity is obvious, but it can hardly be avoided without also giving up, at least partly, the model's advantages. It is important to understand what these are. While some more far-reaching versions of collective rights may indeed clash with individual rights, what is protected by a refusal to afford language rights to a minority group is hardly individual civic equality, as the French position maintains, somewhat disingenuously. Rather, what is protected in this case is indeed the "*unicité*" of the French people, the notion of national identity that may be termed "monocultural." The advantage of this model is that no group of citizens is considered to be outside the nation's mainstream as far as culture, language, and identity go. The more flexible models of civic nationalism make sure that no group of citizens is placed outside the nation in the sense of a shared national identity (of course, all citizens are regarded as part of the "nation" in the civic sense in a democracy). And yet a cultural minority facing a cultural majority is still, virtually by definition, outside the national mainstream in a significant sense. If the constitutional monopoly of French as "the language of the Republic" should be broken, and minority languages recognized, this will come at a price. As the French language is an essential part of French national identity, any group whose language is other than French will, inevitably, become in some significant sense "less French" than others. Officially recognizing it as such would not be costless, both for the group in question and from the viewpoint of the state and society.

Full identification with the nation-state is much more than just political loyalty, or even Habermas' "constitutional patriotism." It encompasses the state's symbols, its shared sense of history and collective identity, its national holidays and days of remembrance, its language and other cultural traits considered essential to its identity. The report of the governmental commission that in 2004 recommended the legislation outlawing, *inter alia*, the Muslim veil in public schools, states that "secularism is a constitutive part of our collective history." According to the commission, the French *laïcité*, secularism, is not just a constitutional principle dating from the early twentieth century, but has a long historical pedigree: "It goes back to ancient Greece, the Renaissance and the Reformation, the Edict of Nantes, the Enlightenment, each of these stages developing, in its way, the autonomy of the individual and the liberty of thought. The [French] Revolution marks the birth of the *laïcité* in its modern understanding." In his statement on the appointment of the commission, President Chirac spoke of the principle of *laïcité* as being "at the heart of our republican identity," "inscribed in our traditions," a basis of "our national cohesion."[13] There is no room in this discourse for the possibility that some French citizens may regard themselves as belonging to any other collective "we," with a different history, culture, and identity. The historical–cultural heritage described in this text (from which Christianity as such is absent, but in some of whose elements it is unmistakably reflected) is fully common to all the regional groups in France. The situation is rather less straightforward, however, as regards both the Muslims and the Jews in the country.

The cultural downside of such a model of nationhood for those people of minority descent who wish to preserve and cultivate a distinct identity are obvious. In today's France, we are talking chiefly about a considerable part of the immigrants from Muslim countries. No less obvious, however, are this model's advantages for those among them who aspire to be fully integrated on such terms. Whether, from the viewpoint of the state and society at large, the costs of adopting such a model in terms of cultural diversity outweigh its advantages in terms of societal and national cohesion is a matter of dispute.

"Civic nationalism" and "protecting the rights of national minorities" surely sound to many as two expressions belonging to the same progressive family, both signifying a commitment to human rights and equality. Yet the former, at least in its pure and unadulterated version, actually makes the very existence of minorities "conceptually impossible," in Kymlicka's words.[14] Under such a model those who might regard themselves as belonging to a distinct minority, so far from being excluded, tend to be strongly invited to become fully-fledged members of the nation on terms that are indeed equal for all citizens, but inevitably reflect the culture (including the historic consciousness) of the majority. The potential for cultural oppression of minorities under such a model is, obviously, considerable, and the border between inclusion and "denying the Other" may sometimes be blurred. Of course, the practical implications of such a model vary greatly from place to place and from group to group, according to the cultural reality on which it is imposed.

Most people would probably agree that when the French Republic considers its Breton citizens as French and French only, denying any possibility of Breton nationalism, this, today, is a case of civic inclusion. By contrast, the fact that the Turkish Republic insists on defining its Kurdish citizens as Turks and denies any possibility of Kurdish nationalism within its borders will often be considered as a case of cultural oppression. It should be noted, however, that this official stance is dictated in both cases by the fundamental logic of inclusive civic nationalism, by the same notion of national identity comprising all the country's citizens. Of course, this official stance is also enforced in Turkey by methods that are considerably more robust than in France. However, the distinct Breton identity, including its language, had been to a large degree successfully erased by France (alongside other local identities that might challenge the "Frenchness" of the French state) by the time that Turkey under Atatürk adopted the model of civic nationalism. The French state had done so by methods that would today be considered wholly illegitimate in any Western democracy, although today's Western democracy may legitimately enjoy the fruits of such a policy practiced generations and centuries ago.

As things stand now, the French notion of civic nationalism based on common culture and language faithfully reflects the actual cultural reality in France as far as the overwhelming majority of its citizens, from all of France's regions, are concerned. Regional affiliations that had in the past the potential to develop under a different historical scenario into fully-fledged national identities are overwhelmingly perceived today as fully compatible with normative mainstream "Frenchness" and do not imply any significant ethnocultural specificity. The fact that the language and culture presently common to the civic nation originated in the (ethnic, in our terms) regional core of the

French state is a historical fact without major emotional and cultural significance for the great majority of those whose ancestors had once accepted this language and culture at the expense of their own. In this respect at least (leaving aside the vexed questions of identity raised by the mass immigration of recent decades, treated below), it cannot be realistically argued today that French civic nationalism functions largely as a disguise for the ethnic nationalism of the majority unwilling to accept the existence of minorities. However, in not a few countries that officially adopt the civic national model things are, arguably, quite different.

Civic nationalism: models and dilemmas

In Turkey, for example, enforcing the same concept of nationhood inevitably means imposing the culture (first and foremost, the language) of an ethnonational majority on a large and, in large part, culturally distinct native ethnonational minority. This is the natural result in such a situation of claiming for the majority culture and language the status of "national" in the inclusive civic sense. Of course, this policy, fundamental to the way the modern Turkish state perceives itself, has been dictated not just by a wish to impose cultural uniformity – thereby ensuring national cohesion and solidarity. It has also been fed by fears of minority (especially Kurdish) separatism. The unity of the nation and the territorial integrity of the state are regarded in Turkey, as they are regarded in many other countries, as two sides of the same coin.

Can the oppressive aspects of applying the pure model of civic nationalism in such a situation be removed by adopting a more flexible model, which accepts the existence of ethnocultural subgroups within what is still perceived as a single national identity? As long as the different minority groups are classified as ethnic, cultural, or linguistic, rather than national, at least the formal conceptual framework of civic nationalism can be maintained. However, abandoning the pure model of civic nationalism in order to get rid of its rigidity and occasional harshness inevitably means also forgoing some of its advantages. If the Turkish nation is perceived as consisting of two ethnocultural subdivisions – the Turkish (Turkish-speaking) majority and the minority that may be defined as Kurdish or Kurdish-speaking – it is clear that the minority, while still regarded as part of the Turkish nation, will in some sense be placed outside its mainstream. The Turkish Republic, under such a scenario, will not be neutral between the two identities. First and foremost, this will apply to the crucial question of language: the main national language of any Turkish nation-state will naturally be Turkish, which is central to the large Turkish majority's culture and identity, rather than Kurdish.

A concept of nationhood defined as including all the citizens of the state, but which at the same time includes an ethnocultural majority that is regarded as the nation's core or mainstream, whose identity is privileged by a special connection with the identity of the state itself, does have the advantage of combining inclusiveness with cultural tolerance and pluralism. But the "civic" nature of such a model of national identity tends to be rather formal, and the partial recognition of the minority's distinct identity that it affords may well be regarded as insufficient by many within that minority. Such a situation exists in Greece vis-à-vis its small Turkish minority, which the state insists on defining as Turkish-speaking rather than Turkish, since no non-Hellenic national identity can officially exist in the Hellenic Republic. This minority community enjoys significant cultural rights and is officially recognized as a religious minority. But its official "inclusion" in a national identity whose character, officially and unofficially, is overwhelmingly imprinted by the culture, language, religion, and historical memory of Greece's Christian Orthodox, Greek-speaking majority is purely formal. While France's secularism can be said to be, in practice as opposed to theory, not entirely neutral between Christianity and Islam, the Greek Republic, with its open and strong link to Greek Orthodox Christianity ("the prevailing religion in Greece," according to the constitution, itself promulgated "in the name of the Holy and Consubstantial and Indivisible Trinity"), is anything but culturally neutral from the viewpoint of its Muslim Turkish-speaking minority. As we have seen, civic nationalism, French style, goes far beyond legal citizenship and has a strong cultural content. But the content of the culture itself is such that it is open, at least in principle, to people of all religions. As far as the centrality of the Greek language is concerned, a Greek civic nationalism, purporting to include all the citizens and "inviting" non-Greek speakers to assimilate, is in principle no different from the French one. However, Greek national culture and identity also has a strong religious aspect. And, of course, for the Turkish community itself, the Muslim religion is not a "private matter" (as the French

Republic would like its citizens to regard their religion) but a central aspect of its own distinct ethnocultural identity. In such a situation, the cultural character of both the majority and the minority is hard to reconcile with any genuine civic nationalism.

If the Turkish-speaking community in Greece is recognized as a national minority, this would accord with cultural reality far better than the present definition, while hardly making its members any less Greek than they are today, both in their own self-perception and in the attitude of the majority. They will continue to be Greek in the sense of being citizens of the Greek Republic, but not in the sense of sharing the Greek national and cultural identity. The status of the small Slav Macedonian community in "civic" Greece is somewhat differently modulated, but the fundamental questions remain. Unlike the Turkish-speaking community, the Slav Macedonian community is not acknowledged as a minority at all, either cultural or national. Since it is Christian Orthodox, its official inclusion in the definition of the Greek nation is more genuine, but at the same time more culturally oppressive to those who refuse to assimilate and wish to preserve their distinct identity, first and foremost, their language.

The Turkish minority in Bulgaria (which is much larger than in Greece) is regarded as an ethnic group within the Bulgarian nation rather than as a national minority. The constitution of the country proclaims in its preamble, "the irrevocable duty to guard the national integrity [along with 'state integrity'] of Bulgaria." It proclaims that the republic is a unitary state, and "autonomous territorial formations" are banned (Article 2.1). The unity of the nation is protected by a ban on "political parties based on ethnic, racial, or religious lines" (Article 11). The status of Bulgarian, beyond it being the official language of the republic, is further elevated by the highly unusual provision that "the study and use of the Bulgarian language is a right and obligation of every Bulgarian citizen" (Article 36.1). Furthermore, while "the religious institutions shall be separate from the state," "Eastern Orthodox Christianity is considered the traditional religion in the Republic of Bulgaria" (Article 13.3), and the state coat-of-arms features the cross. Finally, ethnic Bulgarians abroad ("persons of Bulgarian origin") "shall acquire Bulgarian citizenship through a facilitated procedure" (Article 25.2). At the same time, the constitution officially acknowledges (if somewhat grudgingly and anonymously) the cultural distinctness of the minority: "citizens whose mother tongue is not Bulgarian shall have the right to study and use their own language alongside the compulsory study of the Bulgarian language" (Article 36.2). Indeed, the cultural rights of the minority are respected reasonably well. The potentially oppressive constitutional ban on political parties representing minorities is circumvented in practice, and an overwhelmingly Turkish party plays an important role in the country's politics.

Judging by official definitions alone, it is obvious that it is in name only that the Bulgarian national identity is "civic," in the sense of including all the citizens of the state. As we shall see later, the reason why the state insists on its inclusive civic character is not, in this case, any desire to impose the culture of the majority on the minority, but political apprehensions fed by the complicated history of Turkish–Bulgarian relations. In actuality, there exists in Bulgaria (as in Slovakia) a large ethnonational minority, and, hence, also an ethnonational majority that is distinct from the whole body of citizens and whose identity is expressed by the state. The nominally civic nationalism of this kind lacks both the advantages and the disadvantages of a genuine civic nationalism, being neither comprehensive nor, in this case, oppressive toward minorities.[§]

Whereas in both Greece and Bulgaria the official inclusion of a highly distinct cultural group in the national identity is little more than a way to deny it the status of a national minority, the same cannot be said of Finland and its Swedish-speaking community. The label "Swedish-speaking" rather than "Swedish" reflects the official view – accepted also by the minority community – that there is no Swedish national minority in Finland. Rather, the Finnish nation consists of Finnish-speakers, who happen to be a more than 90 percent majority, and Swedish-speakers. According to the constitution, "The national languages of Finland are Finnish and Swedish" (Article 17.1). The adjective "national," rather than the usual "official," is not accidental in this context. In practice, the status of Swedish is unusually high for a

[§] In the early years of communist rule in Bulgaria, Turks were explicitly recognized as a "national minority" and given considerable language and culture rights. This changed into a policy of forced assimilation and eventually deteriorated into downright persecution in the final years of the regime. The term "national minority" was removed from the constitution in 1971, and later the goal of forging a "unified socialist Bulgarian nation" was proclaimed. These harsh policies were reversed after the establishment of the postcommunist democracy, but the democratic constitution is still based on the concept of a "unified nation."

language spoken by a (small) minority. The historical and political background of the relations between the two language groups is unproblematic, unlike in Greece and in Bulgaria, and they are far closer culturally. And, of course, the Swedish-speaking community does not insist on defining itself as a "national" group. Under such conditions, civic nationalism can play a much more genuinely inclusive role, while still allowing for a high degree of cultural diversity. Nevertheless, although Finnish national identity is not confined to the Finnish ethnocultural majority, the latter is undoubtedly the core of the nation. This is stressed by the fact that Finland officially regards the ethnocultural diaspora of Ingrian Finns in Russia and Estonia as its "kin minority," and, following the collapse of the Soviet Union, granted privileged residence rights to some 25,000 of them. Official ties of a nation-state with an ethnocultural diaspora abroad naturally testify to the ethnocultural character of the national identity involved. In Greece, official ties with the Greek diaspora are much more significant. All the same, in Finland the national identity is considered to include the Swedish-speaking ethnocultural minority, and is in this sense "civic." To the extent that such an inclusion is genuine, as in Finland, it can be said that the national–cultural character of the state is not shaped wholly by that of the ethnocultural majority, though it is still heavily influenced by it. Where this inclusion is merely formal, as in Greece and Bulgaria, the national character of the state is in fact that of the ethnocultural majority.

Returning to Turkey, what would be the result of it recognizing a fully-fledged Kurdish national minority within its borders? Such a definition would certainly accord with the self-perception of many Kurds, who regard themselves as a national community strongly connected with Kurds in neighboring countries, and not merely as a subdivision of the Turkish nation. Recognition of a Kurdish national minority will amount to abandoning the idea of inclusive civic nationalism in favor of accepting the existence of two ethnonationalisms on the territory of the Turkish state: the majority Turkish one and the minority Kurdish one. Ironically, few of those who expect, and sometimes urge, the Turkish state to grant the Kurdish minority greater cultural rights and a full recognition of its distinct identity may realize that they are in fact urging Turkey to adopt an ethnic definition of Turkish nationhood (similar to the Slovak). A Turkish nation-state with an officially recognized Kurdish national minority may be liberal, respectful of individual civil rights, and culturally pluralistic; but it will not be culturally neutral between the Turkish national–cultural identity and the Kurdish one – unless it turns itself into a binational Turkish–Kurdish state, at which point the integrity of the state itself may arguably be endangered. We shall return to this point when we discuss binational and multinational states.

At the same time, if Kurdish citizens of Turkey should no longer be considered, straightforwardly, as "Turks" in the full sense, the emotional power of the statement "we are all Turks (regardless of ethnic origin)" will be lost. The loss may be far from negligible from the point of view of those citizens of Kurdish origin who do accept the notion of inclusive Turkish nationalism, as not a few of them do. Despite the tensions and bitterness generated by the vexed Kurdish question in Turkey, it is very probably far easier for many Turkish Kurds to say "I am a Turk" than for individual Greek Turks to say "I am a Greek (Hellene)." The power of a fully-fledged national bond between a citizen and a state, and its contribution to making the state where one lives "one's own" in the full sense, cannot be doubted. Furthermore, since, as is usually the case, there is no clear territorial boundary between the two groups, any sort of territorial Kurdish self-rule – whether in some autonomous region within a Turkish nation-state, or as part of a barely conceivable binational federation, or even in some Kurdish entity that has seceded from Turkey – will inevitably give rise to a Turkish minority problem. National definitions and political arrangements based on them may be more suited or less suited to a particular cultural reality and people's (often conflicting) aspirations; but none of them is guaranteed to provide an easy answer to the complicated dilemmas that arise in a multi-ethnic situation.

It may, of course, be argued that full integration, less politely called assimilation, of cultural minorities wherever they exist is the right solution to the dilemma. No doubt, this solution often entails important advantages for those involved. It is certainly in the nature of civic nationalism to welcome and facilitate this way of ensuring that no group of citizens is, culturally, outside the national mainstream. However, this solution is obviously problematic from the viewpoint of those who wish to preserve their distinct culture and identity, as well as from the viewpoint of modern attitudes that legitimize and value cultural pluralism.

Immigrant communities

The phenomenon of mass immigration has transformed the map of identities in Western countries in recent decades. Immigrant communities, sometimes referred to as "new minorities," are not easy to classify in traditional national terms. They are not considered as national minorities; this term is reserved to "native" minority groups. Thus, although this is challenged by some radical multiculturalists, immigrant communities are not regarded as entitled to the same degree of recognition of their cultural distinctness on the part of the state. The theory is – or at any rate, used to be – that an immigrant, once naturalized, joins the "host" nation. Multicultural attitudes and practices have challenged this concept without offering an alternative definition of the immigrants' national identity, apart from legal citizenship and civic rights (though the rights of non-citizen immigrants are also stressed). Furthermore, the great diversity of the immigrants' countries of origin and cultures makes it difficult to classify immigrants in national terms. No country can be reasonably described as having as many national minorities as there are countries of origin of its immigrants.

Moreover, the long-term historical impact of this phenomenon is unclear at this stage. Not a few of the immigrants and their descendants are in fact integrating, culturally and socially, well enough for them to be described as "joining the nation" in a more or less traditional sense. This applies even if they preserve, at least for the time being, some degree of cultural distinctness. In Western Europe's experience with previous waves of immigration, successful integration has mostly meant that at any rate the descendants of immigrants do not usually form identifiable cultural minority groups within society. Admittedly, some groups tend to preserve a greater degree of cultural distinctness. Jews and Armenians are salient examples, though in Western Europe they, too, have long since adopted the language of the country where they live. Where the descendants of today's immigrants will stand in this respect in the long run cannot now be predicted with certainty. In the United States and other English-speaking nations of immigrants, a considerably greater degree of cultural distinctness on the part of immigrants and their descendants has come to be accepted and even celebrated. Diversity within a broad cultural common ground is considered a permanent national trait. It is thus uncertain how far, and in what precise way, the map of group identities in the "host" countries will indeed have been permanently transformed by the immigration of recent decades.

In addition, multiculturalism itself, at least in its more radical ideological versions, is now clearly in retreat. This relates specifically to immigrants, as the chief theorist of liberal multiculturalism, Will Kymlicka well recognizes: "there is a widespread perception in Western Europe that multiculturalism 'went too far' in the context of predominantly Muslim immigrants, and there has been a reassertion of more assimilationist or exclusionary policies"; "minority rights provisions for substate national groups and indigenous peoples, by contrast, have not yet suffered any serious backlash in any Western democracy."[15] Still, there is no doubt that immigration has, in recent decades, profoundly transformed Western – in particular, West European – societies.

It can be said that mass immigration and multiculturalism have made the typical West European state less national (at least in the traditional sense of the term), by weakening the connection between national identity and statehood without making the state either binational or multinational (all of which imply recognized national identities: one, two, or several). Nor has the state become non-national, or postnational, for the connection between national identity and state, even if weakened, is still very significant in many ways.[16] Among other things, this connection is crucial to states' self-definition, as they appear in constitutional texts. When these texts refer, in describing the national and cultural character of the state, to minority groups (however defined), they address traditional, non-immigrant minorities. This might include local "indigenous peoples" but not the "new minorities," even if the former are much smaller than the latter.

In fact, the reaction against radical multiculturalism has led to a reemphasizing in many Western countries of the official connection between (majority) culture and polity. "Connection" is the word rather than Gellner's "congruence," since full congruence is not a realistic option (or, necessarily, a desirable aim) in most modern democracies. Language is, again, crucial in this context, both symbolically and practically, as is usually the case in matters of national identity. As a reaction to the appearance of large numbers of immigrants not proficient in the "host" country's language, many of these countries now insist, more than in the past, on strengthening the position of the official language. They make greater demands on immigrants when it comes to mastering the language, among other things as a condition for naturalization and sometimes even for immigration. The latter demand has been introduced by Holland, formerly a bastion of multiculturalism.

These efforts to cultivate a broad cultural common ground among the citizenry are not usually formulated in national terms, except, unsurprisingly, in France. The language of national identity is most readily used in this context by mainstream politicians in France, where national identity and republican citizenship are considered synonymous. Both mastering French and conforming (in some measure) to the French notion of *laïcité* (as exemplified by the refusal to naturalize women who wear the burka) are regarded in France as crucial aspects of adopting the French national identity on the part of immigrants. Other countries usually prefer to emphasize the social, economic, and political benefits of integration and the costs of failing to integrate. This applies, first and foremost, to language. One's chances of finding good employment and ability to communicate with state functionaries and take an active part in public life are typically mentioned in this context. Although the terminology of nationhood is mostly eschewed in these arguments, they bring to mind some standard explanations for the rise of modern nationalism (most notably Gellner's). All these practical issues – largely centered on language and its role in facilitating socioeconomic integration and political participation – have clear implications as regards national identity. By being urged to integrate socially and culturally, the immigrants are being urged to join the nation.

While the immigrants' identity is hard to classify in national terms, there is no difficulty in analyzing in those terms the reactions of "host" societies to immigration. Some of those reactions are quite predictably nationalistic and xenophobic. But most people in Western societies have come to accept, and up to a point welcome, a high degree of cultural pluralism, much higher than in the past. When the German chancellor or the British prime minister announce that multiculturalism has been a failure, they are not trying to bring back some sort of old-fashioned "monoculturalism." However, no democratic electorate is likely to accept things that it regards as fundamentally altering the national and cultural character of the state. If the backlash against radical multiculturalism in Western Europe applies to immigration rather than to traditional national minorities, as Kymlicka notes, this is because questions regarding the overall identity of the society and state are raised by the former rather than by the latter. This results from the sheer numbers involved, the degree of cultural distinctness in the case of some of the immigrants, and the problems of integration.

Of course, accumulated changes over a long period of time may sometimes produce a result that is much more far-reaching than anything that could have been anticipated, or would have been accepted, from the outset. In the United States, the massive non-European immigration – and earlier, the non-English-speaking one – certainly changed the face of society. Whether they have thereby altered the fundamental national and cultural identity of the country may perhaps be disputed from today's perspective, largely depending on the way one interprets these terms. But the whole process has been based on the fact that the immigrants, all in all, have been willing to change in order to accommodate American cultural and societal norms (above all, by adopting English) far more than they have changed these norms – though the latter change has been very considerable as well. That this will also be the case with the massive Hispanic immigration is doubted by some, but judging from past experience seems at least possible.

The national and cultural character of society and state is itself understood today in broad and flexible terms. It is not ethnic in the narrow sense of being confined to a descent or kinship group, yet it is often strongly underpinned by ethnicity and ethnicity-based culture in the broad sense suggested here. Whether the national identity in question is officially "civic" or not is usually, as we have seen, of little practical importance in this respect. In any situation of ethnolinguistic pluralism, and unless the state is binational or multinational, the "idea that liberal-democratic states (or 'civic nations') are ethnoculturally neutral is manifestly false."** To be sure, the connection between the state and a specific national identity and culture is sometimes liable to

---

** Kymlicka, *Politics in the Vernacular*, 24. Kymlicka refers chiefly to language, its centrality to national identity, and the efforts of liberal states – including the United States – to promote their language (*inter alia*, among immigrants). He stresses that these policies should not be seen as "purely a matter of cultural imperialism or ethnocentric prejudice. This sort of nation-building serves a number of important goals": "equal opportunity to work in a modern economy," "generating the sort of solidarity required by a welfare state," and facilitating wide participation in the democratic political system (*ibid.*, 26).

be abused, despite all the mechanisms developed in liberal democracies for containing this danger. Nevertheless, this connection is central to contemporary states and contemporary democracies.

"Imperial nations" and composite identities

As mentioned above, the French model is not the only, or typical, version of civic nationalism. There are other, more flexible models, which acknowledge different levels of identity and different subgroups within what is still regarded as an inclusive civic nation. These subdivisions are usually defined as ethnic, communal, or sometimes linguistic, rather than national. Under such a model the ethnic element is openly acknowledged, not as defining the national identity, but as a significant characteristic of certain subgroups within it. This, for instance, is the case in the United States, where it largely rests on the willingness – often eagerness – of immigrants from various (and faraway) countries of origin to forgo their original national identity and adopt the American one. In the American case, as well as in other immigrant countries, this also means the adoption of the prevailing language of the country. At the same time, one's heritage and ethnicity have come to be accepted and often celebrated as a significant aspect of being an American. Moreover, the civic nationalism of many postcolonial countries with culturally diverse populations is characterized by an officially acknowledged (ethno)linguistic pluralism, while strongly insisting on a single national identity to which all citizens and all groups belong.

Sometimes, however, a certain group may be recognized as having a distinct national (rather than "merely" ethnic) identity of its own, while still being considered as a subcategory within a larger nation. The clearest example of this model is Spain, where the "Spanish nation" is described by the constitution as being made up of "nationalities and regions" (Article 2). Within this framework, the three "historic nationalities" – Catalonia, the Basque country, and Galicia – were from the outset recognized as "nationalities" and set up their autonomous national territorial entities. Later, some of the other regions also claimed a "national" character in this sense. At the same time, the Castilian-speaking majority is clearly dominant, not only *de facto*, due to its numerical superiority, but because of the official and "national" status of its language. The Spanish nation, whose "indissoluble unity" is proclaimed by the constitution (Article 2), is not perceived merely as synonymous with the country as a whole ("the indivisible homeland of all Spaniards") or with the entire civic community, but is clearly endowed with a cultural character by the provision on the official language: "Castilian is the official Spanish language of the State. All Spaniards have the duty to know it and the right to use it" (Article 3.1). On the other hand, the country's autonomous communities can establish their own regional official languages, and have naturally proceeded to do so. A "Spaniard" is thus not merely a citizen of the Spanish state, regardless of national identity. Rather, his or her national and cultural identity, defined through language, is (in the case of minority groups) perceived as two-layered. Language is central to the map of national identities in Spain, as it is in many other places. Of course, differences of language can sometimes be defined as "ethnic" rather than national. There is, needless to say, no "objective" way to distinguish between "mere" ethnicity and national identity, or, indeed, between the different levels of national identity itself. These are all a matter of how people perceive themselves and are perceived by others, and often these perceptions and definitions are conflicting. In the post-Franco democratic Spain, at any rate, non-Castilian-speaking peoples in Spain were officially recognized as "nationalities."

The higher layer of a Spaniard's national identity is the common "Spanishness" stressed not just by making Castilian the language of the nation as a whole, but by adding the unusual provision (similar to the one in Bulgaria) for every citizen's "duty to know it." The lower layer is (in the case of minority groups) his or her "nationality" within this nation. The Castilian-speaking majority is not defined as a (majority) "nationality." Only the minority groups are defined as nationalities, while the majority (split between several regions – there is no region called simply "Castile") receives no appellation distinct from the nation as a whole. The majority is clearly not synonymous with "the Spanish nation," but neither is it merely one of the nation's components. It is the nation's core, and its identity – the national "default option."

This national model combines inclusiveness with a high degree of pluralism, but it still hinges on a denial of a fully-fledged nationhood to the Basques and the Catalans, many of whom insist on this definition. Moreover, it "subsumes" them under an overall national identity within which they inevitably belong to the periphery rather than to the core. This national concept, enshrined in the constitution, is not accepted by the Basque and Catalan nationalists – not merely the radical separatist ones (some of whom, among the Basques, have taken up arms for the cause of separatism) but also the moderate ones. The latter have long commanded a majority in both the autonomous regional parliaments. Both these parliaments have passed resolutions asserting that their respective peoples are "nations" in the full sense, rather than national sub-divisions of some larger nation, and therefore have a right to national self-determination. At present, the regional governments and parliaments controlled by moderate nationalists do not support secession from the Spanish state, but they insist on a right to secede if their nations should freely decide to do so. Accepting this demand – which the central government, supported by the large Castilian-speaking majority, refuses to do – would turn Spain into a fully-fledged multinational state, whose unity, moreover, would no longer be "insoluble."

Thus, according to the definitions enshrined in the constitution, Spain regards itself, despite its officially acknowledged multinational aspect (on the level of the "nationalities") as a nation-state, based on a common "nationhood." This concept of nationhood is avowedly civic in the sense that it purports to include all the subgroups of citizens. However, from the viewpoint of Basque or Catalan nationalists (even moderate ones), the Spanish nation is no more than a majority nation in a state in which they regard themselves as minority nations, and the Spanish state, as such, expresses the identity of the majority. Even according to the official view and official terminology, the common Spanish nationhood is far from being neutral between the majority and the minority groups. The majority, which defines its national identity as simply Spanish (rather than Castilian), has appropriated the name that also stands for the whole. Although historically the name "Hispania" applied to the entire Iberian peninsula, the minority nationalists now regard the "Spanish" national label as referring to another nation and inapplicable to them.

Catalan or Basque nationalists sometimes complain that there is no Spanish parallel to the distinction between Britain and England, which, logically, makes the English component of the overall British nationhood merely one of its components, though it is clearly the overwhelmingly dominant one. There are obvious similarities between the British case and the Spanish one. As we saw in Chapter 5, both may be termed, taking into account their histories and their impact on the present-day map of identities, "imperial nations." Both are large and complex states, constructed, historically, around a core: England and Castile, respectively. In both cases this core has shaped decisively, though not exclusively, the character of the state as a whole, and thus, the character of the state's common "nationhood"; yet it never became fully congruous with the nation. In a typical British (English?) fashion, the terminology used in Britain with regard to national identity is not always consistent and systematic. Britain is sometimes described as a "nation of nations." The widely accepted view, first and foremost among the English but not just among them, is that British identity is an overarching supra-identity and not merely a matter of civic and political affiliation. As such it encompasses all the constituent parts of the United Kingdom, without erasing secondary identities. This is in a way similar to the Spanish two-layered concept of "nation" and "nationalities," with the difference that Scotland is recognized as a fully-fledged "nation," and it is widely accepted that it has a right to secede from the Union if it so chooses. Northern Ireland's right of secession has been recognized by the Anglo-Irish agreement in 1985. This (unofficial) designation of an agreement between Ireland and the United Kingdom (on a par with "Anglo-American friendship" and similar expressions) shows how overwhelmingly English the United Kingdom is in people's perception, both at home and abroad.

England constitutes the bulk of the British state (ruled, as Scottish nationalists like to point out, from London), both territorially and as regards population. English is in fact far more overwhelmingly dominant throughout the United Kingdom than Castilian is in Spain. The English tend to treat "English" and "British" as being more or less interchangeable, or the latter as an extension of the former, although lately displays of Scottish nationalism have prompted talk about English nationalism and calls for an English Parliament. The typical English view of Britain is perhaps most realistically described as "England plus" rather than as a multinational state. British historical consciousness is overwhelmingly English. Significantly, the present queen was crowned Elizabeth II, over the objections of Scottish nationalists who argued that she was the first monarch of the United Kingdom bearing that name. True, Elizabeth I was "merely" the queen of England, yet this argument somehow failed to win the day. The Parliament in Westminster is, historically, the English Parliament later joined by members from other constituent parts. Even England's extremist and xenophobic nationalist party calls itself the "British National Party."

This concept of "Britishness" as an overarching national identity is sufficiently inclusive and flexible to make the English majority regard the state as "theirs" in the full sense, and at the same time guarantee to the non-English constituent peoples a high degree of participation and identification with it. This is borne out by the long list of persons from Scotland and Wales who have occupied leading positions in the British state, including that of prime minister. Some English people may resent what they regard as Scotland's unfair advantages within the Union (obviously designed to compensate the Scots for their minority status), but this does not stop them regarding the British state as "theirs." On the other hand, a significant part of the non-English citizens of the United Kingdom refuse to accept the British label as a definition of their national identity (alongside and above their distinct one), and many of them favor secession. This clearly applies to the nationalist (republican) community in Northern Ireland. The Scottish Nationalists, who won a majority in the Scottish Assembly in 2011, are not content, unlike the moderate Catalan and Basque nationalists in Spain, with the acknowledgment on the part of the English that Scotland is a "nation" (within a "nation of nations") and has a right to secede from the Union if it so chooses. They favor actual secession, although according to the polls there is at present no majority in Scotland for this demand. They regard the British state and the notion of British "super"-nationhood as shorthand for English domination over the non-English peoples of the British Isles. The Welsh nationalists have a similar view, although they are less influential than their counterparts in Scotland.

The model of two-layered or composite nationhood that characterizes in different versions both Spain and Britain is an attempt to square the circle by structuring the state in a way that makes it both national and multinational. That said, the national dimension – inclusive and generous to minorities as well as majority-dominated – is meant to be the decisive one. This model may at this stage be characterized as a partial success, whether one wishes to emphasize the former or the latter. It is probably the best if not the only way to try to keep together nationally diverse countries like Britain and Spain under conditions of a modern democracy. Yet it is surely significant that even this model may in the long run be insufficient to keep them together. The desire to live in a state that is, nationally, "one's own" in the full sense, certainly appears to be a powerful force. This applies even to prosperous Western European democracies in which the rights of minorities and minority nations are well protected, which is not to say that this desire will in every case prove to be stronger than other, conflicting wishes and considerations. States shape ethnic and national identities as well as being shaped by them. Nonetheless, anyone who is overly optimistic about the power of a modern state to shape national identities at its convenience may well wonder about the United Kingdom. The British state – certainly a powerful and largely successful mechanism, as well as a liberal and inclusive one – has been unable to shape Scottish nationalism out of existence in three centuries of full parliamentary Union between the two historic kingdoms.

Would it be correct to say that what constitutes the core of British nationhood is English ethnic nationalism? This, admittedly, sounds rather absurd. Though the challenge of Scottish nationalism naturally tends to make the Englishness of the English more self-consciously distinct and potentially politicized, most people in England will surely find the concept of "English nationalism" quite awkward. English society today, under the influence of mass immigration, is multiethnic to a very significant extent. Nevertheless, it is worth asking how things look from the viewpoint of Scottish nationalists – a far from marginal group in their society. For them, the crux of the matter is that their nation, with its distinct culture, identity, and sense of history, is dominated, by virtue of sheer numerical superiority, by a nation with a different identity, history, and culture. Such a situation between two large groups of citizens in a single state is bound to be defined in usual scholarly terms as a tension between two distinct ethnonationalisms. This perception, however strange it may seem to many, may yet prove to be capable of breaking up a centuries-old polity – one of the world's most liberal and inclusive ones. That both peoples in question speak the same language only goes to show that culture, no less than ethnicity and national identity, is a very broad and flexible concept. While not susceptible to any precise definition from outside, it is nonetheless vitally important for those who regard themselves as sharing it.

Russia is a huge "imperial" country built historically around its Russian core, but including many non-Russian-speaking peoples. Under the communist regime, with its avowed ideological commitment to the right of peoples to national self-determination, the former Russian Empire was reconstructed as the Union of the Soviet Socialist Republics, with the full formal structure of a multinational state. The constituent national republics were regarded as having entered the Union voluntarily and enjoyed a formal right of secession. Russia, which comprised most of the Union's territory (and itself included autonomous national republics for minority peoples), was, formally, merely one of the fifteen republics. In fact, there was never any doubt that Russia was the core of the USSR, both politically and culturally. Russian was the state language of the Union, and, after the initial "internationalist" period, Russian patriotism and national pride became central to the regime's ideology and rhetoric. In post-Soviet Russia, the explicit acknowledgment of minority groups as "nationalities" could not be withheld, if only because this would have meant denying those groups something that was acknowledged under the communist regime. The distinct identity of the minority peoples is respected and their identification with the state is encouraged, but the state itself is unambiguously (though not exclusively) identified with the language, culture, and history of the Russian-speaking majority. The 1993 constitution speaks in the name of "we, the multinational people of the Russian Federation." The unity of the state is guaranteed. Russian is the state language throughout the territory of Russia, while "republics" (of minority peoples) have a right to institute their own state languages (Article 68). The Federation has no component which is "Russian-proper" ("*russkiy*," as distinguished from "*rossiyskiy*," relating to Russia as a whole, regardless of "nationality"; this is carefully differentiated in official and all politically-correct parlance). The "republics" and "national regions" of minority peoples cover only a small portion of the country's territory, and only a small part of its population lives there (though there are also significant minority populations outside them). The sense of historical continuity and identity, in official and unofficial majority discourse, in this vast country ruled from Moscow's Kremlin is overwhelmingly "Russian-proper." The "multinational people of Russia," whose common state language is Russian, may in many ways be compared with the "Spanish nation," with its constituent (minority) nationalities. The "Russian-proper" component is clearly the core of the state. In Western terms, it is the core of the nation, though the constitution does not use this term to describe the whole of which the "Russian-proper" majority is the main component.[††]

[††] In Russia, "nations," as well as "nationalities," are regularly used in an ethnonational sense (applying also to the Russian majority in the country). On

National self-determination and territorial integrity

What makes definitions of national identity in the contemporary world a particularly sensitive matter is the fact that the language of nationhood is apt to raise the question of the right to national self-determination, and at least potentially – of secession. The right of "peoples to self-determination," as it appears in the UN Charter, is a widely acknowledged, though ill-defined, international norm. Whether and under what circumstances this right outweighs the principle of territorial integrity of sovereign states (another fundamental international norm) and includes the right to secede is a subject of a rather inconclusive debate.[17] It is clear, however, that the status of a nation or "a people" (in the sense of a national community) is widely regarded as giving rise to a strong claim to national self-determination. The language of "nationhood" applied to the Scottish identity in Britain reflects the historic fact that the United Kingdom was established by a merger of two kingdoms, but today dovetails with the acceptance of Scotland's right to secede. In recognizing such a right the British state is exceptional. Whatever the different views on the normative scope of the right to self-determination and the different definitions of identity accepted in every country, sovereign states normally regard their territorial integrity as inviolable. The national definitions included in the Spanish constitution represent a certain vision of Spain's culture and history, while also attempting (not entirely successfully) to afford reasonable recognition to minority identities without giving legitimacy to secessionist demands.

But although the Spanish constitution expressly rules out secession by invoking the indivisibility of Spain, one wonders whether Spain would today be willing and able, politically, to use force against Catalonia or the Basque country to keep them within the Spanish state if they were to make a clear and unambiguously democratic choice for secession on the strength of their claim for fully-fledged nationhood. In the re-established democratic Czechoslovakia it appeared inconceivable to oppose the secession of Slovakia by force, even though it had no legally recognized right to secede. The Canadian Supreme Court has

the other hand, the "people" (*"narod"* – etymologically akin, in fact, to the Latin *"natio"*), although it may also denote a substate, ethnonational group, more often means the whole of the population or the civic community.

ruled that although Quebec has no legal right to secede (a right asserted by Quebec on the strength of it being a "nation"), if the province makes a clear democratic choice by a substantial (unspecified) majority, the federal government ought to be willing to negotiate with it in good faith in order to resolve the dispute.[18] The court's language clearly implies, though does not quite say, that in the end the federal government would have a right to insist only on reasonable terms of secession, not to refuse secession outright. The message is clear: you do not have a legal right to secede, but if you really insist we cannot stop you by force. It is highly doubtful whether any Western democracy could today afford to stop by force a determined attempt to secede on the part of a recognized national entity like Quebec, Catalonia, or Scotland, backed by the clearly expressed democratic will of the majority of the people in such a region.

Bulgaria, on the other hand, is probably much more likely to use force in order to stop any conceivable attempt by its Turkish minority, in areas where this minority constitutes the majority of the population, to secede and join Turkey. Of course, such an attempt would not enjoy the democratic legitimacy of a regional referendum or a resolution passed by a regional parliament, which is precisely why Bulgaria's constitution forbids "autonomous territorial formations" within the state. But the fact that Bulgaria also finds it necessary to deny its Turkish citizens the status of a national minority strongly implies that it fears that a recognized "national" status as such, even without the backing of an autonomous territorial entity, might give legitimacy to secessionist demands (or at least demands for territorial autonomy) on the part of a large and culturally distinct population.

The "threat" of national self-determination (no less than genuinely inclusive attitudes) goes a long way to explain the strong tendency in many countries to withhold from minority groups explicit "national" recognition, the preference to define them as ethnic or linguistic, and the insistence on inclusive civic nationalism even when plurality of identities is officially recognized. The Austro-Hungarian Empire could afford to acknowledge that its subjects belonged to various peoples because the emperor, rather than the people, was held to be the highest source of legitimacy and authority. The people's will had, officially, no legitimate claim to prevail against that of the emperor as regards either its internal political arrangements or place vis-à-vis other peoples in the empire. However, as liberalization and democratization progressed in the nineteenth century, the empire found itself under increasing pressures to accommodate various and sometimes conflicting national demands.

In the twentieth century it was paradoxically the communist dictatorships – usurping the people's will rather than openly denying it as the ultimate source of legitimacy – that have found it most easy to acknowledge the multinational character of their state. The USSR, Yugoslavia, and Czechoslovakia had no problem maintaining an officially multinational or binational structure precisely because the regime was powerful enough to prevent not merely its break up but any public expression of secessionist sentiment. It was constantly proclaimed in the name of the "brotherly peoples" how happy they were to live together in their common socialist homeland. The Soviet constitution formally bestowed the right of secession on national republics (though not on the lesser autonomous national entities within them). The Union, it was proclaimed, had been entered upon voluntarily and continued to exist voluntarily. Communist China also defines its minority groups as national minorities or nationalities. But these are considered part of the Chinese nation alongside the Han majority, which is clearly the nation's core, and the unity of the country is officially inviolable.[‡‡] Of course, national distinctness and even national freedom to determine one's future can safely be conceded if the political freedom to ask for anything that is contrary to the government's claim to speak in the people's name is lacking. But where national demands can be voiced more or less openly, there is often great reluctance to define cultural differences – including language differences – between different groups of citizens as national.

Even Belgium, the clearest example of a binational state, officially defines itself in the first Article of its constitution, as "made up of Communities and Regions" (rather than nations). Unsurprisingly, Flemish nationalists who aspire to Flemish independence (though not only them) speak of a Flemish nation. In Canada, it was only in 2006,

---

[‡‡] The theory is that all of China's nationalities exercised their right to self-determination, irrevocably, by voluntarily joining the People's Republic. This was one of Mao Zedong's ideological justifications for abandoning the Communist Party's earlier stance. According to the 1931 constitution of the Chinese Soviet Republic, all the minority nationalities had the full right to self-determination, including secession. See Baogang He, "Minority Rights with Chinese Characteristics," in Kymlicka and He (eds.), *Multiculturalism in Asia*, 61.

after a protracted controversy and long after the country had become *de facto* binational, that the Canadian House of Commons passed a motion recognizing that "the Québécois form a nation within a united Canada."

Postcolonial countries: ethnocultural diversity and "the unity of the nation"

In postcolonial countries, which are often characterized by a high degree of ethnic diversity and not seldom lack an overall ethnocultural majority, it is considered particularly crucial to insist on the "unity of the nation" and to deny any national status to ethnic differences. This is so even though these differences are often recognized and to a greater or lesser degree accommodated by the state, especially in the sphere of language. Concern for their territorial integrity is also displayed by long-established nations. But, as we saw in Chapter 6, in postcolonial countries in particular a "neat" and agreed-upon partition, Czechoslovakia-style, between two clearly defined national groups populating two incontestably delimitated autonomous regions is even less of an option. Rather, there is often every reason to fear the grim consequences of uncontrollable disintegration and fragmentation, accompanied by much violence. In Africa, national claims, even falling short of separatism, on the part of ethnic groups are most often decried as "tribalism." The anti-separatist consensus enjoys wide legitimacy, though secession did occur, as we have seen, in both Eritrea (1993) and South Sudan (2011). Notably, while the South Sudanese struggle for independence had a strong ethnocultural basis vis-à-vis the Arab and Muslim North, the South itself is split between various ethnic groups. It has had its share of interethnic violence and may well have to face separatist challenges of its own.

Obviously, the dangers of separatism, as well as the need to foster social cohesion and avoid ethnic strife, regularly invoked by postcolonial governments, are not the whole story behind their insistence on inclusive nationhood. As in Europe, in cases where an ethnonational core exists, the professed unity of the nation is also useful if one wishes to strengthen the position of a dominant ethnic component. This is habitually done by elevating its language and its other cultural traits to a "national" status, while denying a national character (and, in most cases, a federal autonomy) to the minority identities. In Sri Lanka, for example, the Sinhalese majority (about 75 percent of the population) amended the constitution in order to make Sinhalese the country's sole official language (though this was later modified). The amended constitution similarly confers "the foremost place" on Buddhism (Article 2), associating the state more closely with the majority's ethnocultural identity. At the same time, the government insists on the unity of the nation and on Sri Lanka being a "unitary state," expressly rejecting the claims of the large Tamil minority to be recognized as a distinct "nation." Of course, in Sri Lanka and elsewhere, arguments about constitutional definitions and labels of identity are never the whole story. They give symbolic expression to existing ethnic tensions in various fields, and they can also exacerbate them. The practical demand of Tamil nationalists was originally for an autonomous national entity as part of a federal system. This was rejected in the name of the unitary state. Eventually, radical Tamil nationalists turned to violent separatism. A prolonged and bitter civil war ensued, ending with the defeat of the rebels in 2011.

Malaysia has an ethnocultural Malay majority comprising some 50–60 percent of the population. Alongside it, there is a Chinese minority of about 25 percent, as well as a smaller Indian community and other groups. The Chinese and Indian minorities, unlike the Tamils in Sri Lanka, lack territorial concentration and are in no position to make separatist (or even federalist) demands. The language of the majority, Malay, is, according to the constitution, "the national language" (Article 152), and its religion, Islam, is "the religion of the Federation" (Article 3). Among European democracies, too, as we have seen, it is not rare for an officially "civic" nation to have as its core an ethnocultural majority whose identity is strongly connected with the state. But Malaysia, in addition to this, also practices open preference in favor of the Malay majority in the economic sphere. This preference, justified by the "indigenous" character of the Malays and the need to redress the balance of economic power that has traditionally been concentrated mainly in Chinese hands, is expressly sanctioned by the constitution (Articles 8, 89, 153).

Singapore, which has a Chinese majority of some 75 percent, alongside a large Malay and a smaller Indian minority, is exceptional in that its system reflects a determined effort not to associate the state in any way with the historic identity, culture, and language of the majority. Ethnicity is anything but ignored by the state. The nation is officially subdivided into three ethnic communities (plus a category of "others"), and each citizen is registered as a member of a community. (This is done according to the "race" of the father, and, since 2010, with an option of having a "secondary" communal affiliation for children of mixed couples.) Yet the primacy of the nation over its constituent ethnic communities is strongly emphasized. The government has formulated an official credo setting forth the national ideology and comprising a list of "shared values" adopted by a parliamentary resolution in 1991. These values, it is proclaimed, are essentially "Asian" (and thus, communitarian rather than individualistic). The first of them is "nation before community and society before self"; the last is "racial and religious harmony."[19] Conspicuously absent in this exposition of the nation's cultural common ground is language. It is Singapore rather than France, in which French is a cornerstone of national identity, that should perhaps be regarded as the purest example of "civic nationalism." This is so if "civic nationalism" is understood as signifying a national identity not merely congruous with state citizenship but focused, as far as its content is concerned, wholly on the citizenship and the state rather than on cultural characteristics.

The official languages of Singapore are listed in the constitution as Malay, Chinese (Mandarin), Tamil, and English (Article 153A). But the true state language is English, the language of government, administration, law, and business, as well as the primary language of instruction in all educational institutions (where pupils are also taught their communal "mother tongue"). Various other postcolonial countries make extensive use of the language of the former colonial power. However, these are countries in which the linguistic diversity is such that the European language is the only one common to the different ethnic groups (or rather, to their elites) and no local language is strong enough to be established as a national one. By contrast, in Singapore English has been adopted by the state *in preference* to a local language (Chinese) spoken by the great majority of the people, and the entire population is educated in it, starting from primary school.

Remarkably, Malay is given the symbolic status of the "national language" of Singapore (Article 153A). Article 152 enjoins the government to "exercise its functions in such manner as to recognize the special position of the Malays, who are the indigenous people of Singapore, and [to] ... foster and promote their political, educational, religious, economic, social and cultural interests and the Malay language." Malay is used in the national anthem (which the law expressly forbids being performed in any other language), in the state's coat-of-arms, and in military commands. The Muslim crescent features prominently, though not exclusively, on the national flag. Thus, so far from privileging the cultural identity of the majority, the state, officially and symbolically, privileges that of a minority. The government of Singapore is strong and self-confident enough to offer the native Malay minority far-reaching concessions in the symbolic field, with the obvious aim of stressing its belonging to the nation of Singapore (rather than its ethnocultural affinity with the neighboring Malaysia). The other side of the same coin is that it is willing to suppress with considerable robustness any sign of minority Malay or majority Chinese nationalism challenging the official notion of a single nation.

All the same, the most significant cultural characteristic fostered by the state is the English language. This language has the advantage of not being identified with any community as such, and the advantages that it confers on its users in a world of competitive global economy (in which Singapore has excelled) are obvious. Mastering English to the level of a native speaker had already in colonial times become an important cultural characteristic of the (overwhelmingly Chinese) educated elite. This elite, open also to people from other ethnic backgrounds on a meritocratic basis, has ruled Singapore, firmly and with a considerable measure of success in many fields, since independence. It has shaped Singapore's cultural identity to an extent unimaginable in a liberal democracy. Indeed, its project is unparalleled also in any other regime, which, even if authoritarian, prefers to harness the ethnocultural sentiment of the masses for its purposes rather than to try to control it in such a high-handed way and demand such sacrifices from it. Rather than the people's culture having its usual impact on the cultural character of the nation-state, it is the state in Singapore that has shaped in large measure the cultural character of the people – as regards the majority no less than the minorities. The dominance of English in public education has predictably led to English becoming the main language spoken at home by an increasing number of Singaporeans (though Mandarin, so far from disappearing, has actually benefited from the strong official discouragement of Chinese "dialects"). If brought to its logical conclusion, this process seems destined to produce a paradoxical Singaporean version of Gellner's "congruity of state and culture."

The entire process of nation-building in Singapore, however far removed from ethnic exclusiveness, has obviously been facilitated by the existence of a large Chinese ethnocultural majority. This, as well as the fact that the minority population is subdivided into two distinct groups, means that the danger of ethnic strife had been somewhat less acute than often suggested by the government in justification of the less liberal aspects of its rule. This rule has surely also been helped by the unmistakably Mandarin-like character of the ruling elite and its paternalistic relations with the general public.

The official and unofficial position of English in India is strong, though it cannot be compared with the situation in Singapore. The constitution establishes Hindi – the language spoken by a large plurality, but not a majority, of the population – as "the official language of the Union" (Article 343). English "shall continue to be used for official purposes," a modest formula not reflecting its true importance. At the same time, the various states of the Union are authorized to adopt their own local languages as official, and have proceeded to do so. As we have seen in Chapter 6, the map of Indian states was re-drawn in the 1950s in order to reflect as far as possible the demographic map of the main language groups. Although the original intention of India's founders had been that the federal system would not be connected to language and ethnicity, this idea of nationhood divorced from ethnicity proved to be politically unsustainable. Thus, the various ethnocultural identities are not only recognized for the purpose of language and culture rights, but are given powerful political expression through the federal system. Officially, then, India insists on the primacy of the common Indian national identity over all the particular linguistic and communal ones, and defines itself as a multiethnic and multicultural nation-state. Yet would it not be more realistic to describe India as a *de facto* multinational state? We shall address this question as we turn to deal with binational and multinational states.

Binational and multinational states

A multinational or binational state is the only model that can ensure both objectives: the full recognition of a minority community's distinct national identity, unlike what happens in a "civic" state; and the equal status of this identity vis-à-vis the state, unlike what happens in a nation-state with a national minority, where the minority's identity is recognized but it is the majority's identity that is expressed by the state. As with the other models, this one too is a "package deal" incorporating inherent advantages and disadvantages. Perhaps the greatest disadvantage is that such states are in practice very difficult to keep together. As for the usual classification of nationalisms, the two or more national identities in such a state are obviously not "civic" in the sense of being shared by all citizens. In some sense, this model, with its stress on a plurality of national identities among citizens, is the very opposite of the French one in which "civic" and "national" are perceived as identical. Conspicuously, there are few places in Europe where the importance of one's ethnocultural affiliation trumps the importance of one's state citizenship more than in Belgium – a binational state, though it does not use this term.

Furthermore, the binational or multinational state's official neutrality between its various nationalities does not apply to groups that do not belong to either of the major national components. In binational and multinational federations in particular, the constituent states are anything but neutral toward "stranded minorities," such as the French-speaking minority in Flanders or the English-speaking minority in Quebec. The whole logic of the system makes such less-than-sovereign national entities custodians of their distinct identity, charged with making sure that it finds adequate expression in the public sphere even without full sovereignty. Thus, they tend to be particularly robust in ensuring the hegemonic status of their language and culture within their own territory. In Quebec, this is justified by the French speakers being not just a minority in Canada, but a small minority in an English-speaking North America. In Flanders, this tendency is fed by the still-unforgotten historical grievance against the past domination of the French-speaking elite and the resultant inferior status of the Dutch (Flemish) language. In any case, the English-speaking minority in Quebec and the French-speaking minority in Flanders can testify that the equality of national–cultural identities guaranteed in a federal binational state does not apply to every citizen across the country. Nor does it apply to minority groups that do not belong to any of the constituent components.

Thus, binational Belgium has come under the same criticism as the purely "mononational" France for its failure to adopt (in Belgium's case, to ratify) the European Framework Convention for the Protection of National Minorities. The account of Belgium's position appearing in a report of the Committee on Legal Affairs and Human Rights of the Parliamentary Assembly of the Council of Europe is instructive:

> *At the root of Belgium's reluctance to ratify the Framework Convention ... lies the fear that the principle of territoriality which constitutes the organic principle of Belgium's federal structure would be incompatible with the Framework Convention. This principle entails ... the division of Belgium into four language zones, three of which are unilingual (Dutch-speaking, French-speaking and German-speaking), and one bilingual (Brussels-Capital) ... With the exception [of the] bilingual Zone of Brussels-Capital where Dutch and French are on equal footing, and the recognition of 27 communities with facilities for linguistic minorities, the choice has come down in favour of homogeneous linguistic zones and the assimilation of linguistic minorities.*[20]

It is extremely rare today to hear anyone speak of "assimilation of linguistic minorities," especially when native minorities, rather than immigrant communities, are meant. Even in France, as applied to immigrants, the usual term nowadays is "integration" rather than "assimilation."[21] Still, the same principle of territoriality that is designed to guarantee the equal status of the two main communities in the binational federation that is Belgium (as well as the autonomy of the small German-speaking community) also sanctions the full domination of one ethnocultural identity within both major components of the federation.

Should the constituent "nations" in a multinational state be considered as civic or ethnic? Naturally, they cannot be civic in the strict sense, since by definition they do not include all the citizens of a (sovereign) state. If there is no territorial division between the two (or more) national communities and the state is ruled as a single territorial unit by a kind of partnership between them, it is clear that both national identities must be defined as ethnic *par excellence*. Indeed, the whole system of government in such a state is dominated by questions and considerations of ethnonational identity. Cyprus was established on this basis as a unitary binational state in 1960, but the partnership in government between the two communities broke down after a few years. The constitutional arrangements in Macedonia were adopted in the wake of the 2001 internationally sponsored agreement aimed at ending the conflict by the country's Slav Macedon majority and its large Albanian minority. These arrangements have introduced substantial elements of binationalism, in the form of a partnership between the two main ethnic nationalisms sharing the same territory. It should be noted, however, that Macedonia is not a fully-fledged binational state, as its Slav Macedonian majority has managed to remain the leading force in the country. This is reflected by the clear precedence given to the Macedonian language in Article 7 of the amended constitution. In a declaration that accompanied its signing of the European Convention on National Minorities, Macedonia officially listed its Albanian population as a "national minority," a term that indicates that it regards itself, in the main, as a national rather than a binational state.[22]

In case of a multi- or binational federation consisting of national units, a national identity comprising the entire population of such a unit can, in principle, quite reasonably be defined as civic as it applies to the territorial political entity in question. In practice, however, such a unit, no less than a national state as a whole, is likely to include minority groups significantly differing from the majority. National units within a larger state are prone, no less than national states, to use the rhetoric of inclusive civic nationalism in order to deny such minorities the cultural rights and status that the latter could have claimed had their distinct identity been recognized as "national." Moreover, self-governing national units might be no less concerned than sovereign states with the danger of separatism (or even claims of autonomy, far from always welcome) on the part of minority national groups. Those who contemplate secession are usually very reluctant to accept that anyone has a right to secede from them. By the same token, those who have gained a wide-ranging autonomy from a central government will often stand firm against any demand for autonomy by a minority within the area under their control. The nationalist governments in Quebec, for example, while basing their right to secede from Canada on the claim that the Québécois are a distinct nation, have insisted on this nation's civic and inclusive character. This, for them, justified the imposition of the French language in Quebec's public sphere as a national language of the whole province, rather than merely the language of the ethnonational majority. It also justifies in their eyes the denial of the right claimed by some indigenous groups ("First Nations") to secede from Quebec in case it secedes from Canada. In the case of Belgium, it seems that neither the Flemish nor the Walloon identity can be defined as civic even in a formal sense, since both include, as an important component, people from bilingual Brussels, and thus cannot be said to be congruent with a substate territorial entity. At the same time, translating the principle of "territoriality" into "homogeneous linguistic zones" highlights the oppressive aspect of (enforced) civic nationalism, without the benefit of its inclusive aspect. What can be argued in favor of such an arrangement is that it is apparently considered necessary for the preservation of the delicate balance on which the unity of the Belgian state rests, strongly challenged as it is by the tension between its two constituent ethnonational identities.

The language of inclusive civic nationalism, however manipulative, also obliges, at least in some measure. In 1995, the referendum on sovereignty (in fact, secession) initiated by the separatist *Parti Québécois*, the ruling party in the province, failed by a slim majority of less than 1 percent. The provincial premier and leader of the separatists complained in public that the issue was decided by "[money and] ethnic vote." This remark was correctly interpreted as undermining the notion of the "Québécois nation" as a national identity shared by all the people of the province (although the French language is, avowedly, the main cultural characteristic of that nation). It caused public outrage, which is thought to have contributed (alongside the defeat itself) to the premier's decision to resign.

Of course, the right of non-French-speaking minorities to take part in such a referendum can be easily defended without ascribing to these people a national identity to which many of them obviously do not regard themselves as belonging. This can be done simply by invoking the basic democratic principles. A legitimate democratic decision, whether it is made by a sovereign or a non-sovereign entity, is bound to be made on the basis of universal suffrage, whatever the official or unofficial definitions of group identity prevailing in it. In a nation-state with substantial national minorities, every crucial decision will be taken by a majority vote including the minorities, even when the decision involves the right to national self-determination of the majority people. For example, the decision on the independence of Slovakia, expressly justified, as we have seen, by the right to self-determination of the "Slovak nation" – that is, the Slovak-speaking majority – was, naturally, taken by a parliament elected by the entire population of Slovakia (including the Hungarian minority). However, over and above the democratic principle, there is no denying that in case of an emotionally charged controversy on an issue like this, the language of inclusive civic nationalism, if widely accepted by the majority, has clear advantages. Saying that a certain group has every right to take part in the decision because it is a part of the nation sounds more straight-forward than asserting this right on the basis of a distinction between the group's national identity and its civil rights. This is so even though in other contexts this distinction is crucial to defending the rights of national minorities.§§

How many binational and multinational states are there, and how viable is such a state form? No unambiguous answer is possible, since definitions and labels in this field are apt to be disputed. Not every minority national group that enjoys territorial autonomy affects the overall character of the state enough for it to be reasonably described as binational. The exact border-line is not easy to draw. A diversity of cultural identities (however defined) in a modern state is the rule rather the exception, and this diversity is often officially acknowledged and accommodated. Still, a state that regards itself as embodying in roughly equal measure two or more different national identities – a fully-fledged bi- or multinational state in the sense sug-gested here – is a very rare phenomenon. Moreover, states of this kind, or those that can be said to include a substantial binational or multi-national element, tend to face serious challenges as to their continued existence in that form, even if they are prosperous and long-standing democracies.

---

§§ In Israel in the 1990s, strong opposition was voiced from sectors (though not all) of the political right when Arab deputies were part of the (slim) majority by whose votes the Oslo agreements between Israel and the Palestine Liberation Organisation (PLO) were approved by the Israeli parliament (Knesset). Both the Jews and the Arabs in the country virtually unanimously regard themselves as belonging to two distinct national identities. Furthermore, the minority widely regards itself as part of a wider national community, which is a side to the national conflict which the Oslo agreements were meant to solve – the Arab Palestinian people. Thus, the argument of common nationhood was not available in defence of the minority's right to take part in the decision. It was defended, however, by invoking the democratic rights of all citizens regardless of national identity.

Belgium, which in its present form is structured as an equal partnership between its two ethnonational components – a binational state *par excellence* – functions only with great difficulty on the federal level and would probably have been split in two had it not been for its capital Brussels. Brussels is populated by both communities and situated well within Flanders rather than on the border between the two entities, which makes separation very difficult. In Canada, the combination of Quebec's distinct "nationhood," now expressly recognized by the federal government, and the equal status accorded to English and French on the federal level, produces a situation that can reasonably be defined as binational. It is not, however, binational in quite the same full sense as Belgium, because of the great asymmetry on both population and territory between Quebec and the rest of Canada. That "rest" is English-speaking, yet careful to define itself as multicultural rather than "Anglo-Canadian," and not to adopt any label distinct from the name of the country as a whole. Canada as such could be there if Quebec secedes, but there will be no Belgium if Flanders and Wallonia go their separate ways. In the 1990s, Quebec came very close to seceding, whereas today this seems unlikely. But Quebec has up to now refused to ratify Canada's 1982 constitution – a highly unusual situation in a well-established democracy, where a constitution usually presents a national consensus and a source of legitimacy.

The structure of Britain and Spain, as we have seen, includes a significant multinational element. However, these are not fully-fledged multinational states, both because of their overarching national aspect, at any rate according to the official view (spelled out expressly in the Spanish constitution), and because of the decisive weight in both cases of the main component, which is clearly the core of the state (and, arguably, of the nation) as a whole. Still, in both these countries, secession of constituent parts seems a real possibility, though, of course, it should by no means be regarded as preordained. This is quite remarkable in the case of historic European states that have existed for centuries and have practiced, at any rate in recent decades, both civic equality and a generous measure of national autonomy. Even this may possibly not be enough to contain the desire for full independence among the minority national groups.

No binational or multinational state established during the twentieth century still functioned as a unified state by the century's end. The multinational Soviet Union and Yugoslavia fell apart when the communist regime collapsed. The binational Czechoslovakia was dismantled by a "velvet divorce" when democracy returned. Serbia lost not only Kosovo with its Albanian majority, but also Montenegro. The multinational Bosnia, with its constituent parts both nearly independent and under close international supervision, can hardly be considered as a unified and sovereign political entity. Cyprus, where a binational partnership regime quickly collapsed after independence, has been partitioned for decades. The international peace plans, unsuccessful up to now, speak of a united island, but offer to create two nearly independent entities, loosely confederated under international supervision.

Switzerland has existed for many centuries. It may be debated whether today it is better described as a multinational state or a multilingual nation. The latter seems preferable. It should be noted that there is no Swiss-German or Swiss-French national entity with a government of its own that unites all the cantons speaking either of the languages below the level of the federal government. This is very different from the case in Belgium with Flanders and Wallonia, which unite the Dutch-speaking and French-speaking provinces, respectively. Rather, the particular ethnonational aspect of a Swiss citizen's identity is meant to find expression in his or her canton (all cantons have a single official language), while the federation – officially, confederation – is the focus of the overarching Swiss identity. The latter may well be described as national. Switzerland has never regarded itself as a union between two peoples (with the addition of Italian- and Romansh-speakers), but as a union of the various cantons. At any rate, for reasons described in Chapter 6, the Swiss case is unique. It is hardly an indication that similarly constructed state formations can easily be created or sustained nowadays.

Finally, India. If India's success story is added to the list of multinational states (and democracies), this list will undoubtedly look much more impressive, featuring one – but obviously major – successful example among relatively newly established states. With its ethnocultural diversity reflected in large measure by the country's federal structure, it may be argued that, despite official definitions, India is a *de facto* multinational state.

This argument has some force, but fully accepting it would ride roughshod over much more than just official definitions. The success of the Indian project of democratic nation-building has been based to a large extent precisely on the fact that the notion of Indian nationhood uniting all the country's languages and communities has been accepted by the great majority of the population from the various communities and language groups. Nor is the concept of all-Indian national identity based solely on identification with the Indian Union as a modern state. As explained in Chapter 6, it relies on a widely accepted idea of India as a historical entity with a distinct, though complicated and diverse, cultural character and tradition. Hinduism is certainly a crucial part of the Indian identity as far as the great majority of the population is concerned, though this identity is broad and flexible enough to include non-Hindu communities. Those in India who claim the status of a distinct national identity for their group affiliation reject the Indian state and aspire to secession, sometimes taking up arms in what they regard as their national cause. This applies now, first and foremost, to the Kashmiri nationalists and separatists. In the past, a substantial part of Sikhs in Punjab supported a separatist insurgency aimed at establishing an independent Sikh state. In 2011, the Indian government is headed by a Sikh prime minister. While Scottish politicians serving as British prime ministers have had no difficulty with the notion of Scotland as a nation (within the British "nation of nations"), the Sikh prime minister of India can have nothing to do with any notion of Sikh nationhood. For him, the only legitimate nationalism is the Indian one, which, in Indian terms, is not at all incompatible with taking intense pride in the distinct Sikh identity and heritage.

Such distinctions are not, needless to say, set in stone, but they are unsafe to dismiss as long as they matter to a lot of people. In the final analysis, in the case of India as everywhere, what makes a nation is the will to be a nation. This will is both influenced by ethnicity, in the various senses of this broad term, and impacts the people's consciousness and identity. The will to be a nation is a potent force in politics, well capable of making and breaking state formations, new and old alike.

Conclusion

The *Bolzano/Bozen Recommendations on National Minorities in Inter-State Relations*, a document published in 2008 by the Organization for Security and Cooperation in Europe (OSCE), High Commissioner on National Minorities, states as follows:

Ethno-cultural and State boundaries seldom overlap. Almost all states have minorities of some kind, with many belonging to communities which transcend State frontiers ... The question of national minorities in inter-State relations has often featured between the States of residence and the so-called "Kin-states". This term has been used to describe States whose majority population shares ethnic or cultural characteristics with the minority population of another State ... [European normative documents] explain the conditions under which and the limitations within which States may support citizens of another country based on shared ethnic, cultural or historical ties ... A State may have an interest – even a constitutionally declared responsibility – to support persons belonging to national minorities residing in other States based on ethnic, cultural, linguistic, religious historical or any other ties [while respecting the sovereignty of the countries where those minorities reside].[23]

The *Bolzano* document is one of many European documents that describe the world of the European nation-states at the beginning of the twenty-first century in a way that might well surprise those who are acquainted with much of the scholarly discourse on nationalism, liberal democracy, and contemporary Europe. There is not much that is "postnational" or "culturally neutral" in this description, nor does it appear from it that the European nation-state is on the verge of becoming an anachronism. According to this text, contemporary European states typically have a cultural character that is not shared by all of their citizens. As a result, some of the state citizens are likely to belong to a category that may or may not be expressly defined as a "national minority." Belonging to this category often creates a link between those citizens and another European state, "based on shared ethnic, cultural or historical ties." The inescapable implication is that culture and, indeed, ethnic identity is in such cases highly relevant to the character of both the "state of residence" and the "kin-state," and that this aspect of the state's character is often important enough to find expression in official policies, in laws and constitutions, and in international relations.

That the word "kin" can stand alongside the word "state" when the state in question is a contemporary European liberal democracy might in itself surprise and even shock some people. Of course, what is meant here is not necessarily "kinship" in some literal sense. But the Danish state does regard "ethnic Danes" across the German border as in some important sense "our people," even though they are citizens of a foreign state. Any descriptive theory of modern nation-hood, statehood, and democracy must take this fact, and similar facts, into account. A normative theory may, of course, criticize these facts. But if democracy is a government of the people, by the people, and for the people, then the people's wishes in this respect cannot be ignored. And if democracy is based on respecting the freedom and dignity of the individuals of whom "the people" is comprised, one cannot and should not ignore the fact that many, arguably the majority, of individuals regard their cultural and national identity as a vitally important part of their personality.[24]

Of course, the danger inherent in accepting the legitimacy of the fact that states typically have a national character and that this character typically has a clear ethnocultural underpinning is that this powerful force may be turned against ethnonational minorities. Indeed, great efforts have been made in contemporary democracies, European and non-European, in order to protect the rights of minorities against majoritarian nationalism. These efforts have had the salutary effect of moderating the national (nationalistic) aspect of the nation-state, in so far as this aspect is understood as implying exclusive possession and domination of the state by the (majority) nation. It is worth noting, however, that national or ethnic minorities struggling to improve their lot do not ask for a separation between state and culture. They do not suggest that Esperanto, which is indeed neutral between all ethnicities, should be made the state language, so that the state as such may be culturally neutral. Rather, they try to upgrade the official status of their own particular culture, and, usually, their language. To the extent that they succeed, they enhance the salience of their own culture and language as distinct from that of the majority. Yet this very distinctness also emphasizes their minority status.

The very concept of a national minority throws into sharp relief the fact that the national character of the state in question links it with an identity not shared by all the citizens. If the minority is defined as merely ethnic or linguistic, this, as we have seen, is usually of little practical importance as long as there exists a majority–minority relationship within society. Wherever there is a national minority or national minor-ities, there is *ipso facto* also a national majority. The only way to avoid this situation is to take care that a majority–minority relationship should not exist within the citizen body of the state. The French model of civic nationalism avoids this by insisting on all the citizens sharing, in the full sense, the same national identity. This model, with its advantages and disadvantages, has become rather an exception (most cases of avowed "civic nationalism" are in fact quite different from it), *inter alia* because it is anything but neutral culturally. The other way to avoid, or at least greatly minimize, the effects of a majority–minority relationship is by creating a binational or multinational state. Yet this option is very rarely sustainable.

In the great majority of cases, a stable state is sustained by the feeling on the part of the great majority of the population that the state, in its national and cultural aspect (however broadly and flexibly understood), is "theirs." Affording far-reaching cultural rights (and sometimes territorial autonomy) to minority groups does not in a pluralistic society destroy this feeling. But creating and sustaining a state without a clear national character is an altogether different matter. The borderline between the two situations is not easy to determine in principle. Yet when a democratic electorate identifies it, it will, as a rule, simply refuse to cross it.

According to Kymlicka, "today, virtually all Western states that contain indigenous peoples and substate national groups have become 'multination' states" characterized by "a range of minority and indigenous rights that include regional autonomy and official language rights for national minorities."[25] Western democracies are, indeed, distinguished in today's world by their readiness to afford a "national" status to minority groups, and they often go to great lengths to accommodate minority demands. They are in this sense typically not "mononational." This, however, does not mean that they give up their national character. Neither official language rights for a national minority nor, necessarily, territorial autonomy makes a state multinational. Kymlicka's "multination" states are clearly not, in his own view, the same as "multinational" in the sense suggested here. He stresses that it is wrong to regard "multiculturalism and nationalism [as] sworn enemies." According to him, Western countries, having adopted "liberal multiculturalism" and recognized minority national rights, have not thereby become "postnational." Rather, they "continue to adopt a range of policies to inculcate overarching national identities and loyalties," subject to the limitations imposed by the (now widely accepted) need to allow minorities to preserve their cultural distinctness [26]

The desire for an independent nation-state for one's people is a highly potent force in modern politics based on the popular will – doubly so in democratic politics. This desire is essentially the same in the case of both majority and minority peoples. This is why Europe has today more independent nation-states than ever, even if their sovereignty is limited by the progress of European integration. This is also why attempts to take the European project in the direction that will turn today's nation-states into mere provinces of a federal European state encounter strong popular resistance. Finally, this is why it may be assumed that if the European supra-state does emerge eventually, this will signify not the disappearance of the European nation-state, but the emergence of a European (supra)nation. Such an identity can be expected to have a significant historical depth and cultural content. More broadly, while Europe has played an important role in the history of modern nationalism, as well as in the history of modern democracy, the power of nationalism and democracy – in both their close mutual interrelationship and inherent tensions – is felt far and wide across the globe.

CONCLUSION

Modernism, perennialism, and primordialism, the accepted and largely ossified categories in the study of the nation and national-isms, are all in need of reformulation and synthesis. Although radic-ally transformed and enhanced by modernity, nationalism, the rough congruence – and connection – between state and culture, people or ethnicity, was not invented in the modern era. The national state has been perennial in human history since the beginning of statehood and as one of its major forms, alongside petty-states and empires; and yet human history itself is but a blink of the eye compared with the vast time span of human prehistory, when no states or nations existed. Indeed, nations and nationalism are not primordial; nonetheless, they are rooted in primordial human sentiments of kin–culture affinity, solidarity, and mutual cooperation, evolutionarily engraved in human nature. These attachments, permeating social life and extending beyond family to tribe and ethnos, became integral to politics when states emerged.

Powerfully resonating with the post-1945 climate of ideas and normative atmosphere, modernist precepts have been the most influential, and most misleading, in the current study of the nation and nationalism, exaggerating genuine major developments *ad absurdum*. They thus call for special attention. Losing sight of the ethnonational phenomenon's deep roots, modernist and instrumentalist theorists have regarded the nation and nationalism as a pure sociohistorical construct, if not com-pletely artificially contrived. As a result, they have misinterpreted the ethnonational phenomenon's historical trajectory and have either remained confounded by, or turned a blind eye to, its highly explosive potency, so evidently one of the strongest forces in human history.

Semantic, factual, and normative elements are variably combined in modernist theorizing. Semantics is the least problematic. Most modernists insist that equal citizenship and popular sovereignty, as the practical and legitimizing principle of modern states, are inseparable from the concept of the nation. Indisputably, both have contributed very significantly to the making of *modern* nationalism – indeed, largely by giving priority to the people's wishes and preferences which had always been strongly biased toward the ethnonational collective. Yet precisely because equal citizenship, popular sovereignty, and nationalism have been closely intertwined and mutually reinforcing during the modern era, they are easily confused with one another. Care should be taken not to conflate them at both the empirical and conceptual levels. Furthermore, although definitions are semantic speech conventions and, therefore, ultimately beyond dispute as long as they maintain internal coherence, there is still the question of how much they correspond to the ordinary common understanding of the phenomena they purport to describe. I submit that in ordinary usage nationhood means common identification and solidarity with one's people and state, and the political expression of these sentiments, irrespective of equal citizenship and popular sovereignty. The real question, then, is whether or not the national phenomenon existed in this sense before modern times. And this leads us to a problem more significant than the semantic: the interpretation of history. Facts, as much as definitions, are at stake.

Modernists deny that the population of premodern states – oppressed peasants who rarely left their village environment – had any consciousness of being part of a larger people, let alone felt solidarity with it. Indeed, what many of them in effect deny is the existence of premodern *peoples* (a concept which is increasingly absent from the literature for that very reason). However, both propositions are a caricature of historical realities. Projected by theorists, it is challenged by the great majority of the historians of particular societies who have applied themselves to the subject and possess far more intimate and authoritative knowledge of the societies in question. As we have seen throughout this book, side by side with petty-states and empires, in all of which ethnicity was highly political, there existed large premodern so-called territorial states or dynastic kingdoms. These, in fact, were most often national monarchies, wherein the boundaries of ethnos or people and state largely overlapped. Contrary to the strong narrow European bias of the literature on the national phenomenon, both geographical and temporal, this has been the case around the globe since the emergence of states millennia ago. It is simply that in Europe north of the Mediterranean, states, including national states, only emerged relatively late, during the European "Middle Ages." Far from being a coincidence, the rough congruence of ethnicity, peoplehood, and statehood in national monarchies throughout history was grounded in common identity, affinity, and solidarity, which greatly facilitated and legitimized political rule. Ethnicity has always been political and politicized, ever since the beginning of politics, because people have always been heavily biased toward those they identify as their kin–culture community.

Second only to shared language, the main bonding elements of premodern peoples and a major instrument of nation-building by the state were the premodern mass cultural forms of epos, ritual, and religion. These were widely disseminated by a dense clerical and cultic network spread throughout the countryside and reaching far into its most remote corners. As a number of scholars have shown, holy states and chosen peoples abounded. The holiness, righteousness, and special mission of one's state and people resonated in every parish. This included medieval Christendom, supposedly universalistic religiously but in reality divided politically into national states, with mythologies to match. Herein was the primary medium of the premodern national "imagined community" that Benedict Anderson has so sorely missed. Given its unifying collective bonds, and although premodern national states were monarchic and dominated by the aristocracy, the state could usually rely on the loyalty of its subjects when threatened by a foreign invader. Indeed, even when the state fell prey to a superior imperial power, rebellions repeatedly occurred, often taking the form of mass, desperate, and bloody popular uprisings. These were clearly national rather than social revolts, as the people's social status was unlikely to change after liberation. The "politicization of the masses" on an ethnonational scale regularly manifested itself in these forms of political action. The politicization of the masses and political ethnicity – widely regarded as the hallmark of the national phenomenon – were both intimately connected and as old as statehood itself.

Thus, although nationalism has been vastly enhanced by modernity's sharp increase in social connectivity, political participation, and cultural leveling, it was far from being a creation of the modern era. One way of describing the change from premodern to modern times is the following: having always been cardinal in determining political loyalty and boundaries, but secondary to the dynastic principle and to the right of the conqueror in the legitimization discourse, national identity became the paramount formal, legal, and ideological principle as sovereignty became invested in the people rather than in the ruler. Overly impressed by these revolutionary changes, modernists have construed a false dichotomy whereby national sentiments never existed or played a political role in the premodern world. The idea that the concept of the nation was unknown, unimportant, or devoid of political significance to the people of the premodern world, including medieval Europe, is one of the greatest missteps taken by modern social theory.

Cognitive problems have contributed to the creation of this misconception. Scholars have lacked the theoretical tools to comprehend the deep roots of the ethnic and national phenomenon in naturally evolved human propensities. Even Anthony Smith, with whom this book agrees on so much, is ultimately left with no better answer than modernists to the fundamental puzzle of the ethnic and national phenomenon: his "ethnosymbolic" approach scarcely explains people's explosive devotion and willingness to sacrifice and die for their ethnic and national collective. For much of the twentieth century the idea that human nature had *anything* to do with social realities was anathema to historians and social scientists. And that which we lack the means to comprehend we do not see, even if it is staring us in the face. Repeatedly confounded by the ferocious "atavistic" irruptions of ethnic and national forces, theorists have nonetheless dismissed them as the outcome of manipulation or as an epiphenomenon of something else. Furthermore, they have widely labeled them "irrational." Indeed, the very concept of rationality has been at odds with the ethnonational phenomenon. Ever since Kant (if not Plato), both the rational and the moral have been equated with the universal. To this has been added the liberal and Marxist tendency to identify the good with material gain. Many thinkers in these traditions have failed to realize that the space of loyalty and benefit-sharing extending from the individual to humanity is curved rather than even, and to recognize the rationale explaining why it is so. It has not been clear, nor seriously asked, why the family should play such a favored role between the individual and humanity. And the logic behind favoritism of more remote kin or perceived-as-kin circles has remained not only a mystery, but also lacking in legitimacy. Rationality concerns the adoption of means to achieve a desired end, not a choice between ends, and the aim of benefiting one's closest is as rational as any other. The contrast often drawn between supposedly rational civic principles attributed to the modern state and atavistic and irrational kin–ethnic attachments is little more than a philosophical prejudice.

Finally, there has been deep, genuine, and understandable concern about the horrendous manifestations of chauvinistic and aggressive nationalism. As mentioned in the Introduction, it is hardly a coincidence that nearly all the founding fathers of modernism were immigrant refugees from the horrors of the 1930s and 1940s. Sounder than their claim that nationalism was a superficial craze, a fad with no deep roots in the human psyche, has been the important and highly successful modernist project of imploding often chauvinistic national myths and anachronisms. National myths have come to be seen as not only false, but also as a vehicle for national bigotry. And yet the discrediting project seems to have overshot. Myths abound in the nationalistic discourse, and are an easy target, but counter-myths are almost as easily created. Imagined communities do not mean invented, nor does invented tradition imply wholesale fabrication. Although the latter meanings have usually been denied by the creators of these catch-phrases, they resonate widely in the influential modernist discourse across disciplines. The fashionable shibboleths which have become dominant in the social sciences create a huge obstacle to genuine understanding that social phenomena tend to be *both* deeply-rooted *and* construed. There is nothing mutually exclusive here. Certainly, there has been a pressing need to hedge national traditions by submitting them to historical scrutiny and exposing their intrinsic and often crude ideological biases. But at a higher intellectual level a similar need now exists for the hedging process itself. Indeed, the claim that nations and nationalism are modern constructs invented for ideological purposes is itself a modernist (sometimes postmodernist) ideologically construed concept which requires deconstruction.

This need is as much practical as it is scholarly and academic. The study of the nation and nationalism has been biased by ideological attitudes, has manifested significant "false consciousness," first by nationalists but later also by their critics. The latter as much as the former inevitably affect practical politics, as concepts and perspectives are translated into action. The precept that nationhood equals citizenship, already critiqued by pioneering modernist Carlton Hayes, is very far from universal application. Nonetheless, the notion that different ethnicities in a country should remain together and count as a nation even if they do not perceive themselves as such, or do not get along, is partly derived from the erroneous view that nationhood and ethnicity are *entirely* different concepts that ought to be kept apart.* Of course, the ultimate test of common nationhood is the self-perception of the population in question, Renan's daily plebiscite. However, in actuality the perception of a common nationhood strongly correlates with shared kin–culture identity. The simple reason for this is that people overwhelmingly *choose* to live together in a political community with, and exhibit a strongly preferential solidarity toward, their kin–culture likes. "Constitutional patriotism," in Habermas' phrase, is generally expressed toward one's *own* patria precisely because that particular patria happens to incorporate the above. To be sure, different ethnic communities in a country sometimes view themselves, and therefore are, one nation. However, in other cases, ethnic populations live in one state – voluntarily or involuntarily – without viewing themselves as part of a common nation. Sometimes, their national affinity lies with their kin across the border. In such cases, their citizenship status and national identity do not overlap.

As the alternative to the integrity of multiethnic states is all too often horrendous mayhem, there is a lot of sense in making great efforts to keep together whenever possible mutually alien or even hostile ethnic populations. Ethnicities are often mixed, and attempted partitions frequently entail population transfers, ethnic cleansing, and widespread sectarian violence. There are usually no easy options in complex national situations, and I am the last to underestimate the requirements of practical politics or the utility of constructive hypocrisy in such matters. Still, theory-informed dogmas also play a role in the shaping of policy with respect to problematic multiethnic situations. The world is full of examples, and only a random two will be mentioned here. Given the alternatives, it may or may not be the most desirable option

---

* Student of "consociational" politics Arend Lijphart, for one, attributed this view to "liberal wishful thinking" and called it "unrealistic": Lijphart, "Political Theories and the Explanation of Ethnic Conflict in the Western World: Falsified Predictions and Plausible Postditions," in Esman (ed.), *Ethnic Conflict in the Western World*, 53.

for the various ethnicities in post-Saddam Hussein Iraq to remain together in one state. For this purpose it may even be justified to regard them as one people and nation, which they scarcely are at present but which at least some of them might become over time. However, what about the two ethnic communities in Cyprus, the Greek and Turkish? Historically deeply hostile toward each other on both national and religious grounds, they have been completely separated territorially by a problematic war (1974) and a population movement, some of it forced, with all the injustices that this entailed. In this war the Turkish side may have grabbed more than its proportional share territorially, and this may need to be corrected. All the same, given the existing reality, and leaving aside the obvious interests and pressures involved, is there any point of high principle or practical utility in insisting, as the European Union does, that the two separate ethnic communities must be reunited in one state, albeit confederated?

Ideological dogmas can have a profound, yet ultimately limited, effect on people's thoughts, attitudes, and behavior. The collapse of communism, an ideology so enthusiastically embraced by and worked for by many but going against some deeply ingrained human propensities, is a recent example. Surely there are excellent reasons of both morality and practicality for the abolishment of private property. They are at least as good as the reasons for the abolishment of ethnicity and nationalism, except that all of the above express deep human preferences toward one's *own*. These preferences are subject to great historical variation, of course, and can be socially shaped and adjusted. But attempts to write them off completely out of the best of intentions go against people's natural inclinations, and may require tremendous coercion and cause far greater harm than the ills such attempts set out to remedy. Similarly, major spiritual ideologies throughout history, concerned by the excesses and pains of sexuality, endeavored to curb or suppress it to the point of denial. Denying the deep roots and immense potency of ethnic and national sentiments, declaring them to be a recent invention, contrived manipulation, or an epiphenomenal expression of something else which can be gotten rid of once that something has been removed, are all ideological precepts which may resonate widely but are unlikely to meet with greater success.

Kin–culture identity, solidarity, and cooperation, including their national form, have deep roots in the human psyche and have been among the most powerful forces in human history. Even evolutionary studies of ethnocentrism and nationalism have not grasped how slow-learned complex culture, cultural diversity, and the vital role of shared culture (most notably language) in facilitating social cooperation – all unique to our species – compounded people's stake in and attachment to their extended kin group. Democratization and popular self-determination brought ethnonational bonds of affinity, commonality, and solidarity more overtly to the fore during modernity, as did the liberalization of imperial powers, which de-legitimized rule over other peoples against their will. Thus, the surge of modern nationalism is largely a function of the processes of democratization and liberalization, which allowed people to express and act on their choice. The ostensible weakening of national sentiments in the developed world is in fact a direct result of the triumphant materialization and secure prevalence of the national principle, in a liberal and defensive, seemingly "banal," form. For those espousing the values of the Enlightenment, nationalism has had both emancipating and aggressive-violent aspects. To make the most of the former and contain the latter, a proper understanding of the phenomenon in question is crucial.

NOTES

1 Introduction: is nationalism recent and superficial?

1 This was influentially highlighted by Fredrik Barth, "Ethnic Groups and Boundaries" (1969), *Process and Form in Social Life*, London: Routledge, 1981, 198–227.

2 Walker Connor, "A Nation is a Nation, is a State, is an Ethnic Group, is a … ," *Ethnic and Racial Studies*, 1(4) (1978), 379–388; Walker Connor, *Ethnonationalism: The Quest for Understanding*, Princeton University Press, 1994.

3 Karl Deutsch, *Nationalism and Social Communication: An Inquiry into the Foundations of Nationality*, Cambridge, MA: MIT Press, 1953, 3; Karl Deutsch, *Nationalism and Its Alternative*, New York: Knopf, 1969, 19.

4 Ernest Gellner, *Nations and Nationalism*, Oxford: Blackwell, 1983, 1; Ernest Gellner, "From Kinship to Ethnicity," in *Encounters with Nationalism*, Oxford: Blackwell, 1994, 34–46.

5 Gellner, *Nations and Nationalism*, 70–71, 74.

6 David McCrone, *The Sociology of Nationalism*, London: Routledge, 1998, 7–10; Anthony Smith, *Nations and Nationalism in the Global Era*, Cambridge: Polity, 1995, 97–102; Will Kymlicka, *Politics in the Vernacular: Nationalism, Multiculturalism, and Citizenship*, Oxford University Press, 2001, 243–244; Rogers Smith, *Stories of Peoplehood*, Cambridge University Press, 2003, 74–92; Anthony Marx, *Faith in Nations: Exclusionary Origins of Nations*, Oxford University Press, 2003; Aviel Roshwald, *The Endurance of Nationalism*, New York: Cambridge University Press, 2006, ch. 5; T. Baycroft and M. Hewitson (eds.), *What is a Nation? Europe 1789–1914*, Oxford University Press, 2006, *passim*; Craig Calhoun, *Nations Matter: Culture, History and the Cosmopolitan Dream*, London: Routledge, 2007, ch. 6.

7 Ernest Renan, "What is a Nation" (1882), in H. Bhabha (ed.), *Nations and Narration*, London: Routledge, 1990, 8–22.

8 Carlton Hayes, *Nationalism: A Religion*, New York: Macmillan, 1960, vi–vii.

9 Connor, "A Nation is a Nation, is a State, is an Ethnic Group, is a ... ," and *Ethnonationalism: The Quest for Understanding*; Karl Deutsch, *Tides among Nations*, New York: Free Press, 1979, ch. 7.

10 Hans Kohn, *The Idea of Nationalism: A Study of Its Origins and Background*, Toronto: Collier, [1944] 1969, 4–6.

11 Eric Hobsbawm, *Nations and Nationalism since 1780: Programme, Myth, Reality*, Cambridge University Press, 1990, ch. 2.

12 Kohn, *The Idea of Nationalism*, 6.

13 Gellner, *Nations and Nationalism*, 138.

14 Hobsbawm, *Nations and Nationalism since 1780*, 78; also, e.g., 65, 92.

15 Anthony Smith, *The Ethnic Origins of Nations*, Oxford: Blackwell, 1986; and his many other works.

16 Anthony Smith, *The Antiquity of Nations*, Cambridge: Polity, 2004, esp. 15–17, 38; Anthony Smith, "The Genealogy of Nations: An Ethno-Symbolic Approach," in A. Ichijo and G. Uzelac (eds.), *When is the Nation?*, London: Routledge, 2005, ch. 5; Anthony Smith, *Ethno-Symbolism and Nationalism*, London: Routledge, 2009.

17 Carlton Hayes, *The Historical Evolution of Modern Nationalism*, New York: Russell, [1931] 1968, 292; Hobsbawm, *Nations and Nationalism since 1780*, 48.

18 Michael Petrovich, "Religion and Ethnicity in Eastern Europe" (1980), reprinted in J. Hutchinson and A. Smith (eds.), *Nationalism*, London: Routledge, 2000, vol. IV, 1356–1381; Connor Cruise O'Brien, *God Land: Reflections on Religion and Nationalism*, Cambridge, MA: Harvard University Press, 1988; Adrian Hastings, *The Construction of Nationhood: Ethnicity, Religion and Nationalism*, Cambridge University Press, 1997; Steven Grosby, *Biblical Ideas of Nationality: Ancient and Modern*, Winona Lake, IN: Eisenbrauns, 2002; Philip Gorski, "The Mosaic Moment: An Early Modernist Critique of Modernists Theories of Nationalism," *American Journal of Sociology*, 105 (2000), 1428–1468; Anthony Smith, *Chosen Peoples*, Oxford University Press, 2003; Marx, *Faith in Nations*.

19 Benedict Anderson, *Imagined Communities: Reflections of the Origins and Spread of Nationalism*, London: Verso, 1983. The major effect of print in the consolidation of modern nationalism had already been pointed out by both Hayes, *Nationalism: A Religion*, ch. 4, and Kohn, *The Idea of Nationalism*, 8–9, 123.

20 Anderson, *Imagined Communities*, 20–25.

21 The far-reaching role of the parochial clergy in this respect, in Christianity, Islam, and Judaism, is emphasized by John Armstrong, *Nations before Nationalism*, Chapel Hill, NC: University of North Carolina Press, 1982; and, indeed, it applies more universally to other religions as well.

22 Hobsbawm, *Nations and Nationalism since 1780*, 92.

23 Cf. Rogers Brubaker, "Myths and Misconceptions in the Study of Nationalism," in J. Hall (ed.), *The State of the Nation: Ernest Gellner and the Theory of Nationalism*, Cambridge University Press, 1998, 291.

24 Tom Nairn, "The Curse of Rurality: Limits of Modernization Theory," in Hall (ed.), *The State of the Nation*, 121.

25 Gellner, *Nations and Nationalism*, 34–35.

26 Ernest Gellner, *Nationalism*, London: Weidenfeld & Nicolson, 1997, ix.

27 Gellner, *Nations and Nationalism*, 2, 44–45; also, Joshua Fishman (ed.), *Handbook of Languages and Ethnic Identity*, New York: Oxford University Press, 1999.

28 Smith, *Ethnic Origins*, ch. 2; and often repeated in other books.

29 Max Weber, *Economy and Society*, vol. 2, Berkeley, CA: University of California Press, 1978, 389; Connor, "A Nation is a Nation, is a State, is an Ethnic Group, is a . . . "; Connor, *Ethnonationalism*; Connor, "The Dawning of Nations," in Ichijo and Uzelac (eds.), *When is the Nation?*, ch. 2. Anthony Smith suggests a broader and more flexible concept in his "National Identity and Myths of Ethnic Descent" (1984), reprinted in Hutchinson and Smith (eds.), *Nationalism*, vol. IV, 1394–1429.

30 This is rightly pointed out by Thomas Eriksen, "Place, Kinship and the Case for Non-ethnic Nations," *Nations and Nationalism*, 10(1/2) (2004), 49–62, esp. 59.

31 Friedrich Meinecke, *Cosmopolitanism and the National State*, Princeton University Press, [1928] 1970.

32 John Lie, *Modern Peoplehood*, Cambridge, MA: Harvard University Press, 2004, is a modernist work which refers to peoples as practically synonymous with nations; but Liah Greenfeld, *Nationalism: Five Roads to Modernity*, Cambridge, MA: Harvard University Press, 1993, is sensible here.

33 R. Smith, *Stories of Peoplehood*; also, Margaret Canovan, *The People*, Cambridge: Polity, 2005.

34 For a most useful database, albeit of European ethnicities rather than nations, see: Jaroslav Krejčí and Vítězslav Velímský, *Ethnic and Political Nations in Europe*, London: Croom Helm, 1981, 49–57. The data reveal language to be by far the most distinctive marker.

35 Also an almost universal marker in the European study, Krejčí and Velímský, *Ethnic and Political Nations in Europe*.

36 Krejčí and Velímský, *Ethnic and Political Nations in Europe*.

37 This conclusion also seems to be supported, Krejčí and Velímský, *Ethnic and Political Nations in Europe*.

38 The distinction is occasionally raised in the literature, with some speculation as to its basis. A dedicated study is Maurizio Virdi, *For Love of Country: An Essay on Patriotism and Nationalism*, Oxford University Press, 1995, which wrongly concludes that patriotism exists solely in free societies and is the desire to

protect the institutions of liberty. As his own examples show, patriotism also existed in the French and English absolutist monarchies, as well as, fervently, in many other highly despotic *patriae*. In his Conclusion, Gellner, *Nations and Nationalism*, 138, actually advances a proposition rather similar to mine regarding nationalism as a particular form of patriotism.

2 The evolution of kin–culture communities

1 Pierre van den Berghe, *The Ethnic Phenomenon*, New York: Elsevier, 1981. See also: V. Reynolds, V. Falger, and I. Vine (eds.), *The Sociobiology of Ethnocentrism*, London: Croom Helm, 1987; R. Paul Shaw and Yuwa Wong, *Genetic Seeds of Warfare, Evolution, Nationalism and Patriotism*, Boston, MA: Unwin Hyman, 1989; Tatu Vanhansen, *Ethnic Conflicts Explained by Ethnic Nepotism*, Stamford, CT: JAI, 1999. For the source see Charles Darwin, *The Descent of Man* [1871], ch. 6, in *The Origin of the Species and the Descent of Man*, New York: The Modern Library, n.d., 492.

2 Azar Gat, *War in Human Civilization*, Oxford University Press, 2006.

3 First suggested by Darwin, R. A. Fisher, and J. B. S. Haldane, this idea has become the cornerstone of modern evolutionary theory with W. D. Hamilton, "The Genetical Evolution of Social Behaviour," *Journal of Theoretical Biology*, 7 (1964), 1–16, 17–52. For Darwin see *The Origin of the Species*, ch. 8, and *The Descent of Man*, ch. 5, in *The Origin of the Species and the Descent of Man*, 203–205, 498.

4 W. D. Hamilton, "Innate Social Aptitudes of Man: An Approach from Evolutionary Genetics," in R. Fox (ed.), *Biosocial Anthropology*, New York: Wiley, 1975, 144; Irwin Silverman, "Inclusive Fitness and Ethnocentrism," in Reynolds, Falger, and Vine (eds.), *The Sociobiology of Ethnocentrism*, 113.

5 D. C. Fletcher and C. D. Michener (eds.), *Kin Recognition in Animals*, New York: Wiley, 1987; P. Hepper (ed.), *Kin Recognition*, Cambridge University Press, 1991.

6 Colin Irwin, "A Study in the Evolution of Ethnocentrism," and G. R. Johnson, S. H. Ratwil, and T. J. Sawyer, "The Evocative Significance of Kin Terms in Patriotic Speech," both in Reynolds, Falger, and Vine (eds.), *The Sociobiology of Ethnocentrism*, 131–156, 157–174.

7 Napoleon Chagnon, "Yanomamo Social Organization and Warfare," in M. Fried, M. Harris, and R. Murphy (eds.), *War: The Anthropology of Armed Conflict and Aggression*, Garden City, NY: Natural History, 1968, 128–129.

8 Harry Lourandos, *Continent of Hunter-Gatherers: New Perspectives in Australian Prehistory*, Cambridge University Press, 1979, 38.

9 C. J. Lumsden and E. O. Wilson, *Genes, Mind and Culture*, Cambridge, MA: Harvard University Press, 1981; L. L. Cavalli-Sforza and M. W. Feldman, *Cultural Transmission and Evolution*, Princeton University Press, 1981; Robert

Boyd and Peter Richerson, *Culture and the Evolutionary Process*, University of
Chicago Press, 1985; W. H. Durham, *Coevolution: Genes, Culture, and Human
Diversity*, Stanford University Press, 1991; Peter Richerson and Robert Boyd,
Not by Genes Alone, University of Chicago Press, 2005; John Tooby and Leda
Cosmides, "The Psychological Foundations of Culture," in L. Cosmides,
J. Tooby, and J. Barkow (eds.), *The Adapted Mind: Evolutionary Psychology and
the Generation of Culture*, New York: Oxford University Press, 1992, 19–136.

10 Lawrence Keeley, *War before Civilization*, New York: Oxford University Press,
1996; Steven LeBlanc with Katherine Register, *Constant Battles: The Myth of
the Peaceful Noble Savage*, New York: St. Martin's Press, 2003; Gat, *War in
Human Civilization*; Samuel Bowles, "Did Warfare among Ancestral Hunter-
Gatherers Affect the Evolution of Human Social Behaviors," *Science*, 324
(2009), 1293–1298.

11 Again, this has been pointed out by Hamilton, "The Genetical Evolution of
Social Behavior," 16; and developed by Robert L. Trivers, "Parent–Offspring
Conflict," *American Zoologist*, 14 (1974), 249–264.

12 There have been a couple of classics here, in different fields: Mancur Olson,
The Logic of Collective Action: Public Goods and the Theory of Groups,
Cambridge, MA: Harvard University Press, 1965; Robert L. Trivers, "The
Evolution of Reciprocal Altruism," *Quarterly Review of Biology*, 46 (1971),
35–57. The idea had been suggested by Darwin, *The Descent of Man*, ch. 5,
499–500. See also: Richard Alexander, *The Biology of Moral Systems*, New
York: Aldine, 1987, 77, 85, 93–94, 99–110, 117–126, and *passim*; Robert
Frank, *Passions within Reason: The Strategic Role of the Emotions*, New York:
Norton, 1988; Matt Ridley, *The Origins of Virtue: Human Instincts and the
Evolution of Cooperation*, New York: Viking, 1996.

13 This has been the subject of the most intense debate in modern evolutionary
theory, but the balance of opinion is clearly moving in this direction. Both of the
pioneers of kin altruism, W. D. Hamilton and E. O. Wilson, later come to
acknowledge group selection: Hamilton, "Innate Social Aptitudes"; W. D.
Hamilton, *Narrow Roads of Gene Land*, Oxford: Freeman, 1996; David S.
Wilson and E. Sober, *Unto Others: The Evolution and Psychology of Unselfish
Behavior*, Cambridge, MA: Harvard University Press, 1998; David S. Wilson
and E. O. Wilson, "Rethinking the Theoretical Foundations of Sociobiology,"
Quarterly Review of Biology, 82 (2007), 327–348; Martin Nowak, Corina
Tarnita, and Edward O. Wilson, "The Evolution of Eusociality," *Nature*, 466
(2010), 1057–1062; Samuel Bowles, "Group Competition, Reproductive
Leveling, and the Evolution of Human Altruism," *Science*, 314 (2006),
1569–1572; Bowles, "Did Warfare among Ancestral Hunter-Gatherers Affect
the Evolution of Human Social Behaviors"; Samuel Bowles and Herbert Gintis,
A Cooperative Species: Human Reciprocity and Its Evolution, Princeton
University Press, 2011, crucially highlighting the significance of group

sanctions against defectors and free riders; Oleg Smirnov, Holly Arrow, Douglas Kennett, and John Orbell, "Ancestral War and the Evolutionary Origins of 'Heroism,'" *Journal of Politics*, 69 (2007), 927–940. Darwin suggested the idea in *The Descent of Man*, ch. 5, 496–500.

14 This old idea was first formulated in evolutionary terms by Richard Dawkins, *The Selfish Gene*, Oxford University Press, 2nd edn., 1989, 189–201, 329–331; and developed in his *The God Delusion*, London: Bantam, 2006. See also Pascal Boyer, *Religion Explained: The Evolutionary Origins of Religious Thought*, New York: Basic Books, 2001; Daniel Dennett, *Breaking the Spell: Religion as a Natural Phenomenon*, New York: Viking, 2006. The role of evolutionary by-products of adaptive design were laid out by S. G. Gould and R. C. Lewontin, "The Spandrels of San Marco and the Panglossian Program: A Critique of the Adaptionist Programme," *Proceedings of the Royal Society of London*, 250 (1979), 281–288.

15 Dawkins, *The Selfish Gene*, 331.

16 David S. Wilson, *Darwin's Cathedral: Evolution, Religion, and the Nature of Society*, University of Chicago Press, 2002. Although perceptively pointing out the benefits of religion in fostering cooperation, Wilson overlooks the military aspect.

17 Wendel Oswalt, *Alaskan Eskimos*, San Francisco, CA: Chandler, 1967, xi.

18 Chagnon, "Yanomamo Social Organization and Warfare," 128–129.

19 There is still no substitute for the scope and breadth of L. L. Cavalli-Sforza, P. Menozzi, and A. Piazza, *The History and Geography of Human Genes*, Princeton University Press, 1994. But this monumental work is fast being rendered obsolescent by improving techniques and a legion of specialized studies on specific populations.

20 Joseph Shepher, *Incest: The Biosocial View*, New York: Academic Press, 1983. This finding has been variably disputed over the years, but in my view, given that the incest taboo is strong but never foolproof, it still stands; for a recent critique see: Eran Shor and Dalit Simchai, "Incest Avoidance, the Incest Taboo, and Social Cohesion: Revisiting Westermarck and the Case of the Israeli Kibbutzim," *American Journal of Sociology*, 114 (2009), 1803–1842.

21 Anthony Smith, *Nationalism and Modernism*, London: Routledge, 1998, 147–151; Anthony Smith, *The Nation in History*, Cambridge: Polity, 2000; Smith, *Antiquity of Nations*, 5–6.

3 From tribes to statehood

1 Generally, see Colin McEvedy and Richard Jones, *Atlas of World Population History*, London: Penguin, 1978; Massimo Bacci, *A Concise History of World Population*, Oxford: Blackwell, 1997, e.g., 27, 38, 41–47.

2 For some population figures for these large post-tribal confederate communities (some of which were probably exaggerated, as was customary with enemy

numbers in antiquity), see Caesar, *The Gallic Wars*, 1.29, 2.4, and perhaps the most instructive: 7.75.

3 Barry Cunliffe, *Iron Age Communities in Britain*, London: Routledge, 1974, 105, 114.

4 Malcolm Todd, *The Early Germans*, Oxford: Blackwell, 1992, 8.

5 Kristian Kristiansen, *Europe before History*, Cambridge University Press, 1998, 195.

6 See the various contributions to B. Trigger and W. Washburn (eds.), *The Cambridge History of the Native Peoples of the Americas, vol. I: North America*, Pt 1, New York: Cambridge University Press, 1996, 403, 408, 506.

7 Brian Fagan, *Ancient North America*, New York: Thames & Hudson, 1995, 121, 141–142, 160; John Ewers, "Intertribal Warfare as the Precursor of Indian–White Warfare on the Northern Great Plains," *The Western Historical Quarterly*, 6 (1975), 403–407.

8 Patrick Kirch, *The Evolution of the Polynesian Chiefdoms*, Cambridge University Press, 1984, 98; Marshall Sahlins, "Poor Man, Rich Man, Big-Man, Chief: Political Types in Melanesia and Polynesia," *Comparative Studies in Society and History*, 5 (1963), 287.

9 Andrew Vayda, *Maori Warfare*, Wellington: The Polynesian Society, 1960, 20.

10 M. Fortes and E. Evans-Pritchard (eds.), *African Political Systems*, Oxford University Press, 1940, 7, 36, 198, 239, 276–284; J. Middleton and D. Tait, *Tribes without Rulers: Studies in African Segmentary Systems*, London: Routledge, 1958, 28, 97, 102–104, 164, 167, 203, 207.

11 Jared Diamond, *Guns, Germs, and Steel: The Fate of Human Societies*, New York: Norton, 1997.

12 K. Fukui and D. Turton (eds.), *Warfare among East African Herders*, Osaka: National Museum of Ethnology, 1977, 15, 35; also John Galaty, "Pastoral Orbits and Deadly Jousts: Factors in the Maasai Expansion," in J. Galaty and P. Bonte (eds.), *Herders, Warriors, and Traders*, Boulder, CO: Westview, 1991, 194.

13 Elizabeth Thomas, *Warrior Herdsmen*, New York: Knopf, 1965.

14 P. Bonte, "Non-Stratified Social Formations among Pastoral Nomads," in J. Friedman and M. Rowlands (eds.), *The Evolution of Social Systems*, London: Duckworth, 1977, 192–194, containing important theoretical observations on pastoral tribal structure.

15 Fredrik Barth, *Nomads of South Persia*, London: Oslo University Press, 1961, 1, 50–60, 119.

16 V. Müller, *En Syrie avec les Bédouin*, Paris: Ernest Leroux, 1931; M. von Oppenheim, *Die Beduinen*, vol. 1, Leipzig: Harrassowitz, 1939.

17 Jean Kupper, *Les nomades en Mésopotamie au temps des rois de Mari*, Paris: Société d'Edition "Les Belles Lettres," 1957; J. T. Luke, "Pastoralism and Politics in the Mari Period," doctoral dissertation, Ann Arbor, Michigan, 1965;

Victor Matthews, *Pastoral Nomadism in the Mari Kingdom (c. 1850–1760)*, Cambridge: American School of Oriental Research, 1978; Moshe Anbar, *The Amorite Tribes in Mari*, Tel Aviv University Press, 1985 (in Hebrew; also in French 1991).

18 Israel Finkelstein, *The Archaeology of the Israelite Settlement*, Jerusalem: Israel Exploration Society, 1988, 330–335.

19 This was highlighted by Adam Ferguson's *An Essay on the History of Civil Society*, Cambridge University Press, [1767] 1995, and developed by Lewis Morgan's *Ancient Society*, Chicago, IL: Kerr, [1877] 1907, which greatly impressed Friedrich Engels.

20 See, e.g.: Mervin Meggitt, *Blood is Their Argument: Warfare among the Mae Enga of the New Guinea Highlands*, Palo Alto, CA: Mayfield, 1977, 3–4, 10.

21 Morton Fried, *The Notion of the Tribe*, Menlo Park, CA: Cummings, 1975, following on from his "On the Concepts of 'Tribe' and 'Tribal Society,'" in J. Helm (ed.), *Essays on the Problem of the Tribe*, Seattle, WA: American Ethnological Society, 1968, 3–20. More recently, see R. Brian Ferguson and Neil L. Whitehead, *War in the Tribal Zone: Expanding States and Indigenous Warfare* (School of American Research Advanced Seminar Series), Santa Fe, NM: SAR Press, 2000.

22 Lewis Morgan, *League of the Ho-De-No Sau-Nee or Iroquois*, New Haven, CT: Human Relations Area Files, [1851] 1954, is pioneering. More recently, see Dean Snow, *The Iroquois*, Cambridge, MA: Blackwell, 1994; Daniel Richter, *The Ordeal of the Longhouse: The People of the Iroquois League in the Era of European Colonization*, Chapel Hill, NC: University of North Carolina Press, 1992; Francis Jennings, *The Ambiguous Iroquois Empire*, New York: Norton, 1984; Bruce Trigger, "Maintaining Economic Equality in Opposition to Complexity: An Iroquoian Case Study," in S. Upham (ed.), *The Evolution of Political Systems: Sociopolitics in Small-Scale Sedentary Societies*, Cambridge University Press, 1990, 119–145.

23 Edward James, *The Franks*, Oxford: Blackwell, 1988, 35–36.

24 Dell Hymes, "Linguistic Problems in Defining the Concept of the Tribe," in Helm, *The Problem of the Tribe*, 23–48, overlooks these distinctions between ethnos, language, and tribe. But see, e.g., Fredrick Barth, "Introduction," in F. Barth (ed.), *Ethnic Groups and Boundaries*, London: George Allen, 1969, 9–38.

25 L. L. Cavalli-Sforza *et al.*, *The History and Geography of Human Genes*, Princeton University Press, 1994, 158–194; and more up to date, Gemma Berniell-Lee *et al.*, "Genetic and Demographic Implications of the Bantu Expansion: Insights from Human Paternal Lineages," *Molecular Biology and Evolution*, 26(7) (2009), 1581–1589.

26 A. J. Ammerman and L. L. Cavalli-Sforza, *The Neolithic Transition and the Genetics of Populations in Europe*, Princeton University Press, 1984; Cavalli-Sforza *et al.*, *The History and Geography of Human Genes*; Colin Renfrew,

Archaeology and Language, Cambridge University Press, 1987; Colin Renfrew, "The Origins of World Linguistic Diversity: An Archaeological Perspective," in N. Jablonski and L. Aiello (eds.), *The Origins and Diversification of Language*, San Francisco, CA: California Academy of Sciences, 1998; T. Price, A. Gebauer, and L. Keeley, "The Spread of Farming into Europe North of the Alps," in T. Price and A. Gebauer (eds.), *Last Hunters – First Farmers*, Santa Fe, NM: SAR Press, 1992, 95–126; the contributions by Cavalli-Sforza, Renfrew, J. Thomas, M. Zvelebil, and T. Price, in D. Harris (ed.), *The Origins and Spread of Agriculture and Pastoralism in Eurasia*, Washington, DC: Smithsonian, 1996; Robin Dennell, "The Hunter-Gatherer/Agricultural Frontier in Prehistoric Temperate Europe," in S. Green and S. Perlman (eds.), *The Archaeology of Frontiers and Boundaries*, London: Academic Press, 1985, 113–139; Stephen Oppenheimer, *Out of Eden: The Peopling of the World*, London: Constable, 2003, xxi.

27 J. L. Mountain *et al.*, "Congruence of Genetic and Linguistic Evolution in China," *Journal of Chinese Linguistics*, 20 (1992), 315–331; Ian Glover and Charles Higham, "New Evidence for Early Rice Cultivation in South, Southeast and East Asia," and Peter Bellwood, "The Origins and Spread of Agriculture in the Indo-Pacific Region: Gradualism and Diffusion or Revolution and Colonization," both in Harris (ed.), *The Origins and Spread of Agriculture*, 413–441, 465–498. An excellent synthesis is Jared Diamond and Peter Bellwood, "Farmers and their Languages: The First Expansions," *Science*, April 2003, 597–603.

28 Mark Hudson, *Ruins of Identity: Ethnogenesis in the Japanese Islands*, Honolulu: U. of Hawaii, 1999; Diamond and Bellwood, "Farmers and their Languages", 601.

29 J. P. Mallory, *In Search of the Indo-Europeans*, London: Thames & Hudson, 1989, 76–81; Paul Barford, *The Early Slavs: Culture and Society in Early Medieval Eastern Europe*, London: British Museum, 2001, ch. 1; Zbigniew Kobylinski, "The Slavs," in P. Fouracre (ed.), *The New Cambridge Medieval History*, vol. 1: *c. 500–c. 700*, Cambridge University Press, 2005. A recent genetic study is K. Rebala *et al.*, "Y-STR Variation among Slavs: Evidence for the Slavic Homeland in the Middle Dnieper Basin," *Journal of Human Genetics*, 52(5) (2007), 406–414.

30 For the genetics see again Rebala *et al.*, "Y-STR Variation among Slavs."

31 The leading work on the subject is Anatoly Khazanov, *Nomads and the Outside World*, 2nd edn., Madison, WI: University of Wisconsin Press, 1994, see 119–152, 222–227. See also Roger Cribb, *Nomads in Archaeology*, Cambridge University Press, 1991, 45–54; Thomas Barfield, *The Nomadic Alternative*, Englewood Cliffs, NJ: Prentice Hall, 1993. Fredrik Barth's pioneering "A General Perspective on Nomad–Sedentary Relations in the Middle East," reprinted in his *Process and Form in Social Life: Selected Essays*, vol. 1,

London: Routledge, 1981, 187–197, focuses too narrowly on the economic cause of the pastoralists' advantage.

32 In stark contrast to his co-editor, Pierre Bonte's contribution to John Galaty and Bonte (eds.), *Herders, Warriors, and Traders*, Boulder, CO: Westview, 1991, 62–86, represents 1960s and 1970s trends in rejecting the notion of military domination by ethnically foreign pastoral incomers from the north as the basis for the Great Lakes' societies. There has been an overreaction to late nineteenth- and early twentieth-century theories, best represented by Franz Oppenheimer, *The State*, New York: Vanguard, 1926, which saw conquest by pastoralists as the general mechanism of the original state formation.

33 Giorgio Buccellati, *The Amorites of the Ur III Period*, Naples: Instituto Orientale, 1966; Mario Liverani, "The Amorites," in D. Wiseman (ed.), *Peoples of Old Testament Times*, Oxford University Press, 1973, 100–133; Anbar, *The Amorite Tribes in Mari*.

34 The debate more or less replicates itself with respect to the Amorites, the Aramaeans, and the Israelites. For a summary and references see my *War and Human Civilization*, Oxford: Oxford University Press, 2006, 195–9.

35 The idea that the early Semites were shepherds was widely held in the nineteenth century. More recently it has been mooted, e.g., by James Mellaart, *The Neolithic of the Near East*, London: Thames & Hudson, 1975, 280–282, and is interestingly developed by Mattanyah Zohar, "Pastoralism and the Spread of the Semitic Languages," in O. Bar Yosef and A. Khazanov (eds.), *Pastoralism in the Levant: Archaeological Materials in Anthropological Perspective*, Madison, WI: Prehistory Press, 1992, 43–63.

36 The idea was first demonstrated archaeologically by Marija Gimbutas, *The Kurgan Culture and the Indo-Europeanization of Europe: Selected Articles from 1952 to 1993*, Washington, DC: Institute for the Study of Man, 1997; and is most comprehensively developed by Mallory, *In Search of the Indo-Europeans*, and David Anthony, *The Horse, the Wheel and Language*, Princeton University Press, 2007, both superb.

37 Colin Renfrew, "Language Families and the Spread of Farming," in Harris (ed.), *The Origins and Spread of Agriculture*, esp. 73–76; developing R. Austerlitz, "Language-Family Density in North America and Africa," *Ural-Altaische Jahrbücher*, 52 (1980), 1–10; Johanna Nichols, *Language Diversity in Time and Space*, University of Chicago Press, 1992.

38 Morton Fried, *The Evolution of Political Society*, New York: Random House, 1967; Elman Service, *Origins of the State and Civilization: The Process of Cultural Evolution*, New York: Norton, 1975; William Sanders and David Webster, "Unilinealism, Multilinealism, and the Evolution of Complex Societies," in C. Redman *et al.* (eds.), *Social Archaeology*, New York: Academic Press, 1978, 249–302; T. D. Price and G. Feinman (eds.), *Foundations of Social Inequality*, New York: Plenum, 1995.

39 Sahlins, "Poor Man, Rich Man, Big-Man, Chief"; Marshall Sahlins, *Tribesmen*, Englewood Cliffs, NJ: Prentice Hall, 1968. For Africa, see I. Schapera, *Government and Politics in Tribal Societies*, London: Watts, 1956.

40 This universal relationship has been fully studied in relation to the pre-polis Greeks in Gabriel Herman, *Ritualised Friendship and the Greek City*, Cambridge University Press, 1987.

41 E. A. Thompson, *The Early Germans*, Oxford University Press, 1965, is good on the material underpinning of the transformation of Germanic society.

42 Cf. Colin Newbury, *Patrons, Clients, & Empire: Chieftaincy and Over-rule in Asia, Africa, and the Pacific*, Oxford University Press, 2003.

43 M. I. Finley, *The World of Odysseus*, rev. edn., London: Penguin, [1954] 1978; Jan Morris, "The Use and Abuse of Homer," *Classical Antiquity*, 5 (1986), 81–138.

44 Robert Drews, *Basileus: The Evidence of Kingship in Geometric Greece*, New Haven, CT: Yale University Press, 1983; C. G. Thomas, "From Wanax to Basileus: Kingship in the Greek Dark Age," *Hispania Antiqua*, 6 (1978), 187–206; Chester Starr (ed.), "The Age of Chieftains," *Individual and Community: The Rise of the* Polis *800–500 BC*, New York: Oxford University Press, 1986, 15–33; Walter Donlan, "The Social Groups of Dark Age Greece," *Classical Philology*, 80 (1985), 293–308; developed and revised in Donlan and Carol Thomas, "The Village Community of Ancient Greece: Neolithic, Bronze and Dark Age," *Studi Micenei ed Egeo-Anatolici*, 31 (1993), 61–69; and particularly, Walter Donlan, "The Pre-State Community in Greece," *Symbolae Osloenses*, 64 (1989), 5–29. Also, Yale Ferguson, "Chiefdoms to City-States: The Greek Experience," in T. Earle (ed.), *Chiefdoms: Power, Economy and Ideology*, New York: Cambridge University Press, 1991, 169–192.

45 Mallory, *In Search of the Indo-Europeans*, 125; D. A. Binchy, *Celtic and Anglo-Saxon Kingship*, Oxford University Press, 1970, 1–21; Herwig Wolfram, *History of the Goths*, Berkeley, CA: University of California Press, 1988, 96, 144; D. H. Green, *Language and History in the Early Germanic World*, Cambridge University Press, 1998, 133.

46 For a theoretical discussion, in addition to the studies cited in the following references, see Elman Service, *Primitive Social Organization*, New York: Random House, 1962; Allen Johnson and Timothy Earle, *The Evolution of Human Societies*, Stanford University Press, 1987, chs. 9–10; Earle, *Chiefdoms: Power, Economy and Ideology*; Robert Carneiro, "The Chiefdom: Precursor to the State," in G. Jones and R. Kautz (eds.), *The Transition to Statehood in the New World*, New York: Cambridge University Press, 1981, 37–79.

47 Kirch, *Polynesian Chiefdom*; Marshall Sahlins, *Social Stratification in Polynesia*, Seattle, WA: University of Washington Press, 1958.

48 Herodotus, Bk. v, ss. 66, 69; Aristotle, *The Constitution of the Athenians*, ss. 20–22.

49 T. J. Cornell, *The Beginnings of Rome: Italy and Rome from the Bronze Age to the Punic Wars (c. 1000–264)*, London: Routledge, 1995, 173–196.

50 Max Gluckman, "The Kingdom of the Zulu of South Africa," in M. Fortes and E. Evans-Pritchard (eds.), *African Political Systems*, Oxford University Press, 1940, 25–55; Max Gluckman, "The Rise of the Zulu Empire," *Scientific American*, 202 (1960), 157–168; Keith Otterbein, "The Evolution of Zulu Warfare" (1964), reprinted in his *Feuding and Warfare*, Longhorne, PA: Gordon & Breach, 1994, 25–32; Elman Service, *Origins of the State and Civilization*, New York: Norton, 1975, 104–116.

51 In addition to the references in n. 19 above, see: M. B. Rowton, "Dimorphic Structure and the Parasocial Element," *Journal of Near Eastern Studies*, 36 (1977), 181–198; also, Barth, *Process and Form*, 194.

52 See, e.g., Philip Khoury and Joseph Kostiner (eds.), *Tribes and State Formation in the Middle East*, London: Tauris, 1991; Philip Salzman, *Culture and Conflict in the Middle East*, Amherst, NY: Humanity Books, 2008.

53 Susan Lape, *Race and Citizen Identity in the Classical Athenian Democracy*, Cambridge University Press, 2010.

4 Premodern ethne, peoples, states, and nations around the world

1 Going beyond Weber's original distinction between the "patrimonial" and modern state, modernists hold that only the latter deserves to be designated a state. This is because of its clearer separation between the property of the ruler and ruled, and between the public and private domains in general. More than with the debate over the nation, this is partly a matter of semantics. See Max Weber, *General Economic History*, Blencoe, IL: Free Press, 1950, 313–314, 338ff; Max Weber, *Economy and Society*, New York: Bedminster, 1968, 56, 904–910; J. Shennan, *The Origins of the Modern European State 1450–1725*, London: Hutchinson, 1974; Gianfranco Poggi, *The Development of the Modern State: A Sociological Introduction*, Stanford University Press, 1978; Gianfranco Poggi, *The State: Its Nature, Development and Prospects*, Stanford University Press, 1990, esp. 25; Martin van Creveld, *The Rise and Decline of the State*, Cambridge University Press, 1999.

2 For a broader discussion, see Azar Gat, "Rural Petty-State and Overlordship: Missing Links in the Evolution of the Early State," *Anthropos*, 98(1) (2003), 127–142; Azar Gat, "Why City-States Existed? Riddles and Clues of Urbanization and Fortifications," in M. Hansen (ed.), *Comparative Studies of Six City-State Cultures*, Copenhagen: Royal Danish Academy of Sciences and Letters, 2002, 125–139.

3 Edward Cohen, *The Athenian Nation*, Princeton University Press, 2000; Roshwald, *The Endurance of Nationalism*, 22–30. See also Frank Walbank, "The Problem of Greek Nationality" (1951), *Selected Papers*,

Cambridge University Press, 1985, 1–19. For the restriction of citizenship to "autochthoneous" Athenians only, see Susan Lape, *Race and Citizen Identity in the Classical Athenian Democracy*, Cambridge University Press, 2010.

4 See the end of Chapter 1, and n. 53, above.

5 Gat, "Why City-States Existed?"

6 Gat, "Why City-States Existed?," developing on Colin Renfrew and J. Cherry (eds.), *Peer Polity Interaction and Socio-Political Change*, Cambridge University Press, 1986, particularly Renfrew's "Introduction," 1–18.

7 Stuart Bremer, "Dangerous Dyads: Conditions Affecting the Likelihood of Interstate War, 1816–1965," *Journal of Conflict Resolution*, 36 (1992), 309–341.

8 Aage Westenholz, "The Sumerian City-State," in Hansen, *Six City-State Cultures*, 30.

9 Westenholz, "The Sumerian City-State," 39.

10 Westenholz, "The Sumerian City-State," 39.

11 W. van Soldt (ed.), *Ethnicity in Ancient Mesopotamia*, Leiden: Netherlands Instituut voor het Nabije Oosten, 2005, is an assortment of papers on the subject.

12 For a somewhat different view on Canaanite ethnicity, see Ann Killebrew, *Biblical People and Ethnicity: An Archaeological Study of Egyptians, Canaanites, Philistines, and Early Israel 1300–1100 BC*, Atlanta, GA: Society of Biblical Literature, 2005, who admits, however, that the evidence is very scarce.

13 N. K. Sanders, *The Sea People: Warriors of the Ancient Mediterranean 1250–1150 BC*, London: Thames & Hudson, 1978; Trude Dothan, *The Philistines and their Material Culture*, New Haven, CT: Yale University Press, 1982; John Strange, "The Philistine City-States," in M. Hansen (ed.), *Comparative Studies of Thirty City-State Cultures*, Copenhagen: Royal Danish Academy of Sciences and Letters, 2000, 129–139.

14 The main source for the Sicilian wars is Diodorus Siculus, Bks. 11, 13, 14, 20; and for a few early cases of Greek collaboration with Carthage: Herodotus, Bk. VII, s. 165. For the Phoenicians in general, see Maria Aubet, *The Phoenicians and the West*, Cambridge University Press, 1993; Hans Georg Niemeyer, "The Early Phoenician City-States on the Mediterranean," in Hansen, *Thirty City-State Cultures*, 89–115.

15 A collection of articles, most of them sensible, can be found in I. Malkin (ed.), *Ancient Perceptions of Greek Ethnicity*, Cambridge, MA: Harvard University Press, 2001.

16 Jonathan Hall, *Hellenicity: Between Ethnicity and Culture*, University of Chicago Press, 2002, is knowledgeable but somewhat obscure. Jonathan Hall, *Ethnic Identity in Greek Antiquity*, Cambridge University Press, 1997, is very general. See also, Jan Paul Crielaard, "The Ionians in the Archaic Period: Shifting Identities in a Changing World," in T. Derks and N. Roymans (eds.),

Ethnic Constructs in Antiquity, Amsterdam: Amsterdam University Press, 2009, 37–84.

17 For a case study of Arcadia, see Thomas Nielsen, "Arkadia: City-Ethnicities and Tribalism," in M. Hansen, *Introduction to an Inventory of Poleis*, Copenhagen: Royal Danish Academy, 1996, 117–163. For Boeotia, see Stephanie Larson, *Tales of Epic Ancestry: Boiotian Collective Identity in the Late Archaic and Early Classical Periods*, Stuttgart: Franz Steiner, 2007. Also Crielaard, "The Ionians in the Archaic Period."

18 David Graf, "Medism: Greek Collaboration with Achaemenid Persia," unpublished doctoral dissertation, Ann Arbor, Michigan: University Microfilms, 1979.

19 Herodotus, Cambridge, MA: Harvard University Press/Loeb, 1946, Bk. VIII, s. 144.

20 For the league, see Victor Ehrenberg, *The Greek State*, London: Methuen, 1969, 103–131; Peter Rhodes, "The Greek *Poleis*: Demes, Cities and Leagues," in M. Hansen (ed.), *The Ancient Greek City-State*, Copenhagen: Royal Danish Academy, 1993, 161–182.

21 A. Sherwin-White, *The Roman Citizenship*, 2nd edn., Oxford University Press, 1973; Kurt Raaflaub, "City-State, Territory and Empire in Classical Antiquity," in A. Molho, K. Raaflaub, and J. Emlen (eds.), *City-States in Classical Antiquity and Medieval Italy*, Stuttgart: Franz Steiner, 1991, 565–588; Claude Nicolet, *Rome et la conquête du monde méditerranéen 264–27, Tome 1: Les structures de l'Italie romaine*, Paris: Presses universitaires de France, 1993.

22 T. J. Cornell, *The Beginnings of Rome: Italy and Rome from the Bronze Age to the Punic Wars (c. 1000–264)*, London: Routledge, 1995, 204–208, 320, 351, 380–385.

23 Mary Hodge, "When is a City-State: Archaeological Measures of Aztec City-States and Aztec City-State Systems," in D. Nichols and T. Carlton (eds.), *The Archaeology of City-States: Cross-Cultural Approaches*, Washington, DC: Smithsonian, 1997, 169–207, 209–227; Michael Smith, "Aztec City-States," in Hansen (ed.), *Thirty City-State Cultures*, 581–595; and sensibly in R. Grillo, *Pluralism and the Politics of Difference: State, Culture and Ethnicity in Comparative Perspective*, Oxford University Press, 1998, ch. 3.

24 Ross Hassig, *Aztec Warfare*, Norman, OK: University of Oklahoma Press, 1988, 236, 266–267.

25 Eva Krapf-Askari, *Yoruba Towns and Cities*, Oxford University Press, 1969; Robert Smith, *Kingdoms of the Yoruba*, London: Methuen, 1969; Graham Connah, *African Civilization: Precolonial Cities and States in Tropical Africa: An Archaeological Perspective*, Cambridge University Press; J. Peel, "Yoruba as a City-State Culture," in Hansen (ed.), *Thirty City-State Cultures*, 507–518.

26 Robert Griffeth, "The Hausa City-States from 1450 to 1804," in R. Griffeth and C. Thomas (eds.), *The City-State in Five Cultures*, Santa Barbara, CA: ABC-Clio, 1981, 143–180.

27 Ray Kea, "City-State Culture on the Gold Coast: The Fante City-State Federation in the Seventeenth and Eighteenth Centuries," in Hansen (ed.), *Thirty City-State Cultures*, 519–530.

28 Kingta Princewill, "The City-States of the Eastern Niger Delta," in Hansen (ed.), *Thirty City-State Cultures*, 533–545.

29 Mogens Hansen, "The Kotoko City-States," in Hansen (ed.), *Thirty City-State Cultures*, 531–532.

30 Judith Nagata, "In Defense of Ethnic Boundaries: The Changing Myths and Charters of Malay Identity," in C. Keyes (ed.), *Ethnic Change*, Seattle, WA: University of Washington Press, 1981, 87–116, citations from 97, 99.

31 Anthony Reid, "The Culture of Malay-Speaking City-States of the Fifteenth and Sixteenth Centuries," in Hansen (ed.), *Thirty City-State Cultures*, 417–429, citation from 426.

32 Daniel Waley, *The Italian City Republics*, New York: McGraw-Hill, 1978, 127.

33 Machiavelli, *The Prince*, Cambridge University Press, 1988, ch. 26, 90–91.

34 While this limited longevity is well noted in the Introduction and Conclusion to Griffeth and Thomas (eds.), *The City-State in Five Cultures*, xix, 195–197, 201–202, it remains a puzzle to most of the individual contributors. But see W. Runciman, "Doomed to Extinction: The *polis* as an Evolutionary Dead-End," in O. Murray and S. Price (ed.), *The Greek City*, Oxford University Press, 1990, 347–367; Giorgio Chittolini, "The Italian City-State and Its Territory," in Molho, Raaflaub, and Emlen (eds.), *City-States in Classical Antiquity and Medieval Italy*, 589–602; S. E. Finer, *The History of Government from the Earliest Times*, vol. 1, Oxford University Press, 1997, 369–384; Michael Mann, *The Sources of Social Power*, vol. 1, Cambridge University Press, 1986, 227–228; and Gat, *War in Human Civilization*, 309–322.

35 Gat, "Rural Petty-State and Overlordship: Missing Links in the Evolution of the Early State."

36 Cf. Anthony Smith's two definitions of the nation in his later-day theorizing: *The Antiquity of Nations*, Cambridge: Polity, 2004, 15–17 and *passim*.

37 Michael Hoffman, *Egypt before the Pharaohs*, London: Routledge, 1980; Feki Hassan, "The Predynastic of Egypt," *Journal of World Prehistory*, 2 (1988), 135–185; Michael Rice, *Egypt's Making*, London: Routledge, 1991; A. J. Spencer, *Early Egypt*, Norman, OK: University of Oklahoma Press, 1995.

38 Anthony Smith, *The Ethnic Origins of Nations*, Oxford: Blackwell, 1986, 43, 89.

39 B. Haring, "Occupation: Foreigner: Ethnic Difference and Integration in Pharaonic Egypt," in van Soldt (ed.), *Ethnicity in Ancient Mesopotamia*, 162–172, claims but fails to demonstrate the existence of substantial ethnic diversity within Egypt, other than foreigners.

40 Smith, *The Ethnic Origins of Nations*, 51, citing J. Pritchard (ed.), *Ancient Near Eastern Texts relating to the Old Testament*, Princeton University Press, 1955, 232.

41 Grosby, *Biblical Ideas of Nationality: Ancient and Modern.*

42 For the scant information available see Piotr Bienkowski (ed.), *Early Edom and Moab*, Sheffield: Collis, 1992.

43 Hans Kohn, *The Idea of Nationalism*, Toronto: Collier, [1944] 1969, 27–30, who also includes the ancient Greeks. The case is best made by traditionalists: Anthony Smith in his various works; Grosby, *Biblical Ideas of Nationalism: Ancient and Modern*; Roshwald, *The Endurance of Nationalism*, 14–22; David Goodblatt, *Elements of Ancient Jewish Nationalism*, Cambridge University Press, 2006 (with definitions quite similar to mine: pp. 21–26); and for the Hellenistic period, Doron Mendels, *The Rise and Fall of Jewish Nationalism*, New York, Doubleday, 1992.

44 Hastings, *The Construction of Nationhood.*

45 For an excellent recent work, which addresses much of the debate and serves as a corrective to their own earlier work, see Israel Finkelstein and Neil Silberman, *David and Solomon: In Search of the Bible's Sacred Kings and the Roots of the Western Tradition*, New York: Free Press, 2006.

46 Oded Bustenay, *Mass Deportations and Deportees in the Neo-Assyrian Empire*, Wiesbaden: Ludwig Reichert, 1979.

47 I. M. Diakonoff, "Elam," in I. Gershevitch (ed.), *The Cambridge History of Iran*, vol. II, Cambridge University Press, 1985, 1–24.

48 Thorkild Jacobsen, "Early Political Development of Mesopotamia" (1957), in his *Towards the Image of Tammuz and Other Essays on Mesopotamian History and Culture*, Cambridge, MA: Harvard University Press, 1970, 155–156.

49 Amélie Kuhrt, *The Ancient Near East c. 3000–330 BC*, vol. I, London: Routledge, 1995, 338.

50 Only a selection of works is cited here. For the nationalist reaction to the encounter with the West, see Kai-wing Chow, "Narrating Nation, Race, and National Culture: Imagining the Hanzu Identity in Modern China," in Kai-wing Chow, Kevin Doak, and Poshek Fu (eds.), *Constructing Nationhood in Modern East Asia*, Ann Arbor, MI: University of Michigan Press, 2001, ch. 2; Suisheng Zhao, *A Nation State by Construction: Dynamics of Modern Chinese Nationalism*, Stanford University Press, 2004. The modernist position was most prominently represented by Joseph Levenson, *Confucian China and its Modern Fate*, Berkeley, CA: University of California Press, 1968. For a recent restatement see, e.g.: C. X. G. Wei and Xiaoyuan Liu (eds.), *Exploring Nationalisms of China*, Westport, CT: Greenwood, 2002, especially chs. 1, 2, 7. For a non-dichotomous view of Chinese nationalism, old and modern, see Prasenjit Duara, "Bifurcating Linear History: Nation and History in China and India," *Positions*, 1(3) (1993), 779–804; Prasenjit Duara, *Rescuing History from the Nation: Questioning Narratives of Modern China*, University of Chicago Press, 1995; Michael Ng-Quinn, "National Identity in Premodern

China," and James Watson, "Rites or Beliefs? The Construction of a Unified Culture in Late Imperial China," both in L. Dittmer and S. Kim (eds.), *China's Quest for National Identity*, Ithaca, NY: Cornell University Press, 1993, 32–61, 80–103, respectively; Torbjörn Lodén, "Nationalism Transcending the State: Changing Conceptions of Chinese Identity," in S. Tønneson and H. Antlöv (eds.), *Asian Forms of the Nation*, Richmond: Curzon, 1996, 270–296; James Townsend, "Chinese Nationalism," in J. Unger (ed.), *Chinese Nationalism*, New York: Sharpe, 1996, 1–30; Michael Yahuda, "The Changing Faces of Chinese Nationalism: The Dimensions of Statehood," in Michael Leifer (ed.), *Asian Nationalism*, London: Routledge, 2000, 21–37; Henrietta Harrison, *China*, London: Arnold, 2001.

51 Kwang-Chih Chang, *The Archaeology of Ancient China*, 4th edn., New Haven, CT: Yale University Press, 1986; M. Loewe and E. Shaughnessy (eds.), *The Cambridge History of Ancient China*, Cambridge University Press, 1999; and for the genetics Bo Wen *et al.*, "Genetic Evidence Supports Demic Diffusion of Han Culture," *Nature*, 431 (2004), 302–305; Fuzhong Xue *et al.*, "A Spatial Analysis of Genetic Structure of Human Populations in China Reveals Distinct Difference between Maternal and Paternal Lineages," *European Journal of Human Genetics*, 16 (2008), 705–717.

52 Duara, *Rescuing History from the Nation*, 54.

53 Duara, *Rescuing History from the Nation*, 53.

54 Watson, "Rites or Beliefs?" 82.

55 Hans Bielenstein, *The Bureaucracy of Han Times*, Cambridge University Press, 1980, 114; D. Twitchett and M. Loewe (eds.), *The Cambridge History of China*, vol. 1, Cambridge University Press, 1986, 479.

56 Twitchett and Loewe (eds.), *The Cambridge History of China*, 512, 617–626; Mark Lewis, "The Han Abolition of Universal Military Service," in H. van de Ven (ed.), *Warfare in Chinese History*, Leiden: Brill, 2000, 33–76.

57 Frank Dikötter, *The Discourse of Race in Modern China*, Stanford University Press, 1992, 1–30; Yuri Pines, "Beasts or Humans: Pre-Imperial Origins of Sino-Barbarian Dichotomy," in R. Amitai and M. Biran (eds.), *Mongols, Turks and Others*, Leiden: Brill, 2004, 59–102.

58 Marc Abramson, *Ethnic Identity in Tang China*, Philadelphia, PA: University of Pennsylvania Press, 2008, 2.

59 This dual attitude is exhaustively elaborated with respect to the Manchu by Marc Elliott, *The Manchu Way: The Eight Banners and Ethnic Identity in Late Imperial China*, Stanford University Press, 2001.

60 Rolf Trauzettel, "Sung Patriotism as a Step towards Chinese Nationalism," in J. Haeger (ed.), *Crisis and Prosperity in Sung China*, Tucson, AZ: University of Arizona Press, 1975, 199–213; Hoyt Tillman, "Proto-Nationalism in Twelfth-Century China? The Case of Ch'en Liang," *Harvard Journal of Asiatic Studies*, 39 (1979), 403–428.

61 Trauzettel, "Sung Patriotism as a Step towards Chinese Nationalism," 204.

62 Trauzettel, "Sung Patriotism as a Step towards Chinese Nationalism," 206.

63 Trauzettel, "Sung Patriotism as a Step towards Chinese Nationalism," 207.

64 Jonathan Spence, *Treason by the Book*, New York: Penguin, 2002, 7.

65 Spence, *Treason by the Book*, 41.

66 Pei-kai Cheng and Michael Lestz with Jonathan Spence, *The Search for Modern China: A Documentary Collection*, New York: Norton, 1999, 65.

67 Ray Huang, *1587: The Year of No Significance: The Ming Dynasty in Decline*, New Haven, CT: Yale University Press, 1981, 142.

68 Huang, *1587: The Year of No Significance*, 84.

69 Townsend, "Chinese Nationalism", 13.

70 Chun-shu Chang, *The Rise of the Chinese Empire, vol. 1: Nation, State and Imperialism in Early China, c. 1600 BC–AD 8*, Ann Arbor, MI: University of Michigan Press, 2006, 263.

71 Elliott, *The Manchu Way*, xiv.

72 Elliott, *The Manchu Way*, 23–24.

73 Thomas Barfield, *The Perilous Frontier: Nomadic Empires and China, 221 BC to AD 1757*, Cambridge, MA: Blackwell, 1992.

74 John Duncan, "Proto-Nationalism in Pre-Modern Korea," in Sang-Oak Lee and Duk-Soo Park, *Perspectives on Korea*, Sydney: Wild Peony, 1998, 200–201.

75 Gi-Wook Shin, *Ethnic Nationalism in Korea: Genealogy, Politics, and Legacy*, Stanford University Press, 2006, with an Introduction on the modernist-traditionalist debate with respect to Korea, much of it by Koreans. Hyung Il Pai, *Constructing "Korean" Origins: A Critical Review of Archaeology, Historiography, and Racial Myth in Korean State-Formation Theories*, Cambridge, MA: Harvard University Press, 2000, is a scholarly critique of the myth-making by the Japanese imperial conquerors of Korea and by Korean nationalists regarding Korean prehistory. This has nothing to do with historical, premodern times.

76 Eric Hobsbawm, *Nation and Nationalism since 1780*, Cambridge University Press, 1990, 66.

77 For modernist views of Japanese nationalism see: Demar Brown, *Nationalism in Japan*, New York: Russell, [1955] 1971, a solid historical work that well documents Japanese kin–cultural identity from the beginning of recorded history, while deriving its categories of analysis from modernists Hayes and Kohn; Kosaku Yoshino, "Rethinking Theories of Nationalism: Japan's Nationalism in Marketplace Perspective," in K. Yoshino (ed.), *Consuming Ethnicity and Nationalism: Asian Experiences*, Honolulu, HI: University of Hawaii Press, 1999, 8–28, which nonetheless concludes that popular demand and not government manipulation sustains contemporary Japanese nationalism. See also John Lie, *Modern Peoplehood*, Cambridge, MA: Harvard

University Press, 2004, 140; Ian Nish, "Nationalism in Japan," in Leifer, *Asian Nationalism*, 82–90.

78 Citing the existence of small ethnic minorities in Japan, Tessa Morris-Suzuki, "The Frontiers of Japanese Identity," in Tønneson and Antlöv (eds.), *Asian Forms of the Nation*, 41–66, labors to point out that Japan is not "entirely" homogeneous.

79 See primarily Mark Hudson, *Ruins of Identity: Ethnogenesis in the Japanese Islands*, Honolulu, HI: University of Hawaii Press, 1999; while he walks on eggshells not to violate accepted concepts of ethnicity, his scholarly study basically confirms all the above. See also Joan Piggott, *The Emergence of Japanese Kingship*, Stanford University Press, 1997; Keiji Imamura, *Prehistoric Japan*, Honolulu, HI: University of Hawaii Press, 1996; and the first chapters in D. Brown (ed.), *The Cambridge History of Japan*, vol. 1, Cambridge University Press, 1993. Less useful is Gina Barnes, *China, Korea and Japan: The Rise of Civilization in East Asia*, London: Thames & Hudson, 1993.

80 For Japan's understanding of the world during that period, see Ronald Toby, "Three Realms/Myriad Countries: An 'Ethnography' of Other and the Re-bounding of Japan 1550–1750," in Chow, Doak, and Fu, *Constructing Nationhood in Modern East Asia*, 15–46.

81 Keith Taylor, *The Birth of Vietnam*, Berkeley, CA: University of California Press, 1983.

82 Christopher Goscha, "Anam and Vietnam in the New Indochinese Space, 1887–1945," in Tønneson and Antlöv (eds.), *Asian Forms of the Nation*, 67–92; David Henley, "Ethnographical Integration and Exclusion in Anticolonial Nationalism: Indonesia and Indochina," *Comparative Studies in Society and History*, 37 (1995), 286–324.

83 A massive study of the region is Victor Lieberman, *Strange Parallels: Southeast Asia in Global Context, c. 800–1830*, Cambridge University Press, 2 vols., 2003, 2009.

84 The two studies in the previous note are divided on whether or not the Vietnamese wanted a unified Indochinese state. However, given the attitude of the others, the point remains the same.

85 Hobsbawm, *Nation and Nationalism since 1780*.

86 Anderson, *Imagined Communities*, 158.

87 Mervin Meggitt, *Blood is Their Argument: Warfare among the Mae Enga of the New Guinea Highlands*, Palo Alto, CA: Mayfield, 1977, 2.

88 I. Schapera, *Government and Politics in Tribal Societies*, London: Watts, 1956, 11, 13–16.

89 David Anthony, *The Horse, the Wheel and Language*, Princeton University Press, 2007, ch. 6, esp. 104–108.

90 Crosby, *Biblical Ideas of Nationality*, 3 (and the authorities cited) and ch. 5; Nili Wazana, *All the Boundaries of the Land: The Promised Land in Biblical*

Thought in Light of the Ancient Near East, Grand Rapids, MI: Eisenbrauns, 2010, ch. 1, s. 3.

91 Elie Kedourie (ed.), "Introduction," *Nationalism in Asia and Africa*, New York: New American Library, 1970.

92 For a very effective criticism see Stein Tønneson and Hans Antlöv, "Asia in Theories of Nationalism and National Identity," in Tønneson and Antlöv (eds.), *Asian Forms of the Nation*, 1–39.

93 Most of the evidence comes from the vassal state of Arrapha rather than from Mitanni itself: T. Kendall, *Warfare and Military Matters in the Nuzi Tablets*, Ann Arbor, MI: University Microfilms, 1974. See also Annelies Kammenhuber's skepticism about the Aryan primacy in her *Hippolgia Hethitica*, Wiesbaden: Harrassowitz, 1961, and *Die Arier im Vorderen Orient*, Heidelberg: Winter, 1968, countered by Manfred Mayrhofer, *Die Arier im Vorderen Orient – ein Mythos?*, reprinted in his *Ausgewählte kleine Schriften*, Wiesbaden: L. Reichert, 1979, 48–71; Robert Drews, *The Coming of the Greeks: Indo-European Conquests in the Aegean and the Near East*, Princeton University Press, 1988, 140–147 and *passim*; Gernot Wilhelm, *The Hurrians*, Warminster: Aris, 1989.

94 Trevor Bryce, *The Kingdom of the Hittites*, Oxford University Press, 1998; Michael Beal, *The Organization of the Hittite Military*, Heidelberg: Winter, 1992.

95 Drews, *The Coming of the Greeks*.

96 Bustenay, *Mass Deportations and Deportees in the Neo-Assyrian Empire*.

97 Bustenay, *Mass Deportations and Deportees in the Neo-Assyrian Empire*, 139–140, 147; H. Saggs, *The Might that was Assyria*, London: Sidgwick & Jackson, 1984, 133ff, 243–248; J. Postgate, *Taxation and Conscription in the Assyrian Army*, Rome: Biblical Institute, 1974, esp. 208–211. Cf. Smith, *The Ethnic Origins of Nations*, 100–104.

98 Herodotus, London: Heinemann-Loeb, 1946, I.101.

99 Stuart Brown, "The Medikos Logos of Herodotus and the Evolution of the Median State," in A. Kuhrt and H. Sancisi-Weerdengurg (eds.), *Achaemenid History, vol. III: Method and Theory*, Leiden: Nederland Instituut voor het Nabije Oosten, 1988, 71–86.

100 I. M. Diakonoff, "Media," in Gershevitch, *The Cambridge History of Iran*, vol. II, 36–148.

101 Matthew Stolper, "The Kasr Archive," Ephraim Stern, "New Evidence on the Administrative Division of the Palestine in the Persian Period," and Heleen Sancisi-Weerdenburg, "The Quest for an Elusive Empire," all in Kuhrt and Sancisi-Weerdengurg (eds.), *Achaemenid History*, vol. III, 195–205, 221–226, 263–274, respectively; N. Sekunda, "Achaemenid Settlement in Caria, Lycia and Greater Phrygia," in H. Sancisi-Weerdengurg and A. Kuhrt (eds.), *Achaemenid History, vol. IV: Asia Minor and Egypt: Old Cultures in a New*

Empire, Leiden: Nederland Instituut voor het Nabije Oosten, 1991, 83–143; J. Cook, *The Persian Empire*, London: Dent, 1983, esp. 53,101–112.

102 Graf, "Medism," 36–39.

103 Studies on the size of Persian armies are legion, but in general see: Cook, *The Persian Empire*, 53, 101–125; Muhammad Dandamaev and Vladimir Lukonin, *Ancient Iran*, Cambridge University Press, 1989, 147–152, 222–234.

104 E. Yarshater (ed.), *The Cambridge History of Iran*, vol. III, Cambridge University Press, 1983; Josef Wieshöfer, *Ancient Persia: From 550 BC to AD 650*, London: Tauris, 1996.

105 For today, see Farhad Kazemi, "Ethnicity and the Iranian Peasantry," and David Menashri, "Khomeini's Policy towards Ethnic and Religious Minorities," both in M. Esman and I. Rabinovitz (eds.), *Ethnicity, Pluralism, and the State in the Middle East*, Ithaca, NY: Cornell University Press, 1988, 201–231; Richard Tapper, "Ethnic Identities and Social Categories in Iran and Afghanistan," in E. Tonkin, M. McDonald, and M. Chapman (eds.), *History and Ethnicity*, London: Routledge, 1989, ch. 15.

106 Bernard Lewis, "Rewriting Oneself," *The American Interest*, Spring 2006, 131.

107 Pierre Briant, "Ethno-classe dominante et populations soumises dans l'Empire achéménide: le cas d'Égypte," in Kuhrt and Sancisi-Weerdengurg (eds.), *Achaemenid History*, vol. III, 137–173.

108 R. van der Spek, "Multi-Ethnicity and Ethnic Segregation in Hellenistic Babylon," in Derks and Roymans, *Ethnic Constructs in Antiquity*, 101–115.

109 P. Bilde, T. Engberg-Pedersen, L. Hannestad, and J. Zahle (eds.), *Ethnicity in Hellenistic Egypt*, Aarhus: Aarhus University Press, 1992; Dorothy Thompson, "Hellenistic and Hellenes: The Case of Ptolemaic Egypt," in Malkin (ed.), *Ancient Perceptions of Greek Ethnicity*, 301–322; Mendels, *The Rise and Fall of Jewish Nationalism*, 16–24 and *passim*. Of the more general surveys, Michel Chauveau, *Egypt in the Age of Cleopatra: History and Society under the Ptolemies*, Ithaca, NY: Cornell University Press, 2000 is the most useful.

110 Bilde *et al.*, *Ethnicity in Hellenistic Egypt*.

111 For all the following see Sherwin-White, *The Roman Citizenship*.

112 Sherwin-White, *The Roman Citizenship*, 159.

113 Erich Gruen, *Culture and National Identity in Republican Rome*, London: Duckworth, 1992.

114 See J. N. Adams' monumental, *Bilingualism and the Latin Language*, Cambridge University Press, 2003, xix.

115 Adams, *Bilingualism and the Latin Language*, *passim*, and J. N. Adams' equally monumental, *The Regional Diversity of Latin 200 BC–AD 600*, Cambridge University Press, 2007.

116 For a collection of studies see Pt III in J. Adams, M. Janse and S. Swain (eds.), *Bilingualism in Ancient Society*, Oxford University Press, 2002; also, Sherwin-White, *The Roman Citizenship*, 442–444.

117 V. Parry and M. Yapp (eds.), *War, Technology and Society in the Middle East*, London: Oxford University Press, 1975; Rhoads Murphey, *Ottoman Warfare 1500–1700*, New Brunswick, NJ: Rutgers University Press, 1999, esp. 35–49.

118 Kemal Karpat, "The Ottoman Ethnic and Confessional Legacy in the Middle East," in Esman and Rabinovitz (eds.), *Ethnicity, Pluralism, and the State in the Middle East*, 35–53.

119 Generally, see Esman and Rabinovitz, *Ethnicity, Pluralism, and the State in the Middle East*; Philip Khoury and Joseph Kostiner (eds.), *Tribes and State Formation in the Middle East*, London: Tauris, 1991; Philip Salzman, *Culture and Conflict in the Middle East*, Amherst, NY: Humanity Books, 2008.

120 John Richards, *The Mughal Empire: The New Cambridge History of India*, vol. I, Pt 5, Cambridge University Press, 1993, 145–146.

121 Josephus, *The Jewish War*, vol. II, Cambridge, MA: Harvard University Press-Loeb, 1976, ch. xvi, s. 4.

5 Premodern Europe and the national state

1 Cf. Armstrong, *Nations before Nationalism*, 23–27.

2 More recently, see E. L. Jones, *The European Miracle: Environments, Economies, and Geopolitics in the History of Europe and Asia*, Cambridge University Press, 1987; John Hall, *Power and Liberties: The Causes and Consequences of the Rise of the West*, Oxford: Blackwell, 1985; David Landes, *The Wealth and Poverty of Nations*, New York: Norton, 1999.

3 Charles de Montesquieu, *The Spirit of the Laws*, Cambridge University Press, 1989, 17:6; also 17:4. A rare treatment of these questions is offered in Jared Diamond's Epilogue to his *Guns, Germs, and Steel: The Fate of Human Societies*, New York: Norton, 1997, 411–416.

4 S. Finer, *The History of Government from the Earliest Times*, Oxford University Press, 1997, 1305, recognizes that in Asia "country-states" were swallowed up within empires, whereas in Europe they were not; but he attempts no explanation of that difference. S. Eisenstadt's taxonomy in his *Political System of Empire*, New York: Free Press, 1963, 10–11, and that by Anthony Giddens, *The Nation-State and Violence*, Berkeley, CA: University of California Press, 1985, 79–80, comprise only patrimonial or bureaucratic empires and feudal systems but no premodern national states. By contrast, Charles Tilly, *Coercion, Capital, and European States, AD 990–1992*, Cambridge, MA: Blackwell, 1992, both recognizes a broader and older category of "national state" and attempts to explain its European ascendancy. He fails, however, to take into account both geography and ethnicity.

5 Eugene Borza, *In the Shadow of the Olympus: The Emergence of Macedon*, Princeton University Press, 1990, 281–282.

6 N. Hammond, *The Macedonian State: Origins, Institutions, and History*, Oxford University Press, 1989; Borza, *In the Shadow of the Olympus.*

7 Hammond, *The Macedonian State*, 49–52, 192–196.

8 Hammond, *The Macedonian State*, 53–70, 168–169.

9 Of the ancient sources, Arrian is regarded the most reliable: Bks. v.25–29, vii.8–11.

10 Arrian, Bks. iv.8–14, vii.8–11.

11 Hugh Seton-Watson, *Nations and States: An Inquiry into the Origins of Nations and the Politics of Nationalism*, Boulder, CO: Westview, 1977; Armstrong, *Nations before Nationalism*; Hastings, *The Construction of Nationhood.*

12 See, e.g., W. Pohl and H. Reimitz (eds.), *Strategies of Distinction: The Construction of Ethnic Communities, 300–800*, Leiden: Brill, 1998.

13 Florin Curta, *The Making of the Slavs: History and Archaeology of the Lower Danube Region c. 500–700*, Cambridge University Press, 2001, 344. Similar curious assertions are made in his *Southeastern Europe in the Middle Ages, 500–1250*, Cambridge University Press, 2006, 56, 59, 61; disregarding generations of linguistic and other research, Curta casually suggests that the Slavs did not immigrate to the Danube frontier from the north, but somehow emerged there in the middle of the first millennium. Why their language should be so similar to that of other Slavs in northern and eastern Europe remains unclear. It is unfortunate that these expert studies, well versed in the historical and archaeological evidence, are led astray into such fatuous claims.

14 For scholarly studies on the early Germans see: Thompson, *The Early Germans*; Todd, *The Early Germans*; Green, *Language and History in the Early Germanic World.*

15 Patrick Geary, *The Myth of Nations: The Medieval Origins of Europe*, Princeton University Press, 2002, 11, 41, 73–75, 78.

16 Peter Heather, *The Goths*, Oxford: Blackwell, 1996, xiv.

17 Again, Geary, *The Myth of Nations*, is typical in entirely overlooking the lands outside the old Roman realm.

18 In the theory of nationalism see: Hastings, *The Construction of Nationhood*, for a medieval origin; and Liah Greenfield, *Nationalism: Five Roads to Modernity*, Cambridge, MA: Harvard University Press, 1992, for a sixteenth-century origin and a European and world first.

19 See Stephen Oppenheimer's intriguing *The Origins of the British: A Genetic Detective Story*, New York: Carroll & Graf, 2006, 379.

20 Bede, *Ecclesiastical History of the English People*, London: Loeb, 1930, Bk. 1, ch. 34, 179.

21 Steven Bassett (ed.), *The Origins of Anglo-Saxon Kingdoms*, London: Leicester University Press, 1989; C. J. Arnold, *An Archaeology of the Early Anglo-Saxon*

Kingdoms, 2nd edn., London: Routledge, 1997, esp. ch. 8; Barbara Yorke, *Kings and Kingdoms of Early Anglo-Saxon England*, London: Seaby, 1992, esp. 15–24, 157–172; D. P. Kirby, *The Earliest English Kings*, London: Unwin, 1991. Frank Stenton, *Anglo Saxon England*, 3rd edn., Oxford University Press, 1971, is still a useful narrative.

22 Bede, *Ecclesiastical History of the English People*.

23 Bede, *Ecclesiastical History of the English People*, Bk. 1, ch. 1, 17; Bk. 5, ch. 23, 373. There are several individual accounts of clashes with these people.

24 Richard Abels, *Alfred the Great: War, Kingship and Culture in Anglo-Saxon England*, London: Longman, 1998.

25 Malcolm Godden, in *The Cambridge History of the English Language, vol.* 1: *The Beginnings to 1066*, ed. Richard Hogg, Cambridge University Press, 1992, 513.

26 Godden, *The Cambridge History of the English Language*; see also Patrick Wormald, "Bede, the *Bretwaldas* and the Origins of the *Gens Anglorum*," in P. Wormald (ed.), *Ideal and Reality in Frankish and Anglo-Saxon Society*, Oxford: Blackwell, 1983, 125.

27 Michael Swanton (trans. and ed.), *The Anglo-Saxon Chronicles*, London: Phoenix, 2000, citation from p. xviii.

28 Susan Reynolds, *Kingdoms and Communities in Western Europe 900–1300*, Oxford University Press, 1984, 6.

29 Duara, *Rescuing History from the Nation*, 53.

30 See. e.g., James Campbell, "The United Kingdom of England: The Anglo-Saxon Achievement," in A. Grant and K. Stringer (eds.), *Uniting the Kingdom? The Making of British History*, London: Routledge, 1995, 39–40.

31 Wormald, "Bede, the *Bretwaldas* and the Origins of the *Gens Anglorum*," 103.

32 Wormald, "Bede, the *Bretwaldas* and the Origins of the *Gens Anglorum*," 104; also 122.

33 Wormald, "Bede, the *Bretwaldas* and the Origins of the *Gens Anglorum*," 120.

34 Campbell, "The United Kingdom of England," 31–47; citation from 31.

35 Chris Wickham, *Framing the Early Middle Ages: Europe and the Mediterranean 400–800*, Oxford University Press, 2005, 49.

36 J. Breuilly, "Dating the Nation: How Old is an Old Nation?," in Ichijo and Uzelac (eds.), *When is the Nation*, 25.

37 See Sarah Foot's more cautious assessment: "The Historiography of the Anglo-Saxon 'Nation-State,'" in L. Scales and O. Zimmer (eds.), *Power and the Nation in European History*, Cambridge University Press, 2005, 125–142, esp. 137–138.

38 See, e.g., John Gillingham, "Henry of Huntingdon and the Twelfth-Century Revival of the English Nation," in S. Forde, L. Johnson, and A. Murray (eds.), *Concepts of National Identity in the Middle Ages*, Leeds: Leeds University Press, 1995, 75–101.

39 Charles Barber, *The English Language: A Historical Introduction*, Cambridge University Press, 1993, 142.

40 Reynolds, *Kingdoms and Communities*, 273, and generally 273–276.

41 Generally, see the articles in Grant and Stringer (eds.), *Uniting the Kingdom? The Making of British History*; also Hugh Kearney, *The British Isles: A History of Four Nations*, Cambridge University Press, 1990.

42 A. A. M. Duncan, *The Nation of Scots and the Declaration of Arbroath (1320)*, London: Historical Association, 1970, 14.

43 Duncan, *The Nation of Scots and the Declaration of Arbroath*, 16.

44 Duncan, *The Nation of Scots and the Declaration of Arbroath*, 20–21.

45 For the text, see James Ferguson, *The Declaration of Arbroath*, Edinburgh University Press, n.d., 4–7.

46 Linda Colley, *Britons: Forging the Nation 1707–1837*, New Haven, CT: Yale University Press, 1992.

47 Blair Gibson, "Chiefdoms, Confederacies, and Statehood in Early Ireland," in B. Arnold and B. Gibson (eds.), *Celtic Chiefdom, Celtic State*, Cambridge University Press, 1995, 116–128.

48 Krishan Kumar, *The Making of English National Identity*, Cambridge University Press, 2003, centers on this theme; also, Robert Young, *The Idea of English Ethnicity*, Oxford: Blackwell, 2008, x, 11–14.

49 R. Grillo, *Dominant Languages: Language and Hierarchy in Britain and France*, Cambridge University Press, 1989, 48–62.

50 An authoritative comprehensive history is Knut Helle (ed.), *The Cambridge History of Scandinavia, vol. I: Prehistory to 1520*, Cambridge University Press, 2003.

51 Saxo Gramaticus, *The History of the Danes, Books i–ix*, ed. H. Davidson, tr. P. Fisher, Cambridge: Brewer, 1996, Preface.

52 *Morkinskinna: The Earliest Icelandic Chronicle of the Norwegian Kings (1030–1157)*, trans. T. Andersson and K. Gade, Ithaca, NY: Cornell University Press, 2000, 100.

53 *Morkinskinna*, 101, 104–105, 215–217.

54 *Morkinskinna*, 184.

55 *Morkinskinna*, 187. For more on the patriotic spirit of the sagas see Kåre Lunden, "Was there a Norwegian National Ideology in the Middle Ages?," *Scandinavian Journal of History*, 20(1) (1995), 19–33. The whole issue is dedicated to the question of Scandinavian nationalism since medieval times.

56 Sverre Bagge, "Nationalism in Norway in the Middle Ages," *Scandinavian Journal of History*, 20(1) (1995), 1–18.

57 Ole Feldbaek, "Denmark," in O. Dann and J. Dinwiddy (ed.), *Nationalism in the Age of the French Revolution*, London: Hambledon, 1988, ch. 7. Despite the time frame of the title, the chapter documents the numerous expressions of love for the Danish fatherland in the literature of the early modern period.

58 Rosalind Mitchison (ed.), *The Roots of Nationalism*, Edinburgh: John Donald, 1980, is mostly devoted to Scandinavia.

59 Cf. in a very similar spirit Reynolds, *Kingdoms and Communities*, 289–297.

60 Leonard Krieger, "Germany," in O. Ranum (ed.), *National Consciousness, History, and Political Culture in Early-Modern Europe*, Baltimore, MD: Johns Hopkins University Press, 1975, 67.

61 For numerous such statements in the sources of the time, see Len Scales, "Late Medieval Germany: an Under-Stated Nation?," in Scales and Zimmer, *Power and the Nation in European History*, 172–174.

62 Richard Byrn, "National Stereotypes Reflected in German Literature," in Forde, Johnson, and Murray, *Concepts of National Identity in the Middle Ages*, 137–153.

63 A good study of the various German provinces and identities is Benjamin Arnold, *Medieval Germany 500–1300: A Political Interpretation*, London: Macmillan, 1997, Pt I. Also, on the fragmented linguistic cultural realm, see Scales, "Late Medieval Germany."

64 As Krieger, "Germany", correctly notes.

65 See Chapter 3, n. 29 and adjacent text.

66 A particularly minimalist view is presented by Frantisek Smahel, "The Hussite Movement: An Anomaly of European History?," in Mikuláš Teich (ed.), *Bohemia in History*, Cambridge University Press, 1998, ch. 4.

67 Quoted by Howard Kaminsky, *A History of the Hussite Revolution*, Berkeley, CA: University of California Press, 1967, 138, also 139, from Frantisek Palacky (ed.), *Documenta Mag. Joannis Hus*, Prague: Tempsky, 1869, 531f. Also Derek Sayer, *The Coasts of Bohemia: A Czech History*, Princeton University Press, 1998, 37.

68 Kaminsky, *A History of the Hussite Revolution*, 141–142, from Palacky, *Documenta*, 561f (in Latin).

69 Kaminsky, *A History of the Hussite Revolution*, 298.

70 Quoted by Sayer, *The Coasts of Bohemia*, 38.

71 Quoted by Sayer, *The Coasts of Bohemia*, 41.

72 Sayer, *The Coasts of Bohemia*, 41 (added emphasis).

73 Josef Macek, "The Monarch of the Estates," in Teich (ed.), *Bohemia in History*, ch. 5, esp. 109–111.

74 Josef Petráň and Lydia Petráňová, "The White Mountain as a Symbol in Modern Czech History", in Teich (ed.), *Bohemia in History*, ch. 7.

75 For the eighteenth and early nineteenth centuries see Rita Kruger, *Czech, German and Noble: Status and National Ideology in Habsburg Bohemia*, Oxford University Press, 2009.

76 Serhii Plokhy, *The Origins of the Slavic Nations: Premodern Identities in Russia, Ukraine, and Belarus*, Cambridge University Press, 2006.

77 Norman Davies, *God's Playground: A History of Poland*, Oxford University Press, 1981, 201–202, 206.

78 For a recent example in a long historiographic line, see Timothy Snyder, *The Reconstruction of Nations: Poland, Ukraine, Lithuania, Belarus 1569–1999*, New Haven, CT: Yale University Press, 2003.

79 David Althoen, "*Natione Polonus* and the *Naród Szlachecki*: Two Myths of National Identity and Noble Solidarity," *Zeitschrift für Ostmitteleuropa-Forschung*, 52(4) (2003), 475–508.

80 Plokhy, *The Origins of the Slavic Nations*, 167 (and 168).

81 Janusz Tazbir, "Polish National Consciousness in the Sixteenth to Eighteenth Century," *Harvard Ukrainian Studies*, 10(3–4) (1986), 316–317 and *passim*.

82 Tazbir, "Polish National Consciousness in the Sixteenth to Eighteenth Century," 319–320.

83 Davies, *God's Playground*, 94.

84 Generally, see Teresa Chynczewska-Hennel, "The National Consciousness of Ukrainian Nobles and Cossacks from the End of the Sixteenth to the Mid-Seventeenth Century," *Harvard Ukrainian Studies*, 10(3–4) (1986), 377–392.

85 Frank Sysyn, "Ukrainian–Polish Relations in the Seventeenth Century: The Role of National Consciousness and National Conflict in the Khmelnytsky Movement," in P. Potichnyj (ed.), *Poland and Ukraine*, Edmonton: University of Alberta Press, 1980, 64.

86 Plokhy, *The Origins of the Slavic Nations*, 237.

87 Cf. Tazbir, "Polish National Consciousness in the Sixteenth to Eighteenth Century," 329.

88 Davies, *God's Playground*, 497.

89 Jerzy Ochmański, "The National Idea in Lithuania from the 16th to the First Half of the 19th Century: The Problem of Cultural–Linguistic Differentiation," *Harvard Ukrainian Studies*, 10(3–4) (1986), 300.

90 Ochmański, "The National Idea in Lithuania from the 16th to the First Half of the 19th Century," 303–304, and throughout the article. For a different take see Snyder, *The Reconstruction of Nations: Poland, Ukraine, Lithuania, Belarus*, 18–19, 25.

91 Simon Franklin and Jonathan Shepard, *The Emergence of Rus 750–1200*, London: Longman, 1996, is excellent and covers the latest archaeological finds; the main literary source on this protohistorical process is the oral traditions codified in the *Primary Chronicle* in twelfth-century Kiev.

92 Jaroslaw Pelenski, *The Contest for the Legacy of Kievan Rus*, New York: Columbia University Press, 1998.

93 Michael Cherniavsky, "Russia," in Ranum (ed.), *National Consciousness, History, and Political Culture in Early-Modern Europe*, 119–120.

94 Marshall Poe, *"A People Born to Slavery": Russia in Early Modern European Ethnography, 1476–1748*, Ithaca, NY: Cornell University Press, 2000, 145, 162–164.

95 Nicholas Riasnovsky and Mark Steinberg, *A History of Russia*, New York: Oxford University Press, 2005, 156.

96 Hans Rogger, *National Consciousness in Eighteenth Century Russia*, Cambridge, MA: Harvard University Press, 1960; Greenfield, *Nationalism: Five Roads to Modernity*, ch. 3.

97 Paul Bushkovitch, "The Formation of a National Consciousness in Early Modern Russia," *Harvard Ukrainian Studies*, 10(3–4) (1986), 355.

98 Bushkovitch, "The Formation of a National Consciousness in Early Modern Russia," 355–357 and throughout his article.

99 Geoffrey Hosking, "The State of Russian National Identity," in Scales and Zimmer, *Power and the Nation in European History*, 195.

100 See, e.g., Michael Flier, "Political Ideas and Rituals," in *The Cambridge History of Russia, vol. 1: From Early Rus to 1689*, ed. Maureen Perrie, Cambridge University Press, 2006, ch. 17.

101 J. Basarab, *Pereiaslav 1654: A Historiographical Study*, Edmonton: University of Alberta Press, 1982.

102 Frank Sysyn, "Concepts of Nationhood in Ukrainian History Writing, 1620–1690," *Harvard Ukrainian Studies*, 10(3–4) (1986), 393–423.

103 For Ukrainian resistance in the eighteenth century see Zenon Kohut, "The Development of a Little Russian Identity and Ukrainian Nationbuilding," *Harvard Ukrainian Studies*, 10(3–4) (1986), 559–576.

104 Alexei Miller, *The Ukrainian Question: The Russian Empire and Nationalism in the Nineteenth Century*, Budapest: Central European University Press, 2003.

105 See, e.g., Geoffrey Hosking, *Russia: People and Empire 1552–1917*, Cambridge, MA: Harvard University Press, 1997; James Cracraft, "Empire Versus Nation: Russian Political Theory under Peter I," *Harvard Ukrainian Studies*, 10(3–4) (1986), 524–541; Vera Tolz, *Inventing the Nation: Russia*, London: Arnold, 2001, which accepts, however, that a Russian ethnos had existed since the sixteenth century.

106 For something along these lines see Plokhy, *The Origins of the Slavic Nations*, 289.

107 Aviel Roshwald, *Ethnic Nationalism and the Fall of Empires: Central Europe, Russia and the Middle East 1914–1923*, London: Routledge, 2001, 19.

108 Cited from Oleg Kharkhordin, "What is the State? The Russian Concept of the *gosudarstvo* in the European Context," *History and Theory*, 40 (2001), 206–240, citation from 220.

109 Quoted in Dominic Lieven, *Russia Against Napoleon*, New York: Viking, 2010, 215. See also for the whole subject, Janet Hartley, "Russia and Napoleon: State, Society and the Nation," in Michael Rowe (ed.), *Collaboration and Resistance in Napoleonic Europe*, Houndsmills: Palgrave Macmillan, 2003, 186–202, esp. 192–195.

110 Lieven, *Russia Against Napoleon*, 216.

111 Lieven, *Russia Against Napoleon*, 216.

112 Lieven, *Russia Against Napoleon*, 217.

113 Lieven, *Russia Against Napoleon*, 222.

114 Hosking, *Russia*, 133–137, 199.

115 P. M. Barford, *The Early Slavs*, London: British Museum, 2001, 124.

116 Barford, *The Early Slavs*, 134; also 227, 268.

117 Helmold, priest of Bosau, *The Chronicles of the Slavs*, New York: Octagon, 1966, 45.

118 A recent genetic study is K. Rebala *et al.*, "Y-STR Variation among Slavs: Evidence for the Slavic Homeland in the Middle Dnieper Basin," *Journal of Human Genetics*, 52(5) (2007), 406–414; citation from 406, and for the Poles see 408.

119 Rebala *et al.*, "Y-STR Variation among Slavs," 411–412.

120 G. Tömöry, B. Csányi, E. Bogácsi-Szabó *et al.*, "Comparison of Maternal Lineage and Biogeographic Analyses of Ancient and Modern Hungarian Populations," *American Journal of Physiological Anthropology*, 134(3) (2007), 354–368; citation from 354.

121 László Makkai, "István Bocskai Insurrectionary Army," in J. Bak and B. Király (eds.), *From Hunyadi to Rákóczi: War and Society in Late Medieval and Early Modern Hungary*, New York: Columbia University Press, 1982, 283.

122 Makkai, "István Bocskai Insurrectionary Army." For the early resort to peasant troops as a result of Hungary's desperate straits see Joseph Held, "Peasants in Arms, 1437–1438 & 1456," in Bak and Király (eds.), *From Hunyadi to Rákóczi*, 81–101.

123 Cited in László Benczédi, "Hungarian National Consciousness as Reflected in the Anti-Habsburg and Anti-Ottoman Struggles of the Late Seventeenth Century," *Harvard Ukrainian Studies*, 10(3–4) (1986), 430.

124 Benczédi, "Hungarian National Consciousness," 430.

125 Benczédi, "Hungarian National Consciousness," 431; also 435.

126 Benczédi, "Hungarian National Consciousness," 431.

127 Benczédi, "Hungarian National Consciousness," 436.

128 Ágnes Várkonyi, "Rákóczi's War of Independence and the Peasantry," *Harvard Ukrainian Studies*, 10(3–4) (1986), 369–391; citation from 373.

129 Charles Ingrao, "Guerilla Warfare in Early Modern Europe: The *Kuruc* War (1703–1711)," in B. Király and G. Rothenberg (eds.), *War and Society in East Central Europe, vol. I: Special Topics and Generalizations on the 18th and 19th Centuries*, New York: Columbia University Press, 1979, 48, 49.

130 Ingrao, "Guerilla Warfare in Early Modern Europe," 51.

131 Béla Király, "War and Society in Western and East Central Europe in the Pre-Revolutionary Eighteenth Century," in B. Király and P. Sugar (eds.), *East Central European Society and War in the Pre-Revolutionary Eighteenth Century*, New York: Columbia University Press, 1982, 21.

132 Two useful surveys are M. Harris and N. Vincent (eds.), *The Romance Languages*, London: Croom Helm, 1988; Rebecca Posner, *The Romance Languages*, Cambridge University Press, 1996.

133 See Chapter 4.

134 J. H. Elliott, *The Revolt of the Catalans: A Study in the Decline of Spain 1598–1640*, Cambridge University Press, 1963, 513.

135 Elliott, *The Revolt of the Catalans*, 5, 7, 29, 421–422.

136 Elliott, *The Revolt of the Catalans*, 422.

137 Colette Beaune, *The Birth of an Ideology: Myths and Symbols of Nation in Late Medieval France*, Berkeley, CA: University of California Press, 1991, 308–309.

138 Cf. Reynolds, *Kingdoms and Communities*, 278–289.

139 A. R. Myers (ed.), *English Historical Documents 1327–1485*, Abingdon: Routledge, 1996, 228.

140 Susan Reynolds, "Medieval *Origines Gentium* and the Community of the Realm," in her *Ideas and Solidarities in the Medieval Laity, vol. ii*, Aldershot: Variorum, 1995, 380–381; Margaret Canovan, *The People*, Cambridge: Polity, 2005, 16.

141 Beaune, *The Birth of an Ideology*, 9 (added emphasis).

142 Beaune, *The Birth of an Ideology*, 9–10 (added emphasis).

143 *The Trial of Joan of Arc*, trans. Daniel Hobbins, Cambridge, MA: Harvard University Press, 2005, 134.

144 *The Trial of Joan of Arc*, March 17, 1431, p. 110.

145 Beaune, *The Birth of an Ideology, passim*; also, Marc Bloch, *The Royal Touch: Sacred Monarchy and Scrofula in England and France*, London: Routledge, 1973.

146 Beaune, *The Birth of an Ideology* 19; also 192.

147 Beaune, *The Birth of an Ideology*, 1.

148 Emmanuel Le Roy Ladurie, *The Royal French State 1460–1610*, Oxford: Blackwell, 1994, 54.

149 Le Roy Ladurie, *The Royal French State 1460–1610*, 282.

150 Beaune, *The Birth of an Ideology*, 310.

151 Beaune, *The Birth of an Ideology*, 4–5.

152 William Church, "France," in Ranum (ed.), *National Consciousness, History, and Political Culture in Early-Modern Europe*, 45.

153 Bernard Guenée, "The History of the State in France at the End of the Middle Ages, as seen by French Historians in the Last Hundred Years," in P. Lewis and G. Martin (eds.), *The Recovery of France in the Fifteenth Century*, New York: Harper, 1971, 341.

154 Myriam Yardeni, *La conscience nationale en France pendant les guerres de religion (1559–1598)*, Louvain: Nauwelaerts, 1971, quotation from 332.

155 Eugen Weber, *Peasants into Frenchmen: The Modernization of Rural France, 1870–1914*, Stanford University Press, 1976.

156 Ernest Renan, "What is a Nation" (1882), in H. Bhabha (ed.), *Nations and Narration*, London: Routledge, 1990, 8–22.

157 Cf. Kumar, *The Making of English National Identity*.

158 While drawing the conventional distinction between French "civic" and German "ethnic" concepts originally suggested by Hans Kohn, Rogers Brubaker, *Citizenship and Nationhood in France and Germany*, Cambridge, MA: Harvard University Press, 1992, is well aware that the French model demanded cultural assimilation.

159 See above, Introduction, n. 9 and adjacent text.

160 Also with the same thrust, though of not quite the same quality, is E. D. Marcu, *Sixteenth Century Nationalism*, New York: Abaris, 1976.

161 Len Scales and Oliver Zimmer, "Introduction," in Scales and Zimmer (eds.), *Power and the Nation in European History*, 1.

162 Scales and Zimmer, "Introduction," in Scales and Zimmer (eds.), *Power and the Nation in European History*, 1–2.

163 The claim seems to have been introduced by Guido Zernatt, "Nation: The History of a Word," *Review of Politics*, 6 (1944), 351–366, and then copied from one study to another.

164 Reynolds, *Kingdoms and Communities in Western Europe*, 255–256.

165 Reynolds, *Kingdoms and Communities in Western Europe*, 254; see also Susan Reynolds, "The Idea of the Nation as a Political Community," in Scales and Zimmer, *Power and the Nation in European History*, 54–66.

166 Julia Smith, *Europe after Rome: A New Cultural History 500–1000*, Oxford University Press, 2005, 261, and generally 261–267.

167 Johan Huizinga, "Patriotism and Nationalism in European History" (1940), in his *Men and Ideas*, London: Eyre, 1960, 106–107.

168 Huizinga, "Patriotism and Nationalism in European History," 103–105.

169 Huizinga, "Patriotism and Nationalism in European History," 99.

170 Althoen, "*Natione Polonus* and the *Naród Szlachecki*: Two Myths of National Identity and Noble Solidarity," 500–502.

171 Louis Loomis, "Nationality at the Council of Constance: An Anglo-French Dispute," in S. Thrupp (ed.), *Change in Medieval Society*, New York: Appleton, 1964, 279–296. Although familiar with the subject, Zernatt, "Nation," 358, gets the facts completely wrong.

172 Loomis, "Nationality at the Council of Constance," 291, citing Herman von der Hardt, *Magnum oecumenicum Constantiense Concilium*, vol. v, Frankfurt: 1700, 92.

173 Loomis, "Nationality at the Council of Constance," 293.

174 Loomis, "Nationality at the Council of Constance," 292.

175 This is not the only problem with Shlomo Sand's flawed and tendentious *The Invention of the Jewish People*, London: Verso, 2009.

176 Petrovich, "Religion and Ethnicity in Eastern Europe" (1980), reprinted in Hutchinson and Smith (eds.), *Nationalism*, vol. IV, 1356–1381, citations from 1359, 1361, 1367.

177 Connor Cruise O'Brien, *God Land: Reflections on Religion and Nationalism*, Cambridge, MA: Harvard University Press, 1988; Hastings, *The Construction of Nationhood*; Steven Grosby, *Biblical Ideas of Nationality: Ancient and Modern*; Philip Gorski, "The Mosaic Moment: An Early Modernist Critique of Modernists Theories of Nationalism," *American Journal of Sociology*, 105 (2000), 1428–1468; Anthony Smith, *Chosen Peoples*, Oxford University Press, 2003; Anthony Marx, *Faith in Nation: Exclusionary Origins of Nationalism*, New York: Oxford University Press, 2003.

178 Beaune, *The Birth of an Ideology*, 19.

179 Alexander Grant, *Independence and Nationhood: Scotland 1306–1469*, London: Arnold, 1984, 7.

180 Grant, *Independence and Nationhood: Scotland 1306–1469*, 90, 72.

181 Miroslav Hroch, *Social Preconditions of National Revival in Europe: A Comparative Analysis of the Social Composition of Patriotic Groups among the Smaller European Nations*, Cambridge University Press, 1985, 48–49, 64–69, 100–103, 109–111, 130, 156.

182 See above Chapter 4.

183 Reynolds, "The Idea of the Nation as a Political Community," in Scales and Zimmer (eds.), *Power and the Nation in European History*, 56.

184 Norman Stone, Sergei Podbolotov, and Murat Yasar, "The Russians and the Turks: Imperialism and Nationalism in the Era of Empires," in Miller and Rieber (eds.), *Imperial Rule*, 33–35.

185 Elliott, *The Revolt of the Catalans*, 11, but also 182.

186 Stone, Podbolotov, and Yasar, "The Russians and the Turks."

187 Breuilly "Changes in the Political Uses of the Nation," in Scales and Zimmer (eds.), *Power and the Nation in European History*, 80–81.

188 Michael Walzer, "Pluralism in Political Perspective," in M. Walzer, E. Kantowicz, J. Higham, and M. Harrington (eds.), *The Politics of Ethnicity*, Cambridge, MA: Harvard University Press, 1982, 1.

189 Reynolds, *Kingdoms and Communities*, 251–252.

190 Stanisław Urbańczyk, "The Origins of the Polish Literary Language," in G. Stone and D. Worth (eds.), *The Formation of the Slavonic Literary Languages*, Columbus, OH: Slavica, 1985, 110; also 109 and 113. For other studies, which do not even mention the question of mutual comprehension, see: Edward Stankiewicz (ed.), "The Phonetic Patterns of the Polish Dialects," *The Slavic Languages: Unity in Diversity*, Berlin: Mouton, 1986, 63–83; R. de Bray, *Guide to the Slavonic Languages*, London: Dent, 1969, 601–605.

191 Urbańczyk, "The Origins of the Polish Literary Language," 111.

192 Tazbir, "Polish National Consciousness in the Sixteenth to Eighteenth Century," 319–320.

193 Alexander Schenker, "Polish," in A. Schenker and E. Stankiewicz (eds.), *The Slavonic Literary Languages: Formation and Development*, New Haven, CT: Yale Concilium on International and Area Studies, 1980, 210; Stankiewicz, *The Slavic Languages*, 64; Robert Rothstein, "Polish," in B. Comrie and G. Corbett (eds.), *The Slavonic Languages*, London: Routledge, 1993, 686–758, esp. 754–756.

194 V. Vinogradov, *The History of the Russian Literary Language from the Seventeenth Century to the Nineteenth*, Madison, WI: University of Wisconsin Press, 1969.

195 Robert Auty, "Czech," in Schenker and Stankiewicz (eds.), *The Slavonic Literary Languages*, 165.

196 Charles Tilly (ed.), *The Formations of National States in Western Europe*, Princeton University Press, 1975, 24.

197 Reynolds, *Kingdoms and Communities*, 330–331; her "The Idea of the Nation as a Political Community" is even more emphatic.

198 Sysyn, "Ukrainian–Polish Relations in the Seventeenth Century," 64.

199 Bushkovitch, "The Formation of a National Consciousness in Early Modern Russia," 355.

6 Modernity: nationalism released, transformed, and enhanced

1 See, e.g., Joad Raymond, *The Invention of the Newspaper: English Newsbooks 1641–1649*, Oxford University Press, 1996; Bob Harris, *Politics and the Rise of the Press: Britain and France, 1620–1800*, London: Routledge, 1996.

2 Jan de Vries, *European Urbanization 1500–1800*, Cambridge, MA: Harvard University Press, 1984; Paul Hohenberg and Lynn Lees, *The Making of Urban Europe 1000–1950*, Cambridge, MA: Harvard University Press, 1995.

3 Eugene Weber, *Peasants into Frenchmen: The Modernization of Rural France 1870–1914*, Stanford University Press, 1976, is a superb historical mosaic which covers this process. Surprisingly, however, it fails even to mention earlier stages in the consolidation of French nationalism, most notably the French Revolution.

4 John Stuart Mill, *Considerations on Government by Representatives*, New York: Harper, 1862, ch. 16, 310. For the relationship between democracy and nationalism see Benjamin Akzin, *State and the Nation*, London: Hutchinson, 1964, 51–52; Ghia Nodia, "Nationalism and Democracy" and the other essays in L. Diamond and M. Plattner (eds.), *Nationalism, Ethnic Conflict, and Democracy*, Baltimore, MD: Johns Hopkins University Press, 1994.

5 Ernest Gellner, *Nationalism*, New York: New York University Press, 1997, 41–42.

6 Douglas Dakin, *The Greek Struggle for Independence 1821–1833*, London: Batsford, 1973, e.g., 59; Charles Frazee, *The Orthodox Church and Independent Greece 1821–1852*, Cambridge University Press, 1969, 19, 40, 45 and *passim*.

7 Dakin, *The Greek Struggle for Independence 1821–1833*, 313.

8 Gellner, *Nationalism*, 42.

9 Georges Castellan, *History of the Balkans*, Boulder, CO: East European Monographs, 1992, 253.

10 Gellner, *Nationalism*, 41.

11 I have not been able to find a secure reference for the verse, cited in Wikipedia, available at: http://en.wikipedia.org/wiki/Banat_uprising_of_1594.

12 Leopold von Ranke, *A History of Servia and the Servian Revolution*, New York: Da Capo, 1973 [1848], 36. The father of modern historical scholarship routinely refers to a medieval and early modern Serb *nation*.

13 Castellan, *History of the Balkans*, 233; Misha Glenny, *The Balkans 1804–1999*, London: Granta, 1999, 11.

14 Gellner, *Nationalism*, 42.

15 Castellan, *History of the Balkans*, 343–349; B. Kiraly and G. Stokes (eds.), *Insurrections, Wars, and the Eastern Crisis in the 1870s*, New York: Columbia University Press, 1985, 20–21, 207. Michael Palairet's scholarly and exhaustive, *The Balkan Economies c. 1800–1914: Evolution without Development*, Cambridge University Press, 1997, argues that modernization was actually stronger under the Ottomans and declined after independence.

16 Richard Shannon, *Gladstone and the Bulgarian Agitation 1876*, Hassocks: Harvester, 1975.

17 Bistra Cvetkova, "The Bulgarian Haiduk Movement in the 15th–18th Centuries," in B. Király and P. Sugar (eds.), *East Central European Society and War in the Pre-Revolutionary Eighteenth Century*, New York: Columbia University Press, 1982, 301–338, citation from 329.

18 Aviel Roshwald, *Ethnic Nationalism & the Fall of Empires: Central Europe, Russia and the Middle East, 1914–1923*, London: Routledge, 2001, 22–23; see chs. 2–3 for an excellent comparative overview of the three eastern empires. Also, A. Miller, *The Ukrainian Question*.

19 A very good, nuanced study is Francine Hirsch, *Empire of Nations: Ethnographic Knowledge and the Making of the Soviet Union*, Ithaca, NY: Cornell University Press, 2005. Hirsch emphasizes the genuine Bolshevik belief in the incorporation of the various nationalities and ethnicities in the communist project and the seriousness of their efforts to give the various nationalities political self-expression. Nonetheless, massive coercion was the *sine qua non* of the system.

20 Quoted by Mark Cornwall, "The Habsburg Monarchy," in T. Baycroft and M. Hewitson (eds.), *What is a Nation? Europe 1789–1914*, Oxford University Press, 2006, 171.

21 Roshwald, *Ethnic Nationalism*, 18.

22 There were many such expressions, but see, e.g., the contributions by Jack Snyder and Karen Ballentine, John Mueller, and David Lake and Donald Rothchild, in M. Brown, O. Coté, S. Lynn-Jones, and S. Miller (eds.), *National and Ethnic Conflict*, Cambridge, MA: MIT Press, 2001.

23 A recent invocation of this distinction is Michael Ignatieff, *Blood and Belonging: Journey into the New Nationalism*, New York: Farrar, Straus & Grioux, 1993. W. Kymlicka and M. Opalski (eds.), *Can Liberal Pluralism be Exported? Western Political Theory and Ethnic Realities in Eastern Europe*, Oxford University Press, 2001, offers some considerations on the same issue, although Kymlicka seriously doubts the civic–ethnic divide.

24 For various qualifications and criticisms of the civic–ethnic distinction, see Brubaker, *Citizenship and Nationhood in France and Germany*; Anthony Smith, *Nations and Nationalism in the Global Era*, 97–102; Kymlicka, *Politics in the Vernacular*, 243–244; R. Smith, *Stories of Peoplehood*, 74–92; Roshwald, *The Endurance of Nationalism*, ch. 5; Baycroft and Hewitson, *What is a Nation?*, *passim*.

25 Cf. Mark Hewitson, "Conclusion," in Baycroft and Hewitson (eds.), *What is a Nation?*, 315–316.

26 A detailed study of the differences between the French civic and German ethnic immigration laws since the nineteenth century is Brubaker, *Citizenship and Nationhood in France and Germany*. The author is well aware that the French model demands cultural assimilation.

27 Again compare most notably: A. Smith, *Nations and Nationalism in the Global Era*, 97–102; Kymlicka, *Politics in the Vernacular*, 243–244; R. Smith, *Stories of Peoplehood*; Baycroft and Hewitson (eds.), *What is a Nation?*

28 For the nineteenth century, see Carl Strikwerda, "The Low Countries," in Baycroft and Hewitson (eds.), *What is a Nation?*, 81–99.

29 Jaroslav Krejčí and Vítězslav Velímský, *Ethnic and Political Nations in Europe*, London: Croom Helm, 1981, ch. 7; Ulrich Hof, "Switzerland," in O. Dann and J. Dinwiddy (eds.), *Nationalism in the Age of the French Revolution*, London: Hambledon Press, 1988, 183–198; Jürg Steiner, "Switzerland and the European Union: A Puzzle," in M. Keating and J. McGarry (eds.), *Minority Nationalism and the Changing International Order*, Oxford University Press, 2001, 137–154; Andreas Wimmer, *Nationalist Exclusion and Ethnic Conflict*, Cambridge University Press, 2002, ch. 8; Oliver Zimmer, "Switzerland," in Baycroft and Hewitson (eds.), *What is a Nation?*, 120–151.

30 Steiner, "Switzerland and the European Union," 144–150.

31 Bruce Russett and John Oneal, *Triangulating Peace: Democracy, Interdependence and International Organizations*, New York: Norton, 2001; Azar Gat, *Why Democracy Won in the 20th Century and How it is Still Imperiled*, published for the Hoover Institution, Stanford, by Rowman & Littlefield, 2009.

32 Montserrat Guibernau, *Nations without States: Political Communities in the Global Age*, Cambridge: Polity, 1999; J. McGarry and M. Keating (eds.), *European Integration and the Nationalities Question*, London: Routledge, 2006; A. Smith, *Nations and Nationalism in the Global Era*, 121–143.

33 Cf. Philip Barker, *Religious Nationalism in Modern Europe*, Abingdon: Routledge, 2009.

34 Michael Billig, *Banal Nationalism*, London: Sage, 1995.

35 Much of the following has been foreshadowed by A. Smith, *Nations and Nationalism in the Global Era*, 107–109.

36 Michael Lind, *The Next American Nation*, New York: Free Press, 1995, 57.

37 Lind, *The Next American Nation*, 279.

38 Lind, *The Next American Nation*, 265–277.

39 For this misconception, see Thomas Sowell, *Ethnic America: A History*, New York: Basic Books, 1981, 4. The literature on American ethnicity and ethnic groups is legion. Lawrence Fuchs, *The American Kaleidoscope: Race, Ethnicity and the Civic Culture*, Lebanon, NH: University Press of New England, 1990, celebrates the history of American civic nationhood. Michael Walzer is more discerning and nuanced in recognizing, among other things, that in American history immigrants' assimilation into American culture generally followed naturalization; yet he believes that with the ethnic resurgence this is no longer the case, nor should it be, because the state can and should be neutral about ethnicity: Walzer, "Pluralism in Political Perspective," in Walzer, *et al., The Politics of Ethnicity*, 1–28; M. Walzer, "Comment," in A. Gutmann (ed.), *Multiculturalism: Examining the Politics of Recognition*, Princeton University Press, 1994, 99–103; M. Walzer, *What It Means to be an American*, Delhi: East-West Publishing, 1994. There is a great difference, however, between favorable acceptance of other cultures and neutrality, which the English-speaking United States is far from exercising, nor likely to. Similarly, Rogers Smith, *Civic Ideals: Conflicting Visions of Citizenship in US History*, New Haven, CT: Yale University Press, 1997, dispels the notion of a civic nation by documenting the ethnic exclusionary element of American historical naturalization laws. At the same time, Smith, too, regards only immigrants but not Americans as ethnic; that is, he is aware only of ethnic exclusion but not inclusion. This oversight is largely corrected in his later book, *Stories of Peoplehood*. Noah Pickus, *True Faith and Allegiance: Immigration and American Civic Nationalism*, Princeton University Press, 2005, advocating republican solidarity, is also oblivious to the unifying and nation-creating role of American culture. Thomas Archdeacon, *Becoming American: An Ethnic History*, New York, Free Press, 1983, is general and intelligent, while Roger Daniels, *Coming to America: A History of Immigration and Ethnicity in American Life*, New York: Harper, 1991, is conventional. Ronald Takaki, *A Different Mirror: A History of Multicultural America*, Boston: Little, Brown, 1993, concentrates on the racial aspect.

40 For a most interesting, indeed brilliant, take on this see Yossi Shain, *Marketing the American Creed Abroad: Diasporas in the US and their Homelands*, New York: Cambridge University Press, 1999.

41 Herbert Gans, "Symbolic Ethnicity: The Future of Ethnic Groups and Cultures in America," in Hutchinson and Smith (eds.), *Nationalism*, vol. 4, 1217–1237.

42 Alejandro Portes and Ruben Rumbaut, *Immigrant America: A Portrait*, Los Angeles, CA: University of California Press, 1990, esp. 198–209. Fuchs' discussion of the role of English in his celebration of American civic nationalism, *The American Kaleidoscope: Race, Ethnicity and the Civic Culture*, 458–473, typically misses the language's culturally unifying and nation-building aspect.

43 Joel Perlmann and Mary Waters, "Intermarriage and Multiple Identities," in M. Waters and R. Ueda (eds.), *The New Americans: A Guide to Immigration since 1965*, Cambridge, MA: Harvard University Press, 2007, 114; Jeffrey Passel, Wendy Wang, and Paul Taylor, "Marrying Out: One-in-Seven New US Marriages is Interracial or Interethnic," Pew Research Center: A Social and Demographic Trends Report, 2010; also, Eric Kaufmann, *The Rise and Fall of Anglo-America*, Cambridge, MA: Harvard University Press, 2004, 236–238.

44 Will Herberg, *Protestant, Catholic, Jew*, Garden City, NY: Doubleday, 1955.

45 Perlmann and Waters, "Intermarriage and Multiple Identities," 111.

46 Although her approach is different to mine, Elizabeth Theiss-Morse, *Who Counts as an American?*, Cambridge University Press, 2009, empirically documents, by populations and social categories, the strength of American national identity, its defining aspects, and the degree of inclusion and self-inclusion in it.

47 Rodolfo de la Garza *et al.*, *Latino Voices: Mexican, Puerto Rican, and Cuban Perspectives on American Politics*, Boulder, CO: Westview, 1992; Rodolfo de la Garza, Angelo Falcon, and F. Chris Garcia, "Will the Real Americans Please Stand Up: Anglo and Mexican-American Support of Core American Political Values," *American Journal of Political Science*, 40(2) (1996), 335–351; David Lopez and Vanessa Estrada, "Language," in Waters and Ueda (eds.), *The New Americans: A Guide to Immigration since 1965*, 228–242, esp. 233, 237, 239, 240–241; Richard Alba and Victor Nee, *Remaking the American Mainstream: Assimilation and Contemporary Immigration*, Cambridge, MA: Harvard University Press, 2003.

48 Lind, *The Next American Nation*, 47–48.

49 For the early stages of this process see, e.g., Phillip Buckner, "Nationalism in Canada," in D. Doyle and M. Pampalona (eds.), *Nationalism in the New World*, Athens, GA: University of Georgia Press, 2006, 99–116.

50 Genevieve Heard, Siew-Ean Khoo, and Bob Birrell, "Intermarriage in Australia: Patterns by Birthplace, Ancestry, Religion and Indigenous Status," A Report Using Data from the 2006 Census, Centre for Population and Urban

Research, Monash University for the Australian Bureau of Statistics, Australian Census Analytic Program, available at: www. arts.monash.edu.au/cpur/ publications; Paul Callister, "Ethnicity Measures, Intermarriage and Social Policy," *Social Policy Journal of New Zealand, Te Puna Whakaaro*, Issue 23, December 2004.

51 Kymlicka, *Politics in the Vernacular*, 23–26.

52 Seton-Watson, *Nations and States: An Inquiry into the Origins of Nations and the Politics of Nationalism*, 200; undeservedly neglected, this book, 199–204, 219–226, offers an excellent overview (also of the English-speaking immigrant countries in ch. 5); Wimmer, *Nationalist Exclusion and Ethnic Conflict*, 144.

53 Ofelia Garcia, "Latin America," in J. Fishman (ed.), *Language and Ethnic Identity*, New York: Oxford University Press, 1999, 229.

54 For the extreme case of Argentina, see Jorge Myers, "Language, History, and Politics in Argentine Identity, 1840–1880," in Doyle and Pampalona (eds.), *Nationalism in the New World*, 117–142; more generally, Miguel Centeno, *Blood and Debt: War and the Nation-State in Latin America*, University Park, PA: Penn State University Press, 2002.

55 Anderson, *Imagined Communities*, ch. 4, 50–65. For a critique by several Latin America scholars see: Claudio Lomnitz, "Nationalism as a Practical System: Benedict Anderson's Theory of Nationalism from the Vantage Point of Spanish America," in his *Deep Mexico, Silent Mexico*, Minneapolis, MN: University of Minnesota Press, 2001, 3–34; Centeno, *Blood and Debt: War and the Nation-State in Latin America*, ch. 4, particularly 171–172; Don Doyle and Marco Pampalona, "Introduction: America in the Conversation on Nationalism," in their *Nationalism in the New World*, 4; Eric van Young, "Revolution and Imagined Communities in Mexico, 1810–1821," in Doyle and Pampalona (eds.), *Nationalism in the New World*, 187–189.

56 This is a fast advancing field; see, e.g., S. Wang, N. Ray, W. Rojas *et al.*, "Geographic Patterns of Genome Admixture in Latin American Mestizos," *PLoS Genetics* 4(3) (2008), online; Irma Silva-Zolezzi *et al.*, "Analysis of Genomic Diversity in Mexican Mestizo Populations to Develop Genomic Medicine in Mexico," *Proceedings of the National Academy of Sciences of the United States of America*, (May 11, 2009), online; Isabel Mendizabal *et al.*, "Genetic Origin, Admixture, and Asymmetry in Maternal and Paternal Human Lineages in Cuba," *BMC Evolutionary Biology*, 8(213) (July 21, 2008), online; R. Santos *et al.*, "Color, Race, and Genomic Ancestry in Brazil," *Current Anthropology*, 50(6) (2009), 787–819; T. C. Lins *et al.*, "Genetic Composition of Brazilian Population Samples Based on a Set of Twenty-Eight Ancestry Informative SNPs," *American Journal of Human Biology*, 22(2) (2010), 187–192.

57 Centeno, *Blood and Debt: War and the Nation-State in Latin America*, chs. 4–5, is a very good comprehensive survey.

58 Florencia Mallon, "Indian Communities, Political Cultures, and the State in Latin America, 1780–1990," in Hutchinson and Smith (eds.), *Nationalism*, vol. 4, 1260–1278; Natividad Gutiérrez, *Nationalist Myths and Ethnic Identities: Indigenous Intellectuals and the Mexican State*, Lincoln, NE: University of Nebraska Press, 1999; Wimmer, *Nationalist Exclusion and Ethnic Conflict*, 114–155.

59 *The Guardian*, November 17, 2011.

60 See above, Chapter 4, pp. 78–79 and 127. In my understanding this is also the conclusion of R. D. Grillo, *Pluralism and the Politics of Difference: State, Culture, and Ethnicity in Comparative Perspective*, Oxford University Press, 1998, ch. 2, esp. 53–55. Also see Samuel Obeng and Efurosibina Adegbija, "Sub-Saharan Africa," in Fishman (ed.), *Language and Ethnic Identity*, 355–368, esp. 354.

61 Benyamin Neuberger, *National Self-Determination in Postcolonial Africa*, Boulder, CO: Lynne Rienner, 1984, 25, 34.

62 See p. 19, above. Also searching for more or less the same point, see Benyamin Neuberger, "The Western Nation-State in African Perceptions of Nation-Building," reprinted in Hutchinson and Smith (eds.), *Nationalism*, vol. 3, 946–963.

63 Obeng and Adegbija, "Sub-Saharan Africa," 353; see also Feliks Gross, *The Civic and Tribal State: The State, Ethnicity, and the Multiethnic State*, Westport, CT: Greenwood, 1998, ch. 3.

64 W. Burghardt du Bois, "The Pan-African Movement," in Kedourie (ed.), *Nationalism in Asia and Africa*, 372–387; John Breuilly, *Nationalism and the State*, New York: St. Martin's Press, 1982, 243–245.

65 Breuilly, *Nationalism and the State*, 151–164; Berman, Eyoh, and Kymlicka (eds.), "Introduction," *Ethnicity and Democracy in Africa*, 8, and throughout the book, particularly Githu Muigai, "Jomo Kenyatta & the Rise of the Ethno-Nationalist State in Kenya," 200–217.

66 Deutsch, *Tides among Nations*, ch. 7.

67 David Holloway and Stephen Stedman, "Civil Wars and State-Building in Africa and Eurasia," in M. Beissinger and C. Young (eds.), *Beyond State Crisis? Postcolonial Africa and Post-Soviet Eurasia in Comparative Perspective*, Baltimore, MD: Johns Hopkins University Press, 2002, 161–187; Donald Rothchild, "The Effects of State Crisis on African Interstate Relations," in Beissinger and Young (eds.), *Beyond State Crisis?*, 189–214; Richard Joseph, "War, State-Making, and Democracy in Africa," in Beissinger and Young (eds.), *Beyond State Crisis?*, 241–262; Alexander Johnston, "Ethnic Conflict in Post Cold War Africa," in K. Christie (ed.), *Ethnic Conflict, Tribal Politics: A Global Perspective*, Richmond: Curzon, 1998, 129–152; and a collection of case studies in T. Ali and R. Matthews, *Civil Wars in Africa: Roots and Resolution*, Montreal: McGill University Press, 1999.

68 James Fearon and David Laitin, "Ethnicity, Insurgency, and Civil War," *American Political Science Review*, 97 (2003), 75–90, and David Laitin, *Nations, States, and Violence*, Oxford University Press, 2007, claim on the basis of their statistical database and analysis that economic backwardness and its sociopolitical consequences are the predominant causes of civil wars, whereas ethnic diversity has no effect. I accept the first finding and reject the second. It re-demonstrates that contrary to the pretension of some of their proponents, statistics are a matter of interpretation and can serve any bias. The above authors insist, for example, that ethnic claims by the parties to a civil war are in fact a pretext for something else. Their studies do, however, suggest two important points. First, the incidence of ethnic violence is low in comparison with relatively peaceful ethnic coexistence most of the time. Second, the incidence of civil war does not rise with the *level* of ethnic heterogeneity. Indeed, contrary to the authors' interpretation, this may suggest that ethnic insurgency mainly erupts against a dominant people, rather than in more ethnically diverse ethnic states. For this see pp. 308 and 310 below.

69 See Arend Lijphart's extensive writings on consociational democracy; and with greater emphasis on both sides of the coin: Eric Nordlinger, *Conflict Regulation in Divided Societies*, Cambridge, MA: Harvard University Press, 1972, 31–32; Donald Horowitz, *Ethnic Groups in Conflict*, Berkeley, CA: University of California Press, 1985, ch. 14; Brendan O'Leary, "An Iron Law of Nationalism and Federation? A (neo-Diceyian) Theory of the Necessity of a Federal Staatsvolk, and of Consociational Rescue," *Nations and Nationalism*, 7(3), 2001, 273–296; Berman, Eyoh, and Kymlicka (eds.), *Ethnicity and Democracy in Africa*, 11, 319–320; Seyoum Hameso, *Ethnicity and Nationalism in Africa*, Commack, NY: Nova Science, 1997, ch. 8. David Laitin, *Language Repertoires and State Construction in Africa*, Cambridge University Press, 1992, relying on game theory modeling, concludes that a plural $3+/-1$ language policy is the most likely future outcome in most African states. This may be so, and the book is rich in fascinating detail, but the possibility of political disintegration along ethnic-linguistic lines in some African countries is not suggested as one of the possible outcomes.

70 Larry Diamond, "The State of Democracy in Africa," in *Democratization in Africa: What Progress towards Institutionalization?*, Conference Report, National Intelligence Council, 2008, 1–14; Jeffrey Herbst, "The Institutionalization of Democracy in Africa," *Democratization in Africa*, 61–66. For an older survey, see L. Diamond and M. Plattner (eds.), *Democratization in Africa*, Baltimore, MD: Johns Hopkins University Press, 1999.

71 In addition to the above, see, e.g., Francis Deng, "Beyond Cultural Domination: Institutionalizing Equity in the African State," in Beissinger and Young (eds.), *Beyond State Crisis*, 359–384; Earl Conteh-Morgan,

Democratization in Africa, Westport, CT: Praeger, 1997, ch. 6; the case studies for various countries in Jean-Germain Gros, *Democratization in Late Twentieth-Century Africa*, Westport, CT: Greenwood, 1998; and Berman, Eyoh, and Kymlicka (eds.), *Ethnicity and Democracy in Africa*, 15 and *passim*.

72 Herbst, "The Institutionalization of Democracy in Africa." By contrast and most remarkably, Herbst's *State and Power in Africa*, Princeton University Press, 2000, dealing with state weakness in the continent, scarcely mentions ethnicity at all.

73 Dorina Bekoe, "Democracy and African Conflicts: Inciting, Mitigating, or Reducing Violence?" in *Democratization in Africa*, 29–39, citation from 30.

74 Nordlinger, *Conflict Regulation in Divided Societies*, 110–116; Arend Lijphart, "Political Theories and the Explanation of Ethnic Conflict in the Western World: Falsified Predictions and Plausible Postditions," in M. Esman (ed.), *Ethnic Conflict in the Western World*, Ithaca, NY: Cornell University Press, 1977, 46–64, esp. 55–57; Berman, Eyoh, and Kymlicka (eds.), *Ethnicity and Democracy in Africa*, 6.

75 The best book on this subject, which discusses solutions and ameliorating mechanisms while being deeply conscious of the intricacy of the problems involved, is Horowitz, *Ethnic Groups in Conflict*. Also important, though somewhat marred by a view of ethnicity as artificial and by ideological zeal, are Ted Gurr, *Minority at Risk: A Global View of Ethnopolitical Conflicts*, Washington, DC: US Institute of Peace, 1993; and Ted Gurr and Barbara Harff, *Ethnic Conflict in World Politics*, Boulder, CO: Westview, 1994.

76 Clifford Geertz (ed.), "The Integrative Revolution: Primordial Sentiments and Civil Politics in the New States," *Old Societies and New States*, New York: Free Press, 1963, 105–157.

77 David Henley, "Ethnographic Integration and Exclusion in Anticolonial Nationalism: Indonesia and Indochina," in Hutchinson and Smith (eds.), *Nationalism*, vol. 3, 1041–1082; Michael Leifer (ed.), "The Changing Temper of Indonesian Nationalism", *Asian Nationalism*, 153–169, esp. 159, 167.

78 David Brown, *The State and Ethnic Politics in Southeast Asia*, London: Routledge, 1994, ch. 4; also, John Bowen, "Normative Pluralism in Indonesia: Regions, Religions, and Ethnicities," in W. Kymlicka and B. He (eds.), *Multiculturalism in Asia*, Oxford University Press, 2005, ch. 7.

79 These are the estimates of the CIA's *World Factbook*, available at: https://www.cia.gov/library/publications/the-world-factbook/geos/my.html. The figures in A. B. Shamsul, "Nations of Intent in Malaysia," in Tønneson and Antlöv (eds.), *Asian Forms of the Nation*, 323–347, are somewhat different. Also see C. W. Watson, "The Construction of the Post-Colonial Subject in Malaysia," in Tønneson and Antlöv (eds.), *Asian Forms of the Nation*, 297–322; and for a favorable view of Malaysia's ethnonational policies: N. Ganesan, "Liberal and Structural Ethnic Political Accommodation in Malaysia," in Kymlicka and He (eds.), *Multiculturalism in Asia*, ch. 6.

80 Brown, *The State and Ethnic Politics in Southeast Asia*, ch. 3. Although pursuing a false dichotomy between "primordial" and "construed" ethnicity under the state, the book contains some perceptive case studies, most notably on Singapore. Also see Chua Beng Huat, "The Cost of Membership in Ascribed Community," in Kymlicka and He (eds.), *Multiculturalism in Asia*, ch. 8.

81 Kedourie (ed.), "Introduction," *Nationalism in Asia and Africa*, 77–92; Breuilly, *Nationalism and the State*, chs. 5, 6, and 8.

82 Paul Brass, *Language, Religion and Politics in North India*, Cambridge: Cambridge University Press, 1974, ch. 3 and *passim*.

83 Brass' original protagonist was Francis Robinson, "Islam and Muslim Separatism," in D. Taylor and M. Yapp (eds.), *Political Identity in South Asia*, London: Curzon, 1979, 78–112. A partial revision is Brass, "Elite Groups, Symbol Manipulation and Ethnic Identity among Muslims of South Asia," Taylor and Yapp (eds.), *Political Identity in South Asia*, 35–77; reprinted in his *Ethnicity and Nationalism*, London: Sage, 1991, ch. 3. The most comprehensive study of the relationship between religion and nationalism in India is Peter van der Veer, *Religious Nationalism: Hindus and Muslims in India*, Berkeley, CA: University of California Press, 1994. For more see below.

84 van der Veer, *Religious Nationalism*; Ian Talbot, *Inventing the Nation: India and Pakistan*, London: Arnold, 2000, 12, 60, 75–85 (in my opinion, the best general study of nationalism in the two countries); Lise Mckean, *Divine Enterprise: Gurus and the Hindu National Movement*, University of Chicago Press, 1996.

85 See above, Chapter 4, nn. 52 and 53 and adjacent text.

86 Talbot, *India and Pakistan*, 60.

87 See above, Chapter 4, pp. 125–127.

88 van der Veer, *Religious Nationalism*, 22–23; Meghnad Desai, "Communalism, Secularism and the Dilemma of Indian Nationhood," in Leifer (ed.), *Asian Nationalism*, ch. 6; Ainslie Embree, *Utopias in Conflict: Religion and Nationalism in Modern India*, Berkeley, CA: University of California Press, 1990, ch. 3; Partha Chatterjee, *The Nation and its Fragments: Colonial and Postcolonial Histories*, Princeton University Press, 1993, 6, 120; S. Mitra and R. Lewis, *Subnational Movements in South Asia*, Boulder, CO: Westview, 1996, 108; Talbot, *India and Pakistan*, ch. 2, and p. 194.

89 For the historical roots and development of the idea of Hindu nationalism, see Christophe Jaffrelot, *The Hindu Nationalist Movement and Indian Politics: 1925 to the 1990s*, London: Hurst, 1996.

90 Chatterjee, *The Nation and Its Fragments*; Arild Ruud, "Contradiction and Ambivalence in the Hindu Nationalist Discourse in West Bengal," in Tønneson and Antlöv (eds.), *Asian Forms of the Nation*, 151–180.

91 Mitra and Lewis, *Subnational Movements in South Asia*, ch. 9.

92 Jyotirindra Das Gupta, *Language Conflict and National Development: Group Politics and National Language Policy in India*, Berkeley, CA: University of

California Press, 1970. Also, perhaps a touch idealized, Gurpreet Mahajan, "Indian Exceptionalism or Indian Model: Negotiating Cultural Diversity and Minority Rights in a Democratic Nation-State," in Kymlicka and He (eds.), *Multiculturalism in Asia*, ch. 13.

93 Brass, *Language, Religion and Politics in North India*, chs. 6–8.

94 Mitra and Lewis, *Subnational Movements in South Asia*, ch. 8.

95 See n. 70 above and the following footnote in the text.

96 Arend Lijphart, "The Puzzle of Indian Democracy: A Consociational Interpretation," *American Political Science Review*, 90(2) (1996), 258–268.

97 Tariq Rahman, *Language and Politics in Pakistan*, Karachi: Oxford University Press, 1997; Alyssa Ayres, *Speaking Like a State: Language and Nationalism in Pakistan*, Cambridge University Press, 2009.

98 Katherine Adeney, *Federalism and Ethnic Conflict Regulation in India and Pakistan*, New York, Palgrave Macmillan, 2007, 173–177.

99 See n. 69, above.

100 See the most instructive data for Europe in Krejčí and Velímský, *Ethnic and Political Nations in Europe*, 49–57.

101 Krejčí and Velímský, *Ethnic and Political Nations in Europe*, 49–57.

102 Here also A. Smith, *Nations and Nationalism in the Global Era*, is well-considered and most thoughtful; also Craig Calhoun, *Nations Matter: Culture, History and the Cosmopolitan Dream*, London: Routledge, 2007. I have been pleasantly surprised to read Jerry Muller, "Us and Them: The Enduring Power of Ethnic Nationalism," *Foreign Affairs*, March–April 2008, many of its ideas I share.

103 Melvin Small and David Singer, *Resort to Arms: International and Civil Wars, 1816–1980*, Beverly Hills, CA: Sage, 1982, based on their Correlates of War database, gives no basis for comparison to earlier times and between developed and developing countries. But see Jack Levy, *War in the Modern Great Power System, 1495–1975*, Lexington, KY: University Press of Kentucky, 1983, esp. 112–149. Also Evan Luard, *War in International Society*, London: Tauris, 1986, 53, 67. Recently two new books have brought this trend to the headlines: Joshua Goldstein, *Winning the War on War: The Decline of Armed Conflict Worldwide*, New York: Dutton, 2011; Steven Pinker, *The Better Angels of our Nature: Why Violence has Declined*, New York: Viking, 2011.

104 For more detail, see Gat, *War in Human Civilization*, 524–529, 534–535.

105 The most comprehensive and update estimates are Angus Maddison, *The World Economy: A Millennial Perspective*, Paris: OECD, 2001, 28, 90, 126, 183–186, 264–265. See also Paul Bairoch, "Europe's Gross National Product: 1800–1975," *Journal of European Economic History*, 5 (1976), 301; Paul Bairoch, "International Industrialization Levels from 1750 to 1980," *Journal of European Economic History*, 11 (1982), 269–310, esp. 275, 284, 286;

W. W. Rostow, *The World Economy: History & Prospect*, Austin, TX: University of Texas Press, 1978, 4–7, 48–49.

106 See, e.g., Richard Rosecrance, *The Rise of the Trading State: Commerce and Conquest in the Modern World*, New York: Basic Books, 1986; also Stephen Brooks, "The Globalization of Production and the Changing Benefits of Conquest," *Journal of Conflict Resolution*, 43(5) (1999), 646–670. On the so-called democratic peace, see most notably Russett and Oneal, *Triangulating Peace: Democracy, Interdependence and International Organizations*; and generally on democracy and war: Gat, *Why Democracy Won in the 20th Century and How it is Still Imperiled*. For data, see B. R. Mitchell, *International Historical Statistics, Europe 1750–1988*, New York: Stockton, 1992, 553–562; Maddison, *The World Economy*, 126, 127, 184; Simon Kuznets, *Modern Economic Growth*, New Haven, CT: Yale University Press, 1966, 306–307, 312–314.

107 John Stuart Mill, *Principles of Political Economy*, New York: Kelley, 1961, Bk. iii, ch. xvii, s. 5, p. 582.

108 Andreas Wimmer and Brian Min, "The Location and Purpose of Wars Around the World: A New Global Dataset, 1816–2001," *International Interactions*, 35 (2009), 390–417, esp. 406; Andreas Wimmer, "Waves of War: Nationalism and Ethnic Politics in the Modern World," paper delivered in a conference at McGill, March 2011, p. 4. Similarly, see Kalevi Holsti, *Peace and War: Armed Conflict and International Order 1648–1989*, Cambridge University Press, 1991, 306–334, esp. 307–308. Like every database, each of the above has its own criteria and classification rules which affect the results, and with not all of which I agree. But the general picture is clear. The findings again show how one-sided and narrow are the claims made by James Fearon and David Laitin (n. 69, above).

109 But see most notably Yael Tamir, *Liberal Nationalism*, Princeton University Press, 1993; David Miller, *On Nationality*, Oxford University Press, 1995.

110 Again, cf. Billig, *Banal Nationalism*.

111 For example, Gregory Jusdanis, *The Necessary Nation*, Princeton University Press, 2001.

112 Azar Gat, "The Return of Authoritarian Great Powers," *Foreign Affairs*, 86(4) (2007), 59–69; Azar Gat, "Are Authoritarian China and Russia Doomed? Is Liberal Democracy's Victory Preordained?," *Foreign Affairs*, 88(3) (2009); Gat, *Victorious and Vulnerable*.

113 For a fuller discussion of this complex subject, see Gil Merom, *How Democracies Lose Small Wars: State, Society, and the Failure of France in Algeria, Israel in Lebanon, and the United States in Vietnam*, New York: Cambridge University Press, 2003; Merom and Gat, in Gat (ed.), *Victorious and Vulnerable*, ch. 7.

114 Gat, *Victorious and Vulnerable*, 121, and the references there.

115 Vito Tanzi and Ludger Schuknecht, *Public Spending in the Twentieth Century: A Global Perspective*, Cambridge University Press, 2000; Gat, *War in Human Civilization*, 524–526 and the authorities cited therein.

116 See an overview of the literature in K. Banting and Will Kymlicka (eds.), *Multiculturalism and the Welfare State: Recognition and Redistribution in Contemporary Democracies*, Oxford University Press, 2006, 11–12, 93–94.

117 Rounded figures for the years 2000 and 1998, respectively: Alberto Alesina and Edward Glaeser, *Fighting Poverty in the US and Europe: A World of Difference*, Oxford University Press, 2004, 17, 19.

118 Glaeser, *Fighting Poverty in the US and Europe*, 133–134, 145.

119 Glaeser, *Fighting Poverty in the US and Europe*, 146–166.

120 Glaeser, *Fighting Poverty in the US and Europe*, 41.

121 Daniel Béland and Andre Lécours, *Nationalism and Social Policy: The Politics of Territorial Solidarity*, Oxford University Press, 2008.

122 See most notably the studies in Banting and Kymlicka (eds.), *Multiculturalism and the Welfare State*. However, the book is more concerned with refuting the claim that social solidarity and wealth redistribution are adversely affected by multiculturalist policies, rather than by ethnic heterogeneity in general.

123 Keith Banting, Richard Johnston, Will Kymlicka, and Stuart Soroka, "Do Multiculturalism Policies Erode the Welfare State," in Banting and Kymlicka (eds.), *Multiculturalism and the Welfare State*, ch. 2, especially p. 83.

124 Alesina and Glaeser, *Fighting Poverty in the US and Europe*, 142–144.

125 See http://hdrstats.undp.org/en/indicators/161.html.

126 Jürgen Habermas, *The Postnational Constellation*, Cambridge: Polity, 2001, 58–112, citation from 64–65.

127 Habermas, *The Postnational Constellation*, 80.

128 See most tellingly Habermas, *The Postnational Constellation*, 74.

129 Eric Hobsbawm, interview in *Haaretz* newspaper, June 10, 2010.

7 State, national identity, ethnicity: normative and constitutional aspects

1 See the Introduction, n. 6, above.

2 For the text of the Slovak constitution, and the other constitutions cited here, see International Constitutional Law at: www.servat.unibe.ch./icl.

3 Cf. Kymlicka, *Politics in the Vernacular*, 24–25, arguing, on somewhat different grounds, against the analogy between religion and language in this respect.

4 See Chapter 5.

5 See at: www.ecmi.de/about/history/german-danish-border-region/ bonn-copenhagen-declarations.

6 For the concept of "kin-states" in Europe, see European Commission for Democracy through Law (Venice Commission), *Report on the Preferential*

Treatment of National Minorities by their Kin-State, adopted at the 48th Plenary Meeting, Venice, October 19–20, 2001, available at: www.venice.coe.int/docs/2001/CDL-INF%282001%29019-e.asp; *The Bolzano/Bozen Recommendations on National Minorities in Inter-State Relations & Explanatory Note*, OSCE High Commissioner on National Minorities, Netherlands, 2008, available at: www.osce.org/hcnm/33633.

7 *Report on the Preferential Treatment of National Minorities by their Kin-State*, 42.

8 See, e.g., Council of Europe, Parliamentary Assembly, Resolution 1713 (2010), available at: http://assembly.coe.int/Main.asp?link=/Documents/AdoptedText/ta10/ERES1713.htm.

9 June 15, 1999 (Corsica); May 9, 1991 (Regional Languages); see at: www.conseil-constitutionnel.fr.

10 Council of Europe, Parliamentary Assembly, Doc. 10961, June 12, 2006, *Ratification of the Framework Convention for the Protection of National Minorities by the member states of the Council of Europe*, Report, Committee on Legal Affairs and Human Rights, 5–6.

11 *The Bolzano/Bozen Recommendations*, 3.

12 Will Kymlicka, *Multicultural Odysseys: Navigating the New International Politics of Diversity*, Oxford University Press, 2007, 80.

13 For the text of the report and the President's statement see: www.fil-info-france.com/actualites-monde/rapport-stasi-commission-laicite.htm.

14 Kymlicka, *Multicultural Odysseys*, 42, n. 27, quoting the French Haut Conseil à l'intégration.

15 Kymlicka, *Multicultural Odysseys*, 52.

16 Cf. Kymlicka, *Multicultural Odysseys*, 83–86.

17 See, e.g., M. Moore (ed.), *National Self-Determination and Secession*, Oxford University Press, 1998; Allen Buchanan and Stephen Macedo (eds.), *Secession and Self-Determination*, New York: New York University Press, 2003.

18 Judgments of the Supreme Court of Canada, Reference re Secession of Quebec, [1998] 2 SCR 217, available at: http://csc.lexum.org/en/1998/1998scr2-217/1998scr2-217.html.

19 Chua Beng Huat, "The Cost of Membership in Ascribed Community," in Kymlicka and He (eds.), *Multiculturalism in Asia*, 184.

20 Council of Europe, Parliamentary Assembly, Doc. 10961, June 12, 2006, *Ratification of the Framework Convention for the Protection of National Minorities by the member states of the Council of Europe*, Report, Committee on Legal Affairs and Human Rights, 8.

21 See on this Christian Jopke, "Citizenship between De- and Re-ethnicization," *European Journal of Sociology*, 44 (2003), 440–441.

22 See http://conventions.coe.int/Treaty/Commun/ListeDeclarations.asp?NT=157&CM=&DF=&CL=ENG&VL=1.

23 *Bolzano/Bozen Recommendations*, 1, 2, 3, 5.
24 Cf. Yael Tamir, *Liberal Nationalism*, Princeton University Press, 1993; D. Miller, *On Nationality*.
25 Kymlicka, *Multicultural Odysseys*, 80.
26 Kymlicka, *Multicultural Odysseys*, 83–86; see also Kymlicka, *Politics in the Vernacular*, 23–27.

INDEX